THE COURSE OF LIFE

Volume III

THE COURSE OF LIFE

Volume III

Middle and Late Childhood

Edited by

Stanley I. Greenspan, M.D.
George H. Pollock, M.D., Ph.D.

INTERNATIONAL UNIVERSITIES PRESS, INC.
Madison Connecticut

This is a revised and expanded version of *The Course of Life: Psychoanalytic Contributions Toward Understanding Personality Development,* edited by Stanley I. Greenspan and George H. Pollock, published by the U.S. Government Printing Office, Washington, D.C., 1980.

Library of Congress Cataloging in Publication Data

The Course of Life.

"Revised and expanded version"—T.p. verso.
Includes bibliographies and indexes.
Contents: v. 1. Infancy— — v. 3. Middle
and late childhood— v. 4. Adolescence.
1. Personality development. 2. Psychoanalysis.
I. Greenspan, Stanley I. II. Pollock, George H.
[DNLM: 1. Human Development. 2. Personality Development.
3. Psychoanalytic Theory. WM 460.5.P3 C861]
BF723.P4C68 1991 155 88-28465
ISBN 0-8236-1123-X (v.1)
ISBN 0-8236-1125-6 (v.3)

Manufactured in the United States of America

For information about our audio products, write us at:
Newbridge Book Clubs, 3000 Cindel Drive, Delran, NJ 08370

Contents

List of Contributors

Ronald M. Benson, M.D., Training and Supervising Analyst and President-elect, Michigan Psychoanalytic Institute; Clinical Associate Professor of Psychiatry, University of Michigan and Wayne State University.

Harold P. Blum, M.D., Clinical Professor of Psychiatry, Downstate Medical Center, New York; Executive Director, Sigmund Freud Archives; Past Editor, *Journal of the American Psychoanalytic Association.*

Edith Buxbaum, Ph.D.,† Training Analyst and Child Analyst, Seattle Psychoanalytic Institute; Clinical Professor in Psychiatry at the University of Washington.

Lee Combrinck-Graham, M.D., Associate Professor and Director of Child and Adolescent Psychiatry, Univerisy of Illinois; Director, Institute for Juvenile Research, Chicago, Illinois.

Cecil C. H. Cullander, M.D., Supervising and Training Analyst, The Washington Psychoanalytic Institute, Washington, D.C.; Faculty, University of Virginia Medical School.

Rudolf Ekstein, Ph.D., Clinical Professor of Medical Psychology, UCLA; Training and Supervisory Analyst, Los Angeles and Southern California Psychoanalytic Institutes; Yearly Guest Professor, University of Vienna.

Erna Furman, Member and Faculty, Cleveland Center for Research in Child Development; Assistant Clinical Professor in Child Therapy, Case Western Reserve University School of Medicine.

Robert A. Furman, M.D., Director, Cleveland Center for Research in Child Development and the Hanna Perkins School; Training Analyst, The Cleveland Psychoanalytic Institute.

Stanley I. Greenspan, M.D., Clinical Professor of Psychiatry and Behavioral Sciences, and Child Health and Development, George Washington University Medical Center, Washington, D.C.; Supervising Child Psychoanalyst, Washington Psychoanalytic Institute.

Saul I. Harrison, M.D., Professor of Psychiatry, University of Michigan Medical Center, Ann Arbor, Michigan.

James L. Hatleberg, M.D., Supervising Child Analyst, Washington Psychoanalytic Institute; Assistant Clinical Professor of Psychiatry, Georgetown University Medical School, Washington, D.C.

Hansi Kennedy, Dip Psych., Co-Director, Hampstead Child-Therapy Course and Clinic, now known as the Anna Freud Centre; Graduate Child-Psychotherapist, Hampstead Child-Therapy Course and Clinic, London, England.

Paulina F. Kernberg, M.D., Director, Child and Adolescent Psychiatry, New York Hospital-Cornell Medical Center, Westchester Division; Training Analyst, Columbia University Center for Psychoanalytic Training and Research.

†Deceased

Judith S. Kestenberg, M.D., Clinical Professor of Psychiatry and Training Analyst, New York University, N.Y.; Co-Director, Center for Parents and Children, sponsored by Child Development Research, Sands Point, N.Y.

Selma Kramer, M.D., Professor of Child Psychiatry, Thomas Jefferson University Medical School; Training Supervising Analyst, Philadelphia Psychoanalytic Institute.

Jeanne Lampl-de Groot, M.D.,† Psychoanalyst, Doctor Honoris Causa of the University of Amsterdam; Honorary Vice President of the International Psychoanalytic Association.

Serge Lebovici, M.D., Professeur de Clinique de Psychiatrie de l'Enfant, Universite de Paris-Nord, Faculté de Medecine Experimentale (Professor and Chief, Clinic of Child Psychiatry, University of Paris North, Faculty of Experimental Medicine); Past President of the International Psychoanalytic Association.

Reginald S. Lourie, M.D., Med. Sc.D.,† Professor Emeritus, Child Health and Development, Psychiatry and Behavioral Sciences, George Washington University; Senior Research Scientist, NIMH; Faculty, Baltimore-Washington Institute for Psychoanalysis.

Irwin M. Marcus, M.D., Clinical Professor of Psychiatry, Louisiana State University Medical School; Adjunct Professor, Tulane University; Founding Director of Child/Adolescent Program (now Emeritus); Emeritus Training and Supervising Analyst, New Orleans Psychoanalytic Institute, New Orleans.

Humberto Nagera, M.D., Chief, Youth Services, University of Michigan; Training and Supervising Analyst, The Michigan Psychoanalytic Institute.

Fred Pine, Ph.D., Professor of Psychiatry (Psychology), Albert Einstein College of Medicine, New York City.

Kyle D. Pruett, M.D., Clinical Professor of Psychiatry, Child Study Center, Yale University School of Medicine.

Joseph Rudolph, M.D., Clinical Associate Professor of Pediatrics and Psychiatry, Medical College of Pennsylvania; Supervising Analyst in Child and Adult Psychoanalysis, Philadelphia Psychoanalytic Institute.

Marshall D. Schechter, M.D., Professor Emeritus, Child and Adolescent Psychiatry, University of Pennsylvania School of Medicine, Philadelphia.

Charles Schwarzbeck, III, Ph.D., Clinical Teaching Faculty, Washington (D.C.) School of Psychiatry; Lecturer, Department of Psychiatry, University of Washington School of Medicine, Seattle.

Robert J. Stoller, M.D., Professor of Psychiatry, UCLA School of Medicine.

Heiman van Dam, M.D., Associate Clinical Professor, Psychiatry and Pediatrics, UCLA School of Medicine; Training Analyst and Supervisor in Adult and Child Psychoanalysis, Los Angeles Psychoanalytic Institute; Supervising Analyst in Child Psychoanalysis, Southern California Psychoanalytic Institute.

Stanley Wiseberg, MB ChB MRCPsych DPM, Research Consultant, Hampstead Child-Therapy Course and Clinic, now known as the Anna Freud Centre; Consultant Psychiatrist, Hillingdon General Hospital, Middlesex, England.

Clifford Yorke, FRCPsych DPM, Psychiatrist-in-Charge, The Anna Freud Centre; Training and Supervising Analyst, Institute of Psychoanalysis, London.

Preface

Perhaps the most illusive aspect of human development is the nature of man's innermost wishes, thoughts, and feelings. Until relatively recently, our limited understanding of this aspect of the mind has in part stemmed from a focus on the contributions of only a few developmental phases. Now, a wealth of observational, experimental, and clinical case studies at each stage in the course of life, ranging from early infancy to advanced ages, makes it possible to formulate a truly developmental perspective on mental functioning.

Each stage of development has its own special challenges, organizing properties, and unique meanings. Yet, each new stage builds on former ones, creating a developmental progression characterized by both continuity and opportunity. To understand the unique character of each stage of development, outstanding pioneers, clinical scholars, and researchers have prepared papers on each phase of development. Authors have been given an opportunity to update their original papers from the first edition of *The Course of Life*. Many have written new sections on entirely new papers. In addition, new contributions by outstanding investigators have been added for this revised and expanded edition. These papers have been organized according to stages in the course of life: infancy, early childhood, latency, adolescence, young adulthood, midlife, and the aging process. For each stage, each group of papers will illuminate the special challenges, potentials, and, most importantly, highly personal ways experience is organized.

1

The Four-to-Six-Years Stage

HUMBERTO NAGERA, M.D.

In most earlier textbooks the period between 4 and 6 was labeled the phallic-oedipal phase, a developmental period ending with the child's entry into the latency phase. The earliest age at which the phallic-oedipal phase was thought to begin was 3½. Nowadays, however, it is quite common to observe clear manifestations of this phase in the fantasies, interests, behaviors, and symptoms of children of 2½. Such children, who may be somewhat precocious, are frequently well established in this phase by the age of 3. A brief visit to a normal nursery school in any middle-class neighborhood will provide ample evidence. All that is needed is to observe the children's play and to listen to the fantasies they verbalize. Though initial impressions might suggest that girls are more inclined to such precocity than are boys, careful observation does not bear this out.

It must be clear, then, that there are very significant differences between children 4 years old and children 6 years old. Such differences are to be observed not only in drive development and ego development (including that in cognitive areas) but in superego development as well.

Gesell (1940) described the age of 4 as "the flowering period of language"; the 4-year-old talks "about everything, plays with words, questions persistently, elaborates simple responses into long narratives, comments with approval on his own behavior and criticizes that of others, balances comparison" (p. 204).

He can fashion crude letters and shows a very active imagination while painting, accompanying the activity with much description and shift of ideas. He can hold the brush like an adult, and what he does has a personal value—he wants to take the picture home.

His motor development has advanced significantly; when walking down stairs, he can, at least for the last few steps, place one foot to a step, in contradistinction to the younger child, who places two feet to a step. He can now skip on one foot and can execute either a running or a standing broad jump. He can throw a ball overhand and is able to stand on one foot up to 8 seconds.

He can wash and dry his face and hands and brush his teeth. With some supervision he can dress and undress himself, being able to distinguish the front of his clothes from the back. He can play cooperatively and constructively with other children and is fond of building structures with blocks.

At 4 years the child can repeat three digits on two of three trials but will usually fail the attempt to repeat four digits.

The drawing of a man begins to take form at this time. Head and eyes are portrayed, but other facial features may not be included. Over half of all children this age draw either legs or feet. The child of this age has no fixed formula but modifies his drawing with every attempt.

The 5-year-old not only uses language efficiently, but has developed a sense of social standards and appropriate limitations regarding its use. He frequently asks for the meaning of words.

When painting, he usually begins with an idea in mind, and what he paints is generally recognizable. His pictures have a few simple elements; of these, the most important is drawn largest, so that a flower may be larger than the house it stands next to.

His motor development is well ahead of the 4-year-old's. Thus, he skips using both feet and can stand on one foot for more than 8 seconds. He negotiates stairs a foot to a step with relative ease and can dress and undress himself without any help. At this age he can repeat four digits correctly on one of three trials, a task at which the 4-year-old will usually fail. At 5, the child draws a man clearly. Mouth, eyes, and nose are present, as are body, arms, legs, and feet.

At 4 to 5, the child exhibits as well all the manifestations typical of the oedipal stage. He is involved in triangular concerns and relationships with his parents. For the boy the mother is the object that receives most of his interest—that is, his libidinal cathexis. As the result the father—though a loved object—becomes simultaneously a rival for the mother's affection. The boy's attentions to his mother are those of a young, tender, loving suitor, and because there is nothing he can do but acknowledge the father's prerogatives and privileged position in regard to her, he becomes resentful toward him. This resentment can be circumscribed or reasonably well hidden, or may pervade the boy's relationship with his father and be manifested overtly. This state of affairs characterizes what has been called as the simple positive oedipus complex of the boy.

But this situation is further complicated by the fundamental role that bisexuality plays in the oedipus complex. As Freud (1923) says, because of his bisexual nature the boy "also behaves like a girl and displays an affectionate feminine attitude towards his father, and a corresponding jealousy and hostility towards his mother" (pp. 31–32). Under normal conditions this aspect of the oedipus complex (the negative oedipus complex) is less noticeable and significant than the simple positive oedipus complex. Yet it is always present in some measure and, as I will try to show later on, is the fact that can on occasion, and under certain favorable circumstances, pave the way to the development of a negative oedipus complex that is full-blown and dominant.

The intensity of these behavioral manifestations is very variable indeed, and depends on many factors. Among these are the intensity of conflicts and various favorable or unfavorable circumstances. For example, an excessively seductive mother will exacerbate a situation that is already inherently conflictual. An excessively severe, punitive, nonsupportive, and nonsympathetic father will have a similar effect. Yet even where external conditions are most favorable, conflicts can be quite severe and produce a variety of disturbing symptoms. This tends to be the case when phallic-oedipal impulses are strong and ego and superego objections to them are quite marked.

In some cases the child's preference for certain defense mechanisms heightens conflictual stresses. Take, for example, a situation in which the child resents the father for his privileged position vis-à-vis the mother. Since the father is also a loved object, a conflict arises between love, on the one hand, and negative feelings, on the other. The latter may range from mild to intense hate, with fantasies of disposing of the father, eliminating him from the picture in one way or another, etc. Since the child of this age sees the father as very powerful, he becomes a threatening figure in the child's mind. To the guilt produced by the conflict between love and hate can now be added the fear of the father's response were he to become aware of the child's evil wishes. Given that many children find these wishes highly objectionable, and that some make excessive use of externalization and projection, one can understand how even the most benign father can be transformed by means of such mechanisms into the most threatening and dreaded figure. It is in this way that some children with very lenient parents acquire a very severe conscience. In extreme cases of this type, the child fears for his physical integrity (a displaced manifestation of his castration anxiety) and is convinced in a somewhat "paranoid" manner that the father wants to dispose of him, harm him, and so on. More frequently, of course, and for economic reasons, this fear of the father is displaced onto other objects or situations. Thus they form the basis for many of the fears and phobias typical of this age group.

Intense conflict of the sort just described will not only be florid in its manifestations but may well force maladaptive solutions on the child's ego. Thus, "convinced" that his physical integrity (i.e., his masculinity) is endangered, and wishing to rid himself of the guilt and enormous anxiety he feels, he may repress his phallic-oedipal strivings toward the mother. Instead he turns to the father as the preferred loved object, wanting to occupy the privileged and nonthreatened position that he thinks his mother enjoys in relation to the father. Thus, he arrives at a passive-feminine position vis-à-vis the father or, in other words, at the negative oedipus complex type of solution. This would be an abnormal solution of an otherwise normal developmental conflict. The significance and pathogenic potential of this defensive solution as regards his future sexual identity are determined by many factors—the mother's responsiveness to the child's phallic strivings, his basic constitution in terms of the strength of his instincts, his bisexual genetic balance, the father's attitude, etc. In malignant cases it may lead to a lifelong sexual deviation, as when the outcome is a homosexual position.

For the girl, the phallic-oedipal and oedipal stages proper are much more complex developmental steps to negotiate than for the boy, as girls move into their oedipus complex in two distinct stages. The first one, referred to as the phallic-oedipal stage, is usually reached at around 2½ or 3 years of age. For at least a year the girl, like the boy, takes the mother as the object of her phallic-oedipal strivings, and so far as this is the case the father is the hated rival, though he is also very much loved. This phase is in a way a continuation of the earlier preoedipal relationship with the mother, except that now it acquires the characteristics imposed on it by the newly reached level of development. It is at around 3½ or 4 that the girl must, if her psychosexual development is to proceed normally, transfer her cathexis and ego interests to the father. When she does that, the mother becomes her rival for the father's affection. This, coupled with other changes in the ego fantasies and longings of the little girl, mark her entry into the oedipal stage proper. Generally speaking, this can be expected at around 4 years of age.

This move from the first stage to the second is difficult to negotiate. It is not easy to decathect the preoedipal and phallic-oedipal mother. It helps to have a tolerant, understanding mother and a father who welcomes and encourages the overtures of the little girl without being seductive. The move may be complicated by many factors. A significant one is a fixation at the preoedipal level, particularly at the anal sadistic stage of the relation to the mother. On the one hand, the fixation tends to interfere with the move forward; on the other hand, some girls shy away from the reinforced anal sadistic fantasies occasioned by the mother's having become a hated rival. Clinically, it seems that the one situation reinforces the other to such an extent that some girls cannot take the step.

To complicate matters further, the shift from the object mother (first stage of the girl's oedipus complex) to the object father (second stage) must be accompanied more or less simultaneously by significant changes along other lines of development. These include the modification of active-masculine clitoral strivings with the addition (at a later stage) of the vagina as an important erogenous zone and changes in the concommitant ego fantasies, and an overall change from an active-masculine position to passive-feminine one.[1]

Many of these conflicts are an integral part of growing up and are considered "normal developmental conflicts" typical for the phase and for this age group (Nagera, 1966). They are, nevertheless, the prototype of all later neurotic conflicts and have been designated the "infantile neurosis." Like all conflicts they create tension, stress, anxiety, guilt, shame, and other accompanying affects. Naturally, too, they are attempts at the resolution of these conflicts, and some such attempts lead to symptom formation of a very typical sort. Among the most frequently observed symptoms are sleep disturbances, including nightmares and night terrors frequently leading to attempts to sleep in the parental bedroom or to attempts to separate the parents by having one of them come to the child's room or bed. Reluctance to fall asleep, occasionally amounting to a sleep phobia, is not uncommon. Associated phenomena are fears of the dark, monsters, ghosts, and burglars accompanied by anxious requests to leave the light on, the bedroom door open, etc. Similarly, there are requests for yet another story at bedtime, another glass of water, another hug or kiss, another trip to the bathroom; fears of various people, animals, or "things" hiding in the child's bedroom with clear evil intent; a large variety of phobic symptoms, many of which concern animals that bite (dogs, cats, lions, tigers, etc.); excessive concern about hurts, accidents, and injuries, indicating an increased fear of body damage; and marked anxiety and reactions at the sight of blind, crippled, or otherwise injured people. All of the above are derivative forms of castration anxiety. Observable too are regres-

[1] The terms *active-masculine* position and *passive-feminine* position are understood here strictly in terms of a sexual position. They are in no way meant to equate activity (in the general sense of the word) with masculinity, nor passivity with femininity. For a more detailed account of the polarity see Nagera (1975).

sive moves to wetting, whether transient or more protracted, and occasional regressive moves to soiling. At times there is a marked increase in bedtime ceremonials and ritualistic behaviors, as well as other isolated pieces of obsessive-compulsive behavior.

Within certain limits this is a normal developmental disturbance despite the florid symptomatology. Thus, every child, every human being, has suffered from an "infantile neurosis" in the process of growing up. Like all developmental disturbances and all developmental conflicts, it is usually transitory and tends to disappear spontaneously as the next developmental push takes place. This situation changes the dynamic balance or imbalance between the libidinal (and aggressive) organization of the drives and ego-superego factors. Many such changes, under normal conditions, dissolve or at least diminish considerably the earlier conflictual situation. In this way, the symptoms cease to be produced.

This concept of the infantile neurosis has traditionally been used to cover the normal, expected developmental conflict as well as cases of clear-cut pathology in which "infantile neurosis" has a much more serious connotation. As noted elsewhere (Nagera, 1966), "The difference between these forms are, in part, of a quantitative nature, depending on the one hand on the intensity of the phallic-oedipal conflicts in different individuals, and on the other on the different strength and vicissitudes of the preoedipal elements and their individual contributions to the oedipal phase" (p. 56).

This formulation tends to pose problems concerning the definitions of normality and abnormality, health and illness, which cannot be discussed here. However, the reader should be aware that the term *infantile neurosis* is used here to cover both its normal and its pathological forms. Indeed, the form it takes in both normal and abnormal cases allows for clinical differences and some variability. These will depend on the vicissitudes of the preceding developmental stages. Thus, developmental interferences—developmental and neurotic conflicts that have taken place during earlier phases—form the background and prepare the conditions out of which the infantile neurosis of each human being will develop and acquire its idiosyncratic final shape. This applies to infantile neuroses that are considered still within the realm of the "normal," as well as to those that are distinctly pathological.

Earlier occurrences (developmental interferences, conflicts, etc.) may have led, for example, to a fixation at the anal stage. When this is the case, the development of the drives, the ego (and superego), and object relationships is forced into specific forms of expression. This fixation not only determines the form of expression of the infantile neurosis, which will be characterized by a marked contamination of anal elements (in contrast to its more pure forms), but would also influence its intensity, its fate, and the ego's ability to cope with anxiety and conflictual situations.

In other types of unfavorable circumstances, leading for example to a significant fixation at the phallic-oedipal stage, many of the symptoms will remain. Further, conditions would have been established, by means of a weak spot in the personality, for the possible development in adulthood of specific forms of psychopathology. Fixation at this state predisposes to the possible later development of the various forms of hysteria, hysterical personality and character, and phobias. I am referring here to the most typical and "pure" forms of these disorders, but the simultaneous presence of earlier weak spots and fixations may produce "impure" forms—that is, hysterical disorders with strong oral roots and components. Among the possible forms of the pure type are of course the anxiety neuroses, either free-floating or attached to specific situations, objects, or events. Similarly, disturbances of this phase may lead to extreme cases of castration anxiety, to passivity (passive personality), and to some forms of homosexual outcomes in both sexes.

The favorable resolution of the oedipal stage implies many changes in many lines of development. A particularly important change is the child's increasing ability to displace his interests onto nonincestuous objects of the same sex.

The instinctual aspects of development during this phase have up to now been emphasized, but enormous changes are also occurring in the ego and the superego, changes in large measure responsible for the behavioral changes observed in this age group, as well as for the organization of the first neurosis, the prototype of all later ones.

The infantile neurosis is an attempt on the part of the ego—when it acquires the necessary strength and functional capabilities—to organize into a single structure the manifold neurotic conflicts and developmental shortcomings from earlier phases and to integrate them with the new conflicts typical of the oedipal stage. Its purpose is to make out of this chaos one single organization, one single unit in which everything that has taken place developmentally up to that point gets represented. This is of momentous significance for development and has important economic repercussions. No longer is the ego forced to fight a multiplicity of battles, one at each point at which development was marked by unresolved conflict or developmental shortcomings. Instead it consolidates the manifold conflicts into a single structure, the infantile neurosis, against which it can concentrate all its resources. This type of compromise formation is possible at this age only because of the notable strides made by the ego, particularly in terms of its integrative and synthetic functions. Thus, the oedipal phase is not only an essential turning point in human development but an "organizer" of the highest import (Nagera, 1966, pp. 57–58).

By this time many of the elements for the building up of personality structure have already been contributed. Of course, there are some exceptions, such as those that will come during latency and adolescence. Particularly significant here are the contributions of sexual maturation, with its many implications, both physical and psychological. Nevertheless, such contributions frequently consist essentially of reshapings, recombinations, and rearrangements of elements—or of reinforcements of specific tendencies—which for the most part were already present. Just as changes occur rapidly in the ego during this time, so too the development of the superego quickens. There has always been much debate as to when the superego becomes a functional entity. Those who hold that this structure is not operative until the oedipus complex has been successfully resolved tend to base their position on the following statement by Freud (1923): "The broad general outcome of the sexual phase dominated by the Oedipus complex may, therefore, be taken to be the forming of a precipitate in the ego, consisting of these two identifications in some way united with each other. This modification . . . confronts the other contents of the ego as an ego ideal or super-ego" (p. 34).

Nevertheless, though the final touches to the superego as an enforcement agency take place at this time, especially in relation to oedipal incestuous trends, superego precursors have been active and effective for a long time before this. Indeed, it seems clear that the superego is built gradually, very possibly from the end of the second half of the first year onward.

It is usually around the age of 5 that children (both boys and girls) turn away from the oedipus complex. Freud (1924) described the process as follows:

> The object-cathexes are given up and replaced by identifications. The authority of the father or the parents is introjected into the ego, and there it forms the nucleus of the super-ego, which takes over the severity of the father and perpetuates his prohibition against incest, and so secures the ego from the return of the libidinal object-cathexes. The libidinal trends belonging to the Oedipus complex are in part desexualized and sublimated (a thing which probably happens with transformation into an identification) and in part inhibited in their aim and changed into impulses of affection. . . . this process ushers in the latency period, which now interrupts the child's sexual development. [pp. 176–177]

Just as there were significant differences in the oedipus complex of the boy and the girl, so too, according to Freud, are there marked differences in the forces that lead to its resolution and in the form this resolution takes. "Whereas in boys the Oedipus complex is destroyed by the castration complex, in girls it is made possible and led up to by the castration complex" (Freud 1925, p. 256). In Freud's view, girls blamed their mothers for the absence of the penis, and later on the girl's wish for a penis is exchanged for the wish to be given a baby by the father. Since this wish cannot be fulfilled either, the girl gradually gives up her oedipal attachment to the father and turns to nonincestuous objects. To these factors Freud adds the influence of upbringing and outside intimidation, which threatens her with a loss of love.

Freud (1931, p. 230) suggested that the oedipus complex is all too often not surmounted by the female at all, or is only very slowly surmounted. He thought that the possible consequences of this are that women's superegos are never so inexorable, impersonal, or independent of emotional origins as are those of men (1925, p. 257).

Some of these views are a matter of great controversy nowadays among psychoanalysts, as also among feminists. The latter find them unwarranted and even offensive, particularly such concepts as penis envy, feminine masochism, and the like. The whole matter is in a state of flux and awaits further clarification. As for Freud himself, he frankly stated that "it must be admitted . . . that in general our insight into these developmental processes in girls is unsatisfactory, incomplete and vague" (1924, p. 179).

References

Freud S. (1923), The ego and the id. *Standard Edition,* 19:3–63. London: Hogarth Press, 1961.

——— (1924), The dissolution of the Oedipus complex. *Standard Edition,* 19:173–179. London: Hogarth Press, 1961.

——— (1925), Some psychical consequences of the anatomical distinction between the sexes. *Standard Edition,* 19:243–259. London: Hogarth Press, 1961.

——— (1931), Female sexuality. *Standard Edition,* 21:223–243. London: Hogarth Press, 1961.

Gesell, A. (1940), *The First Five Years of Life.* New York: Harper.

Nagera H. (1966), Early Childhood Disturbances, Neurosis, and the Adult Disturbances (Problems of a Developmental Psychoanalytic Psychology). *Psychoanalytic Study of the Child,* Monograph 2. New York: International Universities Press.

——— (1975), *On Female Sexuality and the Oedipus Complex.* New York: Aronson.

2

The Influence of Early Development on the Oedipal Constellation

JEANNE LAMPL-DE GROOT, M.D.

In observing little children of approximately 4–6 years, we notice a number of similarities in their behavior, but perhaps still more differences. One of the earlier discoveries of Sigmund Freud in treating mentally disturbed patients was the very fact that their symptoms proved to be long-standing and reached back far into the patient's childhood. The inhibitions and disturbances of their love lives, as well as of their working capacities, already had their forerunners in childhood. The events of that period, however, were nearly completely forgotten, repressed, and warded off. They were merely able to come into consciousness through a special procedure, at first by hypnosis. Soon this technique was replaced by the psychoanalytic technique. The patient was requested to communicate his free associations, and the psychoanalyst, making use of this knowledge, tried to determine the origins of the patient's suffering through interpreting the material in collaboration with the patient. The theoretical outcome of Freud's observations was formulated in his statement that the core of neurotic symptoms is to be found in the oedipus complex. In studying "normal" personalities, Freud discovered that every human being passes through an oedipal constellation in his mental development between the age of 3 or 4 to about 6. He described this constellation as follows: A little boy wishes and has fantasies to replace his father as his mother's lover (like Oedipus). A little girl's strivings produce the fantasy of being her father's beloved one in place of her mother. The fate of this early fantasy life is complicated by the fact that in both boys and girls the negative oedipus constellation is present alongside the positive one. Passive sexual strivings in the little boy bring about the fantasy of being the father's beloved one. In the little girl, active sexual urges lead to the wish to be the mother's lover. In "normal" development the positive oedipus constellation will prevail. From the repressed unconscious it influences in some way or other the final love life of the adult.

We can still adhere to Freud's statement that the oedipal constellation is at the core of later neuroses and also of more or less "healthy" sexual love life, only with the addition that the oedipus complex is itself the outcome of complicated maturational and developmental processes in the preoedipal phase (Lampl-de Groot, 1952). The study of the latter was initiated by Freud but further elaborated by analysts, child analysts, and infant observers, partly after Freud's death (Freud, 1909a, pp. 97, 111, 206; 1931).

Children Ages 4–6

Physically healthy newborns with an "average-normal" anlage of the instinctual drives and the potentialities for ego-function development, when adequately mothered in babyhood and educated with understanding love in the family situation, show an active and lively type of behavior in the oedipal phase. The little boy may say, "When I will be big I will marry you, Mommy." His rivalry and hostility toward Daddy will finally be repressed and gradually give way to admiration and love. He will identify with Daddy and strengthen his masculinity. His passive strivings will in latency be sublimated and lead to an ability for learning, accepting knowledge from adults, and communicating with peers. In puberty and adolescence the revival of the old oedipal bonds with the parents will show no more than the usual upheavals and will lead to a more or less healthy adulthood.

The little girl will follow similar developmental lines, which include flexible progression and regression without fixation for both boys and girls (A. Freud, 1965). For the girl, however, there is an additional developmental problem in the fact that she has to give up her original love object (the mother), provoking a stronger hostility. This situation makes it more difficult to arrive at a sublimated, positive relationship and a female identification with the mother. However, both sexes have to cope with the physical impossibility of realizing the heterosexual bond with the beloved parent, and both have to do away with hostility and death wishes experienced toward the parent of the same sex. Nevertheless, healthy children live up to the necessities of human life.

Up to now I have described so-called "normal" development, more or less from a macroscopic viewpoint, and have indicated a number of preconditions, however ill defined and vague. I mentioned physical health. As a matter of fact, gross bodily defects cause a number of disturbances in mental development. Here I put the question whether bodily intact newborns are all alike in their behavior and activities (as quite a few people, including doctors, maintain). I go back to experiences of my own, over fifty years ago, when, as a young medical student, I worked in the obstetrics ward of Amsterdam University.

It sometimes happened that two to five babies were born the same night under similar circumstances. That is, the deliveries were "normal," without artificial intervention, and of an average duration as regards labor. The mothers seemed to enjoy having their babies and wanted to have them near their bodies to cuddle and feed. I shared the mothers' happiness, but I marveled at the wonders of nature. I hasten to add that I also encountered disturbed childbirths, with artificial interventions (sometimes successful, sometimes not), and many tragedies for the mother and other relatives. If the baby was "intact," one could sometimes console a mother who had suffered too much. If the baby was abnormal, with severe physical deformity or brain damage, I often wondered whether it was not inhuman to try to keep it alive, knowing it could never be a "normal" human being.

But here I want to come back to the healthy baby. Though at the time I knew nearly nothing of psychology or psychoanalysis, I was nevertheless fascinated by the observation of how different from one another the newborns were. Some of them, after their first cries had started the breathing process, became very quiet, passive babies, sleeping much and slow to take up the mother's breast (or the bottle, for that matter). On the whole, these babies developed gradually into "normal" babies. Other newborns reacted quite differently. They seemed to be very active, looking around, though I knew they could not yet focus on an object, as myelinization was not yet completed. Nevertheless, they displayed a very different behavior. They were quick in finding the mother's nipple and sucking energetically. The early fascination these observations held for me impressed upon my mind the importance of anlage factors. Of course, no psychoanalyst will deny that anlage plays a role in developmental processes; yet not infrequently one encounters authors who neglect its importance.

I have already mentioned the anlage of the instinctual drives. An imbalance between the sexual-libidinal and the aggressive-destructive drives may have important consequences for developmental processes. An innate excess of aggression is more often mentioned in the literature than an innate weakness of libidinal drives. Perhaps such a weakness is present in the passive, slow newborns mentioned above. After the anlage of the drives, I mentioned the innate potentialities for the development of ego functions. These include intelligence, cognitive functions, sense perception, integration, etc., which come into being only at a later period of development. But they also comprise reaction-formations, defense mechanisms, and defense maneuvers. I also identified adequate mothering as a precondition for healthy growth. This brings us to one of the most important factors: the gradual unfolding of object relations. The human newborn is completely dependent upon the mother for survival. He has to be fed and cared for in order to survive. In contrast to intrauterine life, where there is a constant supply of everything needed, after birth the baby experiences periods during which his needs are not met. The mother determines whether these privations are of short duration or intolerably protracted. We speak of an infant-mother dyad, a symbiotic bond, and of the mother being part of the infant's narcissistic milieu.[1]

In the first weeks and months of life the infant's physical needs are satisfied by a "good-mothering" person. As long as the baby is breast-fed, it is the real mother who is needed. However, not every mother has the capacity for good mothering—many are not aware that providing food and clothes is not sufficient for healthy growth. Love, warm feelings, and empathy are as necessary as bodily care. From observation of babies who have grown up in an institution or who have been hospitalized for long stretches of time, we know that they may become retarded; in some instances they even die (see Spitz, 1965). A baby is greatly in need of being fondled, cuddled, laughed with, spoken to, and moved around. Only when this happens can the little child gradually develop an awareness of the motherly person as a separate individual; "object constancy" (the capacity to retain the bond with the temporarily absent object); and finally a "real" object-love. I will not describe in detail the various phases of development of object relatedness, from symbiosis to the separation-individuation phase with its subphases of rapprochement, etc., because they are so aptly and fully studied by infant observers (see Mahler, 1968, 1972, 1975). Instead I want to mention two other problems, a theoretical one and a practical one.

First the theoretical: I think we should clearly correlate the development of object relatedness with the phase-specific states of the so-called oral, anal, and phallic phases. In the oral phase the infant lives in symbiosis with the mothering object. We know that in the oral phase satisfaction is not only acquired by the infant's being fed and stimulated in the zone of the mouth and

---

[1] The term *narcissism* (and the adjective *narcissistic*) is used in so many different senses that confusion inevitably arises. The term originated in Freud's libido theory and designated the original position of the sexual drive (libido) in the newborn child. Later on the aggressive-destructive drives were included. Although both sexual and aggressive *drives* are present in every living creature, sexual and aggressive acts and fantasies are developmental products and designate modes of *behavior*. Many authors use the term narcissism in reference to behavior (often in a deprecating way), not differentiating it from the underlying drive. Behavior, a developmental product, includes ego functions, however primitive. Finally, sexual impulses lead to love, aggressive ones to hate and to acts of aggression. Both self-love and object-love continue to exist throughout the lifespan, as do aggressive behavior and hate.

the oral cavity, but is also dependent on facial, acoustic, skin-contact, and movement gratifications. When the little child begins to crawl and then walk, a need for autonomy and for separation-individuation coincides with the anal phase of the drives. In this period cleanliness training is usually initiated. It is well known that here the wishes of adults very often run counter to the little child's anal lust. The object bond is the child's need for autonomy combined with a need for "refueling" (nearness of the motherly object), which frequently is grossly disturbed through badly timed and too severe demands by adults for compliance with regulations regarding cleanliness. This state of affairs may lead to severe opposition, stubbornness, and hostile feelings. But, as the little child is powerless, he must eventually submit, sometimes at the expense of loving capacities and sense of self. Aggressive impulses have to be repressed, but residues of his resentment and unhappiness remain in the unconscious and may influence the next developmental phase, the phallic one, where normally object relations take the shape of the oedipal constellation. The developmentally normal progression from one phase to the next is never a smooth and even one. Regressive tendencies are still present. If these are flexible, the progression will occur. If, however, a fixation has become too strong, the normal oedipal constellation may be impaired.

The practical problem involves the modern quest for "emancipation" in adolescents and young adults, a quest having many and varied consequences. I will go into only a few. Both partners of a couple have jobs outside the home; they decide to have a child. Pregnancy and birth are normal. What to do once the parental leave is over? The baby is a few weeks old, and the question arises how to proceed. Both partners want to continue in their jobs. The solution is: "Well, there is a creche in the neighborhood." The baby is brought to the creche at 8 A.M. and is left there until 6 or 7 P.M. We assume that the workers in the creche are decent people and take care of the baby's needs. The baby is confronted with many different caretakers. He scarcely sees his parents. The parents wonder why their baby, a healthy, active newborn, gradually becomes passive, sad, and unresponding to their kindness, and sometimes unmanageably aggressive. They are absolutely unaware of what they have done to their child. We understand the baby's reaction, as a basic experience of trust is lacking; good mothering is the first requirement for the child's healthy development.

In another situation, a young mother, some weeks after the birth of her child, insists on resuming her work. The father, very proud of his son or daughter, may reduce his working time (or choose to be unemployed) and is happy to care for his child. He becomes the mothering person. Instead of speaking of the mother-child dyad, we should in this case use the expression father-child dyad. The only thing a father cannot do is breast-feed the baby. In other aspects of caretaking he may at times be the more motherly person. If the mother does not completely neglect her baby, the triad is already originating, long before the child enters the oedipal situation.

Another very important problem centers around the little child's sexuality. I have already mentioned the need for oral and anal satisfaction. The attitude of the parents vis-à-vis masturbation is of great significance. "Old-fashioned" parents may condemn, with varying degrees of severity, the child's masturbatory activities. The child then either gives them up or, feeling anxious and guilty, absorbs his fantasies into his feelings of guilt and inferiority. By contrast, "modern" parents who claim sexual freedom may "seduce" their child by showing their naked bodies, taking the little child into their bed, and letting him witness their sexual intercourse. They are unaware that the child is being overstimulated and is unable to cope with such overwhelming excitement at this early age. Aside from the parents' attitudes, the little child is unable to actualize his oedipal desires, a fact which makes frustrations unavoidable.

Feeling helpless and powerless, the child takes refuge in fantasies of grandeur and omnipotence. In healthy development, these fantasies may develop into norms and ideals which may give a beneficial direction to the adult's strivings and activities (Lampl-de Groot, 1975, 1982). In my experience, a residue of the original grandeur lives on in the unconscious in everyone. However, relative intensity is decisive for the outcome in adult life. If parents are unaware of the child's inner world (which is usual), the "emotional misunderstanding" between children and adults becomes a fact. The experiential world of little children is very different from that of adults. Children's passionate demands for drive satisfaction are much more powerful than those of adults because ego functions are not yet established; children have still to grow and are very vulnerable. They live according to their need for drive gratification; they are not yet aware of reality factors, the calamities of the wider world that make demands upon the parents and therefore on themselves. Most grownups have forgotten (i.e., repressed) their own infantile experiential world, and lack of empathy with their little children is the consequence.

From both sides ambivalence comes into being. The toddler, who cannot understand why he has to abstain from so many lustful activities, feels abandoned, unloved, and worthless. His awakened aggression cannot be discharged; his powerlessness finds its sole consolation in fantasies of grandeur. The unresponsive parents may feel deceived and disappointed. They have the power to act out their hostility and to punish the child. A vicious circle may arise, and the emotional estrangement between parents and child increases. Luckily this gloomy situation is not always the case. But I do think it occurs more often than is usually assumed, and it is deleterious for the child entering the phallic phase and the oedipal constellation. In extreme cases the latter is not arrived at at all. Sometimes the positive oedipus complex is distorted or reversed, and the negative constellation prevails. Masturbation, if not completely abandoned (which is seldom the case), may give rise to severe guilt feelings and a need for self-punishment. Fantasies often begin to lead a life of their own, and they become very sadomasochistic.

Correlations of an Abnormal Oedipus Constellation with Disturbances in the Preoedipal Phases of Development

I have given only a simplified and sketchy account of the many possible distortions during the first 3 or 4 years of life which may result in an abnormal oedipal situation. My attempt to correlate deficiencies in the preoedipal phase of development with disturbances in the oedipal constellation will be equally fragmentary. I venture the following remarks.

If an infant during the first year of life, though physically normal at birth, is not adequately "mothered," severe disturbance is very likely. The real mother may be absent, or she herself may be mentally disturbed and unable to display any interest or feeling with regard to her baby. A substitute motherly person may bring a favorable outcome, but often this person is not a steady companion to the infant. This situation may impair the normal development of the instinctual drives, which are dependent on a warm object relatedness. The budding ego will not be able to develop its innate potentialities, and a structuration (at first rather primitive) of the baby's mind will not occur. Object relatedness remains symbiotic, and object constancy is not achieved. With severe neglect the child may become a psychotic, a borderline, an addict, or a delinquent.

The baby who has suffered neglect though not too severe, in his first year of life may have reached a kind of object constancy, though often this is rather fragile. Then a failure on the part of the parents to accompany empathically the special tempo of the toddler's developmental processes—for instance, in connection with his readiness to comply with demands for cleanliness—may disturb his maturational processes. The consequence may be fixation in the anal phase, accompanied by strongly ambivalent object relations, an insufficient fusion of aggression and libido, severe envy and rivalry with regard to parents and siblings, and a persistence of archaic grandiose fantasies, magical feelings of omnipotence alternating with a sense of inferiority. It is clear that this state of affairs predisposes to neurotic development, especially the acquisition of an obsessive-compulsive neurosis, often becoming manifest in latency, adolescence, or early adulthood.

If in the phallic phase castration anxiety is too strong, oedipal object relations may be impaired. For instance, a little boy may have given up masturbating together with his masculine fantasies out of fear of retaliation by his rival (the father). By giving up masturbation he unconsciously castrates himself in order to prevent his father from doing it. The boy may then turn to passivity, which may or may not extend to other areas, e.g., to learning inhibitions, difficulties with peers, etc. As a reaction-formation to his fears, outbursts of aggression, uncontrollable rage, or self-damage may occur. Usually, hysterical symptoms are linked to disturbances of the phallic-oedipal phase. In any case, the boy is unable to form a "real" object relation—love for another person on his own merits. The little girl, reaching the phallic phase, has to cope with a special problem, namely, her feeling of being discriminated against and handicapped as compared with little boys, who are allowed and even ordered to touch their genitals in urinating. The little girl often tries to copy the boys, but she feels inferior in having to sit down in order to urinate and in not being able to compete with the boys in producing far-reaching jets of urine. In her so-called penis envy she makes her parents responsible for her imagined inferiority. It is usually said that she resents her mother for this "handicap." In my experience, the father may be resented as well, especially when he feels attracted to his young daughter and in certain ways flirts with her. But when finally he leaves her and accompanies her mother into the bedroom, the little daughter may feel betrayed and full of resentment. In any case, it is difficult for the girl to enter into the "normal" oedipal relationship. Both boys and girls have to fight against special motives for envy. The girl has to struggle with her penis envy; the boy may be intensely envious of his mother and other women, who can produce wonderful, living, and beloved babies, whereas the boy's "products," the excrements, which at first are admired, end by being called "dirty" and "worthless" and are thrown away.

It is little consolation for the girl when she is told that she will later bear a child of her own, an achievement never possible for her brother. A child of 5 or 6 lives in the present and cannot imagine a distant future. The little boy of this age has to find solace in his becoming a father in the distant future, though he will never have a baby in his belly and will never give birth to one. Nor is he told that his future wife will need his semen to become pregnant. In any event, he does not know what that means, even if his parents try to explain it to him. And the 6-year-old boy is as incapable of visualizing a distant future as is the girl.

Here we come upon a special feature of *human* development, different from the growth toward maturity of our brothers in the animal kingdom. Many newborn animals are able to survive independent of their parents' care. With our next of kin, the chimpanzees, we differ in the length of time that dependency is necessary. Chimps need their mother's care for some 2 years, and after a short adolescence are mature and able to realize their own family life. The human child at 5–6 years of age is much further advanced in his emotional and fantasy world than he is in his physical development. He must wait some 8–10 years more before he reaches physical maturity.

Human beings have developed a number of intellectual capacities that are usually considered of inestimable value, one of the most valued being the acquisition of language and symbolic capacity. Over millions of years human beings have acquired a great number of qualities equipping them for conquering the forces of nature and for developing science, technology, and art. Most humans are very proud of these acquisitions and the attending civilization. However, the question arises whether they are strong enough to bear the *emotional* burden this rapid development of knowledge and technique has brought with it.

I have tried to describe the affective misunderstanding between children and grownups, a misunderstanding which may lead to psychopathology, competition, envy, hate, aggression, inhibitions, inertia, and addictions. It seems to me that comparable processes occur in unities larger than a single family. Social groups, countries, continents are fighting each other, not only in words but with deadly weapons. Envy, competition, hate, and lust for power provoke violence, often with lethal outcome.

I set out to describe the healthy development of little children into adulthood. One of the necessary clues is the final prevailing of love over hate and destruction. Let us hope that similarly constructive processes will come into being in the world at large.

References

Freud A. (1965), *Normality and Pathology in Childhood.* New York: International Universities Press.

Freud, S. (1909a), Analysis of a phobia in a five-year-old boy. *Standard Edition,* 10:5–147. London: Hogarth Press, 1955.

——— (1909b), Notes upon a case of obsessional neurosis. *Standard Edition,* 10:155–318. London: Hogarth Press.

——— (1931), Female sexuality. *Standard Edition,* 21:223–243. London: Hogarth Press, 1961.

Lampl-de Groot, J. (1952), Re-evaluation of the role of the Oedipus complex. In: *Development of the Mind.* New York: International Universities Press, 1965, pp. 198–212.

——— (1975), Narcissism and problems of civilization. *The Psychoanalytic Study of the Child,* 30:663–681. New Haven: Yale University Press.

——— (1982), Thoughts on psychoanalytic views of female psychology: 1927–1977. *Psychoanal. Quart.,* 51:1–18.

Mahler, M.S. (1968), *On Human Symbiosis and the Vicissitudes of Individuation.* New York: International Universities Press.

——— (1972), On the first subphases of the separation-individuation process. *Internat. J. Psycho-Anal.,* 53:333–338.

——— (1975), On the current status of the infantile neurosis. *J. Amer. Psychoanal. Assn.,* 23:327–333.

Spitz, R.A. (1965), *The First Year of Life.* New York: International Universities Press.

3

Two-and-a-Half to Four Years: From Disequilibrium to Integration

JUDITH S. KESTENBERG, M.D.

In many ways, the fourth year of life has been a stepchild of psychoanalysis. Helene Deutsch (1944) described a passive phase in girls which followed the pregenital phases and preceded the phallic. Melanie Klein (1928) described a rapidly passing phase in which the boy wanted to have a baby and identified with his mother. The girl, she said, had a much longer feminine phase. The preoedipal wish for a child was associated with anal wishes in the boy and with an "oral vagina" in the girl. Brunswick (1940), who discovered the preoedipal attachment of the girl to her mother, thought it to be part of phallic development. Lampl-de Groot (1947) discussed this phase in detail and assigned it phallic dominance. Freud referred to it in terms of a preoedipal phase; his terminology seems to suggest what is usually considered a phallic and negative oedipal development in the girl, with a sensual attachment to the mother. He never gave up his original idea that a baby is a substitute for a penis and is desired as an heir to penis envy. In his view, the vagina is not really discovered until puberty, at which time the girl has to switch from the clitoris to the vagina. Horney (1926, 1933) was the first to investigate the secondary role of penis envy in the girl's development. She pointed out that the vagina is denied rather than undiscovered. From observations of chil-

This paper discusses preoedipal issues in development and focuses on an early maternal phase concerning the mother-child and their baby. It is suggested that, as the reader reflects on these ideas, they may want to compare them with some of the discussions of preoedipal material in Volume 2.

dren and analyses of young children and adults, I have come to the conclusion that there is a maternal phase that precedes the phallic; its dominant zone is the inner genital (Kestenberg, 1956, 1968). Although my conclusion was based primarily on clinical material, it made a lot of sense to me that ontogenetic development should follow the fetal sequence of female organs developing before the male. Data from hormone assessments in childhood support my thesis, though they cannot be considered conclusive (Kestenberg, 1975). It is not surprising that inner genital dominance cannot compare in flamboyance to oral, anal, or phallic manifestations. The inner genital is cryptic, and it is difficult for the child to pinpoint its location and function. In addition, children are not told its name or function, and it is not easy for them to talk about sensations they can neither properly localize nor name. The situation is worse for boys than for girls. Early psychoanalytic writers reported two sexual centers in men: one inside—an analogue to the vagina—and the other outside—the phallus (Staerke, 1921; Kemper, 1934; Hitschmann, 1940). Fenichel (1931, 1945) concluded from descriptions of the sites of genital sensations that passive men referred to a sensual focus at a point where prostatic contraction propels the semen into the urethra. He referred to it as a special subsection of male sexuality, which he labeled "collicular sexuality." I may add that inner genitality plays a role in the inner genital phase of the boy between 2½ and 4, is revived in prepuberty, and recurs in adult men. The reluctance of parents to discuss the role of the inside with their boys is matched by the silence with which psychoanalytic literature treats the prostate, despite the fact that its disturbance plays an important role in the male reaction to aging, as does the infertility which may result from its removal (Kestenberg, 1968).

It is therefore not surprising that inner genitality as the first phase of genital development has not received recognition and that the sequence of oral, anal, and phallic phases has remained the mainstay of psychoanalytic thinking. In presenting the inner genital phase here, I must emphasize that one cannot look at a phase from the single viewpoint of libido development. In order for a normal phase to be recognized as dominant at a specific time of life, other aspects of psychic life must converge to form a unity. Aggressive drives must be considered; ego and superego development, too, must have a relationship to the predominant drive development. A metapsychological assessment (A. Freud, 1965) of a given phase must show a fit between psychic agencies. Where drives and ego (or superego) are at odds with one another, we expect pathology. For that reason it is incumbent upon us to show a total constellation of the inner genital phase before we can accept it as a distinct phase.

Is there a special organization that characterizes this phase? I have referred to it as a progression from disequilibrium to integration and have endeavored to show that an integration of pregenital with genital drive components must precede phallic development to guarantee a smooth progression into genitality. Several authors, some nonpsychoanalytic, have been concerned with ego development in this phase and have singled it out as a distinct entity.

On the basis of experiments involving the touching and manipulating of objects not seen by the subject, Piaget and Inhelder (1967) identified several stages in the understanding of space. Below 2½ years (Stage 0), experimentation with hidden figures is not possible. In Stage I (from 2½ to 4), there is recognition of familiar objects, then of topological, but not of Euclidean shapes, which begins in Stage II. In substage Ia (2½ to 3), familiar objects are recognized but not shapes. In substage Ib (3 to 4) shapes are recognized on the basis of a distinction between open and closed forms. There is a relative preference for curved shapes.

Proximity, the most elementary spatial relationship, plays a part in the drawings of toddlers who have progressed beyond the level of mere scribbling. Surrounding and enclosure are the relationships most clearly indicated in the case of simple shapes. This can best be seen in examples in which a small circle is put inside, outside, or on the contour of closed figures. There is a progression from simple rhythms to grouping by means of regulatory processes which "begin by coordinating the component parts of the initial rhythms and culminate, as an outcome of their increasing reversibility, in various types of groupings" (Piaget and Inhelder, 1967, p. 59). In the case of one child early in substage Ib, "figures with other shapes inscribed in them all result in an identical closed shape with a scribble inside each one, thus recognizing *the relationship of containment . . .*" (p. 63).

In my investigations of young children's drawings, I have confirmed the observation that from scribbling, crossing and criss-crossing there develops a circular form that eventually can be isolated as a circle. It is characteristic for children 3 to 4 years of age that these circles contain a scribble or another circle inside of them (Figure 1). In many instances these "inside" structures are identified as babies inside Mommy. Thus, there is a development from what seems a chaotic concept of space to a distinction between outside and inside. It is my contention that this realization coincides with the influx of sensations from inside the genital, an influx that helps create in the child the idea that he or she has something contained inside that is neither food, feces, nor urine.

Intellectual and drive development seem interconnected, drives giving impetus to the unfolding of intellectuality according to the stages of cortical maturation. Containment is a form of integration that distinguishes between body boundaries on the outside and on the inside. Hartmann (1939) postulated that aggression leads to differentiation; it may be added that libido is one of the driving forces of integration.

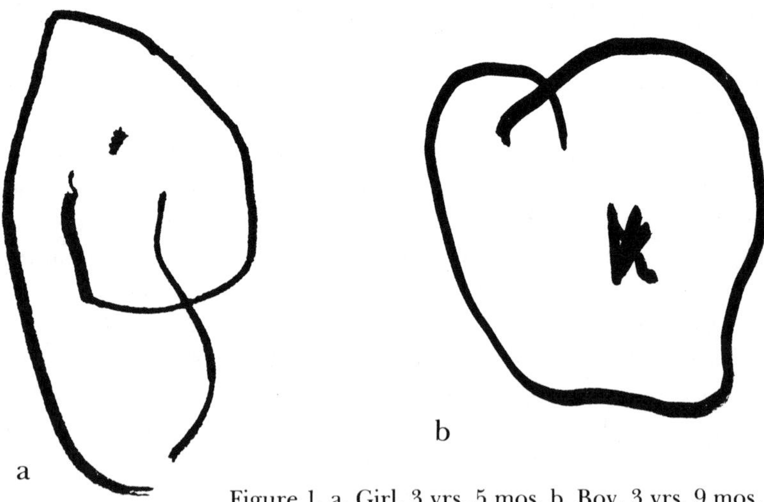

Figure 1. a. Girl, 3 yrs. 5 mos. b. Boy, 3 yrs. 9 mos.

Silvermann, Rees, and Neubauer (1975) seem to speak of the same type of organization when they describe a "central psychic constellation" at the age of 3. I fully agree with their view that this constellation helps determine the form and outcome of later struggles. Out of the coordination, during the first 3 years of life, of preoedipal variables, there arises an organization possessing sufficient cohesion and stability to have an impact on further development. I would add that a coordination between pregenital and inner genital drives and ego functions related to them is, if supported by an integrative environment, the task of the 3-year-old, who must order the ideation and wishes developed in previous phases before a reality orientation can be achieved and coherent images of external and internal reality formed. Greenspan (1981) emphasizes this typical organization of the child between 2½ and 3 years of age, which he refers to as "representational differentiation and consolidation." There is no doubt that differentiation proceeds in every phase, but putting things together and organizing them in a certain order become prominent in the 3-year-old. Toward the end of this phase, when aggression increases, there is a greater trend toward differentiation. Then, in anticipation of the phallic phase, the child begins to see things more in black and white. Greenspan himself gives good examples of the integrative aspects of the prevailing organization. He says that the child between 30 and 48 months begins to frame a number of sentences in order to present cohesive ideas. One notes a sense of cause and effect. However, Greenspan does not doubt that this phase corresponds to what in psychoanalytic literature has been described as the early phallic and beginning phallic-oedipal phases. Our observations suggest that the phallic child, unlike the 3-year-old, is too quick and abrupt to be capable of the kind of painstaking organization that creates a sequential story or leads to a consistent searching for answers to conflicting ideas and unknowns. The phallic child thinks in spurts. Ideas seem to come to him ready-made. He is an adventurer rather than a researcher trying to put things together and make sense out of them, so that they can be contained in units. These units, developed by the 3-year-old, are later used by the phallic child to erupt into flashes of insight that seem to come from nowhere.

Greenspan invokes the idea of integration, which he observed not only in the play of 3-year-olds but also in their interaction with other children and adults. He adds that the complexity of this configuration frequently goes unnoticed. This is a very precise description of the 3-year-old, who cannot always express what he wants to say, but who is capable of complex modes of nonverbal and semiverbal communication to make himself understood.

D., 29 months old, began to play with a doll which he carried around in the Center.[1] He told us that the baby cried and, when pressed to tell the baby's name, said "Crying." He would come to one of the staff and present his baby. At that point he would not tell us whether the baby was a boy or a girl. It seemed to be a third gender, "a baby." His mother had been pregnant for about 6 weeks but had not yet told D. He persisted in this play until his mother explained she was going to have a baby that was growing inside of her. He seemed very happy and pointed to his body, to indicate that the baby was in *him.* When his mother said the baby was inside *her,* he became angry and said he didn't want a brother or sister. He then engaged in a behavior unusual for him. He no longer wanted to be a big boy, but only Mommy's baby. He demanded to be carried and cried a lot. He accepted the notion that the baby was in his mother, but in unguarded moments reverted to his own idea that it grew within him. He made it abundantly clear to us that he wanted a baby in his inside—his own baby and not a sibling.

When his wishing to be a baby subsided a bit, he began to speak about an oven. No matter what the topic of conversation, D. came back to garbled sentences about an oven. A conversation with his mother revealed that D. had pulled out the drawer of their kitchen oven and was interested in knowing how it functioned. We then asked him whether he wanted to know how the baby came out. He nodded. Maybe he thought that Mommy had a drawer inside her, like the oven, and that when the baby was to come out she would pull out the drawer—a

[1] The Center for Parents and Children has two groups of parents and children who meet regularly. It is a research and prevention center for infants, toddlers up to the age of 4, and their parents.

very complex idea that D. could not yet put into words. He agreed that this question was of interest to him. We got a bag and put a doll inside and asked him to find the opening through which the baby would come out. He looked all over the bag, pulling on it until he found the opening. We then let the doll come out by stretching the opening. We had told him that Mommy had a hole between her legs that would be the passage for the baby. His complex questioning and persistent search for an answer would not have come to light had we not discovered the meaning of his preoccupation with the oven. He stopped talking about the oven until he could formulate his next question.

Parens (1980) acknowledged "the biologically determined maturational unfolding of gender related ego as well as drive development" (p. 473), an unfolding which begins to manifest itself in the third year of life. In line with this thinking he postulates an early infantile genital phase, which in the girl should not be called phallic; even then there are differences between boys and girls, whose primary masculinity or femininity is unfolding. It is undoubtedly true that the early genital phase, in which the inner genital is the dominant zone, differs in girls and boys. In the boy it is of shorter duration, and we see more often a breakthrough of phallic impulses that overshadow the inner genital impulses.

In the following sections important issues of this phase are discussed in order to differentiate it from the pregenital phases that precede it and the phallic phase that immediately follows.

Phase Progression

The child emerges from the pregenital phases still a baby and yet a "big boy" or "big girl." His ambition is to be big, to emulate older children and adults in controlling his body, but there is also a regressive pull toward dependency and passivity. The child at 2½ years is, to speak colloquially, "all mixed up." He is in a state of *disequilibrium.* He alternates between "doing it myself," an acquisition of the anal phase; getting time under control ("go for a walk *now*"), an achievement of the last pregenital phase, the urethral (see Kestenberg, 1975); and being a suckling; between being a stubborn asserter of his rights and a child lost in space but dictating where he will be taken and when. Parents are baffled by this inconsistent behavior and often very angry. They expect more from a child who can put many sentences together and understands so many more, and they are offended at the requests made of them to baby this big child. The confusion of the child often frightens them until they begin to understand (usually aided by a preventive intervention) that this is a transition from babyhood to toddlerhood and that the many ups and downs are an expression of confusion rather than a permanent regression. Although regressions are ubiquitous at this time, there is a particularly great tendency to regress or to persist in pregenital habits which were not worked through in the past. When a pregenital developmental task has not been accomplished, its challenge becomes exaggerated in this later phase.

Under the guidance of the *internal organizer* (the increasing influx of inner genital impulses) and the *external organizer* (the mother and to some extent the father), the child quiets down, attempts to resolve problems of the past, and reorganizes pregenital drives and ego traits under the aspect of inner genitality, which is sublimated into motherliness. The unweaned child weans himself; the untrained child trains himself. This can be greatly facilitated if one knows what has impeded previous accomplishments. A child who has been weaned too early may now be more dependent than ever and refuse to separate from his mother. A child whose mother could not provide the authority needed to train a child has now to contend with more temper tantrums than before. If problems of the urethral phase are in the foreground, spilling and urinating on the floor are used to provoke mother and father. It is helpful in such cases to remind mother and child about the early problems and to aid them in finding an accommodation on a new, secondary process basis.

In the Center we frequently ask parents to illustrate books about the child's early development. These are then read and discussed with the child. The pain of weaning when another baby arrived, or the feeling of humiliation when forced to lie during diapering instead of running around, may be the main topic. In one instance, a child would not separate from his mother, who did not protect him when he was a young toddler from a boy who took his things away all the time. In discussing the little book in which his tormentor appeared prominently, this child could verbalize his feelings that his mother liked the other child better. He wanted his mother's protection as a sign of her love. It took a long time, during which his mother protected him, before he stopped feeling like an unprotected, unloved baby.

When the tasks of the pregenital phases have been coped with sufficiently, only minor regressions of a temporary nature occur. These regressions in the service of adaptation (Geleerd, 1964) provide an impetus to reorganization.

The second part of this phase can be characterized as a phase of *integration.* The past is connected with the present, and the feeling of having lost one's babyhood is compensated by an intense identification with the mother that expresses itself in maternal behavior with dolls and babies. Here the difference in behavior between sexes is most pronounced. Boys become preoccupied with moving objects, while girls carry and hug dolls. Both sexes become gentle toward babies—with the exception of their siblings, of whom they are jealous. Both boys and girls spend a lot of time watching babies and stroking them. Helping younger children[2] is a preoccupation for both sexes, but boys are more impulsive than girls and often engage in roughhousing with younger children, in imitation of their fathers. By playing with babylike objects, which include toy cars (in the case of boys) as well as dolls or stuffed animals, children work through their own babyhood and their relation to the mother. From their behavior we can reconstruct how they had been treated by their mothers, not only in babyhood but currently as well. However, both sexes are quite capable now of motherly behavior. Left with infant siblings when their mothers must leave for a short time, these children become protective

[2] In the Center we operate on the principle that families belong together. Siblings are never separated, and 3-year-olds mingle with babies who are their siblings, as well as with other infants.

of the babies and do not let other children come close. A pride develops in having a baby in the family. Many children, girls more often than boys, become attached to a special doll and carry it around or sleep with it.

The end phase, as all end phases, is difficult for the child, as aggression rises and the gentleness of inner genitality recedes in favor of a violent expulsivity. Dolls have all along been mistreated when the child felt mistreated. Now, however, there is an increase of nagging, a characteristic manifestation of unsatisfied inner genital tension throughout life (see Kestenberg, 1968, 1975). There seems to be an increase in inner genital excitement, and the child seems to feel that what is bothering him inside must be expelled. He nags his mother because he can't stand the tension in himself and is trying to spread his excitement out of himself and over to her. This behavior is contagious and leads to many clashes, especially with the father, who is less tolerant of nagging than is the mother, in whom it strikes a responsive chord, even if she is irritated by it. In the end, the child gives up his wish for a child and denies the existence of his inner genital. This need to rid oneself of an inner excitement that has been externalized onto the baby or a baby doll is often expressed in an undue concern with death, both one's own and the mother's. In some cases a ritual "death of the baby" burial (Stevenson, 1954; Kestenberg, 1956) gives expression to what might be called the opposite of the "delivery" of a healthy child, the leading idea of this phase. It is easier for boys than for girls to externalize onto the outer genital and to deny or ignore inner sensations and the existence of genital structures inside the body. Boys can maintain the belief that what is inside is feminine and that they have everything on the outside. By denying the existence of the introitus, the girl can begin to feel that she too is a closed shape, convex like the boy, not concave the way she had felt up till now. Where these mechanisms are successful, children of both sexes can enter the phallic-narcissistic phase (Edgcumbe and Burgner, 1976) and convert their *baby envy* into penis envy. This time the penis envy is almost devoid of pregenital frustrations (oral, anal, and urethral deprivations) that may have been camouflaged earlier as penis envy (Galenson and Roiphe, 1971).

Inner Genitality

Since the inner genitals are not open to inspection, we can only infer the action of inner genitality. One way to do this is to compare behavior resulting from vaginal dissatisfaction in adult women, who can speak about it, with that of 3-year-old girls, and the preoccupation with the inner genital in adult men with a similar preoccupation in 3-year-old boys. Nagging, change of mood, and cryptic masturbation (either by squeezing the thighs together in girls or putting the penis between the legs and squeezing in boys) are observable in 3-year-olds. Furthermore, the analysis of rhythmic movement patterns in children of this age reveals a dominance of "inner genital rhythms." But what are these rhythms? And how can one recognize them?

We can observe in boys, from birth on, changes in tension, from free to bound flow and vice versa. Characteristic rhythms, pure and mixed, whose dominance and frequency change from phase to phase, can be identified.[3] Oral rhythms reveal characteristic sinus rhythm ; oral sadistic rhythms have a sharp peak in snapping and an even top in biting; anal rhythms are flexing and winding; anal sadistic rhythms are characterized by a prolonged phase of remaining on the same level of flow, usually referred to as holding ; urethral rhythms have a running character , and urethral sadistic rhythms have a stop-and-go quality, a rhythm necessary for the mastery of urination. Newborn babies, because of their flooding with maternal hormones, have a preponderance of feminine or inner genital rhythms. These have a quality of being very gradual, of long duration and low intensity. They can be referred to as waves. The aggressive type of inner genital rhythms, observed during the middle phase of delivery, are also very gradual and long-lasting, but they achieve a very high intensity which makes expulsion possible. By contrast, phallic rhythms are of short duration, frequently reach high intensity,

[3] The Kestenberg Movement Profile is based entirely on notations of movement patterns; the results are represented in nine diagrams. One can correlate these with Anna Freud's metapsychological assessment. For a detailed description of the method, see Kestenberg and Sossin, 1979.

and most characteristic, rise and fall with a decided abruptness 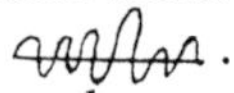 . When their sadistic quality becomes apparent, their peaks are sharp rather than rounded 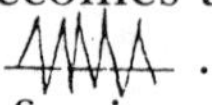 . In addition to these pure rhythms occur mixtures, as for instance oral-feminine  , or urethral-anal-sadistic rhythm forms 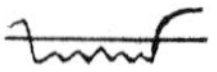 . In the beginning of the inner genital phase at the age of about 2½, we see a great many inner genital rhythms mixed with pregenital types. At the height of this phase inner genital pure rhythms are more frequent and can contain and modify pregenital rhythms. A behavioral manifestation of such a rhythmic mixture can be seen when a very motherly child rocks her "baby," diapers it, and encourages it to defecate, etc.

What evidence shows that these rhythms are indeed the preferred rhythms of certain zones and organs? The description of the very slow and subtle movements inside the proximal part of the vagina (Masters and Johnson, 1965) is identical with what we have classified as an inner genital rhythm. The more intense, sadistic forms of these rhythms can be seen during deliveries. We have discovered the same type of rhythms on the tunica dartos of the scrotum, and the building to a peak before orgasm in men is described in terms very suggestive of the expulsive uterine rhythms seen during deliveries. On the whole, the psychomotor behavior of the 3-year-old can be distinguished with the naked eye from that of the 4-year-old. The 3-year-old is slower, he tends to walk in an undulant fashion, and many of his movements have a wavy quality. In accordance with these rhythms, the 3-year-old tends to be circumspect and delicate, with a body more rounded than that of the springing about, arrowlike body of the 4-year-old.

Since a great many rhythms are available since birth, we can judge phase development only from the preponderance of certain phase-specific rhythms over others and from the way these rhythms organize and modify the other rhythms. The same is true of children's interests and fantasies. In talking about babies sucking, they will emphasize the mother's role as provider of the milk. They play at being mommies and enclose pretend babies in their arms, swaying gently, while making sucking movements themselves.

Quite a few 3-year-olds do not want to part from their

diapers. Whereas many boys confound front and back and think they will lose their penis when the feces is flushed down the toilet, both sexes verbalize that a baby will be found in the toilet and will be lost. A frequent factor in constipation is the overuse of slow, gradual rhythms for defecation, an operation requiring longer holding and quicker release, rather than a prolonged but slight increase and decrease of tension. The inner genital rhythm of low intensity is not conducive to expulsion of feces. When used for defecation it produces a passive type of constipation.

Experimentation with pregenital forms and their incorporation into the newly dominant forms of expression leads to dysfunctions and then to a new way of functioning, at a higher level. In their play, the "mommies," who sucked their thumbs, feed and diaper the "babies," love them and scold them. Boys, who just wet their pants, more frequently wheel them in carriages and walk with them. Boys feel movements inside, while girls seem to feel waves of tension.

At times, especially when the mother is pregnant, a 3-year-old will put a doll under her dress or shorts and walk around pretending she is pregnant. Two-year-olds rarely do this. It was interesting for us in the Center to watch two friends, one of whom had entered the phallic phase while the other was still in the inner genital.

D., 3 years 8 months, supplemented her marching with instruments by putting the instrument under her shorts and having it stick out like an erect penis. R., who had just turned 3, put the instrument under her dress, which did not protrude like a penis but instead simulated pregnancy. D., giggling, pretended she had a penis sticking out in plain view. The difference was striking. R. proudly showed that she had something inside that was rounded and made her full. One child was outside-oriented, while the other was inside-oriented. Both had younger siblings.

Whereas 3-year-olds ask how babies come out, 4- and 5-year-olds ask how they get in. One vantage point is from inside out (How do the hidden babies become visible?), the other is from the outside in (How did you put something into mommy?) While boys seldom ask these questions with the precision and clarity shown by girls, they nevertheless show their preoccupation in their play and acting out. S., a 3-year-old boy concerned with how babies emerge, urinated on the rug. Scolded by his nurse, he replied, "Look, look, it's a baby," and pointed to the shape his urine had created on the rug. When his mother asked where the baby had come from, he unhesitatingly pointed to the side of his groin, where he undoubtedly felt the movement of his spermatic cords. S. was the youngest child in his family and had never seen a pregnant woman.

Hide-and-seek is a game that children of all ages like. However, to hide one's entire self so as not to be seen, is a concept that does not develop before 2 or 3. Being in a contained environment and then coming out of it into plain view has an exhilarating effect on the child. While the 4-year-old pops out of his hiding place suddenly, the 3-year-old allows the seeker to get into a suspense gradually before he appears. The 4-year-old wants to surprise instead.

Evidence of the 3-year-old's preoccupation with the inside is seen in drawings (Kestenberg, 1982) and in verbal as well as nonverbal communications. Evidence of inner genital sensations at this age is seen in the feeling, expressed by children of

Figure 2. A detail of John Singer Sargent's "The Daughters of Edward D. Boit," 1882. Museum of Fine Arts, Boston.

both sexes, that there is a baby inside them; in the idea, frequently expressed by boys, that babies come from their side; and in the frequency with which girls and boys put dolls between their legs, often camouflaging masturbatory activities so gradual as to escape detection by an onlooker (see Figure 2).

The Integrative Influence of Internal and External Organizers

Rhythmic units with a long duration have been shown to have an organizing effect on others. For instance, the anal sadistic straining rhythm, in which tension is held on an even level for some time before being released, can easily incorporate the much shorter oral and anal rhythms. This is even more true of the much longer inner genital rhythms. Children's use of these rhythms in maternallike behavior allows for the evolution of patience and of a tolerance for change. Playing with dolls or dancing, 3-year-olds are predominantly gentle and take their time moving. This is more pronounced in girls than in boys. The hypothesis here is that what is experienced in the lower part of the body, in the immature reproductive organs, is externalized in maternal activities. Unable to experiment with the inside of the body, the child finds suitable objects to stand for inner organs and experiments with these. In the associations of adults and children to their drawings, a babylike object often emerges as a contour of the representation of inner genitalia. However, we also find with some frequency that the image of the mother is included alongside or superimposed on the baby image (Kestenberg, 1982). It seems that the influence of inner genitality motivates the child to investigate patiently—like a researcher—in order to find forms suitable for representing what is felt inside. The representation of internal organs is influenced by the perception of external objects.

The most pervasive fear of the 3-year-old is the fear of annihilation (Jones, 1935), a fear much more archaic than the fear of castration. This fear is understood better when one realizes that the child is afraid of chaos, of a lack of order occasioned by conflicting drives and conflicting ego attitudes and defenses. Prevailing rhythms of movement and thought give the child time to solve inner conflicts, but when external trauma piles up the child cannot cope and becomes terrified of the chaos inside. The 3-year-old needs the external organizer, the mother, to bring order into a confusing and frightening disorder. In following up children who had gone through a very stormy inner genital phase, I discovered that these storms were the forerunners of profound disturbances in adolescence or adulthood.

It is not easy to be a helper to the 3-year-old. Many defenses and coping devices characteristic for the age upset the parent, who then cannot function optimally. What the child needs now is help in expressing the traumas of infancy that while troubling cannot be remembered in words. At the Center we have used books describing and illustrating these traumas to evoke responses in 3-year-olds; often they corrected what we said or drew to conform to what they felt really happened. In one instance a girl who had become very dependent, clingy, and afraid to be alone was entranced when we read a book to her about how she was weaned from the breast at 5 months and was given her bottle by people other than her mother. At one point during the story she began to pull my hair. I asked whether as a baby the girl had pulled her mother's hair. The mother denied it, but the child emphatically insisted that she had. She was able to express her fury at having been left and her infantile attempts to hold on. With her own resources and her mother's new understanding, she could now overcome her fears and coordinate her wishes to be a "big" ballerina with her neediness as the baby she no longer was. For the longest time she kept telling me she would eat me so I would not be able to go away, while at the same time threatening that she would abandon me and that I would never see her again. This helped the mother understand how her daughter must have felt when she was a baby and how this unresolved problem haunted her now. Not all problems, however, are this serious. Usually mothers can help their children integrate conflicting feelings and attitudes without benefit of professional guidance. Three-year-olds reminisce a great deal; they like to look at picture albums and see what they did when they were babies. Mothers are delighted to show them these albums and to help them accept themselves as babies in the past and as the same people now, though older. Three-year-olds can suddenly remember what happened a year earlier and ask questions about it. Many times one cannot understand their questions, even if they pertain to more recent events, without help from their mothers. This is especially true when there is no obvious connection between the current conversation and the child's remarks. The child's attempts to combine and order the relations between objects and their internal representations compounds the difficulty in communication. In preventive work we teach parents to make sense of the child's seemingly unintelligible "primary process" communications.

D., 2½ years old, had been preoccupied with ovens but, as described above, ceased talking about them when the facts of child delivery were explained to him. About a week later I drew a house for the children at the Center. They asked that I draw a room in it and teased me, requesting that I draw the moon and the sun inside the room. Their preoccupation with inside and outside revealed itself in the game they created, in which they laughingly confused what was in the house and what was outdoors. I drew the celestial shapes outside the house and then a moon that could be seen through the window. D. said nothing about it, but participated in a lively and attentive manner. Later that day he asked me to draw with him and was very gratified when I drew circles, something he could not yet do. He had a hard time putting features into the circle without continuing his lines over to the outside. When I drew a square he was disappointed and went to another staff member to have circles drawn. In the midst of this he began to talk about the oven again and assured us that Mommy had an oven, but that he was a little boy and had none. He pointed to the ceiling and said that water was coming down from the sky. With great excitement he told us that the glass was falling and would break. The water and sky may have referred to a rain that had occurred a few days previous (and to his reluctance to be trained) and to the "celestial" drawings we had made earlier that day. He had told us recently that he would not give up his diapers until his mother's baby was born. Still, we did not understand the reference to broken glass until his mother told us that there was a window in her oven door. Hearing her explanation, D. went over to his mother and asked to look inside her "window." Not finding one, he pointed to her belly button, to which he had repeatedly referred as the seat of the baby. It was his mother who guessed then that D. was referring to the delivery of the baby. Again we put a doll in a bag and showed him that he wouldn't let the baby fall out and break. We showed him how slowly the delivery takes place and that it occurs while lying down rather than standing. Still, D. showed us, his arms raised high, how rain and glass would come down from high up. We had to guess that he was speaking of sitting on the toilet and dropping feces and urine into it "from a great height." Relieving himself in the diaper, by contrast, prevented this dangerous fall and so was more acceptable. Reassured, he stopped talking so excitedly. It made sense to us now why he felt he had to wait until the baby was born before he would sit on the toilet. Not yet finished with pregenital concerns, he was still preoccupied with the fantasy that he would deliver the baby with his feces. This fear is frequently seen in girls and even in adult women who were afraid their baby will fall out in a sudden spurt of birth *(Sturzgeburt)*. Three-year-olds who walk around with dolls tucked inside their shirts will also inadvertently lose the doll and not notice it for a while. In the dreams of pregnant women there recurs a theme of losing the baby and not knowing how it happened.

Birth and Death

Nowadays parents often try to explain birth to their children. Some parents even insist that the children be present during home deliveries. This is done out of a lack of understanding that the child needs to test his own birth theories and to weave his own fantasies around a fear-arousing reality that he can view only from a distance. The fear of losing continuity, of ceasing to exist, is very common during this phase. Children urgently ask us where they were before they were born. In one instance, a 3½-year-old girl was told that she was in Mommy's egg. She then asked where she was before Mommy was born. Her grandmother told her that Mommy was in her egg. The persistent little girl then asked where her grandmother was before *she* was born, and so on. Finally the child was reassured that there had always been a predecessor of her—in an egg of her mother, grandmother, great grandmother, etc. Another child, a few months younger, interrogated her mother similarly. In desperation, the mother finally told her that the whole thing started with Adam and Eve, who were created by God (Kestenberg, 1982).

It is important for 3-year-olds to have concrete answers about beginnings and ends. They are afraid of voids, of ceasing to exist, and even when they accept the notion of death—once it is concretely explained and they know where the dead person has been buried (Furman, 1974)—they continue to spin fantasies about rebirth.

Once, when we read to a group of 3-year-olds a story that presented different explanations of what happens to people when they are dead (going to heaven, living in memory, etc.), a child who had wondered why he had no grandfather exclaimed, "I know! When people die they go away so far that we never can see them again." Death is sometimes connected with a feeling of loss, as when a warm "part of the body" (feces or urine) becomes cold and no longer feels like a part of oneself, or with a feeling of feces breaking off. Children equate disappearance with death and begin to worry what happens to their parents when they don't see them. Will they come back, or will they die and never be seen again?

One day a group of children between 2½ and 4 found a dead bird on the steps of the Center. We debated whether the bird was dead and decided that it did not move, did not breathe, and had to be buried. The bird was put in a box which one of the children carried to the back of the playground; there a hole was dug and the box placed in it. The children threw earth on it. But then the oldest and the youngest of the group arrived late and wanted to see the bird. We took the box out, showed them the bird, and reburied it. The oldest child asked again, "Where is the bird?" This time the children answered her that the bird was in the box and the box buried in the earth and she could not see it. Then one creative child suggested, "The bird is dead, but we can be birds." They all began to "fly" on their way back to the Center and two "fell dead," whereupon a staff member was summoned to give them medicine. The identification with the dead bird was obviously a solution to grief and anxiety about the bird's death, which was transformed into a sickness that could be cured. The next day the same creative child invented a story about a worm coming out of the grave and turning into a little bird and flying away. Another day, the child who had had a hard time understanding that his grandfather had died before he was born told us that a bird came out of the grave and flew away. We then said to him, "Your grandpa died a long time ago. Did he ever come back?" The boy smiled and said yes, but he knew that both the bird and his grandpa were dead.

In Furman's experience (1974), the normal 2-year-old can achieve a basic understanding of the meaning of death. However, death is not easily accepted by the 3-year-old, who is caught up in the polarity between death and birth, between the disappearance and the return of people and sensations. Furman reports about 3-year-old Susie, whose mother had died. After being told about it, Susie asked, "Where's my mommy?" Her father reminded her about the dead bird that they had found and buried. She understood. The tendency to deny a loved one's death and the belief in reincarnation ("a bird came out and flew away") remains in the unconscious. Some ethnic groups traditionally name children after deceased parents in order to perpetuate their memory. Analysis of ideas of death and birth reveals that the two ideas are related to falling asleep and waking up, but also to other instances in which excitement dies down and there is a feeling of emptiness or boredom which after a while yields to a new wave of excitation. When inner genital sensations become too disquieting and too intense, there is a great need to get rid of them. There occurs a yearning for the "death" of the inside. Such states are often symbolized in the death and burial of animals or in imaginary funerals for dead dolls. To avoid upsetting and cryptic inner tensions, the child uses a number of defenses but also a number of adaptive measures whereby attention is diverted from the inside to the outside.

Ego Attitudes and Defenses

Externalization is the foremost mechanism of this phase. It is employed both for adaptation and as a defense mechanism against drives. It is the best route by which to achieve the sublimation of inner genital drives into maternal attitudes and behaviors.

Tenderness and care mixed with compassion are shown toward babies and babylike objects. At the same time the child is particularly responsive to slight changes in the mother's feelings and moods. Often, before the mother herself is even aware of her sadness, the child approaches her to ask, "Why are you sad, Mommy?" There is also a desire to make things better, to soothe, as when children say, "Don't worry, Mommy, I will sing to you and make you feel better."

Preoccupation with what is inside the body gets deflected to the exploration of external objects suitable for representing the inner organs: babies, dolls, stuffed animals, but also, especially in boys, hats, cars, toy airplanes, and almost anything that moves in a cryptic way.[4] The mother-baby-child triangle is a unit in which all members are interchangeable. The child alternates between a view of self as a baby, as a mommy, and as a big boy or girl. This triangle is externalized and colors the child's perceptions. For instance, even though there is clear gender differentiation by this time, for the 3-year-old there exist three sexes: men, women, and parents. When asked whether Mommy is a woman, they may say, "No, Mommy." Daddy is not a man but a daddy. The concept of a husband or wife who belong together is way above the young 3-year-old's head and will not be acceptable for another year. To the 3-year-old, the world revolves around him, his parents, his siblings, and his belongings, onto which he can shift and externalize

[4] From this feeling there arises the tendency to call automobiles "baby," a usage popular among adolescents.

inner tensions. Externalization is also used to ward off anxiety about having nothing inside or something too exciting inside. The child then says he is bored and has nothing to do or, when excited, looks for exciting things to do.

Nagging others is the child's affective expression of feeling nagged by what is going on internally. A frequently used mechanism is to spread excitement onto a parent or sibling (Kestenberg, 1975), who then becomes excited as well as the child (or instead of the child). The 3-year-old harbors the belief that excitement and anxiety are like objects that can be taken out of oneself and put in someone else.

The more intense the inner genital excitement, the more frustration there will be, and the more aggression against the child's body (including internal organs) and other people, especially the mother. In a particularly striking case, a vaginal fungus infection made the child feel that she was jumping out of her skin (Kestenberg, 1968). Such situations lead to wishes to eviscerate oneself and to blame a parent for the unbearable tension; anger at one's own inside is sometimes symbolized as the "death of the baby."

Other defenses, developed earlier, are retained and are coordinated now into defense complexes. Denial, ever present, becomes intensified at the end of this phase, which ends with denial of the inside. Reaction-formation makes children stroke babies in a very gentle way. Its breakdown transforms this stroking into pulling and twisting. The magic mechanism of doing and undoing combines with reversal of affect into its opposite and with turning from passive to active (and vice versa). All these mechanisms are put at the disposal of externalization, which leads to acting out in play and in everyday behavior. The acting out is adaptive, as it is a tool for remembering early infantile experiences that cannot be verbalized. Make-believe games transform children into witches, monsters, or princes and princesses.

Identification with the mother, seen in the child's imitation of her maternal qualities and behavior, becomes very distinct during this period. It allows children of this age to care for themselves in spheres where once the mother took responsibility. In this sense, they become their own babies. However, the children's caricaturing of maternal traits and behaviors, used as defense, is not too far removed from aggression. A 3-year-old came to the Center once and said, "You know what, Dr. Kestenberg? My daddy is a beast." Knowing the family, I asked, "Did Mommy say that?" He nodded, embarrassing his mother. Indeed, she had called the father a beast in the midst of an argument. Another 3-year-old mouthed continuously and did not look people in the eye. Careful observation revealed that the child's mother also mouthed slightly and stared in front of her, avoiding contact with others, though in an inconspicuous way. Often such behavior in children results from identification with the aggressor.

Coping with the past and reenacting it, the child will display behavior which is not of recent vintage, but rather something that has been done to him or when he was a baby or toddler. A 3-year-old developed the strange idea that he was unable to climb onto a couch or chair. He seemed to try, but could not quite get there. I observed him alone with his mother and noted that when he approached her she would bend down or stoop down to his level. Had he wanted to climb onto her lap, he could not have—not unless he asked her to straighten up. Although he was quite capable of expressing the desire to climb onto his mother's lap, he behaved as if he were not. I asked the mother whether in the past she had ever been reluctant to take him in her lap. She replied yes, that when he was a little over a year old, and being weaned, she did not want him tugging at her blouse. From his point of view at the time, the mother's lap became unavailable and he could no longer climb on it. At the time of weaning he only realized that he could not climb and he reproduced this feeling at this time when he was trying to put his past in better perspective. In this example, the child did not identify with the mother, but rather acted out what he had experienced as a very young toddler. Through our understanding of the past (with the mother's help), he was able to recoup the lost lap and his ability to climb.

Many other such examples show that one of the adaptive measures taken by 3-year-olds is the reconstruction of the past in action.

The Superego

There is a consensus in psychoanalysis that the superego develops as a cohesive structure after the resolution of the oedipus complex in childhood and later again in adolescence. However, it is recognized that precursors of the superego develop earlier.

By the end of the inner genital phase the child has erected those aspects of the superego which pertain to the acceptance of routines, habits, and limited areas of community responsibility. All the attitudes of the pregenital phases flare up at the beginning of this phase. Grabbing is renewed and eventually given up. Instead of holding on to things, the child begins to share; instead of pushing ahead to be first, he learns to take turns. These new attitudes, which have developed to please the adult, become internalized now, in identification with the preoedipal parents. In addition, basic routines such as eating at the table at specified mealtimes, going to the bathroom rather than soiling or wetting, and going to sleep at bedtime are accepted and internalized. The child is usually ashamed when he has an accident, but he also feels guilty when he spills or messes. These pregenital precursors of the superego now form a sort of a presuperego complex whereby the child adopts a set of rules he has learned from adults. We recognize the struggles with these rules when the child says to a doll or to another child, "You better go to the bathroom now" or "It's time to go to sleep." Rules of fair play are continuously worked through and a sense of justice develops—first, of course, in relation to oneself. For instance, the 3-year-old is offended when his mother gives his friend a larger portion than she gives him. By identification with a fair mother, he learns to distribute equal portions. Most difficult to control are aggressive impulses, especially a desire to upset or hurt others. Here the desire for controlling others, making them cry and hurt, overshadows the demand not to hurt people. Yet this moral issue is being worked through in relation to parents, pets, and friends. The child who is angry at his mother because she has children while he cannot have any overcomes his resentment because of his love for his mother, but also because he is now capable of saying no to himself—"No, I am a little boy (or girl) and cannot have a baby now." To fulfill this demand he forbids himself to "know" his inner genital sensations; he denies the existence of reproductive organs inside his body. The superego constellation I am describing forms the basis for a re-formation of the superego in the resolution of the oedipus complex, when the renouncing of the opposite-sex parent brings also a renewed renunciation of the wish for a baby.

Conclusion

The child between 2½ and 4 years of age has to cope with the loss of babyhood and with becoming a big boy or girl. Pregenital fantasies and attitudes must be reconciled with the new role of a child who is weaned and trained. In the beginning disequilibrium results from the confusion between past and present. Under the influence of internal and external organizers the child succeeds in integrating the conflicting trends in a phase I have called the inner genital. The child becomes preoccupied with the inner genital and with the question of where babies are inside and how they come out. Externalizing inner genital sensations, the child becomes maternal and plays with babylike objects. This is true of both sexes, although the phase lasts longer in girls than in boys. The principal themes of birth and death are important issues of this phase. It ends with a denial of the inner genital and a turn to the outer genital, which ushers in the phallic phase in both sexes.

Briefly, we can see how from the hatching of the self in infancy (Mahler, 1968) there develops a baby-self in contradistinction from the mother; then, at about 3, the child assumes the role of the mother and plays at having babies. Only with the temporary abandonment of motherliness does the 4-year-old become a phallic boy or girl. In this new phase, intrusion into the outer space compensates for the "loss" of the inner space.

References

Brunswick, R.M. (1940), The preoedipal phase of the libido development. *Psychoanal. Quart.*, 9:293–319.

Deutsch, H. (1944), *The Psychology of Women,* Vol. 1. New York: Grune & Stratton.

Edgcumbe, R., & Burgner, M. (1976), The phallic-narcissistic phase: A differentiation between preoedipal and oedipal aspects of phallic development. *The Psychoanalytic Study of the Child,* 30:161–180. New Haven: Yale University Press.

Fenichel, O. (1931), The pregenital antecedents of the Oedipus complex. *Internat. J. Psycho-Anal.,* 12:141–166.

——— (1945), *The Psychoanalytic Theory of Neurosis.* New York: Norton.

Freud, A. (1965), *Normality and Pathology in Childhood.* New York: International Universities Press.

Furman, E. (1974), *A Child's Parent Dies.* New Haven: Yale University Press.

Galenson, E., & Roiphe, H. (1971), The impact of early sexual discovery on mood, defensive organization, and symbolization. *The Psychoanalytic Study of the Child,* 26:195–216. New York: International Universities Press.

Geleerd, E.R. (1964), Adolescence and adaptive regression. *Bull. Menninger Clinic,* 35:467–468.

Greenspan, S. (1981), *Psychopathology and Adaptation in Infancy and Early Childhood: Principles of Clinical Diagnosis and Preventive Intervention.* New York: International Universities Press.

Hartmann, H. (1939), *Ego Psychology and the Problem of Adaptation.* New York: International Universities Press, 1958.

Hitschmann, E. (1940), Beitrage zur Aetiologie und Konstitution der Spermatorrhoe. *Internationale Zeitschrift fur Psychoanalyse,* 25:197–205.

Horney, K. (1926), The flight from womanhood. *Internat. J. Psycho-Anal.,* 7:324–339.

——— (1933), The denial of the vagina. *Internat. J. Psycho-Anal.,* 14:57–70.

Jones, E. (1935), Early female sexuality. In: *Papers on Psycho-Analysis.* London: Bailliere, Tindall & Cox, pp. 485–495.

Kemper, W. (1934), Zur Genese der Genitalien Erogeneitat und des Orgasmus. *Internationale Zeitschrift fur Psychoanalyse,* 30:287–312.

Kestenberg, J. (1956), Vicissitudes of female sexuality. *J. Amer. Psychoanal. Assn.,* 4:453–476.

——— (1968), Acting out in the analysis of children and adults. *Internat. J. Psycho-Anal.,* 49:341–346.

——— (1975), *Children and Parents.* New York: Aronson.

——— (1982), Inner-genital phase: Prephallic and preoedipal. In: *Early Female Development,* ed. D. Mendell. New York: Spectrum, pp. 81–125.

——— & Sossin, K.M. (1979), *Movement Patterns in Development.* New York: Dance Notation Bureau.

Klein, M. (1928), Early stages of the oedipus conflict. *Internat. J. Psycho-Anal.,* 9:167–180.

Lampl-de Groot, J. (1947), The preoedipal phase in the development of the male child. *The Psychoanalytic Study of the Child,* 2:75–113. New York: International Universities Press.

Mahler, M. (1968), *On Human Symbiosis and the Vicissitudes of Individuation.* New York: International Universities Press.

Masters, W., & Johnson, V. (1965), The sexual response cycle of the human male and female: Comparative anatomy and physiology. In: *Sex and Behavior,* ed. F.A. Beach. New York: Wiley, pp. 512–535.

Parens, H. (1980), Psychic development during the second and third years of life. In: *The Course of Life: Psychoanalytic Contributions Toward Understanding Personality Development, Vol. 1,* ed. S. Greenspan & G. Pollock. Washington, D.C.: National Institute of Mental Health.

Piaget, J., & Inhelder, B. (1967), *The Child's Conception of Space.* London: Routledge & Kegan Paul.

Silvermann, M., Rees, K.A., & Neubauer, P.B. (1975), On a central psychic constellation. *The Psychoanalytic Study of the Child,* 30:127–157. New Haven: Yale University Press.

Staerke, A. (1921), The castration complex. *Internat. J. Psycho-Anal.,* 2:179–201.

Stevenson, O. (1954), The first treasured possession. *The Psychoanalytic Study of the Child,* 9:199–217. New York: International Universities Press.

4

Ages Four to Six: The Oedipus Complex Revisited

HEIMAN VAN DAM, M.D.

In 1905, Freud published *Three Essays on Sexuality* (1905b), in which he startled the scientific world by describing the existence of a sexual development in children during the first 6 years of life and its aftereffects in later development and adult sex life. Strachey (1953), in his editor's note, quite rightly considers this paper, together with *The Interpretation of Dreams,* Freud's "most momentous and original contributions to human knowledge" (p. 126).

The facts of infantile sexuality had been denied by most observers up to that time, partly because of repression, the observers' own infantile amnesia.

Freud had formed his own ideas on infantile sexuality primarily on the basis of his self-analysis and analyses of adult patients, including the content of dreams. In addition, he had some limited access to direct infant and child observation plus an encyclopedic knowledge of art, history, mythology, and anthropology. As his own fund of data increased, Freud became aware of "deficiencies and obscurities" in his discovery. As he stated in the preface to the second edition, he wished "that what was once new in it may become generally accepted, and that what is imperfect in it may be replaced by something better" (p. 130). What has become generally accepted are the facts of infantile sexuality and its reverberations in later life. The details of what that infantile sexuality consists of and how it affects later life have been revised, corrected, expanded, "replaced by something better," elaborated, and, in many instances, confirmed. Investigators who have found themselves at odds with some of Freud's reconstructions have sometimes felt, erroneously I believe, that they were attacking the essence of psychoanalysis. This has been true especially of many outside the field of psychoanalysis, including some leaders of the women's movement. As Freud himself was quick to admit, he may not in each instance have described correctly the details of infantile sexuality. However, the basic essentials—namely, an early sexual life that becomes partially repressed and that affects adult life in a variety of ways—have survived the last 70-odd years remarkably well. It is in this spirit that this chapter is written; it will begin with a brief outline of how Freud developed his ideas about the oedipus complex, and what recent research has discovered to be at variance with his formulations. For a more detailed description of the development of Freud's ideas, the reader is referred to Calogeras and Schupper (1972). Briefly, as early as 1897 Freud regarded falling in love with the parent of the opposite sex and jealousy of the parent of the same sex to be a universal phenomenon in children (1897, p. 265). He felt more certain of his observations on the male child than on the female.

Freud became aware of constitutional factors as early as the Dora case (1905a). This case also served as a clinical demonstration of the resurgence of oedipal strivings in adolescence. His "On the Sexual Theories of Children" (1908) and the analysis of Little Hans (1909) brought into direct focus children's preoccupation with their oedipal conflicts. He became aware of the role of sexual stimulation (the doctor game, etc.) and trauma (e.g., the birth of a sibling) in the development of the oedipus complex. Freud maintained throughout that the oedipus complex in boys is initiated as a developmental sequence, and likened it to the child's deciduous and permanent teeth. For the little girl, by contrast, he maintained that the oedipus complex was initiated by a trauma, namely, the discovery of the fact that males have penises. This would turn the little girl away from her mother in anger and disappointment. As a consequence, she gives up her wish for a penis and turns to her father with a wish for a baby, adopting a feminine attitude toward him. The wish for a penis would lead to the character trait of jealousy.

Even rather late, Freud (1925) was uncertain about his formulations, especially about female oedipal development: "This opinion can only be maintained if my findings, which are based on a handful of cases, turn out to have general validity and to be typical" (p. 258). In other words, Freud struggled between adherence to a biological theory—anatomy as destiny—and the acknowledgment of psychological factors in the epigenetic unfolding of the child's personality. The discovery of the penis by the little girl supposedly led not only to her entry into the oedipal phase, loosening her tie to her mother and turning her toward her father; it led also to jealousy, the wish for a baby, and a sense of inferiority, especially about her clitoris, that resulted in her abandoning masturbation. The belief that she has lost her penis due to masturbation also played an important role.

As noted with regard to the little boy, oedipal conflict was thought for the most part to develop ontogenetically. At times Freud assumed that it began around the age of 2 (Freud, 1940); at other times around age 4 (Freud, 1925). It would intensify the child's attachment to his mother, but now it was no longer the dyadic relationship of the preoedipal period but a triadic one, with the father as rival. Castration threats and especially the sight of the vagina would put an end to the boy's oedipal wishes and to his masturbation at around age 6, whereupon he would enter latency. In addition to fear of castration, Freud cites the influence of painful disappointments: the boy (or girl) does not see the oedipal wishes fulfilled. Freud (1924) believed that the resolution of the oedipus complex, like its development, also followed a preordained hereditary pattern.

By 1924 the influence of preceding phases of development (oral and anal) on the manifestations of the succeeding oedipal phase had become part of Freud's thought. Also, the study of ego and superego began to have its influence on his formulations. Namely, the superego now became the heir to the oedipus complex (Freud, 1925, p. 257). In the boy, the ending of the oedipal phase was more sharply defined, and Freud therefore assumed that the male superego would be a more independent structure than the female one. As noted above, Freud made these statements with considerable hesitation, a fact sometimes overlooked by his critics. In 1931 Freud stressed the importance of the preoedipal attachment to the mother and how it subsequently shows up in the oedipal development of the girl. He was influenced by, or responding to, the observations of a number of female analysts, including Helene Deutsch, Ruth Mack Brunswick, Melanie Klein, Karen Horney, and Jeanne Lampl-de Groot.

His awareness that the preoedipal phase of development had a great influence on the nature of subsequent neurosis compelled Freud to retract as a universal thesis the idea that the oedipus complex is the nucleus of the neurosis (Freud, 1931, p. 226). He tried to reassure those who would feel reluctant to make that correction by calling the preoedipal periods the negative oedipus complex. The obvious problem with this formulation is that the oedipus complex implies a triadic relationship and the existence of a fantasy life.

Nagera (1975) has commented on the confusion surrounding the term *preoedipal.* In the case of the girl it would, according to Nagera, describe three phases (oral, anal, and negative oedipal); in the case of the boy, only two (oral and anal). Nagera prefers to limit the term to the dyadic situation and rightly assigns the term *oedipal* when fantasies are of a phallic, triadic nature.

In his 1931 paper Freud makes clear that a woman's strong dependence on her father is the heir to an earlier, equally strong attachment to her mother. Conversely, a strongly negative attachment to a father could be the heir to an earlier negative attachment to the mother. Freud was able to clear up why so many of his female adult patients believed they had been sexually seduced in childhood by their father; the so-called seduction, he argued, dates back to preoedipal phases in which the mother's bathing and cleaning of the vaginal region had been stimulating for the little girl. (Feeding should be added to this source of early drive stimulation.) In later life the object of the stimulation had been shifted from the mother to the father. The mechanism of displacement from one object to another is phase-appropriate for the little girl in the oedipal period. As a result of his increasing awareness of the influence of preoedipal phases, Freud made the bisexual nature of the oedipus complex much more explicit. For the little girl, the vagina, according to Freud (1931) remains "nonexistent and possibly does not produce sensations until puberty" (p. 228), a view that can no longer be maintained. The castration complex may lead to an attitude of revulsion toward sexuality. Freud did not include in his description of the complex the contributions which, for instance, the anal phase may make in developing this attitude. Both the vagina and the penis may be looked upon by the child as excretory organs. Castration strongly denied by the girl may lead to homosexuality.

So much for Freud's changing views on the oedipus complex. It is hardly any wonder that after 1939 discoveries and reformulations continued to be made. Perhaps one of the most important ones was anticipated by Freud on numerous occasions. I am referring to the concept of developmental lines. Freud constantly referred to the developmental line of the libidinal drive (oral, anal, phallic, latency, puberty, adolescence, and adulthood). It was not until Anna Freud (1963) published "The Concept of Developmental Lines" that the idea was made explicit that there were many developmental lines, each with its own history and its own vicissitudes. These developmental lines may influence each other. Especially influential is the libidinal line of development.

We have already observed the influence of the libidinal drive on object choice and object cathexis during the oedipal phase. We are equally aware of the influence of the oedipal phase on other aspects of ego development, such as memory, ego organization, and defense. Identifications and the development of superego and ego ideal are strongly influenced by oedipal libidinal strivings. More than any other line of development, sexuality deserves a special position in our view of human development. The oedipal phase remains an organizer—a momentous event in the child's life. Its outcome determines, as mentioned above, not only libidinal and aggressive development, but also the child's capacity to participate in such latency tasks as academic learning, relating to peers, and modifying the contents of the superego and ego ideal. Thus, the outcome of a child's oedipal conflicts remains nuclear for later neurotic solutions. Freud's frequent comments on the relative failure of the female superego were in part made because he did not take into account that ego and superego begin to develop well before the oedipal phase. This does not mean that the resolution of the oedipus complex does not have a tremendous influence on both. For instance, during the preoedipal period, specific, circumscribed superego injunctions can be observed, such as that against biting the maternal nipple in the first year of life. As early as the end of the first year one can see infants who already derive pleasure from completely finishing their meals; this precursor of the ego ideal does not carry over yet to other activities, and must still receive external reinforcement.

Similarly, during the anal phase "sphincter morality" is laid down. Here one can begin to see some tendency toward generalization: these children may show signs of orderliness and feelings of shame in connection with the spilling of food, finger paint, etc. It is not until the resolution of the oedipus complex that one sees an organized superego—partially because of increased cognitive development, but also because of the many identifications with the parent, especially the parent of the same sex. It is because of these and similar tremendous changes, both quantitative and qualitative, in many areas of the child's functioning that the oedipal phase should not be put on a par with other lines of development. Also, it continues to make sense to call superego developments prior to the oedipal phase superego precursors. Glenn (1977) recently demonstrated the existence of a strong superego in a young girl who began her analysis at age 3½. Schafer (1974), in questioning whether women's superegos are indeed frail, followed in some of his objections the reasoning used by Glenn—that preoedipal drives contribute to superego formation.

Another line of development of great importance is that of object relatedness which begins in the autistic phase. Mahler and her coworkers (Mahler, Pine, and Bergman, 1975) have studied separation-individuation during the dyadic phase that precedes and makes possible the development of a triadic one.

The citation here of Anna Freud, Nagera, Mahler, and

Glenn aptly demonstrates that today we have access to much more than the reconstructions of early childhood from adult analysis, the material on which Freud relied so heavily. It remains a testimony to his genius that so much of what he wrote is still valid today. Contemporary child analysts have not only the data from their analytic interpretations and reconstructions to verify or correct either understanding of the oedipal phase; in addition, they can make direct observations on the small children they have in treatment, including their development during the oedipal phase. They also have the reports of parents and teachers on these children. The child analytic literature today is full of such data on children 4 to 6 years old (Edgcumbe, 1976). These reports amply corroborate the main findings of Freud: the existence of an infantile sexuality that reaches a peak during the oedipal phase. This is followed by a relatively dormant period during latency. This dormancy ends with the prepuberty phase, in which infantile drives find renewed expression. With the onset of puberty, the adult sexual genital drive, with its own characteristics (primacy, ejaculation, orgasm), appears. Oedipal and preoedipal issues may be recapitulated. Once again one sees the influences of this drive development on other lines of development (e.g., ego, superego, ego ideal, object removal) in adolescence. Unresolved issues from the oedipal phase, such as traumata (Greenacre, 1952), may be repeated at that time.

Child analysts would find it difficult to corroborate Freud's statements to the effect that prior to the oedipal phase little girls behave like little boys. The difficulty is due in part to the phenomenon of phase dominance. For instance, one may already find oedipal strivings during what is predominantly an anal phase. As a result of this fact alone, the preoedipal girl is not like the little boy. Another factor to be considered is what Stoller (1973) and Kleeman (1976) have called the assignment of gender at birth, namely, the effect of the environment on the infant's development. For instance, when young parents cover their newborn baby with a pink or a blue blanket, it sets in motion in the parents certain attitudes, fantasies, and expectations, many of them of an oedipal nature, which contribute to the shaping of the child's personality long before the oedipal phase: very early on, the child is encouraged to identify with the parent of the same sex. More observation and research are necessary to resolve the question of the relative contributions made by biological and environmental factors in determining the gender identity of the young child. One remains impressed, however, with the many psychological factors that can be elicited in cases of nursery school children who have problems with gender identity. Childhood traumata and parental attitudes can often be identified. The fluidity of childhood symptoms in general applies equally to children who wish to dress like the opposite sex or who claim or wish to be of the opposite sex. The fluidity of these symptoms would tend to point to the importance of psychological events over biological factors in problems related to gender identity. These problems usually do not become fixed until adolescence. At any rate, Freud's idea that a girl is like a little boy until puberty can no longer be maintained.

Any similarity in the behavior of little boys with that of little girls is due primarily to the boy's identifications with his mother and sisters. Similarly, most masculine behavior in girls is due to identification with the father and brothers. An instructive example is that of a little boy who had been successfully toilet trained by his divorced mother, with the exception that no matter what she tried, he would urinate only sitting on the toilet. But within a few weeks after entering nursery school at age 3, he spontaneously stood up for his urination.

Recently, increased attention has been focused on penis envy. It has been pointed out that the little boy has a pregnancy envy that has vicissitudes similar to those of penis envy in the girl. For instance, little boys may deny that only women can become pregnant. Such boys may entertain fantasies that girls have girl babies and boys have boy babies. One is reminded of the parthenogenetic pregnancy fantasies in girls in whom a preoedipal or oedipal cathexis to the mother predominates.

Jacobson (1950) has noted correctly that the wish for a baby originates during preoedipal development and it has oral and anal components in all children. It is interesting that the wish for a penis and genital masturbation in girls very likely also predate the oedipal phase. All these themes and activities become readily a part of the fantasy life of the oedipal child. It is little wonder, therefore, that in reconstructions from adult analysis only the oedipal aspects of these fantasies have aroused the attention of most analysts. One is dealing here with the phenomenon of telescoping of events. In actuality, these themes antedate the oedipal phase in most cases. Edgcumbe and Burgner (1975) recently drew attention to the fact that phallic drive development and the oedipal level of object relatedness do not necessarily coincide.

The wish for a pregnancy in boys may become sublimated. For instance, it may become transformed into learning or artistic creativity. If the wish remains strong, perhaps because of traumatization (e.g., the birth of a sibling), it may lead to symptomatology, such as encopresis, where the retained stool becomes equated with the wished-for pregnancy. Freud (1908, p. 220) had already drawn attention to the equation of feces with baby, and to the fact that it was valid for both boys and girls. For a more recent review of anal fantasies see Hayman (1974). In most boys, reaction-formations against this wish for a child are set up and lead to a disinterest in babies that may last a lifetime. Due to changing social attitudes, men are now more able to express their wish for a child than in times gone by. They attend their wives' deliveries and participate actively in rearing the infant. Conversely, many "modern" women have sublimated their wish for a child by means of creative careers, to the point that the wish for a child is diminished. The fate of this wish for a child in boys is, of course, determined by many factors, such as the outcome of the oedipal relationships, sibling rivalries, the ego's capacity for sublimation, and the attainment of a stable identification with the father. In girls, the pregnancy wish may be fulfilled as well as sublimated but may also lead to symptomatology (Moore, 1976).

A recent line of research has focused on the origin of penis envy in the little girl. Galenson and Roiphe (1976) in a careful direct observational study have noted an object-directed masturbation with fantasies on a nonverbal visual-motor level which would indicate an awareness of castration and turning to the father. This, however, is preoedipal in the sense that a dyadic relationship is involved. These observations were made on infants in the second half of their second year of life, during ongoing separation-individuation from the mothers. Galenson and Roiphe agree with Freud that penis envy and the female castration complex do exert crucial influences upon female development. However, these events occur during the anal urethral period of development and exert their influence on various other lines of development, including the subsequent oedipal phase; i.e., they precede the oedipus complex itself, as does genital masturbation and the wish for a baby.

Child analysts have been impressed with the correctness of what Freud called the "preordained" appearance of developmental landmarks, as well as with the possibility of developmental interferences on the part of the environment. The environment may be too stimulating or too depriving for ordinary development to proceed according to schedule. Understandably, Freud described the development of children in intact homes. Today, however, many children are reared in one-parent homes. Neubauer (1960) has studied the effect of such environments on the oedipal child. There are, of course, no two cases alike. Some children lose a parent through death, others through divorce. Sometimes the absent parent visits; in other situations this is not the case. Substitutes for the absent parent may be available, such as an older brother, an uncle, or a grandfather in the case of an absent father. The sex life of the remaining parent is also of importance. Does the parent date, is the child aware of it, does the child have a relationship with the dates, etc.? In the case of the child living with the parent of the same sex, the oedipal attachment to that parent is more difficult to overcome. For instance, the female child may as a result become fixated on what Nagera would define as the first stage of the phallic oedipal phase with a negative oedipal constellation. She would become a masculine lover to her mother and become at risk for homosexuality. The wish for a penis may be expressed quite openly in these girls. Or she could advance to the second stage and develop an inverted oedipal constellation. The child will appear quite feminine, but her main cathexis is still toward the mother. Men, including the male therapist, are perceived as rivals who are not to be trusted. The positive oedipal constellation in these girls is weaker than the inverted one. They identify with the mother, act flirtatiously toward men, and often express a manifest wish for a baby, but the mother remains the main object toward whom it is directed.

In the case of boys who are living with their mothers, either active or passive positive oedipal wishes are predominant, depending on the influence of preoedipal developments, including when the father left the home, etc. As in the case of girls, development beyond the oedipal phase meets considerable difficulties. In the case of the girl, the major obstacle is the relative weakness of cathexis to figures of the opposite sex; in the case of the boy, it is the hypercathexis to the mother plus the lack of male identification. Oedipal guilt is increased in both the boy and the girl. The excessive guilt may become repressed, with the result that the superego appears defective. The reason for the severity of the superego lies in the fact that oedipal and preoedipal wishes remain so strong in these children. In addition, in the case of boys, male figures may be lacking from whom they could derive more benign introjects into their superegos. Overidealization of the absent parent also contributes to setting very high standards in the superego. In addition, rage toward this parent can become the rage of the superego against the drives. It should be stressed again that the availability of substitute parents may alter this outcome considerably. The question of availability is not only an external one; it depends also on internal factors in the child, such as the ego's adaptiveness, its capacity to accept substitutes, etc.

My own limited experience with children reared by a father is in cases in which a female housekeeper was present. The traumatic loss of the mother through death, illness, or divorce had its impact in the sense that the father became heir to the child's attachment to the mother, which was only partially undone by the presence of a mother substitute. Because my own experience is limited, however, I cannot draw any general conclusions. The few reports available in the literature on the effect of an absent mother have in common that mother substitutes were quickly provided, which is much easier to accomplish in our society than to find father substitutes. The loss of the mother may well be more traumatic for the boy than for the girl. The reason lies in the fact that it is normal for the girl to make the father her main love object.

The marked increase in the divorce rate in recent years has become an added developmental interference to resolution of the oedipus complex.

Parens, Pollock, Stern, and Kramer (1976) have used the observational method to study Freud's hypothesis that the little girl enters the oedipal phase after the discovery of the castration complex, with a consequent turning to the father with a wish for a baby. Their observations on the behavior "of only a handful of normal girls" do not confirm Freud's hypothesis. Their findings are somewhat at odds with those of Galenson and Roiphe. One would have expected that the castration complex preceded the onset of the oedipus complex. In one child, Jane, there was only a mild awareness of genital difference; yet the evidence for entry into an oedipal phase seemed available (p. 96). In another child, Candy, the wish for a baby preceded awareness of castration. It is obvious that much more research along the lines pioneered by Parens and Galenson is necessary before definite conclusions can be drawn. Parens's work, if confirmed, would indicate that the girl enters the oedipal phase similarly to a boy, namely, on the basis of a "preordained" drive development aided by environmental facilitation. This would make Freud's theory more internally consistent. The combined approach of reconstructions from adult and child analyses and the judicious use of the direct observational method should eventually clarify the various issues raised by Freud's discoveries.

Some of what Galenson, Kleeman, and Parens have discovered was available all along. As Freud (1923) put it, it is "possible, in spite of whole decades of unremitting observation, to overlook features that are of general occurrence and situations that are characteristic, until at last they confront one in an unmistakable form" (p. 141). For instance, Bornstein (1935) described a 2½-year-old girl who was in the midst of her castration complex, who had oedipal fantasies, and who was actively masturbating.

The modern research described in this paper needs to be confirmed by other researchers, and additional data obtained. For instance, the shift from mother to father should be studied in both sexes. Very likely it has its precursors already in the first half of the first year of life and is of a dyadic nature. A good beginning was the report of the 1977 panel of the American Psychoanalytic Association, "The Role of the Father in the Preoedipal Years" (Prall, 1978).

Recently I was able to observe a 4-month-old female infant who had experienced the traumatic temporary loss of her mother. She had developed a transient symptom, namely a selective mutism. It consisted of an inability to respond with the usual cooing and babbling when stimulated by the maternal voice or the voice of other women. The infant did respond readily to vocal stimulation by her father, her 5-year-old brother, myself, and other males. What can be deduced from this kind of observation is that the shift from mother to father in the oedipus complex for the little girl has an antecedent development that reaches back into the first year of life. The preoedipal attachment to the father obviously influences the subsequent oedipal attachment.

An additional area that needs further study is masturbation. Marcus and Francis (1975) have collected in a series of papers most of the current psychoanalytic research regarding masturbation. It has become abundantly clear that masturbation, like many other phenomena, has its precursors and starts earlier than was first reconstructed. Its precursor, genital play, begins in the first year of life and serves a dual function. It aids the developing ego in its increasing awareness of the body self, and it also serves for purposes of pleasure. Perhaps, by the end of the second year, fantasies that are object-directed in a dyadic way become associated with the genital play, and one can then begin to speak of masturbation and the beginnings of the phallic drive. Oral and anal drives are likely to be dominant during this period. In the third year of life the fantasies associated with masturbation become triadic in nature. This, then, can be considered the onset of the oedipal level of development of object relatedness. This is also in agreement with the findings of Edgcumbe and Burgner (1975).

Contemporary social and cultural changes have given analysts the opportunity to study the influence of environmental factors on male and female sexual development. The opportunities provided women in today's society, and the demands made on them, create "experiments provided by fate" (Freud and Dann, 1951). Consequently, it may be possible to better answer what is biologically determined ("anatomy is destiny") and what is culturally modifiable. When analysts were first confronted with the so-called social and cultural revolution, they were poorly prepared for it. Even now, though many changes in female sexual attitudes have become the focus of analysts' attention, other changes, such as teenage pregnancy and the planned pregnancies of single adult women, have so far received no analytic attention. As Parens and his colleagues have suggested, the wish for a baby may well antedate the onset of the oedipal phase. Perhaps it is an inborn given that in the course of development becomes enmeshed with the various psychosexual stages and their conflicts. One can only wonder why teenage pregnancies are on the rise and those of married women continue their decline.

Today women are very different from what they were at the turn of the century. To give just one example, Freud described oral fixations in 1905 and predicted that in male adults it would become "a powerful motive for drinking and smoking" (1905b, p. 182). Women in 1905 simply did not smoke or drink. Many of Freud's statements about women have to be considered as probably valid for the time in which they were written. As has been pointed out by Ticho (1976) and others, women before World War I rarely lived independently. They lived in the parental home until their marriage, obeying first their fathers and mothers and subsequently their husbands. It is not surprising that Freud found that under these conditions the female oedipus complex never was completely resolved, and that female superegos had not acquired the degree of independence found in men who to a much greater extent ventured out into the world on their own. Women's active strivings had to be channeled into identifications with their husband's activities. The husband would become the wished-for penis, and other regressive ego functions would also be encouraged. Motherhood was more valued then, and as long as a woman produced and reared children she felt valued. Women past 30 in Freud's experience were difficult to work with; their future indeed was bleak. The idea of a woman earning money was a disgrace unless she belonged to the lower economic strata. By contrast, today's woman is valued for her ability to pursue a career, while a woman producing and rearing children has diminished in value in the eyes of society. For the male, raising children and doing housework have increased his value in today's world.

All this has had a tremendous effect on the outcome of oedipal conflicts. We mentioned how in a boy the wish for a child no longer needs to be sublimated or defended against. To an extent, it can now find an outlet in participation in the rearing of one's children. For the girl, the wish for a baby has now gone very much like that wish in the boy. One can almost paraphrase Freud by saying that before puberty boys and girls are different, but not so after puberty. The girl nowadays, like the boy, can be conscious of her wish for a child. She will, also like the boy, sublimate some of it in her career, and some of it is defended against in the form of a reaction-formation—a disinterest in having children—or a rationalization on the basis of population zero, etc. One can understand the popular phrase "unisex" now. However, it seems that by and large women still have a much stronger conscious wish for a baby than do men. It would seem that this stronger wish is at least partially based on biological grounds. However, the mere fact that in just a few years' time such profound changes in the incidence of child-bearing have come about is indicative of the strength of cultural factors, which in turn are affecting drive, ego, superego, and ego ideal formations.[1]

As was indicated earlier, in the discussion of the fate of the wish for a child in a boy, the wish for a child in a woman may also be affected by many internal conflicts: bisexual conflicts; the resolution of her oedipal rivalry with her mother, permitting identifications to take its place; resolution of the oedipal tie to her father in order to overcome the guilt over the "oedipal child"; the reworking through of these conflicts in adolescence in order to achieve "object removal"; the relative capacity of the

[1] In a similar vein, some members of the women's liberation movement assert currently that concepts like penis envy are instilled in girls entirely because of cultural factors, i.e., a male-oriented and male-dominated society. Although this assertion can easily be accommodated within current psychoanalytic thinking, it still needs to be proven.

ego to form sublimations and identifications in regard to the wish to create a child, etc. Some parents have actually tried to prepare their children during latency for culturally modified tasks of adulthood. For instance, doll play by girls both before and during latency is discouraged in some homes. If permitted to play with dolls at all, they are encouraged to play with ones that represent working women, etc. Nevertheless, dolls that represent babies or brides continue to be the most popular ones. Dolls with phallic attributes such as long flowing hair or protruding breasts have also become popular in recent years. It would seem, therefore, that the working through of oedipal conflicts is more powerful than direct parental influence. Similarly, encouraging latency boys into doll play and cooking classes takes a second seat to their needs for identifications with male figures in their latency games. The resolution of oedipal conflicts through spontaneous latency play activities seems to be the best guarantee that a child will adapt to whatever role he may be called upon to play in adult life.

A good example of how the oedipus complex affects lines of development other than the libidinal is the line which Anna Freud (1963, p. 258) has described as beginning with play with the infant's own body and eventually reaching the ability to work. Freud himself had already drawn attention to the fact that the criteria for health lay in the capacity for love and work. More recently, Applegarth (1976) has discussed the problems women have in regard to their careers. Instead of work just being work, i.e., being a conflict-free ego activity, it has become invaded by many conflicts, especially those associated with the oedipal phase. For instance, women who feel castrated believe they lack an essential feature for success. Penis envy may show itself in a hostile, envious, contemptuous attitude toward men, as well as in a sense of low self-esteem and a belief that careers are "masculine" and that success makes a woman sexually unattractive to men. Part of what contributes to these problems is the fact that up to now success in most fields was attained only by men. As a result, career women often have to identify with and learn from successful men in their careers in order to attain success themselves. As Applegarth points out, the mother may be looked upon as castrated and stupid, and the father as phallic and smart. If such associations are made, the woman would feel more masculine if she were to be successful. Men, of course, may have similar fears. The resulting conflict may lead to interferences with work. In child analysis, one can see similarly how unresolved oedipal conflicts lead to learning disturbances and even inhibitions.

Among the many other questions that can also be studied more closely now is the problem of masochism as it relates to women. If one again calls to mind the position of women in the year 1900, one can see that labels such as passive and masochistic may well have been a universal truth at that time. Circumstances were more difficult then for the full unfolding of female development. Women were much more dependent, and the turning of aggression upon the self was selectively encouraged. Today, by contrast, girls are encouraged to play the more active roles in childhood games at home and at school. In former times, to use Freud's words (1933) the suppression of women's aggressiveness "is prescribed for them constitutionally and imposed on them socially" (p. 116). The social impositions are pretty well gone, and so the question of how much is constitutional can be approached now. It is obvious that an even better view of what constitutes a woman will be possible 25 years from now. Blum (1976) has summarized succinctly current analytic thought about female development. In brief, much of contemporary analytic work indicates that the girl's feminine development begins early, well before the oedipal phase. If penis envy is not too much of a narcissistic injury, the girl can enter full oedipal development, and feminine identifications in the ego, superego, and ego ideal can occur as part of ongoing, conflict-free development. On the basis of observation and clinical data, Blum also rejects the idea of girls having a weak superego. As for masochism, Blum makes the distinction between enduring pain for the goal of childbirth and motherhood as contrasted with masochistic goals, i.e., pain for pain's sake. Nor is being sexually receptive synonymous with masochistic submission. Masochism is not necessary for adult feminine sexuality any more than sadism is necessary for masculinity. Rather, both are indications of unresolved oedipal conflicts. Blum also points out how in times past a woman experienced the death of many close female relatives and siblings. She also could anticipate the death of some of her own children as well as her own death in childbirth. This external traumatizing factor may have contributed greatly to the universal masochistic fixations which Freud saw. As Blum notes, a masochistic concept of the primal scene was usually based on reality in Freud's time. It can be said that today it is questionable whether women are more masochistic than men. In either sex, it is a sign of unresolved oedipal conflict.

As all the aspects of what was considered to be masculine or feminine are becoming open to renewed questioning, one ends up with where Freud left us in 1933 in regard to femininity (and of course the same can be said for masculinity): "If you want to know more about femininity, enquire from your own experiences of life, or turn to the poets, or wait until science can give you deeper and more coherent information" (p. 135).

References

Applegarth, A. (1976), Some observations on work inhibitions in women. *J. Amer. Psychoanal. Assn.,* 24(Suppl.): 251–268.

Blum, H.P. (1976), Masochism, the ego ideal and the psychology of women. *J. Amer. Psychoanal. Assn.,* 24(Suppl.):157–192.

Bornstein, B. (1935), Phobia in a two-and-a-half-year-old child. *Psychoanal. Quart.,* 4:93–119.

Calogeras, R.C., & Schupper F.X. (1972), Origins and early formulations of the Oedipus complex. *J. Amer. Psychoanal. Assn.,* 20:751–775.

Edgcumbe, R. (1976), Some comments on the concept of the negative oedipal phase in girls. *The Psychoanalytic Study of the Child,* 31:35–61. New Haven: Yale University Press.

——— & Burgner, M. (1975), The phallic narcissistic phase. *The Psychoanalytic Study of the Child,* 30:161–180. New Haven: Yale University Press.

Freud, A. (1963), The concept of developmental lines. *The Psychoanalytic Study of the Child,* 18:245–265. New York: International Universities Press.

——— & Dann, S. (1951), An experiment in group upbringing. *Psychoanalytic Study of the Child,* 6:127–168.

Freud, S. (1897), Extracts from the Fliess papers. *Standard Edition,* 1:177–280. London: Hogarth Press, 1966.

——— (1905a), Fragment of an analysis of a case of hysteria. *Standard Edition,* 7:3–122. London: Hogarth Press, 1953.

——— (1905b), Three essays on sexuality. *Standard Edition,* 7:130–243. London: Hogarth Press, 1953.

——— (1908), On the sexual theories of children. *Standard Edition,* 9:207–226. London: Hogarth Press, 1962.

——— (1909), Analysis of a phobia in a five-year-old boy. *Standard Edition,* 10:3–147. London: Hogarth Press, 1962.

——— (1923), The infantile genital organization. *Standard Edition,* 19:141–145. London: Hogarth Press, 1962.

——— (1924), Dissolution of the Oedipus complex. *Standard Edition,* 19:173–179. London: Hogarth Press, 1962.

——— (1925), Some psychical consequences of the anatomical distinction between the sexes. *Standard Edition,* 19:248–258. London: Hogarth Press, 1962.

——— (1931), Female sexuality. *Standard Edition,* 21:225–243. London: Hogarth Press, 1964.

——— (1933), Femininity. *Standard Edition,* 22:112–185. London: Hogarth Press, 1964.

——— (1940), An outline of psycho-analysis. *Standard Edition,* 23:144–207. London: Hogarth Press, 1964.

Galenson, E., & Roiphe, H. (1976), Some suggested revisions concerning early female development. *J. Amer. Psychoanal. Assn.,* 24(Suppl.):29–55.

Glenn, J. (1977), Psychoanalysis of a constipated girl. *J. Amer. Psychoanal. Assn.,* 25:141–162.

Greenacre, P. (1952), Prepuberty trauma in girls. In: *Trauma, Growth and Personality.* New York: Norton, pp. 204–223.

Hayman, A. (1974), Unusual anal fantasies. *The Psychoanalytic Study of the Child,* 29:265–276. New Haven: Yale University Press.

Jacobson, E. (1950), The wish for a child in boys. *The Psychoanalytic Study of the Child,* 5:139–152. New York: International Universities Press.

Kleeman, J.A. (1976), Freud's views on early female sexuality in the light of direct child observation. *J. Amer. Psychoanal. Assn.,* 24(Suppl.):3–28.

Mahler, M.S., Pine, F., & Bergman, A. (1975), *The Psychological Birth of the Human Infant.* New York: Basic Books.

Marcus, I.M., & Francis, J.J., eds. (1975), *Masturbation from Infancy to Senescence.* New York: International Universities Press.

Moore, W.T. (1976), The wish to steal a baby in a 15-year-old girl. *The Psychoanalytic Study of the Child,* 31:349–388. New Haven: Yale University Press.

Nagera, H. (1975), *Female Sexuality.* New York: Aronson.

Neubauer, P. (1960), The one parent child. *The Psychoanalytic Study of the Child,* 15:286–309. New York: International Universities Press.

Parens, H., Pollock, L., Stern, J., & Kramer, S. (1976), On the girl's entry into the oedipal complex. *J. Amer. Psychoanal. Assn.,* 24:79–108.

Prall, R.C., rep. (1978), Panel: The role of the father in the preoedipal years. *J. Amer. Psychoanal. Assn.,* 26:143–161.

Schafer, R. (1974), Problems in Freud's psychology of women. *J. Amer. Psychoanal. Assn.,* 22:459–486.

Stoller, R.J. (1973), The impact of new advances in sex research on psychoanalytic theory. *Amer. J. Psychiat.,* 130:241–251.

Strachey, J. (1953), Editor's note to three essays on sexuality. *Standard Edition,* 7:125–129. London: Hogarth Press.

Ticho, G.R. (1976), Female autonomy and young adult women. *J. Amer. Psychoanal. Assn.,* 24(Suppl.):139–156.

5

Consequences of Primary Paternal Care: Fathers and Babies in the First Six Years

KYLE D. PRUETT, M.D.

The last decade has been the first to witness significant scholarly contributions to the understanding of the effect of direct, ongoing paternal involvement on child development (Russell, 1982; Pruett, 1983, 1985, 1987; Radin and Goldsmith, 1985; Chused, 1986). An historical shift has brought increasing numbers of men into increased contact with their children, whether or not they choose to be there. It is incumbent upon researchers of the psychoanalytic developmental persuasion to continue to examine, observe, and follow this phenomenon carefully. Until very recently, intimate father-child interaction in the early years has enjoyed a dubious status. Early evidence from some studies, however, suggests this nurturing arrangement, even when the father is the primary caregiver, may be quite adequate for the task of providing competent care.

In order to address the question whether intimate paternal care was good for children developmentally, six years ago I began a small longitudinal study of intact families in which fathers served as primary caretaker (Pruett, 1983). The study addressed the development of infants from 2 to 22 months (the ages of the children who presented for study), the psychological characteristics of the fathers and the mothers, the father's nurturing patterns, and marital relationship patterns.

Portions of this chapter first appeared in *The Nurturing Father,* by Kyle D. Pruett, Warner Books, New York, 1987.

Seventeen families were recruited from around the large New England industrial and academic community in which I worked. The families ranged across the socioeconomic spectrum from those on welfare to blue- and white-collar workers and professionals. Eight fathers were unemployed, but the other nine included a graduate student, a blue-collar worker, a sales representative, an artist, a computer programmer, a real estate broker, a lawyer, a writer, and a small businessman. Among the employed, incomes ranged from $7,000 to $125,000 a year. The mothers included a nurse, two teachers, two secretaries, a lawyer, a taxi driver, two sales representatives, three real estate brokers, three blue-collar workers, and two welfare recipients. Among those employed, incomes ranged from $8,000 to $75,000 yearly.

Of the 17 infants, 8 were male and 9 female. The parents ranged in age from 19 to 36 with a mean age of 24 for fathers and 25 for mothers. Surprisingly, all the children except one were firstborn, although this was not part of the research design.

The average age at marriage had been 23 for men and 24 for women. Of the 34 adults, 2 had been married previously, both of them women. One 30-year-old had been married for 3 years when her first husband died. The other woman was 22; her marriage had lasted less than a year and had ended in an uncontested, mutually agreed upon divorce.

The fathers were first interviewed at home while caring for their children. Detailed histories were taken of their own lives and family of origin, their parents, their growing up, and their previous experience with children. The history of the choice to stay home also was reviewed. During this first visit, usually 90 minutes in length, observations were recorded of the father-infant interaction in the natural setting of the process of typical child care. The main focus, however, was on the stories the men told of their own lives and experiences. Would some recurring factor emerge that would predict this unique parental behavior?

All 17 fathers reported themselves as having been reared traditionally. Their fathers were breadwinners, while their mothers raised chlidren and cared for the home. Thirteen of the group came from intact families. The other 4 had lived predominantly with their mothers before beginning their own families (one had lived with his father from the age of 12, after a bitter divorce). They had an average of 2 siblings, with a range from 0 to 7.

Six of the men had attended private school for all or part of their secondary education. Fifteen of the 17 men had spent most of their post-high-school years living away from home, while the other 2 had remained with their families. Of these, one worked and the other commuted to college.

All 17 fathers reported that as teenagers they seemed headed toward the expected role of breadwinner, protector, or provider. Few considered fathering an important role. None would have predicted as teens that they would be rearing their own children.

As would be expected of adolescent males, few recalled giving any thought as teenagers to what might be gained or lost by actively nurturing a child. The immediate task of controlling their own instinctual needs during this agitated phase seemed to eclipse interest in the needs of any children in their lives, present or future. Often when these men did think about fathering as teenagers, it was in terms of pride in fertile potency, not of fulfilling a dream to nurture competently or of gaining immortality.

Only 4 of the 17 fathers reported active memories of anything more than casual involvement with young children or infants as teenagers. Three of these were involved with infants born into their immediate families. One father lived transiently during his adolescence with a family friend who sheltered at-risk foster children.

The bulk of these men regarded themselves as having developed normally (based on their own stories) and in step with their traditional social and familial values. Taken as a whole, this was an unremarkable group, with little to distinguish it from any other predominantly middle-class collection of young men who would self-select for such a study (Pruett, 1987).

Some subtle subgrouping emerged with regard to *when* during the conception and pregnancy process the families decided that the fathers would "mother." When asked *when* the families decided on this child care arrangement, there was only one decision characteristic they all shared. *None* of the families considered this a permanent situation at its inception.

At the outset, the families' "decision phase" allowed them to be grouped roughly into thirds: the first third (6 families) decided prior to the pregnancy that the father would be the primary caregiver; the second third (another 6 families), during the pregnancy; and the final third (5 families), during the neonatal period.

The early-deciding group of men tended to be professionals or others of upper socioeconomic status. A typical example was the father who decided to "take some time off from his career" (education) to care for the baby while his wife pursued hers (retail sales) because it seemed either "fair or interesting or both to do for a while." The attempt to time conception carefully was a hallmark of this group. They tended to plan everything ahead of time.

The middle third was similar in reasoning but typically was influenced by some change in the mother's feeling about staying home with a baby after she'd begun carrying it. Sometimes it had become increasingly clear that the mother's job or career would be jeopardized seriously by extended maternity leave. Meanwhile, the father's economic status was changing anyway, or his established career could better withstand a prolonged leave of absence.

The late-deciding third was in some ways the most interesting. These families often had the decision "forced" upon them at the last moment, usually for economic reasons; as when a father lost his job while his wife retained hers. Not surprisingly, this group contained the highest number of initially reluctant, uncertain fathers.

Mothers in the study ranged in age from 22 to 36, the mean age being 25. They came from families as culturally and socioeconomically diverse as those of their husbands. Three of the men had been only children, whereas 2 of the women were. The number of siblings was slightly higher for the men than for the women, the average father's family having 5.2 members, and the mother's 4.3.

Six of the 17 mothers were firstborn, compared to 4 of the

men. One man and one woman were adopted (they were not married to each other). One couple I have included as married because they had lived together for 5 years before becoming parents.

Fifteen of the 17 women had mothers still living. Thirteen of these mothers initially disapproved of their daughters' and sons-in-laws' child care arrangements. Thirteen of the 17 women had had mothers who worked outside the home, either full or part time, at some point during their childhoods.

The women's educations ranged from eighth grade to graduate degrees in medicine, law, and business. This distribution held generally for the husbands, too, though two Ph.D.'s were also to be counted among them.

As noted above, those women who made the child care decision earliest tended to have higher incomes and more education. Several of these women were at "critical" phases in their careers or educations and had had their babies sooner than they might have preferred. The middle group (who made the fathering decision during the pregnancy) tended to talk about their child care plans as temporary measures. For example, Mrs. James, a real estate broker, had asked her husband "to take over for a few months" while she made her new promotion secure.

The late-deciding group had the lowest income and least education. There were two disadvantaged families in this group whose mothers were earning income "illegally" because of limitations placed on allowable income by state welfare regulations. This was a kind of double jeopardy for these women: they could not take pride in their work, as it was so tenuous. Another late-deciding couple had arranged for the wife to take her husband's nonunion construction job, as he had injured himself. Although unable to bend over to lift bricks, he *could* manage a baby. The foreman accepted this man's sturdily built wife as his replacement on the job site! Five years later, *she* was the foreman.

As a group, the women were no more or less homogeneous than the men. One life choice did separate out one subgroup from the rest, i.e., those who chose to leave or suspend work and stay home full time to care for the children after the birth of a second child. These women had mothers who were somewhat similar. When I looked back at the early histories they gave at the first interview, I discovered that as a group they had tended to describe their own mothers as being "unhappy . . . cold . . . unavailable." One of the group said the only time she ever heard her mother laugh was when she watched "The Honeymooners" on TV. This group of women seemed to identify more strongly with their fathers, whom they generally regarded as more nurturing and supportive, "more available" to them emotionally then their mothers. Such women also reported feeling less competitive with their spouses, and tended to identify positively with their husband's nurturing of the first baby.

A formal assessment focused primarily on the children was done in the more laboratorylike setting of the Child Development Unit of the Yale Child Study Center. The children were accompanied by the father and usually by the mother for the standardized assessment. The Yale Developmental Schedule was used to evaluate each child's development. This schedule is a comprehensive tool originally created at the Yale Child Study Center by Dr. Sally Provence some 25 years ago (Provence and Naylor, 1983). It is a composite protocol used widely for research and clinical purposes, and consists of carefully chosen items from several standardized scales (e.g., Gesell, Stanford-Binet, and Merrill-Palmer). It provides a reliable matrix for assessing, recording, and following over time a young child's performance in motor function, problem solving, language, and personal and social skills. It allows the clinician or researcher to compare an individual child's developmental performance with the expected range of competence for children of the same age. The development of the infant or very young child is so complex and so rapid in the early years that one has to evaluate skills and competence carefully in many areas in order to have a valid picture of how any child is maturing at a given moment in time.

The Yale Schedule has one feature, unique among standardized instruments, which made it quite useful for this study. As it can be used to follow a child from birth to the sixth birthday without changing assessment tools, it lends itself quite well to longitudinal studies.

The developmental examiner (frequently my role) provides a supportive interaction so that the child can become comfortable enough to do his best at some familiar tasks and some novel ones. Developmental competence is assessed in several areas simultaneously; first, the child's large and small muscle skills, strength, and dexterity are assessed. Second, adaptive skills are measured. Persistence and comprehension of novel tasks are required to solve problems. Third, language skills, both receptive and expressive, are measured. Fourth, personal and social functions are evaluated. Here we look at how involved the child is emotionally with the important people in his life and how competent he is in eliciting, with and without the use of language, the social interactions so critical to his survival. Frequently two sessions were required to complete the assessment.

Some of the children warmed quickly to the developmental procedure, as though the evaluation itself were an enjoyable game. Others waited and watched carefully, seeming to seek assurance that the examiner or their performance was okay. Eventually, the profiles began to take shape. The developmental competence of these babies was compared to the age-expected competence of the more typically raised babies represented on the standardized schedules. While there was little homogeneity among the group socially, economically, or culturally, some intriguing trends emerged.

First, these children raised primarily by men were active, vigorous, robust, and thriving infants. They also were competent. The majority functioned somewhat above the expected norms on several of the standardized tests of development. The youngest group of infants (2 to 12 months) performed certain problem-solving tasks on the same level as babies 2 to 4 months their seniors; personal and social skills were also ahead of schedule. The older babies in the group (12 to 22 months) performed equally well.

Second, apart from the quantitative aspects of these babies' performance, certain qualitative or stylistic characteristics emerged quite frequently; for example, these infants seemed especially comfortable with—indeed attracted to—stimulation from the external environment.

A third finding, hard to quantify, looked something like this: many of the babies seemed to expect that their curiosity, persistence, or challenging behavior would be tolerated, even appreciated by the adults in their environment, whether parents, examiners, or observers. The expectation that play would be rich, exciting, and reciprocated, or that block designs or puzzles would eventually succumb to sheer determination was widespread in this group of babies. One of the older children, 22-month-old Amy, knocked over her tower of ten small red cubes (which she had so carefully and proudly constructed only a moment before) with a broad sweep of her closed fist. She sat forward quickly on the edge of her baby chair and, with a broad, open-mouthed smile, fixed her eyes with excited anticipation on the face of the examiner; she seemed eagerly to await the next challenge.

I had expected that the fathers' uncertainty and lack of preparation for their job as primary nurturing parent, especially in the less economically advantaged families, would somehow be observable in their babies' developmental profiles. When the data were analyzed, however, the timing of the decision to be the primary caretaker could not be correlated with how well the child did on developmental examination. The babies of the late-deciding families could not be distinguished from those of the early deciders.

So, the babies were doing well. The fathers demonstrated a capacity to nurture another being so as to insure its survival and assure its humanity. They "read" and understood their babies well enough to feed, change, nap, and comfort on time. Their responses conformed reasonably to the babies' most complex needs.

Although as a group they achieved the relationship at different rates, all the fathers had formed the deep, reciprocal nurturing attachment so crucial to the early development of the thriving human baby. The depth and rapidity of the attachment amazed even them. *How* it was achieved varied, of course, from man to man and baby to baby.

The fathers as a group reported a similar sequence of feelings as they gradually took charge of their babies' lives. Most of the families began life with their babies with a period of from

3 to 8 weeks in which the mother was the primary, or at least coequal, caretaker of the infant. Afterward the mother returned to work or school. This was a critical transition for both parents and babies. But a curiously consistent sequence of realizations was reported by the men.

When the everyday troubles began—the crying or inconsolable infant—the father would think to himself, "What would my wife do?"

Anywhere from 10 days to a few months later, these men had completely abandoned this mental portrait of themselves as being a "stand-in for Mom." Unique caregiving styles emerged as the men gradually began to think of themselves as parents in their own right. Most of the men kept this feeling to themselves, as though they couldn't quite believe it, or trust it, or maybe shouldn't even have it.

The changes within the families over the initial two years were far-reaching. Second children had been born into 7 families. Fathers had continued to serve as the primary caregiving parent in 8 families, including 4 in which there now were 2 siblings. Mothers had become the primary parent in 3 families, all of whom had second children. Fathers had returned to work or school in 6 families (3 with second children) and had ceased to function as the primary parent. There had been one parental separation, in which the father had retained custody.

All the children were tested again using the Yale Developmental Schedule. As a group, the children, now toddlers and preschoolers, continued to perform well on these measurements, especially in the two areas seen before. Some individual children excelled at others level as well. Three of the older children (2 girls and 1 boy) tested noticeably above the expected norms on language expression and comprehension. These children were all from the early-deciding families and seemed to have been reared in quite fertile verbal environments. Two of the younger children from the late-deciding families (1 boy and 1 girl) were especially gifted in motor function and agility. Both were from families in which physical strength, coordination, and participation in sports were highly valued and practiced by one or both parents. On average, the entire group's capacity to use cognitive skills and intellect to sole novel problems was better than expected, as was personal-social competence.

Seeing this finding repeated two years later makes us turn to a search for explanations. I had initially speculated that these babies may have performed especially well on certain developmental tasks as a result of a more particularly stimulating, vigorous, and unpredictable handling style possibly characteristic of fathers. This quality was observed throughout the study and did not diminish over time, adding support for the idea that it may be a characteristic of the American father-infant pair. Then, 2 years later, when neither infrequent interaction nor lack of familiarity were remotely valid as explanations, we found the fathers and babies in our study still "carrying on" to some extent, probably because they enjoyed it. This fact tends to confirm my speculation that this quality may be responsible for the babies' repeated strong performance on the developmental testing. (It should be noted here that so-called "father-released" behaviors, such as persistence and curiosity, are singled out not necessarily because they are more valuable than other behaviors, but because they are measured more easily on testing.)

We may point to yet another factor that perhaps explains why these babies develop so vigorously. As noted, the children in this study were all firstborns. It has been shown repeatedly that fathers tend to be more involved with firstborn babies, especially when they are male. Birth order, then, must be acknowledged as a contributing factor.

Further, does parenting of the father carry an extra valence because, unlike the mother, the father has had no lifelong role identification to nurture, raise, or take responsibility for a baby? Is it because for men primary nurturing is a choice, not a fate, an option that if not exercised occasions none of that sense of having denied a lifelong role expectation that often afflicts women in similar circumstances? This gives men a certain *freedom* to parent not often enjoyed by women. We human beings tend to pursue more joyfully and creatively the things we choose to do than the things we feel we must do. *Or are these babies thriving because of the abiding commitment of 2 parents (instead of the traditional 1½)?* For example, a majority of the 17 mothers breast-fed, often at great inconvenience to themselves, for at least 2 months.

Four years into the study I made another thorough assessment of 15 of the original families. Another family had left the area, making direct evaluation of the child impossible, although the family remained in frequent touch by mail and provided a steady stream of snapshots.

It should be stated that by now no reasonable claim of objectivity could be made by this researcher. These families and I had come to know one another very well over the 4 years. We had spent dozens of hours together, much of it in their homes or apartments, as they tolerated my endless inquiries with affection. Over the years they had revealed much about themselves and their deep concern for their children, as well as their aspirations and uncertainties.

The children now ranged in age from 4 to 6, and the Yale Schedule was at the outer limit of its usefulness for the older children. Some supplemental testing, especially in the areas of language competence (Peabody Picture Vocabulary Test), was required for them. In an attempt to protect the validity of the evaluation—the children by now were so accustomed to me and my interest in them and their families that they could almost be considered collaborators—I now used other developmental examiners whenever possible.

As a group, the children continued to develop vigorously. Their problem-solving and social skills remained especially strong, although the degree of advanced functioning had waned somewhat. Now their scores were 2 to 4 months ahead of expected norms, instead of the 6 to 10 seen earlier. The test findings supported my clinical impression that the rate of precocious function had slowed for the entire population.

Eleven of the original children now were over the age of 5. Of these, 4 were still primarily in the care of their fathers but in intact families. One was in the sole custody of his father. The other 6 children in this older group were now mainly in the care of their mothers; all of these now had siblings. Two of the fathers of the younger, under 5 children were serving as primary caregivers. This meant that 4 years after the study began, 7 of the 16 families with whom I maintained contact had fathers still serving as primary caregivers. Of the 9 remaining, 6 were families in which the mother served as primary caregiver, 5 of these with second children. The other 3 used supplemental day care, nursery school, or babysitting arrangements and described themselves as sharing child care "roughly" equally.

So, after hundreds of hours of testing, playing, interviewing, visiting, and watching, we concluded the study after 4 years (5 including follow-up contact). What could we say about these men, their babies, and their families?

First, there were as yet no signs of big trouble, either intellectual or emotional, in this group of children, suggesting that men as primary nurturing caregivers can do a creditable job. Father care need not be considered hazardous to one's health.

Second, if these children were not troubled, were they different in some way? The answer is both yes and no. When one looks at the level and range of emotional maturity, quality of human relationships, and ability to handle the stress of everyday life, there were no gross personality characteristics to differentiate reliably these children from their more traditionally raised peers. Comfortable dependency, zest for life, assertiveness, a vigorous drive for mastery, and the usual childhood worries all were clearly present in both boys and girls.

There also seemed to be no significant lack of emotional flexibility in any of these children. Nor could one call them as a group inhibited or constricted. If anything, there were rudimentary signs that these children might in fact be developing more flexible personalities, particularly in the ease with which they moved back and forth between feminine and masculine behavioral roles.

If there is anything unique about their internal images of themselves or their parents, it may be the prevalence in their play of the father as a nurturing force. Over the entire study there was empirical evidence to strengthen the initial speculation that having a father as a primary nurturing figure stimulates greater curiosity and interest in the father as procreator than is found in more traditionally reared children. For the children in the study, the father is seen as a *maker* of human beings along with the mother, who makes *and* births them.

It also was clear by now that in these children's images of the world, men and women were not very interchangeable in their roles. The study children tended not to make much of their family's differentness, sometimes to the point of portraying their parents' roles as quite traditional. Their family drawings depicted Dad with a briefcase going off to work, when often he did not even own one, or Mother cooking dinner, when she had not done so for years.

Social anthropologists would not find this very surprising. They contend that socialization pressures in school and society as a whole are so powerful as to eclipse the portrayal of the real details of these children's lives.

Before we look at what happened to the children and their parents in this study after another 2 years, we are well advised to review carefully the developmental phenomena and idiosyncratic requirements of this next particular stage in personality formation. The next major developmental gauntlet to be run by the child is the period between 6 and 11, generally characterized as latency. Benson and Harrison (1980) have referred to this stage as the "eye of the hurricane," others, as the "golden age of childhood" because of its characteristic stability, flexibility, and relative calm. Theoretically, this period of calm stands, psychosexually, between the *sturm* of the oedipal phase and the *drang* of adolescence. The ego is given a brief respite from the bombardment of instinctual demands, and the self increasingly enjoys larger shares of daylight.

Erna Furman (see chapter 9, this volume) summarizes the characteristic requirements and transitions of early latency. First, there is the onset of infantile amnesia, highlighted by the often palpable sense of loss to the child of large segments of his past life and history. Second, the child becomes aware of the new voice of conscience as superego formation proceeds, often experiencing difficulty defining its origin or identity as external or internal. Third, object relationships, though secure, are often buffeted by the narcissistic injury of the child's rejection, inherent in the oedipal resolution; this leads to a temporary downgrading of parental images. Instead of being part of the oedipal child's vigorous interaction with the external world, latency parents find themselves drifting toward the cheap seats.

This often coincides with increasingly narcissistic object choices with regard to peers, who are chosen carefully for particular characteristics often desired, and sometimes feared, by the child himself. Fourth, ego function begins to accelerate in the face of the relative recession in instinctual demands, permitting the independent maintenance of certain functions which previously rested in the parent, such as the capacity to neutralize instinctual energy, to mediate structural conflicts, to establish the secondary autonomy of function and activities, and to effect more advanced forms of identification. This is particularly true as regards the capacity to identify with the aggressor, with its special combination, according to Anna Freud (1937), of introjection, projection, and turning passive into active to avoid guilt. These functions are particularly characteristic of early latency as defined by Bornstein (1951), who originally suggested the subdivision of latency into two periods, the years 5½ to 8, and 9 to pubescence.

One typically sees in latency a number of intensive defense operations designed to prevent the breakthrough of oedipal libidinal wishes toward the parent of the opposite sex. Girls may present a swaggering tomboyishness or an omnipotent, imperious attitude toward boys. Boys may become especially provocative and manipulative of adult women and sarcastic, devaluing, and abusive with girls their own age. In fact, Anna Freud points out that intense relationships with peers who share the same attitudes are based more on identification than on object love (1965).

As for the parental response to latency, mothers and fathers often remember rather fondly their own latencies because of the sense of mastery of experience and the amount of energy available for adventure and exploration. It often is a time they remember as the beginning of "friendships" with *their* parents, characterized by Erna Furman (see chapter 9) as "a time when a child can be an easy friend and congenial companion for peers and adults alike, with few of the heart-rending heights and depths of emotion which tend to accompany the earlier infantile and later adolescent relationships."

Schecter and Combrinck-Graham (see chapter 13, this volume) further describe the opportunity for mastery inherent in latency: "This period is one of growing self-esteem, a capacity to separate from family and interact with peers and other adults, a shift from primary process to secondary process thinking, an ability to undertake formal schooling, a greater joy in bodily control, the development of sexual identity, the control of primitive impulses leading to sublimated pleasures and gratification in learning, a growing sense of humor, and a sense of mastery and competence. . . ."

It is important to remember that the latency period we are discussing is at the earlier, oedipal end of the continuum, rather than at the later, prepubescent end. Here the ego finds itself under greater instinctual pressure than later on. It also is under close scrutiny from the superego as well. Regression is still used frequently to defend against certain primitive impulses. Identification with the aggressor is particularly helpful during this period, as it permits an alliance between the parental superego and the child's newly forming conscience to keep such impulses at bay.

It is abundantly clear to contemporary clinicians that sexual *interest* persists during latency in a variety of vigorous forms. Nevertheless, sexual *impulse* life is expressed less directly during this period than in the one immediately preceding. Sarnoff (1976), in particular, has championed the point of view that drive pressure continues unabated during this period.

Having reviewed the central processes at work during this period of personality formation, let us now return to the clinical investigation to see whether these children are dealing with such issues according to expectations.

Assessment at this stage in the longitudinal study no longer could make use of the Yale Developmental Schedule in a universal way because of its upward limitation to subjects 72 months of age. Consequently, the assessment now made use of the Stanford-Binet and certain projective items, such as Family Drawing and Sentence Completion forms, to assist in the ongoing measurement of cognitive and psychological functioning within the research population. Two diagnostic play sessions lasting an hour each continued as part of the protocol, as well as one lengthy, two-hour parental interview. Although some of the instruments had to be changed, the central focus on overall personality formation within these children remained unchanged. Narrative reports were prepared on each child and assessments made of various aspects of personality functioning, such as basic intactness of the child's ego (as represented by basic ego functions); flexibility of personality as reflected in the capacity to play and learn; the ability to form relationships, organize intrapsychic experience, and provide autonomous and conflict-free spheres; appropriateness of superego function; basic affective capacities; age-appropriate defenses; and, whenever possible, drive organization (see chapter 12, this volume).

The following results have emerged in the 15 children still available for study at 6 years. As noted above, the cognitive assessment was conducted whenever possible by a psychologist unknown to the child, in order to obviate the familiarity occasioned by my long-term involvement with these children. However, I did conduct the diagnostic play interviews for the sake of continuity. Stanford-Binet scores ranged from 106 to 138. Projective techniques yielded no significant or worrisome signs of anxiety, depression, or other clinically significant conditions.

As usual, it was in the play and in the histories of the children that we find the most useful and important material. To illustrate a case in depth, I will discuss Helen, now 7½, a child who at 4 was reported in a previous communication (Pruett, 1983). Her sister was now 3½; her mother, 34; her father, 31. The parental care system was described as "joint" now, as both parents were working full time. Her sister was in a combination nursery school/day care facility five mornings and two afternoons a week, and her father cared for her on the remaining three afternoons. Helen once again demonstrated the best language performance of all the children in the study. She also was one of those children whose mother, after the second child, had joined much more actively in her care. Her IQ on the Stanford-Binet was 120.

When I saw Helen again after a two-year hiatus, she took my hand on the long walk to the playroom and said that she had wanted to tell me how she'd been "growing up." So I asked her after a bit of a silence, "Well, how *have* you been growing up?" Helen: "I have grown 11 pounds and 4 inches, and now

I can watch dirty movies!" I registered some surprise, to which she responded, "Well, not *real* dirty movies—just some with bad words in them!" Upon entering the playroom, she surveyed the toy inventory and decided to pull out the combination chess and checkers set. Although it soon was obvious that she knew the rules of "chest," as she called the game, it was equally clear, as soon as we began moving pieces about the board, that it was going to be very difficult for her to tolerate losing. It seemed that the aggressive aspects of her play were not yet integrated with real interest in the game, so that the fun of the play was being threatened constantly. After a period of frustration at the chess board, I suggested a game of cards, something simple like Fish, but Helen would have none of it. She asked if I knew how to play gin rummy and, without awaiting an answer, proceeded to shuffle and deal the cards. It soon became clear that we would never finish the game because of interminable discussions of rules. She finally said, "Let's not *play* with things; let's talk."

She began by telling me of her uncle's death some months before. I had heard of this event from her mother and father, who had called during the time of Helen's mourning for her Uncle Jack, who had died at age 36 of a sudden, massive heart attack. They briefly had become concerned about how depressed she appeared.

Helen slumped back into the playroom chair and said sadly but with animation, "I can just hear my Uncle Jack . . . in my heart. He and I used to tell secrets. And I remember every single one that he ever told me—*every single one.* If I ever died and went to heaven and saw him, I'm sure I'd cry my heart out. I wonder if he'll ever come down from heaven and visit me. He told me once I was his 'bestest' friend. He taught me how to drive a tractor and feed the chickens." Her affect during these revelations was intense, labored, and her eye contact almost piercing, as though she needed my complete and undivided attention to be able to tell her story. She continued, "He's in his own grave, all alone, way, way in the back of the grave place. I got to miss school to go see them put him in the ground. Even my grandpa and my daddy and my mommy—everyone cried. It just broke my heart! I just don't have a Jack anymore."

I asked whether it ever comforted her just to think of him. She replied, after seemingly ignoring my question, "I thought I saw him blowing by our house one day when we had a hurricane." (We, indeed, had had a moderately severe hurricane about three months after her uncle's death.)

Though poignant and sad to hear, Helen's story is an articulation of the capacities of a maturing latency ego. Throughout her two play sessions she was able to use the intellectual and analytic defenses typical of early latency, such as reaction-formation, denial, and identification with the aggressor. But regressive retreat in the face of real insult never is far away. During the period immediately following her uncle's death, she had begun to sleep longer periods of time, though less restfully and efficiently. Her appetite had decreased for four or five days. She had become clingy and demanding of her father, in particular, and had developed some milk somatic complaints as well. She had, however, begun to recover more quickly from Jack's sudden death than her parents had. A decreased psychological dependence on her parents, typical in latency, had been coupled with an increased intensity of *non*parental relationships which had rendered Jack, as well as her schoolteachers, more vital and vigorous objects and sources of gratification in her life. This undoubtedly made her uncle's loss all the more poignant.

When not preoccupied or saddened by loss, Helen continued to develop in myriad ways, including her unique brand of humor, now enriched by a number of "dirty jokes." The sense of mastery and competence she had demonstrated as a 2-year-old was now displayed less narcissistically and seemed more evenly distributed throughout her personality.

Helen's relationships with her peers were strong, though neither predictable nor dependable. She was popular and sought after as a friend and play companion in her second grade class. At the end of first grade, however, she had run into some difficulty with her peer group when she briefly challenged established gender roles and rules. Although she certainly preferred to play with girls, she tried to introduce boys' games to the girls, as well as sports-oriented clubs and activities. She even joined in a few contact sports, such as playing touch football with the boys. But when none of these efforts came to fruition, she decided to change her tactics and joined the Brownies.

Meanwhile, Helen's mother had come to feel that her competent, popular little girl was a much more easy friend and comfortable companion. She reported that her daughter had "evened out a lot." Her mother seemed able to enjoy her much more empathically now because her humor and sense of competence rendered her much easier to be with. Her relationship with her father continued to be strong and vigorous. She would call him at work daily at the end of school to "shoot the breeze."

Let us now look at 8-year-old David, now head of the largest sibling group in the cohort. He and his 4-year-old brother recently had been joined by twin baby sisters. His parents were both 33 years of age, and his father continued as his primary caregiver. David was a cognitively competent child with an IQ of 118 on the Stanford-Binet, popular and well liked in his second grade class. His play was rich, varied, and characterized by a number of war and battle sequences in which he served as a highly competent and sought-after medic.

This theme apparently was quite prominent in David's play at school. He organized elaborate war games during recess which at first blush seemed classically latency-aged and bellicose. But as the play evolved over the course of the year, a complex series of events led to the formation of a field hospital. The boys carried bodies, operated, reattached limbs, applied pretend bandages, hung IV bottles, etc. For nearly two months at the beginning of second grade, David had directed and produced this play, which included almost all of the boys in the class. He "saved" and "repaired" and "dressed up" (dressing wounds), "saving" repeated numbers of his classmates.

David's mother was employed full time as an operating room head nurse, and his father had spent four years in the Army prior to David's birth. His father was one of the six men who still remained as primary caregivers in the longitudinal study. His father occasionally was surprised to see how lovingly David dealt with his siblings. His recollections of his own growing up were that his relationships with siblings were much more angry and "battling." It troubled him a little that his son was arranging his militaristic fantasies along the lines of a M.A.S.H. officer, rather than General Patton. It was his wife who pointed out the identification compromise David had achieved so economically between war and healing.

David's parents described feeling a palpable calm settling into their relationship with him, which was a great contrast to what they were experiencing with his 4-year-old brother. They recently had noticed a strong trend toward David's eliciting shared caregiving from the two of them. He seemed to be differentiating less between them and would bring similar problems and requests to either of them, depending more on who happened to be handy than on "who had first place in his heart," as his mother put it. He now seemed to be "easier and more predictable," according to his father.

David's parents seemed to be describing a phenomenon experienced by most parents of latency-age children. Fairly regular resolutions of rough-and-tumble, id-versus-ego oedipal skirmishes seem to occur across all latency populations assessed to date.

Although the male-male and female-female alignments among peers typical of latency certainly were present among the subjects of the study, the flexibility in gender identity and role which we saw in these children during their oedipal years seems to have remained intact. Helen's attempts to organize touch football games among her girlfriends, and David's attempts to run a field hospital were not unusual. It is important to underscore that this is a subtle finding, not obvious in wholesale ways to the casual observer.

Another subtle finding was suggested by one of the fathers in the study; it seemed to be shared by a number of other families, but was particularly obvious in the stories of the fathers. One of the hallmarks of the pleasure of latency parenting is the pleasant recollection of one's own latency period relationships with one's parents. But David's father pointed out that he felt an "odd kind of distance from what David's growing up is like at this age." It had struck him that David was having a very different life than he'd had at this age. It seemed to trouble him that he could not identify easily or readily with David's style of play, its content, or the joy he took in it. He even found himself on occasion encouraging him to be "tougher"; when he "caught himself doing it," he talked with his wife about it. What he discovered in his conversations with her was that he could not identify readily with David's latency experience because he was having an experience that he'd never had in his own life, i.e., having a father deeply involved in his care. This partial empathic obstacle probably had existed during the oedipal years as well, but the instinctual pressure of that phase, and the reciprocal defensive activity of both parent and child at that time, made this "difference" consciously accessible only during latency. This seemed the first clinical evidence of a none-too-surprising dissonance between latency parenting as a developmental phase, and the nurturing ego ideals these fathers used as guides for their own parental behavior and experience.

It is important to point out, however, that this is a subtle finding that had not led to psychopathological constructs (as yet) and that has been described by only half of the fathers. By far the most powerful experience reported by parents regarding the latency-age children in this study is a kind of joyful relief at the return of a less challenging closeness with one's child. Nevertheless, the nurturing ideal toward which the fathers, in particular, aspired still was a highly individual one.

The difference in their children's experience as compared to their own, as expressed by fathers particularly but also by mothers, though less poignantly, I tend not to see as empathic failure. Instead, I see it as a kind of endless variation on the nurturing experience, which undoubtedly will broaden the experience of both parent and child.

In closing, the children we have seen to date do seem to be entering the "eye of the hurricane" in appropriate style. They are hard at work at age-appropriate adaptations. The unusual path chosen by their parents in arranging their care hardly seems to preoccupy them, or even to interest them much.

Ultimately, it must be recognized that these children's lives are just beginning, and the long-term effects of such intimate paternal care await further longitudinal study. Yet, the first six years are seminal in the formulation of personality. The fact that these children are rigorous, thriving, competent, and complex reassures the clinician that early, intense paternal involvement need not be considered inherently problematic developmentally. In fact, it may well enrich both the child and the parent's nurturing experience in enduring and positive ways—ways which may be particularly profound for the father.

References

Benson, R., & Harrison, S. (1980), The eye of the hurricane: From seven to ten. In: *The Course of Life: Psychoanalytic Contributions Toward Understanding Personality Development, Vol. 2, Latency, Adolescence and Youth,* ed. S. Greenspan & G. Pollock. Bethesda, Md.: NIMH, pp. 137–144.

Bornstein, B. (1951), On latency. *The Psychoanalytic Study of the Child,* 6:279–285. New York: International Universities Press.

Chused, J. (1986), Consequences of paternal nurturing. *The Psychoanalytic Study of the Child,* 41:419–438. New Haven: Yale University Press.

Freud, A. (1937), *The Ego and the Mechanisms of Defense.* New York: International Universities Press, 1966.

——— (1965), *Normality and Pathology in Childhood.* New York: International Universities Press.

Provence, S., & Naylor, A. (1983), *Working with Disadvantaged Parents and Their Children.* New Haven: Yale University Press.

Pruett, K.D. (1983), Infants of primary nurturing fathers. *The Psychoanalytic Study of the Child,* 38:257–277. New Haven: Yale University Press.

——— (1985), Oedipal configurations in father-raised children. *The Psychoanalytic Study of the Child,* 40:435–456. New Haven: Yale University Press.

——— (1987), The nurturing male: A longitudinal study of primary nuturing fathers. In: *Fathers and Their Families,* ed. S. Cath, A. Gurwitt, & L. Gunsberg. Hillsdale, NJ: Analytic Press.

Radin, N., & Goldsmith, R. (1985), Caregiving fathers of preschoolers: Four years later. *Merrill-Palmer Quart.,* 31:375–383.

Russell, G. (1982), Shared-caregiving families: An Australian study. In: *Nontraditional Families: Parenting and Child Development,* ed. M. Lamb. Hillsdale, N.J.: Erlbaum, pp. 139–171.

Sarnoff, C. (1976), *Latency.* New York: Aronson.

6

A Different View of Oedipal Conflict

ROBERT J. STOLLER, M.D.

From the beginning of his work to the end, no subject more persistently occupied Freud than that of the origins, development, and maintenance of masculinity and femininity. Although he changed and expanded his ideas, he always took the position that gender identity resulted from the interplay of biological and environmental ("accidental") factors. Over the last 20 years or so, data have emerged that amplify and modify his theories on this subject. Let me, as a way of presenting this newer material, review his positions and compare them with recent ideas.

Regarding the biological, Freud recognized that his theory building was limited by the rudimentary knowledge then available from laboratory researchers or from observers of animal behavior. He could nonetheless point to the evidence that in all mammals, man included, both male and female anatomical and physiological features are present, regardless of the individual's sex. As with other aspects of personality, he spoke of a "complemental series," a range of possible origins ranging from those in which the biological predominates to those in which the "accidental" does. Recognizing that psychoanalysis is not equipped to study anatomy and physiology, Freud concentrated on intrapsychic and interpersonal perspectives, with the oedipus complex as the central issue.

He established that maleness and masculinity[1] are recog-

[1] Maleness and femaleness are biological states made up from chromosomes, external genitals, internal sexual apparatuses (e.g., prostate, uterus), gonads, hormonal state, secondary sex characteristics, and brain differences; by contrast, masculinity and femininity are psychological, personality states reflecting one's identification with behaviors defined by societies, families, and individuals as masculine or feminine.

nized by mankind (perhaps at even the profoundest level: the racial unconscious) as superior to femaleness and femininity. Although males accept this superiority, they believe their maleness and masculinity are endangered throughout childhood. This fear—castration anxiety—is due especially to the boy's awareness that his father can attack, even destroy him for wanting to possess his mother. Females have a different set of problems; recognizing male superiority from infancy on, they suffer envy of males' better equipment and status, forever trying to end their despair at not having a penis, or perhaps, at having had their penis taken from them, by finding a substitute for this absent penis. These two central features of personality development—castration anxiety in males and penis envy in females—set the form, he said, of all normal and aberrant personality formation, not just masculinity and femininity; almost all psychopathology—neurotic or psychotic—is the result of these conflicts.

Beyond this, women get off to a bad start because their first relationship—that with their mother—is homosexual, while males from the first are heterosexual and have only to preserve, not create, that orientation in the rivalry with their fathers for their mothers. Therefore, males have an intrinsically simpler task; to become masculine they need not change their desire, as do females if they are to become feminine, from a person of the same sex to one of the opposite sex. But females must make this great shift, must find a reason to give up their primordial love for the mother and somehow find a way to commit their affection and eroticism to a profoundly different sort of object—their father. The chance for slippage in females is therefore so great that one can expect only a few to negotiate the double obstacles of penis envy and primary homosexuality. Femininity, Freud felt, is a secondary, defensive state, acquired rather late in development and more the product of renunciation of hope than of pleasurable experiences or expectations.

To support this description Freud and many later analysts have offered data derived from the analyses of uncounted men and women (and, later, boys and girls), data said to confirm the hypotheses. Challenge from within analysis came from a few workers (Horney, 1924; Jones, 1927; Zilboorg, 1944) who disagreed with Freud in this one area, in insisting that there was in girls a primary femininity, beginning from earliest life on, and not the product of a secondary revision of one's history for the purpose of defense against trauma and conflict. In addition, the absoluteness of the superior male status was questioned by those (e.g., Boehm, 1930) who suggested that one also finds male envy of female capacities (such as procreation) and anatomy (breasts).

Newer Biological Data

Recent findings put in doubt the theory that maleness is inherently superior (as would be indicated, for instance, in the belief that the clitoris is a hypotrophic or vestigial penis). It is now known that all mammalian tissue—brain, genitals, any—is at first female. That is the "resting state," the elemental condition; until male hormones exert their influence (as they normally do in males because of the Y chromosome), maleness does not occur. Even when the animal is chromosomally male (XY), it will not develop as a male and act in a masculine way unless androgens are present at the right time in fetal life. And the converse is true; if, when the animal is chromosomally female, androgens are added, then maleness and masculinity result. The fundament is female; maleness requires an additional step. All animal experiments confirm these findings, but obviously we must turn to "natural experiments" in order to study humans. Although these do not test the rule as rigorously as would experimentation, none contradict it.[2] The following are examples.

Klinefelter's syndrome. In this condition, although the body appears male, the chromosomes are abnormal in that there is an extra X (female). Not only may this anatomically and physiologically impair maleness, but an unexpected number of these men develop feminine behavior.

Turner's syndrome. In this condition there is only one rather

[2] The above findings and the following examples are reviewed in Money and Ehrhardt (1972).

than the normal two sex chromosomes (XX for females, XY for males). At birth the infant appears unremarkably female, and in the absence of the maleness-inducing Y chromosome, these girls invariably grow up feminine in behavior by their culture's standards. In fact, they are more feminine than a control group of girls.

Androgen insensitivity syndrome. In this condition, although there is no sex chromosome defect (these people are XY, i.e., chromosomally male), there is a flaw (probably genetic). Normal amounts of normally constituted androgens are present from fetal life on, but the tissues are incapable of responding. The result, as the rule would predict, is that the habitus is female and the behavior feminine. Once again, when compared to a control group of biologically normal girls, these girls are more feminine than the controls.

Progestin-induced androgenization. When, some years ago, women with threatened abortions were treated with progestins, an occasional female infant was born with androgenized genitals.[3] Although they were recognized to be unquestionably female, they nonetheless grew up more aggressive, more tomboyish than a control group.

In bisexual states such as these, then, it seems that hormonal influences modify the fetal brain, permanently changing gender behavior from that expected toward that typical of the opposite sex. These data should brake enthusiasts of male superiority who rely on untestable biological arguments. Nonetheless, our evidence at present confirms Freud's belief that biological bisexuality is present in humans, that it can be a measurable influence on psychological development, and that in some cases it may be the dominating cause of cross-gender behavior.

Newer Psychological Data

As we move along Freud's "complemental series," we find conditions in which both the biological and the postnatal en-

[3] Progestins, though female substances, at times aberrantly act in a male direction.

vironmental (psychological) forces influence gender development. Here is an example.

Androgenital syndrome in females. In this disorder, excessive amounts of androgens are produced by the adrenals in an otherwise normal female fetus. The fetal brain is apparently[4] androgenized. As a result, although all these females have an unquestioned sense of being female, they are more tomboyish than a control group. On the other hand, the postnatal environmental effects (rearing) are even more powerful. Because the external genitals are androgenized, they will be hermaphroditic, that is, with male-appearing attributes. If the infant is assigned at birth to the female sex because the proper diagnosis of sex is made, she will grow up with no question she is a female (but with the tomboy qualities just noted). But such an infant unequivocally assigned as a male grows up masculine and with no question he is a male. Both, the one brought up as a male and the one who believes she is female, are biologically the same. The difference is simply the product of one set of parents believing their child is male and the other that their child is female.

Hermaphroditism without CNS involvement. The next step along our continuum is exemplified by the "natural experiment" in which the infant is born with hermaphroditic genitals not the result of a prenatal pathology that also affects the brain. In this circumstance, the sex assignment is the essential factor in starting the development of gender identity. When, on the basis of external genital appearance, the infant is assigned as female, it grows up in no doubt that it is female and is appropriately feminine. And if it is unequivocally assigned as male, it grows up in no doubt that it is male and with appropriate masculinity. An act in the environment—sex assignment—made the difference, not biology.

So, as Freud made clear and as we see from the new data, biological "forces" are not the whole story. Although fetal hormones are the essential factor for postnatal behavior in lower animals, environmental factors are increasingly important as

[4] "Apparently" is the best we can say, because we cannot experiment on the human fetal brain.

one moves up the evolutionary scale. In humans, these postnatal effects from birth on not only influence, but can even at times overpower, as we shall soon see, biological anlagen.

Sex Assignment

At birth, infants are assigned to the male or female sex on the basis of the appearance of the external genitals. This act is made valid by the authority who delivers the baby and is confirmed by what parents see. It starts the process—different in each family and for each child—in which endless communications pass from parents, especially mothers, to the infant. In these are represented attitudes about the infant's sex. Whatever subtleties are transmitted in this regard to the infant—for instance, whether a parent likes or dislikes the fact that the infant is male or female—we can at least be sure that the baby receives clearly the message as to which sex it is assigned to.

This holds even for children with ambiguous genitals —hermaphrodites. In that case, unless parents are told and believe otherwise, the child will learn that its sex assignment was not clearly to the male or to the female sex but, unfortunately, unequivocally to something else, a sex in which one is neither simply male nor simply female.

Parental Influences

Sex assignment cannot of itself create gender development. Its importance is that the infant has now been permanently categorized and that everyone—the mother at first, then both parents, siblings, peers—incessantly confirms the assignment. In doing so they also inform the infant which behaviors they like and which they dislike, thus shaping aspects of personality. As the months pass, with increasing complexity the infant is encouraged, coerced, frustrated, and otherwise moved to begin creating itself as an individual separate from, and (in the boy's case) different in sex from, its mother.

Core Gender Identity

As early as the end of the first year, generally by the end of the second year, and almost always and unalterably by the fourth year (Money, Hampson, and Hampson, 1957; Stoller,

1968), an aspect of character structure has been developing in the child, an unquestioned, unthinking conviction—a piece of identity—that one is a male or female. And in the rare case where the family thought the child an hermaphrodite, it develops an hermaphroditic identity. This sense of maleness or femaleness, or of being an hermaphrodite, is the core gender identity. It is, we have seen, the product of prenatal brain influences, sex assignment, and parental influences. In addition, these communications are confirmed for the child as it gradually comes to know the dimensions and capacities of its body: body ego. This awareness of its body will then be further confirmed—and threatened—as the child sees the anatomy of other children and of adults. And the knowledge that one is male or female can be confirmed—and threatened—only after one knows one is male or female.

At this point we are back again on ground familiar from Freud's descriptions. Now we can see the development of penis envy in girls, breast and reproductive envy in boys, and fear of body and gender damage ("castration anxiety"); the child has advanced so far, has learned so much, has become so able to remember and to fantasize that it can invent its oedipal conflict.

The Oedipal Conflict

Freud (1905, 1932) had a theory of gender development to fit his belief that women are less moral, more envious, more insincere, and more narcissistic than men, and therefore inferior to them. In brief, this theory held that the psychology that is uniquely women's is the sum of the efforts made to adjust to not being male. Because they lack penises, women know they are doomed to inferiority. The development of femininity in females is the effort made to salvage something of value from this fateful, originally biological fact. There is, then, nothing that could be called primary femininity, a naturally occurring state bolstered by conflict-free, traumaless development, both biological and psychological. Rather, males are favored with primary masculinity, for they are born anatomically superior and do not have to change their first sex object in order to develop their masculinity or become heterosexual.

In addition, identification plays its part. Here again, Freud felt that the advantage went to the boy. Seeing fathers as the powerful, respected, and envied person and mothers as the loved but inadequate, inferior, and damaged parent, he thought identification with the parent of the same sex would naturally be augmented between a son and his father. On the other hand, the girl would have mixed feelings about identifying with her mother, a diminished and disparaged creature. The path leading to a mature gender identity in the boy is therefore more straightforward than in the girl. The only obstacle between the boy and his desired mother is his powerful father. Yet even this conflict has its built-in solution. Although father forbids access to mother, his admirable strength serves as a model for heterosexual and masculine identification. In boys, the oedipal conflict arises spontaneously and can be successfully resolved.

The girl's situation, Freud said, is different. She is in such jeopardy that she may fail even to advance enough to enter an oedipal conflict. She believes herself either a castrated male or a member of a deficient sex; she is possessed by penis envy, discouraged from identifying with her mother because of her mother's inferiority, and engulfed in homosexual love from birth on. Before she can find herself in a rivalrous situation with her mother (comparable to the boy's rivalry with his father), she must undergo an added struggle: to disengage herself from loving her mother and turn to her father.

The great difference between men and women, then, is that men usually succeed, more or less, in the tasks created by the oedipal complex and women usually fail, more or less.

Primary Femininity

This theoretical edifice will not stand if there is a primary femininity—an unquestioned, unconflicted, ego-syntonic acceptance of oneself as female—or if primary masculinity should be less stable than Freud described. In testing a hypothesis, we know that we should do more than shake the theory with more theory and see if it falls; the ultimate test must be observations. In this regard, there are some, at least enough to let us question Freud's convictions.

When we look at infants, we find differences in response in girls as compared to boys, from the first months of life on. Although these are not marked, they are measurable (see Green, 1976). Some are the result of biological differences between male and female infants, and some seem to result from differential handling of the sexes by mothers. At any rate, simple observation of a child by a year or so of age can distinguish behavior typical of girls from that typical of boys (Kleeman, 1971, 1976). Although penis envy is ubiquitous in girls and appears even earlier than Freud had noted (Roiphe and Galenson, 1972), we also know that many months pass, from birth on, before the girl will see a penis or have enough knowledge and sufficiently complex fantasies to make judgments regarding genital superiority.

For most infants there are many stretches of nontraumatic, nonfrustrating, nonconflictual intimacy and pleasure with mother. In such exchanges, mothers encourage behavior they consider feminine in their daughters, and feminine behavior results. How could Freud have missed this obvious finding? In fact, he did not; he only ignored what he observed. We recognize this when we look at his exact words. (I use italics to indicate his awareness.) "*At some time or other* the little girl makes the discovery of her organic inferiority" (Freud, 1931, p. 232); "*when* the little girl discovers her own deficiency, from seeing a male genital, it is only with hesitation and reluctance that she accepts the unwelcome knowledge" (p. 233); "*when* she comes to understand the general nature of this characteristic, it follows that femaleness—and with it, of course, her mother—suffers a great depreciation in her eyes" (p. 233). But in theorizing on the origins and nature of masculinity and femininity, he left out that first stage implied in his use of "when."

Primary Masculinity

It is no longer easy to argue for primary masculinity on the basis of superior biology; but we must still confront Freud's thesis that the boy is better off than the girl in that, from birth on, his love object is a person of the opposite sex. Although one cannot argue against that truth, another piece must nonetheless be inserted in the argument. It is this: the first stage in an infant's relationship with its mother is a matter of being as if one with her rather than of finding her from birth on to be an object, clearly perceived as separate from oneself, of different sex, and erotically desirable. Once again, Freud seems to have ignored his own observations, in this case that the start of life is a state of symbiosis between mother and infant, in which the infant only gradually emerges—separates and then individuates (Mahler, 1968)—from the original oneness. Freud forever emphasized the presence throughout life of the first, objectless state, of the pull toward merging again into mother. This suggests that in all infants the first stage of development is one of "protoidentification"[5] with the mother. If that is so, the tendency to merge with the mother would—her being female—augment the development of femininity, a favorable consequence in girls but a threat to further gender development in boys.

There is suggestive evidence for this hypothesis. It is well known, for instance, that in most societies men have innumerable techniques in ritual, custom, neurosis, and erotism to maintain vigilance ("symbiosis anxiety") against what are perceived as the dangers of intimacy with women. One can speculate that the greater part of manifest masculinity in many cultures is constructed from fear of intimacy with—worse, of becoming like—women. This might even be one of the sources of the finding that most of the perversions are rare or not found at all in women. Another speculation: are there differences between the erotic style and sensibilities of men and women that are influenced by the possibility that a kind of femininity is the first state in both boys and girls?

A "natural experiment"—primary male transsexualism—tests the hypothesis that mother-infant intimacy promotes feminin-

[5] The quotation marks serve to indicate that I do not know the real nature of the earliest processes by which the infant perceives, takes in, and converts the external world into its own self.

ity. This condition, which is only one of many that can bring a person to ask for a change of sex, is defined as follows: an anatomically normal male who has been feminine since earliest childhood, who has never shown masculine behavior or lived successfully in a role typical for boys or men in his society, and who at present—whether child, adolescent, or adult—is the most feminine of males. Such a person shows what can happen in a male infant if the process of separation-individuation is impeded, if the "protoidentification" with the mother is encouraged. Despite its rarity, I shall expand on this transsexualism, since the aberrance of such a family's oedipal relationships and the boy's resulting femininity illuminates more ordinary development. (A less manifest reason for describing this condition is to give an example of how psychoanalytic research helps us understand personality development.)

Transsexualism

One must study three generations in order to understand the process. The transsexual boy's maternal grandmother is a cold, harsh woman with no love for the daughter who is to be the transsexual's mother. The girl, although unquestionably female, is made to feel from birth on that being female is worthless. She is treated with no affection or respect by her mother but serves simply as a slave for household tasks. On the other hand, her father loves her; they are close for a few years. Unfortunately for her femininity, however, the attachment is one in which the father has his daughter join him in his masculine interests, encouraging her to be like him. Then somewhere between age 6 and puberty he abandons her, through such events as death, separation, divorce, or going into the service.

With the father's desertion, the girl, sometimes within days, begins acting like a boy. She refuses to wear girls' clothes, insisting on dressing only in boys' clothes from underwear out. She cuts her hair short, in the manner of boys. She refuses to play with girls and will play with boys only in exclusively boys' games; she becomes a fine athlete, better than most of the boys. Even more, she wants to become male, talks of sex change, and prays to God for a penis. Up to this point the story sounds much as that of females who grow up to be transsexuals. But, with the changes of puberty and their proof of oncoming adult femaleness, these girls stop waiting for maleness, become manifestly depressed, and put on a feminine facade, giving up their boyish ways. In time, without romance, heterosexual fantasies, or premarital sexual enthusiasms for men, they marry. Having decided they must act as if feminine, they have pushed themselves toward marriage, but their wish to be males, although consciously renounced, and their hatred and envy because they are not persist.

The men they marry are chosen by them to fulfill their unhappy needs. These men are not effeminate, but they are distant and passive. (It is unlikely that a more manly man would marry such a woman.) They are not involved with their families, not respected by their wives, and not physically present most of the time. When the transsexual-to-be is young, his father—hard working—leaves home before the boy is awake and does not return until the child is already in bed. On weekends, having worked so hard, he wishes to relax; his wife encourages him in this so long as relaxation continues to keep him removed from the family. He is therefore not present even on weekends; for instance, he spends his time in a photographic darkroom or drinking beer and watching football, with the children instructed not to disturb him; or he is a painter, isolated in his studio.

It is likely, of course, that not everyone of this sort marries and has children. And those who do, do not have a houseful of transsexuals. In fact, for years I was puzzled that all the families observed had only one transsexual son, and there were no reports of families in whom more than one case was reported. The reason why only one was appearing, despite there often being more than one son born, was revealed in each mother's story, as we shall see shortly.

Contrary to what we might expect, these mothers are happy to give birth to this son. One might think that very feminine boys are the result of a mother who was disappointed not to have had a girl. Yet these mothers were overjoyed. In addition, each boy is given a strongly masculine, phallic name at birth, which hardly seems to predict a continuing impulse in the mother to have her boy be feminine. And when one recalls that these are women who hate men and who learn to despise the penises they envy, one is surprised to learn that the proximate cause of the femininity is an excessively intimate symbiosis, present from birth indefinitely onward until external forces end it, in which the mother is trying to produce a frustrationless, traumaless, blissful state. Nothing is to split them apart.

Why then is this infant spared his mother's hatred of males? This intimacy, more complete than any reported elsewhere, is set off by the infant's perceived beauty and gracefulness. If his mother finds the baby to be ideal—beautiful, cuddly, responsive to her—he becomes the beautiful phallus for which she has yearned since her sad, hopeless girlhood. Finally, from her own body has been produced—just as she had hoped for and then despised of ever getting—the perfect penis. Although all others—her husband's, her other sons', all other men's—are ugly, this one is not. Because her other sons are not considered beautiful and graceful, they are spared this intense symbiosis and are not feminized.

With this cure for her lifelong depression in her arms, she is not about to let go of it. There is nothing complex about this motivation. When she holds the baby, she feels marvelous; when he is out of reach, she feels less so. If he were out of sight, she would be anxious. Therefore, she simply acts on her desire and keeps him unendingly in contact with her. This is actually skin-to-skin, day and night, with almost no interruption. Father is driven from the marriage bed, the infant taking his place for extended periods. In time, and at appropriate ages, though, the mother allows ego functions to develop—sitting, crawling, standing, walking, talking. None is aborted or delayed in the symbiosis. Rather, in her love and pride, she encourages her son to develop his intelligence and creativity. However, she does so only with him constantly within sight and reach.

When one hears of a mother and infant in a blissful relationship in the first months of life, one thinks only that this is normal, even ideal. However, one does not expect it to go on day and night, with the mother trying to keep it from being interrupted; and especially one does not expect it to persist for years. But in these families this excessive intimacy is still active when the children are first seen for evaluation, around age 4 or 5. Every impetus to referral is indicative of the process. By this age the boys act and look like beautiful girls, but the mothers refuse to recognize this; they consciously cannot understand how everyone is able to mistake their child for a girl. So they do not often spontaneously bring their sons for evaluation but are driven to only after months of seeing the boys identified as girls by strangers. Between 4 and 5, in our society, children begin moving out into the world, especially to school, and it is then that pressure builds up for the mother to consider her child abnormal and to get help.

The mother, thus, does all she can to maintain the close relationship with this ideal product of her body. At this point one would expect the father to interrupt the process. But he was already chosen as a person who is not there; and he is not. (He is not even willing to participate in the treatment.) With him out of the way, the mother is free to continue the symbiosis uninterrupted; no one moves in as a shield between mother and son. The father's second main function—to serve as a model for his son's masculinity, as most fathers do—is also not possible. He simply is not present, and, additionally, masculinity is so constantly disparaged in the family by the mother's remarks about this weak and absent father that the boy is never encouraged to look on masculinity as a state he would admire and wish to identify with.

Once the femininity begins to appear, somewhere around 1 to 2 years, mother is thrilled to see it, all the while denying that it is strange behavior for her phallicly named, undoubtedly male son. She defines it as lovely, fine, adorable, creative, not as feminine, and so encourages him to continue.

Crucial data are missing from this explanation: never observed by an outsider and not articulated by mothers or their transsexual sons is the process by which, within the first year or so of life, the little boy draws forth his femininity. One can presume that the pleasures of the symbiosis are transmitted in measurable ways: the mother's soft and cradling arms, warm skin, pillowy muscles and bosom, cooing voice, and the innumerable other movements, behaviors, and attitudes that, though minute, pass clearly on to the infant's body so that he is in an ambiance molded for constant bliss. But does this lead to feminine behavior? And if so, how?

Here may be a clue. All the mothers mention that these sons' eyes are large and beautiful, which draws the mothers to look constantly into the babies' eyes. There probably is no more intense way available to humans for merging with each other than to look deeply into each other's eyes; lovers have always known this, as have mothers. It is a powerful process, so intense that few persist for more than moments. Yet these mothers keep it up as long as possible; in no other way do they so profoundly sense their unbroken connection with this beloved infant. Perhaps in this way, especially, the boys "drink in," merge with, sense they are part of, their mothers' femaleness.

A most odd oedipal situation develops in these families: there is no oedipal conflict. Other boys emerge from the mother-infant symbiosis to become separate persons. They then desire their mothers as sexual objects and fear their fathers' retaliation for such wishes. The conflict between desire and fear complicates—deepens—their developing masculinity, especially when resolved by identification with the father. This helps boys to delay consummation of this first heterosexuality, displacing it out of the family and to a later time. Father thus converts from overpowering rival to ally when he encourages his son to identify with him, while mother serves the process of renunciation by being a model for future love objects. Heterosexual masculinity is the consequence.

None of this occurs with the extremely feminine boy. His mother, not his father, is the model for his gender identification, and she is not the object of his erotism. He wants *to be* like rather than *to have* her (Greenson, 1968). His father, all too absent, is neither rival nor model. The boy is deprived of the needed conflict. (For more details see Stoller, 1968, 1975.)

Female Transsexualism

Extreme masculinity in females also tests hypotheses about the development of masculinity and femininity in males and females. Let us define the female transsexual as an anatomically normal female who has been masculine from earliest age on, has never had episodes of femininity or living in typical female roles, and is at the time of evaluation the most masculine of all females. If too much mother and too little father lead to femininity in boys, then masculinity in girls could result from too little mother-infant intimacy and a father who is all-too-present as a model for identification and not used as an object for opposite-sexed love. And that is what is found. Girls who become transsexuals are not considered beautiful at birth and, in their first few years, do not have a mother who is available for good enough mothering. Instead this mother, although physically present within the house, is made frustratingly unavailable to her daughter; mother is an invalid who must not be disturbed, or is clinically depressed, or is overtly paranoid. The child in infancy is given only physical care adequate to keep her growing. She does, however, develop a close relationship with her father; unfortunately, he is interested in this daughter only if she functions as if she were a boy, joining him in all his masculine interests. (For more details see Stoller, 1975.) Note the similarity to the childhood of the transsexual boy's mother, who also, in later childhood, is powerfully masculine.

Implications for Normative Behavior

Hypothesis: if a woman like the described mother of the primary male transsexual marries a man like the described father and has a beautiful, graceful son, she will create the above-described symbiosis, making her son feminine by a year or so of age. She will then encourage the femininity, and father will fail to intervene, so that the boy (in the absence of treatment or other circumstances that disrupt these family dynamics) will continue to develop in a feminine way. He will be feminine throughout his life, never having episodes of natural-appearing masculinity. He will not dress, walk, or talk like a man, want sexual relations with women, desire to be a father, seek out a masculine profession, or otherwise live in roles his society defines as masculine. No exigencies of life will get him to turn from his femininity. In time he will try to change his sex.

If this hypothesis is to be tested, we must turn it around as follows. If we have an adult, biologically normal male who is at present the most feminine of all males and has been so without interruption since earliest life, then he will have a mother as described, a father as described, have been perceived in infancy by his mother as being beautiful and graceful, and will have been excessively close to her.

Corollary: to the extent that any element in this constellation is less strong or absent, the femininity will be lessened.

Corollary: the less these family dynamics are at work, the more likely is masculinity to occur.

What do these hypotheses say about normative behavior? It is well known that a study of extreme cases can teach one about mechanisms of similar nature but lesser degree. In other words, one begins to make sense of ordinary behavior. If an excessively close and blissful symbiosis leads to femininity and if a less intimate symbiosis is followed by less femininity, does the ordinary mother-infant symbiosis also put boys a bit at risk for femininity? The answer may be yes (Stoller, 1975).

Conclusions

The data suggest that Freud's description of oedipal conflict can be modified. First, we find that maleness is not the primary state of animals; femaleness is. More to the point for the present-day analyst, we are no longer sure that masculinity is the more stable state. The evidence from feminine males suggests that we look, in all boys, to see if the earliest stage of gender development is the heterosexual one Freud postulated. I think it is not. Rather, there is an earlier period during which the boy is merged with his mother. Only gradually, and with his parents' help, will he separate from her, in time to know her as a separate, desired, opposite-sexed person. But at first he is susceptible to femininity. (The same merging with mother will make the first stage of gender development a protofeminine one in girls as well, a good start if one is to grow up feminine.)

From there on, Freud's theories are compatible with what we observe. A girl has to contend with her first love object being female, and so she must make the profound shift to erotic preference for her father—for males. In addition, the evidence that girls suffer penis envy is clear and underlines important issues with which women may have endless problems. But, if my hypotheses are correct, these struggles take place on a solid base of primary femininity, making unlikely Freud's belief that femininity is only a secondary state reached after trauma and conflict. On the contrary, that may be, in part, the situation with the development of masculinity in males.

We can be assured, however, that even if these suggested shifts in our understanding of oedipal conflict are correct, neither sex is deprived of a full share of developmental struggle.

References

Boehm, R. (1930), The femininity complex in men. *Internat. J. Psycho-Anal.*, 11:444–469.

Freud, S. (1905), Three essays on the theory of sexuality. *Standard Edition*, 7:135–243. London: Hogarth Press, 1953.

——— (1931), Female sexuality. *Standard Edition*, 21:225–243. London: Hogarth Press, 1961.

——— (1932), Femininity. *Standard Edition*, 22:112–135. London: Hogarth Press, 1964.

Green, R. (1976), Human sexuality: Research and treatment frontiers. In: *American Handbook of Psychiatry*, ed. S. Arieti. 2nd ed. New York: Basic Books, pp. 665–691.

Greenson, R.R. (1968), Disidentifying from mother. *Internat. J. Psycho-Anal.*, 49:370–374.

Horney, K. (1924), On the genesis of the castration complex in women. *Internat. J. Psycho-Anal.*, 5:50–65.

Jones, E. (1927), The early development of female sexuality. *Internat. J. Psycho-Anal.*, 8:459–472.

Kleeman, J.A. (1971), The establishment of core gender identity in normal girls: I. (a) introduction; (b) development of the ego capacity to differentiate. II. how meanings are conveyed between parent and child in the first 3 years. *Arch. Sex. Behav.*, 1:103–129.

——— (1976), Freud's views on early female sexuality in the light of direct child observation. *J. Amer. Psychoanal. Assn.*, 24:3–27.

Mahler, M.S. (1968), *On Human Symbiosis and the Vicissitudes of Individuation.* New York: International Universities Press.

Money, J., & Ehrhardt, A. (1972), *Man and Woman, Boy and Girl.* Baltimore: Johns Hopkins Press.

——— Hampson, J.G., & Hampson, J.L. (1957), Imprinting and the establishment of gender role. *Arch. Neurol. & Psychiat.*, 77:333–336.

Roiphe, H., & Galenson, E. (1972), Early genital activity and the castration complex. *Psychoanal. Quart.*, 42:334–347.

Stoller, R.J. (1968), *Sex and Gender.* Vol. 1. New York: Science House.

——— (1975), *Sex and Gender.* Vol. 2. New York: Aronson.

Zilboorg, G. (1944), Masculine and feminine. *Psychiatry*, 7:257–296.

7

Childhood Psychosis: A Psychoanalytic Perspective

PAULINA F. KERNBERG, M.D.

Working with psychotic children is the greatest challenge to the child therapist. The intense turmoil presented by children suffering from autism or schizophrenic illness suggests that their internal world is a fragmented, unstable, and awesome chaos. No matter what etiological theories are used (Erikson, 1959; O'Gorman, 1970; Gunderson and Feinsilver, 1972; Garmezy, 1974a, 1974b; Miller, 1975; Rutter, 1975; Mahler, 1976; Ritvo, 1976), understanding the subjective experience of the child remains a major challenge.

The Object Relations Theory Approach

I will attempt to conceptualize the phenomenology of the psychotic child's experience in terms of psychoanalytic object relations theory. The potential usefulness of this task is to suggest that, clinically, object relations theory may be the most relevant aspect of psychoanalytic psychotherapy as applied to psychotic children. Formulating phenomena from an object relations theory perspective allows the therapist a more practical framework than that provided by the traditional theory of drives, superego pressures, defense mechanisms, ego functions, ego strength, and ego weakness.

As a prelude to a consideration of object relations theory in its connection with psychosis, I will present a general definition of object relations theory, one that will provide a point of reference from which to describe the particular kinds of objects and self-representations that an autistic or schizophrenic child may have (Mahler, 1968; Tustin, 1972). According to Otto Kernberg (1976), object relations theory has various meanings, which can be summarized as follows.

In general, object relations theory is a theory of the structures in the mind which derive from, preserve, and organize interpersonal experiences. In addition, it is the theory of the mutual influences of the intrapsychic structures and the vicissitudes of expression of instinctual needs in the psychosocial environment. Seen in this way, object relations theory occupies an intermediate field between classical psychoanalytic metapsychology and the phenomenological clinical description of normal and pathological function. Psychoanalytic object relations focuses upon the internalization of interpersonal relations and their contribution to normal and pathological ego and superego development and should therefore be differentiated from a theory of interpersonal relations, that is, interactions or relations between people.

A second, more restricted, definition views object relations theory as a special approach within psychoanalytic metapsychology, one stressing the building up of bipolar units (object images and self-images) linked by affect as a reflection of the original infant-mother relationship and its development from dyadic to triangular and multiple interpersonal relationships, internal and external. The object images and self-images that are simultaneously built up in the context of a particular affective link constitute the units that will become primary determinants of the overall structures of the mind (ego, id, and superego). Various developmental schemas have been outlined in terms of object relations theory, those of Erikson, Jacobson, Otto Kernberg, Mahler, Winnicott, and Melanie Klein.

The interesting implication of this second definition of object relations theory is that it accounts for the various ways in which an individual's representational world can be constructed (Sandler and Rosenblatt, 1962), taking into account the child's concrete level of thinking (including the subjective experience of himself and his relations to others), the intactness of cognitive apparatuses (Ritvo, 1976), levels of development, pressures of instinctual drives, and experiences with external objects (Sandler and Rosenblatt, 1962). Here the various theories of childhood autism and childhood schizophrenia (Mahler, 1968; Laufer and Gair, 1969; Ekstein, 1971; Mednick, Schulsinger, Higgins, and Bell, 1974; Meltzer, Bermer, Hoxter, Weddell, and Wittenberg, 1974; Freeman, 1975; King, 1975; Blatt and Wild, 1976; Diatkine, Lang, Lebovici, and Mises, 1977) find a common conceptual framework: no matter what determines the particular path toward the autistic syndrome or the schizophrenic syndrome—genetic predisposition, congenital factors, cognitive dysfunction, maternal deficiencies, or family pathology—the end point will be a pathologically distorted subjective world.

What is the subjective pathological world of the psychotic child like? Before attempting to describe it, I would first like to discuss three concepts formulated by Sandler and Rosenblatt (1962), Escalona (1968), and Isaacs (1948) bearing direct relevance to the formulation of the individual's subjective world.

According to Sandler and Rosenblatt (1962), the concept of the representational world, in addition to containing images and organizations of the internal and external environment, includes the body representation and the self-representation. A representation can be considered to have a more or less enduring existence as an organization or schema constructed out of a multitude of impressions. A child experiences many images of his mother throughout the course of his life, on the basis of which he creates a mother representation; in the same way, a body representation and a self-representation are built up gradually of body and self-images, which, by definition, are more temporary expressions of a particular body state or self-state.

The construction of the representational world is a product of ego functions, and the self- and object representations are part of the representational world. In talking about self- and object representations being replayed in external reality, I will be referring to object relations theory within the second of the definitions given above, namely, as a special approach within psychoanalytic metapsychology, one which stresses the building up of bipolar representations (self- and object) linked by a particular affect, these constituting the primary units determining the formation of superego and id (Kernberg, 1976). The following corollaries of object relations theory will be outlined: (a) The external object does not correspond exactly with its representation as an internalized object. Object representations and self-representations are a complicated mosaic, far more complicated than the perception of the external object. As Brierly (1944) described, "Even a 2-year-old child's memory of its mother will not be a simple system, but the result of 2 years of life with her. The conscious memory will then be accessible as part of the more extensive unconscious mother-child system and its affect, having its roots in early infancy." (b) Concomitant with each object representation is a self-representation linking the former to itself through a specific affect. (c) Both sides of this bipolar unit are reenacted in the internal world of the child—in dreams, in play, in the transference, and in behavior generally.

The representational world is a concept that can be related to Escalona's concept of pattern of concrete experience (1968). This is defined as the accumulation of sensations, body feelings, and affective states experienced by the infant, and the manner in which fluctuations in awareness are linked to perceptual input. During the first few months of life the particular juxtaposition of subjective states and their perceptual concomitants leads to the emergence of recognitions, anticipations, memories, and the like. I might add that in this beginning emergence of recognition and memories, the representational world of self- and object images linked by affect begins to be built.

Escalona has stated that the infant's experience comes to include the psychic processes that accompany and begin to guide behavior. To the degree to which this is the case, the young child's goals and fears, his established inclination and aversions, are all forms of ideation and later thought that become part and parcel of his experience. The world of internal object relations is therefore a model, an organizational frame, being built in an individualized way by the child. The model makes it possible for the various subjective inputs in instinctual development, the growth of ego and its various subsystems (cognitive structures, defense mechanisms, tolerance for anxiety, etc.), and the external world to meet on an intermediary common ground, which Sandler describes as the representational world, Escalona as pattern of concrete experience, and Isaacs as unconscious fantasy.

Indeed, in "The Nature and Function of Phantasy" Isaacs (1948) explains that the common expression and meeting ground of drives and ego development are in the realm of a product: the formation of unconscious fantasies which mediate the relation of the individual to the outside world, determining the perception of the outside world and accessible to modification by external reality. She assumes that even defense mechanisms can reflect unconscious fantasies and describes a subject, an object, an affect, and an action. Thus, in the case of repression, it is as if the subject were saying "I do not want to remember my attraction for my father because my positive feelings for him would not meet with the approval of my mother, who would feel angry for my stealing him away. Therefore, I have to 'forget' and put away my wish to have Daddy all to myself in order to keep my relationship with my Mommy." Or, in the case of displacement, projection, and denial in a phobic symptom, one might say that these mechanisms are an abbreviated way of saying, "I don't want to think about my destructive feelings toward my mother, so I will think they come from another source, which I will avoid—the teacher, the dangers of the street. In fact, I don't want to experience any such feelings because I may get punished, so, therefore, I will pretend I do not feel anything negative about my mother."

Representational world, pattern of concrete experience, unconscious fantasy—none of these can be assessed directly. An assessment can be made or a reconstruction formulated, first of all, through the phenomena of transference—the patient's relationship with the analyst, the patient's perception of the analytic situation, and the patient's perception of himself in the analytic situation. Secondly, the representational world can be glimpsed by paying utmost attention to details from the child's behavior. Third, some insight into this subject world can be gained through the contents of the child's fantasies as expressed verbally or through play.

In psychotic children the level of pathology is such that the representational world is fragmented; there is no integration of self- or whole object representations, but only of part objects, that is, components or fragments of the representational world. As defined by Anna Freud, a part object is usually related to the infantile dependence of the child, who sees the mother in terms of her need-satisfying role. In psychosis, however, the part object implies a further breakdown of part object images and concomitant partial self-images, as well as a crucial qualitative difference in the accompanying affects (intensity, modulation). This representational world has a typical instability—it invades and permeates the external reality, sometimes to an overwhelming degree.

Application of the Concept of Representational World to Autism and Childhood Schizophrenia

The representational world of psychotic children may be seen in the qualitative experience of these children as described by Mahler (1968), Tustin (1972), and Winnicott (1958). Despite the fact that psychotic children lack an integrated superego, age-appropriate ego development, and advanced defense mechanisms such as repression, reaction-formation, undoing, and isolation, to view them as lacking psychic structure is in my opinion misconceived. These deficits do not mean that these children lack psychic structure; rather, my hypothesis, as illustrated by the authors mentioned above, is that they use primitive defense mechanisms to deal with extremely primitive conflicts and that they have established object relations which, though they exist in an uncanny mixture of self- and object images, can become intelligible upon close scrutiny.

Typical Anxieties

The anxieties of psychotic patients are of a different nature from those of neurotics. They are not intersystemic conflicts that have to do with fear of the superego on the part of the ego, for example, or with conflicts between ego and id, but rather are intrasystemic conflicts involving various contradictory, dissociated self- and object representations of the most fragmentary and primitive nature.

One of the first anxieties, described by Winnicott as early as 1958, is the one related to *falling infinitely*. That this is a primitive anxiety is illustrated by the fact that falling or fear of falling releases an inborn behavior mechanism already available to the prelocomotor infant. In experiments involving the visual cliff (Walk and Gibson, 1961), in which an infant is placed on a flat, checkered surface creating the optical illusion of going down another level, the infant stops short right at the edge. The fears of vacuum, darkness, solitude, and silence are fears related to the fear of falling.

That this anxiety has physical and psychological determinants is evident in the fact that the holding function of the mother's arms and the supportive holding function of her primary maternal preoccupation with the infant are important factors allaying this anxiety (Winnicott, 1958). The persistent presence of this anxiety may indicate that these protective factors are missing—because of environmental factors related to deficiencies in the nurturing figures, because of impediments in the child which do not allow him to use available maternal care to fulfill his needs for support, or, as is most frequently the case, because of an interweaving of these factors.

In our observations of children 6 to 12 years old in an inpatient ward at Bronx Municipal Hospital Center, Albert Einstein College of Medicine, a high incidence of suicide attempts was seen. Frequently, these were attempts to jump out of a window on a high floor. To some extent this may represent the actualization of the child's hopelessness, the feeling that he is indeed falling out of maternal supports and into the arms of a black void—the absent mother.

Mahler (1976) describes the *fear of loss of body boundaries*—in a most real sense the body of the schizophrenic and autistic child felt to be both a body self and a psychological self concretely dispersed and fragmented in the environment. Rank and McNaughton (1950), as quoted by Tustin (1972), describe an "atypical child, who, after a tantrum-like explosion of panic and rage, sobbed as she laid in her therapist's arms and shouted 'A piece fell out! A piece fell out!' " (p. 31). As Tustin describes it, the experience is that of a break in bodily continuity, as if the child had a hole in his body.

In this context, anxiety over lack of support has to do not only with the absence of the good supportive mother, a lack which at this level of regression is felt concretely, as the lack of the nipple or of good body feelings of comfort, smoothness, softness, and harmonious sounds, all of which are experienced as intrinsic parts of the child's organism; the anxiety also involves the presence of a bad object. The mother is experienced as a nasty, hard, discomforting, rough physical presence, out of control and doing unexpected and scary things. Panic and rage accompany this particular anxiety—affects that are experienced as bodily explosions. Because of the lack of differentiation between self and object, the bad object is simultaneously felt as a threat of annihilation of the self.

The anxieties described above are those for which secondary autism (Mahler, 1968), a withdrawal to forestall rage and terror about falling apart and losing boundaries, is a solution.

Another variation of the fear of losing body boundaries or of dispersion of the self is the fantasy that the body self and fragmented self-images are made of fluid, that one may, for example, lose one's boundaries by emptying one's self through a body orifice or scratch in the skin, which may be perceived by the child as an orifice. For instance, a 7-year-old autistic child became quite concerned when a hernia operation was secondarily complicated by chronic infection due to an allergic reaction to the material used in suturing. Because his body boundaries were so unstable, he felt terrorized that the "holes" in his skin, draining pus, would drain all of him, as if he were made of fluid. This led to feelings of depersonalization and a secondary anxiety that he was losing himself in his mother, his siblings, and others; in addition, the inanimate world was permeated with his self-representations, forming what Bion (1967) has called bizarre objects.

Impending damage to the whole body, through generalization or spread of oral traumas experienced during early infancy in the perioral cavity, is illustrated by another vignette. An autistic child, exhibiting a combination of abnormal primary autism and encapsulated secondary autism as defined by Tustin, went to the dentist. In reenacting this experience in subsequent play with a therapist, he reproduced not only the usual turning of passive into active that one sees in the better-integrated child, but his subjective experience of the entire event. He had the therapist, playing dental patient, sit on a pillow that was supposed to be hot and prickly; the child, playing denist, poked around in her mouth with some sticks that simulated dental instruments. Thus, the child arranged the examination so that the therapist would feel pain not only in her mouth but around the buttocks. At the same time, excited with sadistic pleasure, he pretended to poke holes all over her skin. In acting out his experience, he showed how the examination of his mouth permeated his entire body and became both traumatic and exciting in a chaotic blending of oral and anal pain, oral and anal excitement.

To continue with the enumeration of anxieties in psychotic children, *castration anxiety* is not localized in the genitals as it is in neurotic children but is instead expressed as anxiety related to explosive body disintegration or multiple mutilation.

Because the psychotic child's concept of body is so primitive, there is the fantasy of a primal cavity which is felt to be an empty sack (Furer, 1969). This gives rise to the fear that feces and food will mix together. Whatever the libidinal quality of feces or food, because of the fear that good part-objects will be contaminated by bad ones, many psychotic children have extreme conflicts over processes of intake and output, conflicts manifested in bowel disturbances, peculiar eating habits, anorexia, and vomiting.

A particular oral anxiety in psychotic children has been noted by Tustin (1972) as an aspect of the Isakower phenomenon. In 1938 Isakower described the essence of the sensory quality of the phenomenon as something dry, soft, and gritty or wrinkled seeming to fill the mouth and feeling close to the skin surface of the body, to be manipulated with the fingers. There is sometimes also a visual sensation of a shadowing mask, indefinite and mostly round, approaching and growing enormous and then shrinking to practically nothing. Isakower associated this phenomenon with predormescent states and linked it with reminiscences of the infant's falling asleep at the breast. Both Benjamin (1963) and Stern (1961), Tustin (1972) notes, related this phenomenon to situations of oral deprivation. They observed that these experiences of gritty feelings attributed to eyes and skin are associated with traumatic experiences during early infancy and with the fear of falling infinitely, and that they represent the primitive reaction to the lack of the nurturing mother.

Tustin describes a young patient who commented, upon leaving the last therapy session before her planned vacation, that he felt horrible and that his body hurt: "I got grit all over me and I got grit in my mouth." This bodily feeling of grit or gravel, which is related to other sensations described as "prickles," tiny broken-up bits of "crunchy stuff" and bits of broken glass, suggests that brief separations from the mother are experienced literally as broken things put into one's body and may explain some of the self-cutting behavior seen in late-onset childhood schizophrenia.

A symbiotic psychotic child who was reenacting with his therapist his anxieties about separation from his mother began to enter the practicing subphase of separation-individuation. During this phase there is an unstable sense of self and a lack of object constancy. In one session, as the child asked the therapist to leave the room, he literally put plastic sticks around the therapist's leg and arms "to make her suffer" for leaving him. In so doing, he concretely conveyed to the therapist what it was like for him to go through the process of beginning bodily and psychological individuation from his mother, a psychotic, apprehensive woman.

The Concept of the Self in the Psychotic Child

Instead of appropriate ego boundaries, which carry with them the feeling that one is held together by a psychological skin formed as the normal infant internalizes sufficiently soothing and sheltering experiences with the mother, the psychotic child develops a "second skin" (Bick, 1968). In this second-skin phenomenon, the skin either becomes muscular, with rigidity and stereotyped behavior, or it becomes part of the clothing the child wears and does not want to part from. In discussing this phenomenon Tustin (1972, pp. 48, 49) describes the case of David, who is bound by an outside armor. She quotes Mahler (1961): "once the autistic armor has been pierced, the children become particularly vulnerable to emotional frustration, helplessness, and despair" (p. 51).

For the psychotic child, the self is also felt to be an embryonic self, held back in its development because of a lack of the necessary satisfying experiences of encircling the nipple in the mouth, of being encircled in the mother's arms, or, at a higher level, of being held within the ambiance of mother's caring attention—experiences that are vital for beginning integration. Instead, the experience of self is peculiar and relatively unshareable using normal modes of communication. The experienced lack of good mothering is an insufferable nightmare.

The autistic solution produces a child who looks comfortable for much of the time, as autism produces a sense of pseudo self-sufficiency by the formation of autistic objects (Tustin) which are parts of the child's own body or parts of the outside world experienced by the child as if they were his body. A clear example of being held together in a second psychological skin is presented by a 5-year-old psychotic child who frantically put pieces of sticks into a cardboard cylinder together with globs of glue—"milky stuff"—and worked eagerly for more than half an hour to pick up all of the sticks available in the room, gluing them all together. The fragments contained in the milky glue and in the cardboard box reflected his fragmented experiences of himself and his wish to be contained by the therapist, to be put back together permanently.

Sometimes, because splitting mechanisms are used, various self-representations coexist simultaneously; for example, an autistic child used several registers of voice in order to communicate with me. He had a shrieky, high-pitched voice which seemed an imitation of his mother and sister, a "monster" voice which was low-pitched and throaty, a regular voice, and several which were imitations of various real and fictional characters. When these voices were pointed out to him, he recognized only one of them as himself, the one that seemed most appropriate for his age.

The Role of the Tongue

According to Winnicott (1958), the mother's nipple and the baby's tongue work together to produce in the infant the illusion of continuity and to confirm it, thus avoiding a primitive sense of separateness. If for any reason there is a break in this bodily continuity, it is experienced as a loss of part of the body and precipitates the need for an armor or second skin or, at yet another level, a pseudoself.

In discussing this topic in her work, Tustin (1972) quotes Bonnard (1960), who characterized the tongue as our first major "scanner." The feeling of the tongue in the mouth brings the child his first experience of space. Initially, the tongue would be the infant's whole experience of being and would not be experienced as part of the body. It seems that early oral trauma may be associated with the feeling of the tongue's suddenly being in space without the lulling continuation of the mother's body afforded by the nipple. The awareness of separateness is inseparable from awareness of space and brings with it awareness of outside and inside. It seems feasible that "inside the mouth" is the primary experience of "inside the body."

Austistic children who have blotted out awareness of separateness and of inside and outside have little or no inner life, which accounts for the impression they give of emptiness and vacancy. According to Tustin, the child's autistic self is a primitively omnipotent one in which he has the illusion of permeating the environment with his fluid body self. In that way he controls the mother in fantasy or involves her beneath the crust of the autistic barrier.

Object Representations

External objects are felt to be invaded by the autistic child's production, whether of feces, gases, hot air, or words. The objects are empty receptacles waiting to be filled up by him; they are brought into existence by him and for him. Anything not bounded by him in this way is experienced as "not me" and dangerous.

The autistic child's object representations are not only fragmented but coated by projections of his own fluid self in rather bizarre combinations. Because these projections into the outside world include external inanimate objects with self-images, only with an object relations perspective can one begin to decipher the particular relationships of the child to his world of objects.

The aspects of self that are projected can be described at this level as eruptions from the body, on the model of such reflex bodily activities (Tustin, 1972) as spitting, defecation, vomiting, coughing, or sneezing, activities which take a piece of the subject with them. States of rage are also expelled onto the environment, turning it into a threatening and monstrous world. The not-me experience is abrupt and traumatic. Bodily separateness is like a feeling of containing poisonous substances and having gritty sensations all over one's body.

A schizophrenic 5-year-old child of superior intelligence had the urge to pour paints, glue, and water on the floor, and on both the mother and the therapist; at times he rubbed the glue on his own skin and on the therapist's, and put it into his mouth, as if to take in a sense of togetherness. In order to deal with an abrupt and traumatic separateness, the child produces the autistic object.

The normal transitional object is distinguished by the child as separate from its body, partly representing the mother; this is not the case with the austistic object. The function of the latter is to obviate completely any awareness of the not-me, which is felt to be unbearably threatening. By contrast, in the normal child's use of a transitional object, the not-me is not completely shut out, although awareness of it may be diminished.

Mahler (1968) describes the use of these autistic objects or psychotic fetishes as precursors of the normal transitional object, which involves a higher level of differentiation and presupposes a positive relationship with the mother figure, to be preserved in a realm intermediate to the me and the not-me. By contrast, the autistic object is felt to be filling the gap in mothering in a specific and bizarre way; that is, it is filling up a vacuum or discontinuity (hole) in the body self.

Various combinations of object-images occur. Bion (1967) has described the projection of multiple fragments of object-images which condense with aspects of the self and get dispersed in the external reality, as if the patient would feel more protected with the expulsion of multiple fragments of rejected and feared self- and object-images. Sometimes the part objects of psychotic patients belong to the class of what Bion describes as bizarre objects, in which combinations of self-images and distorted object-images are expelled violently, coating external objects, as it were, while acquiring a life of their own.

Animate and inanimate objects may become condensed and reenacted, as in the case of a chronically self-mutilating girl who vividly described her subjective experience of the presence of her mother as glass cutting into her skin. This, according to Tustin's views, corresponds to experiences of early deprivation and separateness.

The evacuation and loss of the representational world through the sense organs, body orifices, or cuts in the skin may explain both hallucinatory experiences and panic reactions to minor abrasions.

Early autism is characterized by global, undifferentiated, and omnipotent object representations or broken object representations. In childhood schizophrenia, by contrast, object representations are more frequently fragmented and bizarre.

Oedipal Configurations and Part-Objects

Tustin describes the case of a recovering autistic child who had reached the stage of being able to dream; he described seeing a bowl of creamy milk in which there suddenly appeared a tuft of male pubic hair, at the sight of which he felt sick and terrified. This is an illustration of the primitive and bizarre forms taken by oedipal constellations in the rudimentary object relations of these children.

According to Tustin, psychotic children dramatically react to the uprooting from the primal illusion of oneness with the mother. Because of a lack of self-object differentiation, certain aspects of the mouth are felt to disappear, from the infant's point of view, along with the mother and the breast. This loss of continuity with the mother, through the nipple, is felt as a black hole in the mouth. Behaviors such as mutism may be understood as efforts to have a closed mouth and so avoid the black hole; putting all the fingers in the mouth may be seen as an attempt to bridge the gap. Displacement of this black hole onto other parts of the body, such as the anus, the vagina, or the eyes (whereby occurs the dread of looking at the black holes of other people's eyes), can occur. Children use saliva in the mouth as well as urine and feces, which can be smeared, in efforts to fill up these holes.

A 7½-year-old psychotic child drew a ship with a black hole whose blackness eventually covered the entire ship and swallowed up the little boy, who was playing the captain. Initially, the boy had put his finger in this hole, but it soon was not enough, and the blackness invaded the whole ship, killing his crew. The hole, as Tustin (1972) has described it, the sense of hole, is a disaster that separates him from the mother and affects both simultaneously because of the characteristic state of undifferentiation between self and object.

Fantasies of the Self and the Object World

During treatment many psychotic children begin to hallucinate, to have positive hallucinations as precursors of remembering and negative hallucinations as precursors of ignoring and forgetting, and, in the case of one child at least, to have fears of his own shadow, as if it were an explosively projective, enormous defecation threatening and burdening him—a kind of "dirty nappy" he cannot rid himself of. All of these developments indicate that the child is engaged in a process of resolution, in the context of the therapy, whereby primitive fantasies are gradually replaced by such ego functions as imagining, remembering, and thinking.

Affects

The typical affects of psychotic children are global, intense, and unmodulated, characterized by panic states and rage attacks. This description of affects brings us to problems of a secondary nature built into the mother-child relationship, namely, the fact that the child's anxieties are so intense that the mother is called literally to rescue the child from psychological death.

Defenses

In the psychotic child's representational world, specific defenses are used which do not form part of the general spectrum of defenses of higher-level pathology. First, in the defense of deanimation described by Mahler, the world of persons is experienced as inanimate, as a protection from dangerous projections.

Tustin (1972) discusses how animism and autism seem to be opposite modes of operation of the primitive mind. Animism consists of endowing objects with life. Pathological autism is a death-dealing process which blocks out things to make them nonexistent; it also reduces living beings to the state of inanimate things. Distinguishing between living and nonliving objects would seem to be a critical state in the development of the child. In pathological autism this distinction either has not been made with any clarity or has been blotted out secondarily. Thus, the function of the mother as an animating agent in the environment is made either nonexistent or is deactivated by the child due to intrinsic limitations. Whatever the cause, the outcome is the deanimation of the environment as a primitive defense maneuver.

The child uses the smashing of objects or the shedding of clothes as a way of destroying the painful, anxious, and fragmented parts of himself. Falling and biting himself may be interpreted in the same manner.

In a second primitive defense, bad objects are blotted out, while the sense of the body is enhanced by the regular kinesthetic stimulation.

Through other behavior—for example, sucking on the tongue or on the soft pads of the cheek, or listening to the beating of one's own heart—the child attempts to preserve sameness and give some security to the extremely unstable, explosive quality of the representational world by making external reality correspond to the reality of his own body.

In order to relieve anxiety, the body is used as an autistic object; therefore, primary objects remain parts of the body. The hands moving in stereotypical fashion through space can be comforting, as if the separateness of the fingers were a way of dealing with the dread of separateness in general.

Two Vignettes

An autistic child insisted on being kissed if he sustained even the most minute injury to his skin and expected his mother to snap up his pants after he urinated, refusing to touch them himself. After laborious work, his anxieties about being emptied through whatever minute hole existed were relieved by seeking the omnipotent mother to protect him from this fluid evacuation of himself and from his fear by that by snapping his pants he would also snap his skin, as he had not differentiated his clothing from his skin. The mother had contributed to preserving both these behaviors, as she could not understand the underlying anxieties. Because the child's IQ was normal, it was possible for the therapist to verbalize these fantasies and explain them to him, to his great relief.

Another autistic child had been playing on his own, lying on the floor, looking at the monsterlike rubber figures he had laid on the floor against each other, biting each other, swallowing each other. This play became interactional after a few sessions, indirectly through the rubber monsters. The patient dared to pretend to bite, chew, and swallow pieces of the therapist's nose, arms, body, and breasts. As he was "eating" the therapist up and enjoying it, what was a dead therapist became a good thing to eat up, becoming now a part of himself, equally alive.

Conclusion

The psychoanalytic understanding of childhood involves psychosis from an object relations point of view and provides a theoretical framework for psychoanalytic psychotherapy of psychosis. The treatment of these children implies the tasks of deciphering the components of self and object, as they are fragmented, bizarre, projected, or introjected in the most unexpected combinations, and of exploring primitive fantasies to render them accessible to interpersonal sharing and secondary processes.

References

Benjamin, J.D. (1963), Further comments on some developmental aspects of anxiety. In: *Counterpoint,* ed. H.S. Gaskill. New York: International Universities Press.

Bick, E. (1968), The experience of the skin in early object relations. *Internat. J. Psycho-Anal.,* 49:484–486.

Bion, W.R. (1967), *Second Thoughts: Selected Papers on Psycho-Analysis.* London: Heinemann.

Blatt, S.J., & Wild, C.M. (1976), *Schizophrenia: A Developmental Analysis.* New York: Academic Press.

Bonnard, A. (1960), The primal significance of the tongue. *Internat. J. Psycho-Anal.,* 41.

Bosch, G. (1970), *Infantile Autism.* New York: Springer Verlag.

Bower, G.R. (1965), Stimulus variables determining space perception in infants. *Science,* 149:88–89.

Brierly, M. (1944), Notes on metapsychology as process theory. *Internat. J. Psycho-Anal.,* 25:103–104.

Campos, J.J., Langer, A., & Karowitz, A. (1970), Cardiac responses on the visual cliff in prelocomotor human infants. *Science,* 154:196–197.

Clancy, H., & McBridge, G. (1969), The autistic process and its treatment. *J. Child Psychol.,* 10:233–244.

DeMyer, M.K. (1977), Research in infantile autism: A strategy and its results. In: *Annual Progress in Child Psychiatry and Child Development,* ed. S. Chess & A. Thomas. New York: Brunner/Mazel, pp. 393–415.

Despert, J.L. (1968), *Schizophrenia in Children.* New York: Brunner/Mazel.

Diatkine, R., Lang, J.L., Lebovici, S., & Mises, R. (1977), Therapeutic experiences with psychotic children. In: *Long Term Treatments of Psychotic States,* ed. C. Chiland & P. Beguert. New York: Human Sciences Press, pp. 250–265.

Ekstein, R. (1971), *The Challenge: Despair and Hope in the Conquest of Inner Space.* New York: Brunner/Mazel.

——— Bryant, K., & Seymour, F.W. (1958), Childhood schizophrenia and allied conditions. In: *Schizophrenia: A Review of the Syndrome,* ed. L. Bellak. New York: Grune & Stratton, pp. 555–693.

Erikson, E.H. (1959), Identity and the life cycle. *Psychological Issues* Monograph 1. New York: International Universities Press.

Escalona, S. (1968), *The Roots of Individuality.* Chicago: Aldine.

Freeman, T. (1975), *Childhood Psychology and Adult Psychosis.* New York: International Universities Press.

Furer, M. (1969), The Development of a pre-school symbiotic psychotic box. *The Psychoanalytic Study of the Child,* 19:448–469. New York: International Universities Press.

Garmezy, N. (1974a), Children at risk: The search for the antecedents of schizophrenia. Part I. Conceptual models and research models. *Schizophrenia Bull.,* 8:14–90. Bethesda, Md.: NIMH.

——— (1974b), Children at risk: The search for the antecedents of schizophrenia. Part II. Conceptual models and research methods. *Schizophrenia Bull.,* 9:55–125. Bethesda, Md.: NIMH.

Gunderson, J., & Feinsilver, D. (1972), Psychotherapy for schizophrenics: Is it indicated? A review of the relevant literature. *Schizophrenia Bull.,* 6:11–23. Bethesda, Md.: NIMH.

Isaacs, S. (1948), The nature and function of phantasy. *Internat. J. Psycho-Anal.*, 29:73–97.

Kernberg, O. (1976), *Object Relations Theory and Clinical Psychoanalysis*. New York: Aronson.

King, K.P. (1975), Early infantile autism relative to schizophrenia. *J. Amer. Acad. Child Psychiat.*, 14:666–682.

Laufer, M., & Gair, D.S. (1969), Childhood schizophrenia. In: *The Schizophrenic Syndrome*, ed. L. Bellak & L. Loeb. New York: Grune & Stratton, pp. 378–461.

Mahler, M. (1961), On sadness and grief in infancy and childhood: Loss and restoration of the symbiotic love object. *The Psychoanalytic Study of the Child*, 16: 332–351. New York: International Universities Press.

——— (1968), *On Human Symbiosis and the Vicissitudes of Individuation*. New York: International Universities Press.

——— (1976), Longitudinal study of the treatment of a psychotic child with the tripartite design. *J. Phila. Assn. Psychoanal.*, 3:21–46.

Mednick, S., Schulsinger, F., Higgins, J., & Bell, B., eds. (1974), Studies of children at high risk for schizophrenia. In: *Genetics, Environment and Psychopathology*. New York: North Holland Publishing, pp. 103–116.

Meltzer, D., Bermer, J., Hoxter, S., Weddell, D., & Wittenberg, I., eds. (1974), *Explorations in Autism*. Perthshire: Clunie Press.

Miller, R.T. (1975), Childhood schizophrenia: A review of selected literature. In: *Annual Progress in Child Psychiatry and Child Development*, ed. S. Chess & A. Thomas. New York: Brunner/Mazel, pp. 357–401.

O'Gorman, G. (1970), *The Nature of Autism*. New York: Appleton-Century-Crofts.

Rank, B., & McNaughton, D. (1950), A clinical contribution to early ego development. *The Psychoanalytic Study of the Child*, 5:53–65. New York: International Universities Press.

Ritvo, E.R., ed. (1976), *Autism: Diagnosis, Current Research and Management*. New York: Spectrum Publications.

Rutter, M. (1975), The Development of infantile autism. In: *Annual Progress in Child Psychiatry and Child Development*, ed. S. Chess & A. Thomas. New York: Brunner/Mazel, pp. 327–356.

Sandler J., & Nagera, H. (1963), Aspects of the metapsychology of fantasy. *The Psychoanalytic Study of the Child*, 18:159–194. New York: International Universities Press.

——— & Rosenblatt, B. (1962), The concept of the representational world. *The Psychoanalytic Study of the Child*, 17:128–145. New York: International Universities Press.

Schulz, C.G. (1975), An individualized psychotherapeutic approach with the schizophrenic patient. *Schizophrenia Bull.*, 13:46–69. Bethesda, Md.: NIMH.

Stern, M.M. (1961), Blank hallucinations: Remarks about trauma and perpetual disturbances. *Internat. J. Psycho-Anal.*, 42.

Tustin, F. (1972), *Autism and Childhood Psychosis*. New York: Science House.

Walk, R.D., & Gibson, E.J. (1961), A comparative and analytic study of visual depth perception. *Psychological Monographs,* 15:1–49.

Wenar, C., Ruthenberg, B., Dratman, M., & Wolf, F. (1967), Changing autistic behavior. *Arch. Gen. Psychiat.,* 17:26–35.

Winnicott, D.W. (1958), Metapsychological and clinical aspects of regression within the psychoanalytic set-up. In: *Collected Papers: Through Paediatrics to Psycho-Analysis.* New York: Basic Books, pp. 278–294.

8

Clinical and Theoretical Aspects of Two Developmental Lines

CLIFFORD YORKE, FRC PSYCH, DPM,
HANSI KENNEDY, DIP PSYCH
STANLEY WISEBERG, FRC PSYCH, DPM

At first sight some of the developmental lines delineated by Anna Freud (1963) are misleadingly descriptive. Take, for example, the line which leads from egocentricity to companionship. The steps on this line are easily enumerated. To begin with, the child is wholly self-centered; other children have no importance for him or, if they are at all significant, are experienced as interlopers who interfere with his relationship with his mother or as rivals for her attention. The second step on the line is taken when the child begins to look on other children as useful for the needs of the moment, exclusively for immediate satisfaction, to be discarded as soon as the need has passed. There is as yet no sense of cooperation, as this would require the recognition that the playmate has wishes of his own. Such a recognition is achieved in the next stage, when a helpmate is wanted to take part in a joint effort, whether constructive or destructive, helpful or mischievous. Finally, other children are seen as objects in their own right, as friends with whom the child can identify, to be loved or hated, feared or admired, with whom he engages on a more or less equal basis and with whom he can share—in short, a true companion.

Progress along this developmental line is such that every step, in terms of outward manifestations, is readily identifiable. Yet what is seen is in fact the outcome of the interaction of the various developing internal agencies, both with each other and with the external world. Furthermore, these mutations are collectively subject to the synthetic function of the ego, with results for better or for worse. In the line which leads from egocentricity to companionship, every step described is an indication of developmental progression. The drives are increasingly curbed as the id becomes subject to the checks and controls of the ego; ego functions of exploration and construction are put at the service of the furtherance of the line; and the emotional needs for partnership are met by the provision of appropriate opportunities.

While lines of this kind are helpful in assessing normal personality development, there are others which are particularly important in deciding whether the prerequisites for treatment exist. For example, object relationships should have progressed beyond the stage of object constancy if a treatment relationship is to be established. Some degree of affective awareness and some capacity for self-observation likewise are prerequisites, while a potential capacity to restrict and contain anxiety is also a necessary condition for interpretive treatment. Even quite young children may respond affirmatively to an offer of help with their worries, although the child's understanding of the internal nature of the disturbance generally comes about through treatment rather than preceding it.

Unlike the line which leads from egocentricity to companionship, or the line from play to work, or, yet again, the line which leads from irresponsibility to responsibility in body management (A. Freud, 1963), there are others which are by no means so readily demonstrable in terms of overt behavior. The line which leads from the experience of primitive and vegetative excitation to the capacity to restrict anxiety to signal level (Yorke and Wiseberg, 1976) and the line which leads from early infantile awareness to a wish for self-understanding (Kennedy, 1979) are less readily discernible from the standpoint of the everyday observer. Recently, our attention has been extended to lines of this kind, since they are not only of considerable scientific interest but are also of special importance to the practicing psychoanalyst or psychotherapist. We begin with a brief account of the developmental line of anxiety and continue with a short survey of the line which leads from primitive self-awareness to the capacity for insight in the adult.

The Developmental Line of Anxiety

We regard the human infant, at the beginning of life, as utterly helpless and completely dependent on his mother for the assuagement of his needs. He repeatedly undergoes periods of apparent distress, alleviated when he is cuddled or fed. Sleep usually supervenes, and he remains in a calm and peaceful state until discomfort awakens him and distress begins to mount.

While we cannot with certainty know much about the psychic life of the infant, we assume that it is built up very slowly from only the humblest of beginnings. Whatever the nature of the infantile sensorium, we see little evidence in the first weeks of anything beyond states of excitation of a crudely unpleasurable kind, followed by evident relief and satisfaction. It seems reasonable to refer to what is seen in these early states as organismic or vegetative excitation and its discharge, rather than true affect.

During the first year, big strides have been taken when, around the age of 3 months, the infant smiles on seeing its mother's face, whatever fragmentary precursors of this the mother may have observed. Equally impressive is the elaboration of this "smiling response" in the ready interchange of smiles between child and object. By this time, too, the infant has developed wider and more varied ways of indicating distress. These responses are not dependent on the stimuli aroused by a particular person, such as the mother or father, and are therefore unselective. But, at a later stage—between 7 and 9 months of age, as a rule—a much more specific response can be observed. The child, approached by a stranger, no longer responds with pleasure. On the contrary, he shows clear evidence of perplexity or anxiety. He may cry and bury his face in his mother. This response, termed by Spitz (1965) "stranger-anxiety," is the first unequivocal sign of mentalized anxiety, however much this may have been taken along a developmental line leading from vegetative excitation to a true affect of anxiety.

Let us turn from these first steps along the line of anxiety to the end point. Writing with the adult in mind, Freud conceptualized anxiety in terms of a signal, seated in the ego, which gave warning to the latter that it faced an imminent threat of overwhelming panic and a concomitant reduction to helplessness. This concept will be clear if we approach it by way of example. A housewife mentioned to her doctor that she always cut up the baby's food with a spoon, and she was puzzled by her reluctance to use a knife. Early impulses to cut and damage, appropriate enough at a certain stage of development in a young child, had long since vanished from this woman's consciousness. However, a remnant (a fixation) endured, and was in danger of rearousal by a new experience in her life when she found herself responsible for the protection of a small and vulnerable infant. Although the repression barrier had effectively kept the unwanted impulse at bay over the years, her awareness of all the dangers confronting the child remobilized the fantasy, determined by her fixation, that the child could be harmed by a sharp instrument. Only this remote derivative of her unconscious impulse had approached awareness, and it had aroused a highly restricted measure of anxiety in the face of her loving and nurturing motherhood. Recognition of such an impulse would have been deeply repugnant and would have led to helpless panic. But, in fact, only a fractional measure of anxiety had been experienced and had served to call on defensive maneuvers. By avoiding the use of a knife, the danger of recognizing the impulse had been effectively reduced. Repression was reinforced in response to the signal. The fear of a slip with the knife could now remain isolated from a mutilating or murderous wish; the derivative remained a derivative, and a displacement (the food) remained an effective displacement.

This illustrates the effective use of the signal function of anxiety. There is no danger of escalation to panic. Its operation has, notwithstanding, resulted in a symptom, however minor. Simple puzzlement at the need to use a spoon is the only conscious psychic consequence. If, hypothetically, the signal had resulted in immediate repression of the derivative, the psychic operation would have remained silent and would have left no conscious trace of its existence. Indeed, in the normal adult we assume that silent operations of this kind constantly and repeatedly occur and recur in the maintenance of the mental economy in the service of efficient adaptation. By the same token, it is easy to envisage the supervention of more severe pathology in response to the anxiety signal where simpler measures are either ineffective or cannot be maintained in the face of further pressures.

We can see, therefore, that the developmental line of anxiety leads from the vegetative excitations of the first weeks of life, through the mentalized and pervasive anxiety clearly demonstrable in the presence of strangers at around 8 months, through further refinements until an end point is reached at which, ideally, anxiety can readily function at signal level. The process by which progress can be made along this line does not simply involve the increasing mentalization of anxiety. It involves, concomitantly, the capacity to restrict and contain that unique affect.

During the first period of life, covering roughly the first year, the child's needs and wishes arise and are met within the context of a functional mother-baby unit. It is axiomatic that if, in a major particular, this unit is defective—as in the case of a depressed and unresponsive mother—then normal development cannot occur, and foundations are laid for pathology. No matter how active the child may become within this context, the serious environmental failure means that, in common with other lines, the developmental line of anxiety will be deviant or arrested. The crude pain-pleasure series is interfered with, and refinement by mentalization is less likely to occur. Similarly, a repeated change of partner in the dyad may, in the later months, mean that there is insufficient consistency of handling to lay a basis for predictability and some degree of safety. Or again, physical illness involving, for example, gastrointestinal disturbances or operations may, by interfering with the normal pleasure-pain series from the standpoint of the body, interfere with the normally expectable shifts from body to mind and therefore with the mentalization of the anxiety response. But while, in different children, the outcome of these early interferences will vary, it is safe to say that the future course of the developmental line will be delayed, deviant, erratic, or otherwise gravely imperiled.

Indeed, it may be helpful to refer to the case of a child in which a pathological interference with the line had clearly occurred. Norma was a psychotic child of 9 who, in spite of her chronological age, had not yet entered the third period of life when she was taken into intensive treatment by a colleague. She was repeatedly subject to severe and pervasive anxiety which was almost uncontrollable. This anxiety led to a good deal of overactivity and aggressive attacks on objects, both animate and inanimate. It was clear that Norma had failed to reach certain achievements normally to be expected in the second period of development. She had failed to develop a capacity to use speech adequately in the service of secondary process thinking; and her reality testing was tenuous and defective.

Evidence suggested that there were defects in the operation of the mother-child dyad. Although subsequently she had made relationships with housemothers and others, she had been subject to repeated episodes of separation and loss. In this connection, an episode in her treatment was particularly instructive. On a journey to her treatment session, her vehicle missed a turn on a roundabout (traffic circle) and had to go around a second time. Norma became terrified that it would go around and around and never stop, that she would never see her therapist again. Her safe arrival at the clinic brought only limited relief, and for months afterward the trauma of the situation brought repeated panics. At this time of her life, much of Norma's fear became attached to particular words—her "worry words." Following the roundabout experience the word *round* and, indeed, any round object became the focus and apparent source of panic. On one occasion she picked up a round ashtray and shattered it on the floor without warning because, she said, she was "afraid of the roundabout." On another occasion she tried to damage the word *roundabout* by shouting it, and she also wanted to put cotton wool in her ears so that she would not hear the word. She confused the contents of her body with the contents of her mind. She felt she was full of bad urine which would leak out of her, and she tried to tip out bad thoughts by standing on her head.

It may be assumed that if Norma's distinction between the actual word and what the word represented had been clearer, she would have been able to express directly her fear of loss of her therapist and that she would have been able, in time, to increase her mastery over such fears. Effective thinking (secondary process) would have enabled her better to comprehend the nature of different threats both from within and without. Similarly, the process of thinking would have been able to serve one of its essential functions—the delay of instinctual discharge. Thought could have been used in a more mature way as "trial action," and this in turn would have permitted the sampling of the affect of anxiety and the institution of defensive measures against the danger situation.

We have previously remarked on the interdependence of the anxiety line and the body-mind line. Norma's confusion between what pertained to body and what to mind clearly impaired her capacity to learn adaptive ways of coping with her "bad thoughts" and her anxiety.

This fascinating and complex case illustrates the crucial importance of secondary process thinking and the associated capacity for delay ("trial action") and anticipation, for the developmental line of anxiety to proceed normally during the second period of life. This period comes to an end with the resolution of the oedipus complex and the firm establishment of a structured superego. Superego anxiety, or guilt, is now experienced and implies a further differentiation of affect.

The third period of life comprises latency, and at the beginning of this period signal anxiety should be reasonably well established. But the child still needs the support of parents and teachers to maintain reasonable containment of anxiety. In any case, it is important to bear in mind that, as in any other developmental line, advances are uneven, and reversions take place from time to time. These will still occur even in the adult.

A boy of 10 years who was in analysis showed an apparently excellent control of anxiety. He had achieved a signal level of functioning. However, this did not prevent anxiety symptoms (which, nevertheless, did not approach panic). His previously excellent learning ability was interfered with by the intrusion of distracting sexual fantasies involving monsters which, in analysis, appeared to derive from the primal scene. Defense mechanisms, to wit, displacement, were deployed, in part successfully, under the influence of the anxiety signal. At the end of one of his sessions, his father, who was always there to collect him, was missing, and a panic attack ensued. It emerged that, the day before, his father had been involved in a motor accident which had resurrected a fear that the father would be killed. The fear of monsters indicates in the first place a relative instability of signal function, which the later episode illustrates a temporary reversion to pervasive anxiety under the pressure of oedipal death wishes.

In our view it is useful to consider adolescence as a fourth and adulthood a fifth period in the extension and consolidation of developmental lines; we proceed on this basis. The relative peace of latency becomes disturbed with the biological maturation of puberty and the psychological changes of adolesence. A mental economy which, with the help of auxiliary egos, formerly dealt adequately enough with the pressures of latency can no longer cope with the intensified urgencies of the drives, without far-reaching changes. Furthermore, during the fourth period of growth encompassed by adolescence, old dangers reemerge with fresh force. If, therefore, anxiety is to remain operative at signal level, there must be a restructuring of defensive measures and coping mechanisms. The increase in the instinctual cathexes, both sexual and aggressive, involves a remobilization of all the pregenital trends before they become incorporated in, and subordinated to, adult genitality, thereby contributing, in the end, to its enrichment. But, in the meantime, repression barriers are threatened and the defensive organization broached, now here, now there, as the increased instinctual cathexes add force to pregenital trends and rearouse oedipal fears, with the added danger that the increase in physical size and sexual function at last makes possible the physical realization of the instinctual wishes of childhood.

Inevitably, all this has consequences for the anxiety line. The intensified anxieties of adolescence, often increased to the point of panic, indicate the instability of the line during this period of development, so that regressions (reversions) readily recur along it, partly in line with the instinctual regressions themselves, with alternating readvances and progressions of varying degrees as the ego struggles to reassert its mastery. It is, indeed, vicissitudes of this nature which give adolescence its storm-tossed character, and it is precisely the restabilization of this line which, in terms of anxiety, is such a cardinal task in this phase of development, if maladaptions such as neurosis, delinquency, drug taking, or the reexternalizations of conflict resulting in war with the outside world are not to become established. What is it that makes restabilization possible?

Paradoxically, it is the repeated reversions and regressions which provide the motivations for fresh advances and which foster moves toward mastery. In this respect, the outcome of such backward steps differs strikingly from neurosis. Indeed, moves of this kind in adolescence can more accurately be regarded as regressions in the service of the ego, although, admittedly, this feature is by no means unique to adolescence. The urge toward mastery and independence prompted by every regressive experience leads to the step-by-step working through to the point of resolution, of the prephallic and oedipal anxieties. All this involves the reordering of the defensive organization, the emergence of the structures of the ego and superego, in increasingly adaptive and therefore more mature form. As the part instincts are modified as they are met by more stable defenses and are integrated more holistically, a new quality of object relations emerges, and true genitality in its widest sense begins to make an appearance. The stability of the anxiety line becomes more enduring as the end station on that line is reached.

None of this means, of course, that this attachment is proof against all trials and tribulations, whether inner or outer. In the nature of things, fixations and developmental disharmonies persist and will always predispose to pathology. In this case, the signal function of anxiety may persist and subserve neurotic symptom formation, or it may be lost altogether. Since every forward move in adolescence is of necessity tenuous, followed as it is by further backward steps, and since every progression awaits further consolidation, risks of this kind prevail at every turn.

For example, the reawakening of negative oedipal trends,

particularly in early adolescence, may reveal themselves in poorly controlled anxieties. A 13-year-old boy who had hitherto enjoyed male companionship, especially in relation to team sports, began to dread games day, especially the naked propinquities of the changing room. These fears were reinforced by the presence of the games master, who took his shower with the boys. The anxiety was no longer restricted to signal level. In such a situation, where the mental content is uneasily divorced from the affect, a sudden breakthrough of panic may indicate a greater reversion to pervasive anxiety.

A degree of reversion approaching pervasion appeared during the course of treatment of an 18-year-old girl. It was of some interest that a fear of boys persisted alongside a repugnance for her father. She would tell the therapist with great indignation that her father had revealed his disgusting character by attempting to put his arm around her. She dealt with her fear of boys through the rationalization that her person would be repellent to them, until, despite her best endeavors, repeated advances on their part made her conviction increasingly untenable. In due course she formed a friendship with a young man with whom she would not allow sexual intercourse. She was in some awe of the boy's able and aggressive personality, which was also reassuring to her, as he could not easily be damaged. When the boy became seriously ill and was hospitalized, she showed an expected and understandable concern. But when he was convalescent, he was, for a time, unable to stand upright, and she was devastated by his helplessness. She could not contain her anxiety or deal with it by effective action. She could avoid panic only by staying away; and although she kept in touch with him by telephone, she was unable to allow herself to see him until he was better. It was only through this avoidance that she could prevent pervasion by her fears.

We have described reversion along the developmental line to the point of pervasive anxiety. Can there be a further reversion to a yet more primitive state—that is, to vegetative excitation itself and a concomitant suspension of ego functions?

There are, in fact, at least four conditions, each of them widely recognized, in which such a reversion occurs. The first of these is the posttraumatic state, by which we mean the initial stage ("shock") of the traumatic neurosis. The second is "battle exhaustion"; the third, pavor nocturnus in children; and the fourth, the Stage IV nightmare. For our present purposes it is sufficient to illustrate the first and last of these conditions; and we leave aside the question of whether or not the third and fourth can be differentiated (see Fisher, Byrne, Edwards, and Kahn, 1970). Let us turn first to the traumatic neurosis.

One day a motorist pulled off the road. He was sitting in his car, engrossed in a newspaper when, without any warning, another car skidded, left the road, and crashed into him. He suffered only minor physical injuries but was found slumped in a dazed condition. He remained off work for many months and showed the classical symptoms of the traumatic neurosis. He was restless, tense, and irritable and was plagued by recurrent dreams, as well as recollections in which the car crash was reexperienced. In contrast with the vividness with which the crash was repeatedly recalled, inquiry showed that *he had no memory for the period immediately after the crash,* no memory, that is, for the posttraumatic state. His friends told him that, for a period of time, he had been immobile, pale, and tremorous.

The last example typifies the Stage IV nightmare, although the immediate outcome of one of the episodes was singularly unfortunate. The young woman who suffered from such nightmares would awake in the night with a start and hurtle herself from her bed in a state of confusion and terror. Unhappily, while on holiday in Germany she went straight through the window, landed on the ground, and fractured both legs.

The processes involved in the traumatic neurosis are well known and were described by Freud (1920). Here we are concerned only with the immediate posttraumatic state. The ego is totally unprepared for the trauma; under its impact, ego functioning is suspended, and precisely for this reason memory for the posttraumatic period is impossible. (The state of affairs is therefore quite different from repression.) Since the ego functions are knocked out during the period immediately following the trauma we cannot speak of anxiety—which requires ego functioning for its existence—but only of vegetative excitation.

The sleep laboratory has made possible the refined study

of the Stage IV nightmare. Stage IV refers to the electrical level of sleep as shown by the EEG. It occurs during a non-REM stage when secondary process functioning occurs and a brief but terrifying thought or fantasy is experienced. The ego is flooded by excitation, sleep fails to prevent motor discharge, the patient awakes in a state of utter confusion, and it may be some minutes before the ego recovers its functioning sufficiently for an observer to get in touch with him. A reversion from terror to vegetative excitation has taken place in the meantime.

These two examples are taken from adult patients, and they may serve to remind us that, even when development has been consolidated in postadolescence and adulthood and the anxiety signal has come to operate with a fair degree of refinement, these achievements are easily lost, at least temporarily. Indeed, when a reversion along the anxiety line results in an anxiety neurosis, as some have argued elsewhere (Yorke and Wiseberg, 1976), the result may have a more permanent character and settle into chronicity. The circumstances, both internal and external, in which this happens require further study.

Lastly, we should perhaps remind ourselves that conditions which bring about brain damage, and therefore loss of at least some ego functions, may also result in the loss of signal function. In the early stages of certain chronic organic syndromes, such a loss may be strikingly apparent—notably, for example, in the Alzheimer type of presenile dementia and in cerebral atherosclerosis. In these conditions, reversion along the line of anxiety is a common feature.

We now turn to a further example of a developmental line traced and described in some detail elsewhere (Kennedy, 1979), which is of special interest to all who practice therapy with children or adults. It is only in the process of psychoanalytic work that this line, concerned with the growth of the capacity for "insight," can clearly reveal itself.

The Development of the Capacity for Insight as Illustrated in the Psychoanalytic Process

In psychoanalytic therapy the work of interpretation aims, inter alia, at making unconscious conflicts conscious. The assumption is made that insight gained through the analytic process uncovers such conflicts, exposes their infantile origins, assists in their resolution, and so comes to the help of the patient's more mature ego in the task of finding new and more adaptive solutions to his difficulties. In the psychoanalytic view, the capacity for insight is linked with the work of the ego's integrative and adaptive functions. Nevertheless, it is indisputable that treatment results cannot be evaluated by the degree of insight attained, particularly in children. In some cases the results of analysis do seem connected with a lasting awareness which patients have of their problems and with an increased ability for critical and appraising self-scrutiny, while others fail to achieve this. Certainly, many children put out of their minds whatever insights they may have acquired during their analysis, even though the obstacles in the path of their developmental progress have been removed and their more pressing conflicts seemingly resolved. The capacity for insight and self-observation depends as much on ego maturity as it does on a positive wish for self-understanding. A developmental approach to the manner in which this capacity is acquired may also offer a fruitful contribution to the elucidation and clarification of the role of insight in the psychoanalytic process itself.

It is clear that the capacity for self-observation and insight is to be found in many people who have not undergone analysis. Since, however, psychoanalytic technique uses, and even actively encourages, the patient to use his capacity to observe himself, and since the analytic work addresses itself to the task of exploring the psychic processes which interfere with the patient's awareness of inner experiences, the analyst has an unusual vantage point from which to assess the developmental level at which these functions operate and the extent to which they are capable of improvement. Furthermore, the practitioner of child analysis has the additional opportunity to observe each step in the growth of these capacities as it arises. It is to the elucidation of these steps that the rest of this chapter is addressed.

A Developmental Line Which Leads from Early Infantile Awareness to a Wish for Self-Understanding

In our earlier discussion we emphasized the point that the infant's earliest experiences can amount to little more than fluctuating feeling states. But, at the same time, as affective experiences of pleasure, unpleasure, and primitive anxiety slowly differentiate, the infant begins to build rudimentary psychic representations on the basis of his experiences. The task of establishing boundaries between inside and outside, between me and not-me, can now begin. Initially these boundaries are determined by the wish to attribute pleasurable experiences to the me and unpleasurable ones to the not-me. At this primitive stage of structural foundation, the infant's "experiential awareness" can only be subjective. There can be no objective understanding of the internal source of experience, and the capacity for self-observation, which is dependent on a split in the ego between an experiencing and an observing part, cannot be said to exist during the preverbal stage of development.

Structural development is facilitated through the acquisition of language. Greater control over the discharge of affects is possible when action can be short-circuited through thought and verbal expression. Armed with these new tools, the child's comprehension of his world rapidly increases; and some capacity for self-observation and self-reflection can now begin to develop. But affective control must precede it. Let us take, as a case in point, a 2-year-old whose mother has just been blessed with a new baby. From the child's point of view, the blessing, to say the least, will be mixed. A little girl of our acquaintance, who had ostensibly looked forward to the new baby's arrival and sat on her mother's bed shortly afterward, betrayed her distress; as her little brother was fed, her lower lip quivered in an effort to hold back her tears. Soon afterward, she repeatedly attempted to get into the baby's carry-cot; and she entreated her mother to "put him in the dustbin." Under the impact of jealous rage and anger, and with the baby's continued presence in the house, the child lost her precocious adaptation and reverted to direct drive gratification by sucking, wetting, and attacking the baby, whom she hit with a teddy bear.

A child who had undergone similar experiences and whose

sleep was disturbed by fears of insects and monsters came into analysis shortly before she was 3. Her jealousy was unremitting and was repeatedly in evidence both in her direct physical attacks on her little sister and in her insistence that she herself was a baby. In treatment she crawled on the floor, talked baby language, and thereby sought the therapist's admiration. "Look at me!" she would say with evident glee, "I'm a baby!" Within a short time, however, her precocious ego development, of which her verbal ability was only one reflection, allowed her to recount in her session events occurring in the home or nursery school and to put her fantasies vividly into words. On one occasion, after she had opened the session with her usual babylike activities, the therapist verbalized the child's wish to be the baby sister whom she felt to be better loved. After a moment she stood up in reply and said confidingly: "I get cross with the baby and shove her down the hole and she comes out again and I get cross." On another occasion she attacked a doll with some excitement and asked the analyst to help her flush it down the lavatory. The anal stamp of her concrete thinking was extended into a phase of increasing ability for reflection during which she surprised and delighted her therapist by saying, "Yes, I have hurts," and went on to say, "I'm afraid of bugs and monsters, and I don't like being sad and naughty." Then her sadness lifted, and her face brightened as she said, "Let's throw all the *hurts* out of the window."

This example illustrates the fact that young children of this age have some ability for self-observation and reflection, but that it is tenuous and readily overthrown by the impact of instinctual needs. Moreover, their level of thinking bears the characteristics of the instinctual phase through which they are passing.

With the growing internalization of parental demands and disapproval, with the establishment of superego precursors, the capacity for self-observation becomes directly involved in the conflicts which begin to arise between the need to gratify wishes on the one hand and the fear of displeasing the loved parent on the other. Although a potential for the recognition of the internal sources of wishes and feelings now exists, it is frequently interfered with by the child's need to avoid the painful experience of conflict. Instinctual wishes which mobilize anxiety and fears of retaliation are repeatedly dealt with through denial, displacement, externalization, reversal, or other defensive maneuvers.

A little boy of 3 provides an example. The patient struggled to defend himself against any awareness of his intense anger with his mother, who was his only caretaker and whom he blamed for sending away his father. He strongly denied such feelings whenever they were suggested to him in his analysis. After several months his treatment was interrupted through the therapist's unexpected illness. He returned in an angry mood. He responded with the usual denial to the therapist's interpretation of his anger with her for keeping him away. A moment later, however, he kicked a chair and said, with a smile, "Naughty chair kicked me." Thus his wish to kick the therapist was first diverted toward an inanimate object; but even this maneuver was unacceptable, had to be reversed, and was explained by him as an attack on himself. His "knowing" smile conveyed some awareness of his anger and at least a measure of insight into his need to defend himself against its acknowledgment.

Although the young child's capacity to reflect may be accelerated and his self-knowledge widened as a result of analytic work, they are difficult to mobilize in the service of a treatment alliance because of the child's enduring search for gratification rather than understanding and because control over instinctual wishes and affects is at best very precarious.

While self-reflection is more in evidence in children with precocious ego development, a more pathological form of premature self-observation is to be found in children with obsessional tendencies who feel particularly divided by conflicting wishes and heightened ambivalence. In such children, introspective self-observation is often very pronounced and exploited for purposes of self-criticism. But this does not lead to insightful understanding, because it is used to meet punitive and masochistic needs.

During the first year of analysis of a 4-year-old boy, his ritualistic behavior was frequently interpreted as a response to massive anxiety mobilized by hostile and destructive wishes toward his mother. At this stage in treatment, he often complained about his lack of control over the compelling force which made him perform these rituals. He would call out angrily to the therapist, "See what my worries are making me do!" as he rushed round the room picking up pieces of paper. As his anger and destructive fantasies emerged more openly in the transference, he developed aches and pains which kept him away from treatment. After considerable work on these resistances, he again revealed his capacity for self-observation by sending a message through his mother, saying, "I know my headaches are from my worries, but I don't want to talk about them yet." Although in this he anticipated a future alliance with the therapist, this first step in his acquisition of insight was extremely limited if not, indeed, spurious. It was only after his self-punishing tendencies could be worked through that he was able to relinquish some of these defenses.

Once in latency (Anna Freud's third period of development), the child has more effective defenses available for the containment of instinctual pressures. Just as the child has acquired the potential ability to observe himself and to reflect on his inner experiences, the developmental thrust manifest during latency counters his ability to use it. This new developmental impetus directs the child's energies and attention toward the external world and away from his inner experiences. He develops sublimatory interests, engages in peer-group activities, and generally turns his curiosity and interests away from inner concerns. As a rule, the latency child resists introspection and insight into inner conflicts and looks for environmental solutions and external changes.

A 7-year-old boy was so terrified of the dark that he needed one of his parents to sit with him every night for some two hours before he could fall asleep. His fears spread, and he soon found it impossible to move freely about the home. He explained that the house where the family lived was old and rambling so that ghosts and monsters of murderous intent could conceal themselves effectively. Although he readily agreed that he needed help with his fears, he was convinced that the only possible solution was to move out of the house. In treatment, as his anger with his siblings moved into awareness, he described dreams in which burglars broke into the house at night, tried to kidnap him, and chased him so far away from the home that he could not get back to his mother. These dreams heralded the emergence of oedipal anxieties, and, as these appeared in the transference, strong resistances were mobilized.

His symptoms improved, and he now complained that his only source of unhappiness was that treatment interfered with his leisure and made it impossible for him to attend the Junior Scouts. He made desperate efforts to become a good child rather than a good patient. To this end, negative and hostile feelings had to be avoided. He strictly adhered to the rules of any games he played. He studied Scout rules and practiced making knots to improve his skills to the required level. But at this point he began to express concern about whether he could perform the "daily good deed" demanded by the Scouts and whether or not it would be "good enough." In the end, he could hardly bring himself to attend a Scout meeting; and when his parents told him that he need not be a Scout if he did not wish to be, he withdrew with great relief. He no longer had to face the anguished problem of making the "Scout's promise," which he felt he could not live up to.

However, with the internalization of the superego at the start of latency, self-observation acquires a special function. Indeed, the capacity to experience guilt may further objective insight. A 7-year-old girl who frequently became violent, and who attacked the therapist and the furniture in the treatment room, always became extremely frightened and contrite afterward. She would confess her misdeeds to everyone, especially her mother, and sometimes even ask her therapist to make a physical retaliation. The guilty feelings which followed the loss of instinctual control were the subject of much analytic work. When, during the second year of analysis, such a situation recurred, the therapist told her, "I have an idea that you feel so bad about yourself that you believe you ought to be killed." The patient said in reply, "I shouldn't be killed, but in my thoughts I feel I ought to be."

Adolescents are introspective, think about themselves, and use their intellectual capacities to further their knowledge about themselves. But, for all that, they cannot bring themselves to surrender ego control, even temporarily, and, in analysis, to submit themselves passively to transference experiences and free associations. They remain terrified of the intensity of id pressures and the emotional turmoil of their inner world. The adolescent turns his scrutiny upon himself, certainly; but he remains blind in one eye.

Let us turn for illustration to the treatment of a 13-year-old boy. Whereas, in the first months of treatment, he fought off any awareness of feeling, by the middle of the first year he was speaking freely about feelings of sadness or happiness. He would follow these acknowledgments with a musing self-questioning about the reasons for his affective state. Much of this introspection was a function of his identification with his therapist and a reflection of the treatment alliance; but it also served a defensive purpose. By his activity in the interpretive process he avoided the passive "endurance" of interpretation at the hands of the therapist. But as the analytic work progressed, he began to express his delight when he discovered that with the lifting of defenses against affect he began to remember things which, somewhere, had always been known to him, yet now had the quality of "newness." When he recognized that he turned passive into active when he laughed to avoid the feeling that someone would laugh at him, he said, with real delight, "It makes me feel so good and it is something so simple, too. I don't understand why I did not see it before."

In this chapter we have regarded adolescence as the fourth period of human development and adulthood as the fifth. As far as insight is concerned, it is only in the adult that we encounter a potential for the attainment of an optimal degree of objective self-understanding, since this presupposes maturity of ego functions and a genuine wish for self-knowledge. Self-observation, having progressed from infantile experiential self-awareness to cognition of self, now moves beyond the stage of critical self-evaluation to become an autonomous function.

Such an "ideal" adult patient will form a strong treatment alliance. Integrative comprehension will bring the insights gained into meaningful contexts. In the course of analysis, the patient's material is "worked through": fresh links between drive derivatives and defensive maneuvers and shifts are repeatedly and variously established as these are manifested in different situations. As part of the psychoanalytic process, self-knowledge becomes a self-ideal, and, at the end of the analysis, the analyzing function often becomes internalized. The ego's synthetic function, nonetheless, must allow insights to proceed to a point from which they can form a basis for adaptive solutions.

It must be assumed that the capacity for objective self-assessment exists, at least as a potential, in most adults. They may not have a great need to use it in a self-conscious way, nor the opportunity to demonstrate it, except in such special circumstances as an adult treatment situation. We may not know with certainty, when faced with the end result, whether a failure to develop this capacity belongs with certain types of personality formation, whether it results from developmental disharmonies or results from defensive measures organized against the emergence of neurosis. This is a matter for further study. But, since we have suggested that the capacity itself is most readily demonstrated in the terminal phase of a successful analysis, we shall attempt to justify this view with the help of case material.

The patient, an attractive and intelligent woman of 30, had sought help on account of a disabling social phobia. Her station in life demanded that she entertain and be entertained, but she could face these social occasions, if at all, only with the help of a few stiff drinks. Not surprisingly, this circumstance proved a considerable resistance in the analysis: whenever she had negotiated a difficult social crisis it was difficult to know whether she had done so on the basis of her insights or whether the alcohol had proved of greater help. But by the time of the terminal phase, the prophylactic drinking had been reduced to two Anadin tablets (a combination of mild analgesics) taken together with a minute drop of martini. We had not at this point understood the meaning of this. Lastly, it is necessary to know, in appreciating what follows, that she came from a working class background which contrasted sharply with her present situation, and that she had spent much of the earlier part of her analysis in berating her father and his supposedly unspeakably bad character.

Toward the end of her analysis, it was agreed that she

would take an extended weekend break. On her return she described a number of social activities in which she had taken part with evident enjoyment. She had been symptom free. Before the first social occasion, however, she had taken two Anadins and a tiny martini. This appeared to give her "complete confidence."

She then described how, on her way to London that day, she had averted an accident by quick thinking. She felt quite calm. Suddenly she felt an entirely new symptom—a tightness in the chest, as if she had difficulty in breathing. Then, as if making a discovery, she went on: "It's as if I was in the grip of . . . a giant."

She left this train of thought and returned to the Anadins. "I know what you will say," she told the analyst, "they're breasts. But I'm sure they're not. . . . A funny thought occurs to me—that it's the combination which matters. It's something to do with the *taste* produced by mixing them with the martini. It's a combination of bitterness and something I can't describe. It makes me feel marvelous."

She continued her introspection: "The feeling has something to do with the mixture of the tablets and the *gin* in the martini. . . . Gin is made from juniper berries. When I was a child I had a fantasy of living in open country and eating wild berries." She paused then: "Father once lived in the open and kept himself alive on wild berries." She paused again. The analyst said: "So when you take the Anadins and the martini it's as if you are your father." She nodded, and the session came to an end.

The following day she began by accusing the analyst of being a few minutes late. She was extremely critical. Soon, however, her tone of voice changed as she reported a social occasion which she had attended the previous day. Force of circumstance had denied her the opportunity of taking the tablets and alcohol beforehand. Nevertheless she remained symptom free.

She began to wonder once more why Anadins and martini together should bestow such a magical sense of assurance and power. The analyst responded: "It's as if you're drinking through your father's penis and taking his strength into you." She suddenly thought of a liqueur her father used to give her.

"On feast days and special occasions he would let me *taste* it, not drink it, as I was just a little girl," she explained. "It was a kind of slivovitz. I thought it was marvelous. . . . I'd forgotten all about it until now. *That's* what the Anadins and martini remind me of."

She continued: "The wild berries—Father used to tell me lots of stories of danger and excitement in the Carpathians. . . ." She stopped. "I've just thought of something else," she went on, "the Giant. There was said to be a red Giant who had a red beard and lived in the Carpathians. He was a good giant . . . well, I used to think of Father living in the Carpathians when he escaped from the East. I pictured him hunting bears and living off wild berries." The analyst intervened: "So now we know why you felt as if you couldn't breathe yesterday."

The patient nodded but continued as if the comment was unnecessary. She thought of a visit to the Italian Alps she had once made with her husband. She visualized the scene. "It was twilight. A ray of red sunshine shone on the trees and on the green grass." She stopped. The analyst said, after a moment, "I wonder why you have to stop." She said, unconvincingly: "I'm not going to cry." Nevertheless, she did. After a few moments she was able to say that she had remarked to her husband: "It's so beautiful, it's painful."

"This can't be right," she went on. "I always used to say that Father was useless, just a drunken beast. But now—other people's fathers seem to have led a dull life by comparison. Now it's almost as if I'm *glad* he's my father." "Yes," said the analyst, "it's always been easier to see him as the bad giant rather than the good one. You reexperience the same conflict here. You begin the session by feeling I'm bad and neglectful—it's still sometimes easier than feeling you draw any strength from me." And so the analysis continued.

If we have given an extended extract from the treatment account of this case, it is because we feel that the highest point on the line of development with which we are concerned is to be found there; and if what has been described illustrates not only the wish for self-knowledge but the excitement as the capacity for self-discovery manifests itself, we are content to let the material speak for itself in terms of all that has been said about the developmental line of insight leading through childhood and beyond.

There is, perhaps, one last point which needs to be made before we recapitulate, by way of conclusion, the steps along the lines which lead to signal anxiety and the adult capacity for insight. What our adult patient now has at her disposal is an internalized capacity which can come to her aid whenever she needs it. This is not to say that she could not *lose* this capacity or that its availability may not at times be suspended. As in all developmental lines, the potential for insight may revert to an earlier and more limited level at any time; equally, arrests along the line may occur.

Recapitulation: The Steps on the Two Developmental Lines in Terms of the Five Periods

The Line Leading to Signal Anxiety

During the first year of life the line leads from the crude vegetative excitation of the neonatal period to clear signs of mentalized anxiety at around 8 months. This early ability to experience pervasive anxiety will develop further by the end of the first year.

The acquisition of secondary process thinking and the concomitant capacity for delayed drive discharge through "trial action," the organization of defenses and, with these forward shifts, the general strengthening of the ego in relation to the drives, will normally ensure the acquisition of reasonably well-functioning signal anxiety by the time the oedipal conflicts resolve, the superego is established, and the child is about to embark on latency.

In the third period of life, which comprises latency, the successful reinforcement of defenses, especially repression, means that signal anxiety will normally be well established. Sublimations of instinct further external adaptation and help to reduce the sense of internal discord. But the child still needs support from parents and teachers to maintain reasonable containment of anxiety.

With the biological maturation of puberty the child begins

to enter adolescence as the relative peace of latency gives way to intensified drive urges with which the ego cannot cope without substantial developmental modifications. Reversions along the developmental line of anxiety can be expected to occur repeatedly, alternating with further forward moves. The repeated working through of prephallic and oedipal anxieties is a vital developmental task if some of these gains are not to remain under substantial threat.

It is only in postadolescence and adulthood, in the attainment of a more enduring genitality, that the highest achievements on the line can be regarded as consolidated.

The Line Leading to a Wish for Self-Understanding

1. During the first year of life the child cannot be expected to attain more than subjective experiential awareness.

2 a. Ego structures are gradually evolved which enable the child to acquire a fluctuating ability for self-observation and reflection. Since, however, the ego is still very immature, this capacity is tenuous and readily undermined by the pressure of instinctual needs.

2 b. The capacity for self-observation is extended as the internalization of parental demands and approval proceeds. The increasing capacity for self-observation is used to maintain an inner state of well-being and reduced anxiety. The child deals with disapproved instinctual wishes and their derivatives by externalization, displacement, or denial.

3. In latency, conflicts are fully internalized. Repression and other defense mechanisms are employed to seal off unacceptable drive derivatives. With the resolution of oedipal conflicts and consolidation of an internalized superego, as well as the increased ego maturity of the latency child, the capacities for self-observation and self-reflection are further secured. Superego introjects ensure that self-observation will not serve to maintain control over unacceptable wishes and feelings. With the successful operation of defenses, in particular the repression which is responsible for the so-called infantile amnesia, the child turns his interests and curiosity away from conflicts and the inner world and toward the outside world. He looks for

external causes and solutions to his problems and not for self-understanding.

4. The adolescent becomes introspective and self-reflective, but is also terrified by the intensity of his sexual and aggressive wishes and by his dependency. He therefore defends himself strenuously against recognition of the revival of past conflicts in the present, which limit his capacity for insight.

5. It is only in the adult that we encounter a potential for the attainment of an optimal degree of objective self-observation and, with it, the wish for self-understanding. Self-observation becomes an autonomous function. In the adult who has completed a successful analysis, self-understanding can reach beyond everyday conscious experience—beyond, that is, the normal end point on the line.

In her discussion, Anna Freud has drawn attention to the interdependence of developmental lines and has pointed out that many of them cannot manifest themselves without the preexistence or support of others. We have indicated, for example, that the anxiety line is intimately linked with the pathway which leads from body to mind. It is obvious that the two lines described above are closely interconnected.

Poorly controlled anxiety interferes in the normal functioning of self-observation and self-reflection. Panic is the enemy of insight. Well-controlled anxiety is a human attainment which, among other things, fosters self-observation and self-understanding in the interests of internal and external harmony.

References

Fisher, C., Byrne, J., Edwards A., & Kahn, E. (1970), A psychophysiological study of nightmares. *J. Amer. Psychoanal.,* 18:747–782.

Freud, A. (1963), The concept of developmental lines. *The Psychoanalytic Study of the Child,* 18:245–265. New York: International Universities Press.

Freud, S. (1920), Beyond the pleasure principle. *Standard Edition,* 18:1–64. London: Hogarth Press, 1955.

Kennedy, H. (1979), The Role of insight in child analysis: A developmental viewpoint. *J. Amer. Psychoanal. Assn.,* 27(Suppl.):9–28.

Spitz, R.A. (1965), *The First Year of Life.* New York: International Universities Press.

Yorke, C., & Wiseberg, S. (1976), A developmental view of anxiety. *The Psychoanalytic Study of the Child,* 31:107–135. New Haven: Yale Universities Press.

9

Early Latency: Normal and Pathological Aspects

ERNA FURMAN

The psychoanalytic concept of the latency period originates with Freud. He introduced and formally defined it for the first time in 1905 as a phase in the sexual development of children. From then until the end of his life, Freud essentially maintained his initial view of latency and repeatedly stressed its importance for the understanding of normal and abnormal psychological growth. His many references to the topic of latency also show, however, that he continued to grapple with the concept, adjusting his formulation to clinical findings and weighing the role of biological, phylogenetic, cultural and individual psychological factors (Freud, 1905b, 1908, 1909a, 1911, 1916a, 1921, 1923a, 1923b, 1923c, 1924a, 1924b, 1925, 1926a, 1926b, 1926c, 1939, 1940).

Freud described the latency period as following the phallic-oedipal crest of infantile sexual development and extending until the onset of puberty. Although he several times altered the exact age limits, the indicated span of time coincides roughly with elementary school in this country. Structurally, Freud viewed the latency period as "characterized by the dissolution of the oedipus complex, the creation or consolidation of the superego and the erection of ethical and aesthetic barriers in the ego" (1926a, p. 114). From a dynamic point of view he stressed the role of castration anxiety in bringing about repression and/or dissolution of the oedipus complex and the increasing importance of guilt emanating from the newly formed superego. He saw the latency child's conflict focus on the struggle against masturbation, with its attendant oedipal and preoedipal fantasies. Although Freud observed a "halt and retrogression" (1916a, p. 326; see also 1939) in psychic sexual development and hence a relative diminution in drive energy, he pointed out from the start that instinctual breakthroughs do occur and that latency "need not bring with it any interruption of sexual activity and sexual interest" (1916a, p. 326). Depending on the cultural setting and individual personality, however, the latency child's adaptation is more usually marked by expanding relationships with peers and adults outside the family, by growth in ego functions, skills, activities, and sublimatory interests, and by conformity to the rules of family and community.

Freud's metapsychological definition of the latency period has stood the test of later psychoanalytic clinical investigations and theoretical developments. There are only a few additions: Anna Freud's work on defenses (1936) paved the way for Bornstein's suggestion (1951) to subdivide latency into two periods. This division is based on differences in the structural equilibrium of the personality and implies technical therapeutic considerations. The early latency period extends roughly from ages 6 to 8; late latency covers the subsequent 2 to 3 years and is characterized by a solidification of the preceding ego and superego developments and by greater internal harmony. More recently, Williams (1972) proposed a triphasic division of latency, again based on theoretical and therapeutic criteria, but

> emphasizing the influence of the preceding phase of prelatency on early latency development, and in delineating the impact of the phase that follows latency—namely, prepuberty. Without trying to schematize, one can roughly describe early latency as lasting from 5 to 7, latency proper from 7 to about 9, and late latency from approximately 9 to 11. It should be understood that this scheme does not represent a strict categorization: In some children the prelatency period, chronologically speaking, extends far into what we would regard as latency proper; others show an early thrust into prepuberty [p. 600].

Katan (1978) stresses that chronological demarcations of the latency period, and of subdivisions within it, are misleading because of the normally wide variation among children. The child's entry into latency and transition into prepuberty is characterized by the same overlapping of phases as at earlier developmental stages. The actual timing of the beginning and end of latency is therefore difficult to determine and differs greatly from child to child. She notes that in some children the onset of latency may normally occur as late as the seventh or eighth year, depending on factors of endowment, personality development, and environmental influence; e.g., children to whom a father becomes available only at age 6 may experience a delayed oedipal period, followed by a delayed but normal latency and puberty.

Several authors have noted that the clinical picture of latency is sometimes far from calm. Instinctual breakthroughs may be quite frequent; they may occur to a marked degree during the earliest and latest years of latency; there may be no diminution in instinctual interests and activity (Alpert, 1941; Clower, 1976; Sarnoff, 1976). Maenchen (1970) suggests that during recent years in this country latency appears to be less long and its characteristics less evident. Such findings help us to understand the many vicissitudes of latency but do not invalidate the concept of latency. Freud himself referred to these phenomena and understood them in terms of variations in individual personalities, familial influences, and cultural patterns. It is not the presence or absence of instinctual manifestations that defines latency; rather, it is the emergence within the child's personality of the superego, changes in the ego, and their position vis-à-vis the oedipus complex and its derivatives.

Freud saw the importance of the latency period in the context of human sexual development, which is marked by a diphasic onset. Latency represents a halt to, and interruption of, the progression of infantile sexuality. The child's libidinal attachment to his infantile parental love objects culminates in the oedipus complex and is repressed or dissolved with the onset of latency. Adolescence represents the second onset of sexual development, leading to genital maturity and libidinal investment in love objects outside the family. Freud (1905b, 1939) noted that this diphasic onset of sexual life was peculiar to man and that its psychological manifestations were paralleled, and even caused, by comparable physiological and biological phenomena in the maturation of the sexual organs. Indeed, he sometimes called it the physiological period of latency (Freud, 1939).

The causes of this diphasic onset are to be found in biological and historical factors. Following Ferenczi's suggestion (1913), Freud (1923a) considered the glacial epoch a key factor; the diphasic onset, he wrote, "which seems to be peculiar to man, is a heritage of the cultural development necessitated by the glacial epoch" (p. 35), and he reiterates this view later (1926a). Whereas this hypothesis may appear strictly Lamarckian in genetic terms and as yet unproven by scientific findings, Lampl (1953) discusses its plausibility. He shows how, more recently, evolutional phenomena have been explained by a combination of Darwinian and Lamarckian theories, and he explores the close interaction of biological and psychological factors in the development of latency and other areas. Sarnoff (1976), by contrast, disputes biological and physiological factors affecting latency and focuses on the cultural-historical development of the human race. Clower (1976) stresses the role of society.

In Freud's view, the historical factor is defined by the lengthy helplessness and dependency of the human infant, by the formation and subsequent repression of the oedipus complex (both byproducts of the close and extended parent-child relationship), by the superego that emerges out of the preceding developments, and by the variable cultural utilization and reinforcement of the child's psychological status in the developmental phase of latency (1905b, 1908, 1916a, 1923a, 1923c, 1939). Freud pointed to the important personality achievements during the latency period, especially the emergence of values, ideals, and sublimations, and their positive implications for human cultural development. He stressed, however, that, at the same time, the latency period and its attendant psychological developments constitute "the determining factor for the origin of the neuroses" (1923b, p. 246; 1939). The interruption in sexual development and repression or dissolution of the oedipus complex can be "most propitious culturally" (Freud,

1916a, p. 326) but also makes man vulnerable to neurotic diseases.

Later psychoanalytic writers have not followed up Freud's particular areas of interest in the latency period. In 1959, Fries found that the word "latency" appears in the titles of but a few psychoanalytic publications, although the topic of latency is taken up in many. Her observation still holds true now, with some notable exceptions. Psychoanalytic investigators have concerned themselves mainly with the treatment and elucidation of pathology in latency children. Many articles trace the prelatency genesis of latency symptomatology; many others contribute to the technique of therapy with this age group. Relatively few writers have focused on the theory of latency, on normal developmental steps and masteries, and on the multiple pathogenic determinants, internal and external, which operate specifically during the latency period and affect its course and outcome.

The following discussion of normal and pathological development in early latency incorporates many existing psychoanalytic contributions. In addition, it introduces several concepts which I have previously described (E. Furman, 1980) and whose significance has not been assessed in the context of this developmental phase. For purposes of clarity these concepts are pinpointed below and further amplified in the appropriate sections of the text:

1. The onset of infantile amnesia, characterized by the forgetting of prelatency experiences, causes many children inner disharmony, bewilderment, and distress. The loss of a familiar part of the self—one's past—is sometimes experienced as an inadequacy, leading to dissatisfaction and concern with himself, or as shameful. It may also affect the child's relationships if he is unaware of the source of discomfort and perceives it as stemming from without or expects it to be alleviated by his loved ones. When the parents recognize this developmental phenomenon, they can then extend appropriate educational help to the child by explaining the universal and limited nature of this form of forgetting.

2. The early latency child normally experiences difficulty in recognizing the "voice of conscience" as stemming from

within; he can be helped educationally to reach this awareness, which in turn will assist him in integrating and mediating the newly internalized superego demands.

3. Externalization of superego to ward off inner conflict may be regarded as a phase-specific transitional defense in early latency; it becomes pathological only if it exceeds certain limits in intensity and/or becomes so rigid as to preclude progress toward mature and appropriate integration of superego demands.

4. Partial regression of the libido to the anal sadistic level is known to be a normal phenomenon in early latency. Observation and clinical material from analytic treatments show that the libidinal regression to the phallic-narcissistic level is equally if not more prominent in normal development. It is linked to the narcissistic hurt of the oedipal rejection and affects the normal course of object relationships in latency: the turning away from the parents, the relative "downgrading" of the parents, the narcissistic object choice of peers, and the defensive attitude to peers of the opposite sex.

5. The postoedipal regression to the phallic-narcissistic level is more marked and may assume pathological dimensions in cases with a previously established phallic-narcissistic fixation point and in cases where, in early latency, the child experiences a hurt in his relationships with the parents which then constitutes a developmental interference. These latter instances were studied in cases where a satisfactory age-appropriate relationship with father or mother was not available during early latency because of physical absence or emotional unavailability. The effects of earlier fixation and current developmental interference may overlap and reinforce one another.

6. Whereas the father's role during the child's oedipal phase is well recognized, his importance to the child in early latency has not been stressed—as a love object, as a model for identification, and as regards his attitude to the child's growing up. Even subtle and manifestly minor paternal pathologies constitute very significant developmental interferences at this level.

7. The partial libidinal regression in early latency presents a special diagnostic difficulty in that it makes it difficult to distinguish isolated neurotic problems carried over from con-

flicts at previous levels from those which result from the current regression. This affects the differential diagnoses between phase-appropriate and neurotic conflicts.

8. Early latency is an important time for the differential diagnosis of atypical (borderline and psychotic) disturbances in cases that are not too severe and/or that responded well to therapeutic intervention in the preschool years. This applies particularly to the assessment of such ego functions as the capacity to neutralize instinctual energy, to establish secondary autonomy of functions and activities, to mediate structural conflicts, to effect advanced forms of identification, and to take over and independently maintain functions which, in early years, were vested in the parents.

Some Developmental Characteristics of Early Latency

Superego Formation

Superego formation is one of the crucial developmental achievements of the latency child. Since Freud (1923a), many writers have contributed to our understanding of the various aspects of the superego. Some have researched the specific mechanisms by which it is built up following dissolution of the oedipus complex and how this process is related to, or differs from, preoedipal precursors (Jacobson, 1954; Sandler,1960). Anna Freud's work on the defenses (1936), especially the defense of identification with the aggressor, is a cornerstone to the understanding of the intermediate stage in superego formation. In early latency the child's superego is not yet fully internalized or integrated with the rest of the personality, drive pressure is still strong, and ego functions are often inadequate to the task of mediating to achieve inner harmony.

Intense psychic conflict gives rise to anxiety which in turn is warded off by a variety of defenses. Identification with the aggressor—a combination of introjection, projection, and turning passive into active—is phase-appropriate and is used to avoid feelings of guilt. The child's use of this defense may show in unexpected attacks on others by word or deed. Another phase-specific defense is the externalization of the superego, the warding off of internal conflict by attributing the superego to another person—usually one in a position of authority. The use of this defense may result in the unruly aggressive or sexual behavior we customarily expect in much younger children. The casual observer then finds it difficult to appreciate how close such a child is dynamically to the responsive and obedient latency child whose superego demands regulate his behavior more effectively. Indeed, these very different behaviors may alternate or manifest themselves in separate settings; for example, the child may be difficult to live with in the family but adapt well at school. As Anna Freud (1930) noted, "If [the teacher] does succeed in representing [the children's] superego, the ideal of the group, the compulsory obedience changes into voluntary submission" (p. 120).

Even when full internalization does take place, the newly formed superego tends to be harsh and uncompromising. Bornstein (1949, 1951, 1953a, 1953b) and later Williams (1972) were particularly attuned to the early latency child's heightened sensitivity to criticism, his tendency to experience even the slightest implied disapproval as a vicious punitive attack, and to respond with intensified defensive maneuvers. Both writers described therapeutic techniques to deal with the early latency child's special resistances. Bornstein's work on the interpretation of defenses and affects actually revolutionized child analytic technique in general and made the use of an introductory phase redundant.

Masturbation

The internal prohibitions, reproaches, and threats of punishment emanating from the newly formed superego are of course primarily directed against the instinctual drives and drive derivatives associated with the oedipus complex. The diminution of the drives is not a sudden phenomenon. Moreover, as stressed by Freud (1916a, 1919, 1926a, 1939), Anna Freud (1965), and Bornstein (1951, 1953b), there is a measure of drive regression, partly defensive. As a result, the early latency child's masturbation and accompanying fantasies contain both oedipal and preoedipal elements. This further intensifies the conflict with the superego, as the latter finds itself particularly opposed to the sadomasochistic regressive aspects.

My own findings in working with children in this phase suggest that the regression from the oedipal to the phallic-narcissistic level (Edgcumbe and Burgner, 1975) is especially prevalent. The child's experience of rejection by the oedipal love object leads to a renewed emphasis on the phallic-narcissistic components and revives related conflicts around sexual differences, penis envy, and castration fear.

Since a greater or lesser degree of drive activity continues throughout latency and since the oedipus complex is usually not fully dissolved but merely kept unconscious, the ego has to channel direct and indirect drive expression. Most writers consider the struggle against masturbation among the latency child's main developmental conflicts. Periodic instinctual breakthroughs are regarded as normal. Some of these occur in the form of displaced activities with preoedipal admixtures (such as nailbiting); others involve genital feelings and genital manipulation. There is no consensus as to the exact nature of the latency child's capacity for genital discharge. Especially in girls there appears to be considerable variation within the range of normality. Lampl-de Groot (1950) finds that latency girls masturbate clitorally and do not reach an orgastic climax. Clower (1976) stresses the prevalence of nonmanual clitoral masturbation and the orgastic discharge potential of the clitoris in latency. Bornstein (1953b) and Fraiberg (1972) report cases of vaginal arousal and orgastic experiences. Bernstein (1976) reports on the role of masochistic fantasies of being penetrated in shaping the latency girl's masturbation and related conflict.

The child in early latency usually exhibits in his behavior both instinctual derivatives and the struggle against them, alternately or in combination; for example, his room may be very messy at one time and obsessively tidy at another; his plea to "stay up late" expresses both his wish to share the parents' evening time and his fight against masturbatory temptations in bed. Bornstein (1953b), Anna Freud (1965), and Nagera (1966b) describe these sleep disturbances of the latency period, as well as the child's own newly acquired measures for coping with them, for example, by reading in bed.

The latency child finds himself in special difficulty when his struggle against masturbation is too successful, i.e., when his personality allows no voluntary or involuntary episodes of bodily instinctual gratification. Anna Freud (1949b) described how, in such cases, the child's sexuality may invade his ego functioning, causing severe disturbances in relationships and activities (see the section on character disorders below).

Fantasy

The growing ego, however, also makes accommodations with the drives in phase-appropriate activities, provides for indirect discharge, and increasingly converts id energy for use in developing ego functions, such as thought and speech (Kolansky, 1967).

Many writers have discussed the development by which fantasies become separated from masturbatory activity and undergo changes which disguise their oedipal and preoedipal contents (Freud, 1919; A. Freud, 1922, 1949b). Eventually these daydreams and fantasies contribute to the development of thinking and some of its creative aspects, to playing and attendant skills and social relations, to artistic activities, and to the enjoyment of literature (Freud, 1911; A. Freud, 1922, 1965; Friedlander, 1942; Burlingham, 1945; Blanchard, 1946; Lampl-de Groot, 1950; Bornstein, 1951, 1953b; Peller, 1954, 1959; E.B. Kaplan, 1965; Kramer, 1971; Goldings, 1974).

The latency child's fantasies, separated from the act of masturbation, do not always lead to ego gains. Anna Freud (1949b) showed how they can be transferred from the family to the school and the wider community and result in various forms of social maladjustment or of interference in ego activities, such as learning inhibitions, feelings of being disliked or persecuted, provocativeness, struggles with authorities, and disruptive exhibitionism.

The fantasies most characteristic of this phase, e.g., the family romance (Freud, 1909a) and the fantasy of having a twin (Burlingham, 1945), crystallize and flourish in late latency. Many children's books dealing with related themes, however, become favorites already in early latency (Friedlander, 1942; Peller, 1959; Widzer, 1977). E.B. Kaplan (1965) and Goldings

(1974) have shown that some of these fantasies are also expressed in well-known children's rhymes, beloved in latency and chanted rhythmically to accompany the motoric games of this phase, e.g., jump rope.

Motility plays an important part in latency and is another area in which the ego harmoniously includes id derivatives and gradually gains ascendancy over them. E.B. Kaplan (1965) and Kestenberg (1975) have drawn attention to the early latency child's characteristic psychomotor activities. They have shown how normal development of these activities depends on the close interaction of physiological and psychological maturation, and how it serves as a vehicle for phase-appropriate instinctual discharge, furthers social relationships, and increases ego skills. Goldings (1974) and Sarnoff (1976) stress the significance of these rhymes and rhythms for the transmission of cultural traditions, blending individual oedipal and preoedipal contents with societal lore and myths. Failure or deviation in this area of ego functioning can be taken as a serious sign of developmental pathology, affecting many aspects of the latency child's personality.

Play

Postoedipal play in general has received attention as a developmental line in which all parts of the latency child's personality harmoniously interact. E.B. Kaplan (1965), Goldings (1974), and especially Peller (1954) have traced the oedipal and preoedipal contents of social games (e.g., team sports and board games) and individual hobbies (e.g., model building, crafts, collecting). In his charming and instructive autobiographical book, "*Where Did You Go?*" "*Out*" "*What Did You Do?*" "*Nothing*," Smith (1957) described in detail the many solitary and social games of his latency years, both formal and improvised. He brought out the interaction of fantasy and reality and the extent to which the child deals with them on his own or shares them with peers but, phase-appropriately, keeps them at a distance from adults.

In early latency the instinctual aspects of these games are often still so poorly integrated with the rest of the personality that they tend to interfere with the enjoyment of playing; e.g., the child can't bear to lose, insists on being first in all things, or can only collect kings in a card game. At better moments and increasingly with the transition into late latency, the main point of the games is their elaborate defensive nature; here is seen an insistence on rules and fairness, on the skill of playing as opposed to the thrill of winning, and on cooperative effort versus individual rivalry. As a matter of fact, many games never get started or fail to get finished because of interminable discussions about the rules. Even some early latency games focus primarily on defense, such as hopscotch and "Step on a crack, break your mother's back." In games and hobbies, the obsessive ritualistic defenses of this phase tend to stand out, but the overall increase and solidification of reaction-formations and rationalization are also evident.

Defenses and Sublimations

The very onset of latency is associated with repression of the oedipus complex. It is primarily the mechanism of repression which the ego uses to ward off the castration anxiety associated with oedipal strivings and to serve as a countercathectic measure against the reemergence of infantile sexuality. This brings about the infantile amnesia, the forgetting of the bulk of prelatency experiences so characteristic of human mental development. Freud (1905a) pointed out that in the hysteric, the glaring gaps in memory which are caused by the use of repression are gradually filled or bridged so as to produce a conscious continuum of the person's life history. With phase-appropriate repression at the beginning of latency, it is usually a positive sign when it occurs piecemeal over a prolonged period rather than obliterating memories suddenly and totally. The slower selective process indicates better integration and does not make excessive demands on the ego's energies. However, even when repression initially wipes out only some memories, this can be very upsetting to the young latency child. He finds that he can no longer share in the family's conversation about a past happy vacation; he cannot recognize the babysitter who remembers *him* so well, and he struggles in vain to reproduce for himself the continuity of "where I was when" and "what happened next." As they affect the child's synthetic function, these experiences are not only disconcerting but may also be felt as a narcissistic injury which lowers his self-esteem or as an imperfection of which he is ashamed. Some children also worry that their memory is altogether impaired, that they will be unable to remember what they learn at school or experience at home.

The inner disharmony which results from the loss of a familiar part of the self—one's past—is further intensified by having to integrate the new superego—an as yet unfamiliar part of the self. This unsettled and distressing mental state sometimes leads to irritability, excessive demandingness, or withdrawal from love objects when the cause of the painful feelings is perceived to lie in the external rather than the internal world. Adults sometimes contribute to the child's discomfort by laughing at his forgetting or by prompting him to remember, as though he could do so if only he were not so lazy, stupid, or uncooperative—"But *surely* you remember Auntie May! Why, she was *so* nice to you when we visited her." I found that, when parents are helped to recognize the phenomenon of infantile amnesia and the puzzlement it causes youngsters at the time of its onset, they can be most helpful to their children. It is very reassuring to children to be told that these lapses of memory are part of growing up, that it happens to everyone, including all grownups when they were young, and that they can learn again about many things in their early lives by looking at photos or home movies or simply by asking the older members of the family to tell them about past events. And, above all, children need to know that they will not go on forgetting; from here on in, they will be able to remember what they learn and experience.

Latency is of course best known for the characterological integration of such defenses as the reaction-formations of pity, cleanliness, and shame, all of which aid in socialization and become part of the child's ego ideal. Freud (1905b, 1908, 1923b, 1926a) and other writers have stressed the concomitant development of sublimations utilizing newly neutralized energy (A. Freud, 1930, 1965; Blanchard, 1946; Lampl-de Groot, 1950; Bornstein, 1953b; Jacobson, 1954; Kaplan, 1957; Fries, 1959; Becker, 1965; E.B. Kaplan, 1965; Williams, 1972).

The child's pleasure in learning is closely linked to sublimations and to a phase-appropriate teacher-pupil relationship. It is most important for the child's development that this relationship focus on and support these ego activities and serve as a model for identification in this area; by contrast, when the teacher presents himself or herself as a parent substitute and encourages elements of the parent-child relationship in the teacher-pupil interaction, this may constitute a developmental interference (Nagera, 1966a) and lead to pathology in the child (A. Freud 1949b; E. Furman, 1977, 1986). At times in the past the strictness and rigidity of the school environment allowed no opportunity for a phase-appropriate relationship with the teacher. The young latency child's libidinal strivings were then turned back onto himself, leading to an increase in autoerotic activities, or were focused in full force on his peer relations. Such lack of opportunity for a teacher-pupil relationship also discouraged the development of suitable identifications and sublimations and detracted from a joyful investment in learning. More recently, some progressive educational trends have erred in the opposite direction. By encouraging the transfer of family relationships to the teachers and by meeting the child's emotional needs instead of expecting him to work toward the attainment of skills and behavioral norms, the school becomes an arena in which prelatency conflicts are perpetuated and progressive latency development is interfered with.

Object Relationships

The intense libidinal attachment to the parents is dissolved and repressed. The parents themselves are no longer considered all-important and almighty. Adults outside the family begin to assume a greater role in the child's life. The oft-repeated "My teacher said . . ." testifies to this and suggests that ego and superego aspects enter into these new relationships to a significant extent (Freud, 1914). The diminished psychological dependency on the parents and the increased importance of relationships with other adults not only contribute to the child's schooling but also affect his performance in the psychotherapeutic setting, especially the transference relationship. Theoretical and technical aspects of the transference in latency analyses have been discussed by several authors. Some of them point to increased transference manifestations; others speak of the development of a transference neurosis in some latency children (Bornstein, 1949, 1953a; Harley, 1962; A. Freud, 1965; Fraiberg, 1966, 1967; Maenchen, 1970; Novick, 1970; Williams, 1972; Sandler, Kennedy, and Tyson, 1975).

With peers, too, real friendships begin to develop and constitute an important part of the child's life (Pearson, 1966). These relationships as well as the many group and social activities are now limited to children of the same sex, while those of the opposite sex tend to be kept at a distance, sometimes despised or teased. The early latency child still struggles with these developmental steps. Remnants of oedipal libidinal interest may show in the boy's love for his woman teacher or in play with girlfriends. Commonly we also see intense defensive measures against such breakthroughs, e.g., boy's provocative or boisterous defiance with adult women, their abusive and belittling attitudes to girls; with girls we note similar difficulties, e.g., fearfulness of men, tomboyishness, or bossy and "holier than thou" behavior with boys.

The early latency child's retreat to phallic-narcissistic concerns, occasioned in part by the narcissistic hurt of the oedipal rejection and defense against oedipal ties, was referred to earlier. My observations and therapeutic work with children in the Hanna Perkins Kindergarten[1] suggest that the effects of this regression are particularly noticeable in the area of object relationships. It contributes to the disappointed "downgrading" of the parents, the preference for peers of the same sex, and the defensive attitude to those of the opposite sex. Anna Freud (1965) notes that relationships with contemporaries in latency are based on identification, not on object love. Preference for friends of the same sex in this phase is likely to be succeeded by heterosexual object choice in adolescence. The boy who seeks out girls and the girl who seeks out boys are more likely to experience difficulties with heterosexuality later on.

[1] Many of the clinical data and theoretical formulations in this paper derive from my work at the Hanna Perkins Nursery School and Kindergarten (see R.A. Furman and Katan, 1969) and from what I have learned there both from and with my colleagues.

Assessment

These briefly summarized psychoanalytic contributions to normal development in early latency highlight selected areas. The overall metapsychological assessment of the latency child is facilitated by the use of the diagnostic profile and developmental lines (A. Freud, 1965), as illustrated in the literature by Meers (1966). R.A. Furman and Katan (1969) utilized the profile in their follow-up study of youngsters treated in the Hanna Perkins Therapeutic Nursery School and included a "Scheme for Lines of Development and Mastery of Tasks in Latency" to aid in the assessment of latency children.

Latency Pathology

In private psychiatric practice as well as in mental health agencies, latency-age children constitute a large proportion of cases referred and treated. The reasons for this are in part familial and societal. Although emotional difficulties in preschoolers are the rule rather than the exception, the parent-child relationship during the earliest years is so close and exclusive that the child's problems cause the parent especially marked guilt and narcissistic injury (E. Furman, 1969). These painful feelings tend to be warded off by defensive measures (denial, rationalization) against recognizing the child's difficulties and against seeking professional advice. The parents' reluctance is abetted by the fact that the young child's troubles manifest themselves primarily within the family setting and are largely hidden from the scrutiny of outsiders.

The latency child, by contrast, is less close to the parents (Kestenberg, 1975). They view his maladjustments at a somewhat greater emotional distance; moreover, his school attendance exposes him to interaction with, and expectations from, an outside authority. Many referrals of latency children are indeed prompted by the school or occur in consultation with it. Evaluations show that many of the children seen in this age group suffer not from disturbances which developed with the onset of latency but from conditions which were overlooked during the preschool years and only now are surfacing undeniably as the children fail to master phase-appropriate tasks.

By contrast, both parents and teachers often wish for psychiatric help for preadolescent and adolescent youngsters who are caught in the emotional upheavals of growth; but effective referrals and, even more so, treatment programs run afoul of the children's resistances. Unlike the latency child, the adolescent cannot be "taken" to get help.

In addition to these external factors, there are significant internal and phase-specific reasons that account for the large number and variety of latency problems. The review of latency development above gives an inkling of the magnitude of the structural changes within the personality, the extent and intensity of new conflicts, and the variety of ego functions to be mastered. It is not surprising that the early phase of latency, in particular, gives rise to much inner stress, with attendant ups and downs in behavioral adjustment, and that it also serves as the matrix for the formation of lasting pathology (Freud, 1926a; A. Freud, 1945).

Some presenting difficulties are especially characteristic for the latency child. Among these are learning problems, troubles with peer relations, school phobias, and homesickness. But these problems are not necessarily caused by current conflicts. They may represent complex psychic reactions to stresses at several developmental levels and may be indicative of various types of disturbance (Klein, 1945, 1949; Blanchard, 1946; Pearson, 1952; Sperling, 1967). Conversely, the most diverse complaints may be the outcome of developmental latency conflicts—be they bodily aches, fears, delinquencies, wetting and soiling, obsessions, tempers, or maladaptive character traits. Anna Freud (1970) has shown that symptoms can be diagnostically revealing of the underlying nature of the pathology if we study them analytically; but even well-understood symptoms are only one part of a metapsychological assessment. For the purpose of this chapter, I shall attempt to group latency pathology within the diagnostic categories introduced by Anna Freud (1965) and extended for use with young children by Daunton (1969, pp. 213–214):

Essentially Healthy Personality Growth Despite Manifest Disturbances

The earlier description of the developmental aspects of latency includes examples of phase-appropriate behavioral difficulties and relates them to conflicts in several areas of personality functioning. Individual variations are so great that it would be impossible to compile an exhaustive list of manifest maladjustments. In each case, however, phase-appropriate signs of inner stress as well as the areas of adequate functioning show that the child has entered latency and is grappling with its developmental tasks—an important indication of emotional progression.

Some phase-specific manifestations cause so much friction in the child's relationships and are so deceptive as to their psychic origin that parents and teachers tend to misinterpret them and to respond in an unhelpful fashion. This is particularly marked with difficulties arising from the initial internalization of the superego.

In observing young children during entry into latency, one is struck with how uneasy they feel with their newly acquired superego, how little it as yet feels a part of them, and how hard it is for them to understand its signals and use them effectively in controlling behavior. In the Hanna Perkins Kindergarten there are usually several children who complain that their mothers constantly "yell" at them or that their teachers are "mean" to them. Closer scrutiny shows that these children attribute the harsh voice of conscience to outside authorities. When it is pointed out that the mother or teacher was actually very encouraging and soft-spoken and that perhaps something inside the children is very angry at them, they sometimes listen, half-bewildered, half-thoughtful, with an inward-looking expression on their faces. As they become more aware of what goes on inside them, they learn better to distinguish inner and outer reality, recognize more readily the demands of conscience, and their relationships suffer less interference. Some weeks or months later these children occasionally comment, "My conscience is yelling at me today," or "You like my writing, but I think it's terrible." At the earlier stage, attributing criticism to the outside is not a defense but a sign of unfamiliarity with the new inner agency and its lack of integration into the rest of the personality.

The newly formed superego is indeed hard to integrate because it is usually quite harsh and uncompromising. The slightest mistake is judged to be a major crime. It takes time and educational help for a new conscience to become "liveable" with; as we often tell our kindergarten children and first graders, one's conscience has to learn that one does not have to be perfect and that there are big, medium, and little crimes. We also find that the children's superego integration is furthered when we make them more aware of the "loving" inner voice and raised self-esteem at times when they succeed in achieving their ideals; for example, the parent or teacher may comment on the child's pleased expression on completing a hard assignment or conforming to a "difficult" rule. "You look so happy. Perhaps something inside you told you what a good job you did."

Since it is so hard to come to terms with the new superego, it is not surprising that children use a variety of defense mechanisms to ward off the intense anxiety and painful guilt feelings. As mentioned earlier, Anna Freud (1936) noted in this connection the defense of identification with the aggressor, which can lead to unexpected angry attacks. Projection and denial are also not uncommon, nor are their conscious counterparts—tattling, shifting the blame onto others, and lying. Perhaps the most widely used mechanism in this age group is externalization of the superego to ward off internal conflict (Brodey, 1965; A. Freud, 1965; Novick and Kelly, 1970), often combined with a need to seek punishment. This combination of mechanisms is similar to that seen in Freud's description (1916b) of the adult criminality arising from a sense of guilt.

The case of Jimmy illustrates the use of these defenses and how his parents helped him to become more aware of them and to achieve better mastery of his conflicts.

Case 1

Jimmy was a very "good" first grader, always well behaved in class, somewhat timid, and easily hurt by the least unkind remark, but fairly glowing when praised and appreciated. His work was generally very good, but sometimes he hurried through it to be "the first finished" and then felt guilty and crestfallen when he found that his rush had produced a few mistakes or sloppy writing. At home Jimmy was less concerned with criticism and perfection, and enjoyed his activities and relationships with the family. Every now and then, however, Jimmy became quite "naughty" with his parents.

His "naughty" times appeared to start with minor disobediences, e.g., playing rambunctiously with a peer and not heeding the first call to come into the house, or mishaps such as accidentally spilling a dish. Instead of an apology or an effort to put matters right, Jimmy would at such times become inappropriately angry and provocative. He defied his parents' admonitions and requests, loudly proclaimed how little he cared about their expectations, and insisted that he would do just as he pleased. When his parents were very firm, and especially when they sent him to his room or instituted a sanction, Jimmy's outburst eventually subsided; but when they tried to reason with him or kindly disregarded his misbehavior, his naughtiness crescendoed as he yelled abusively, sometimes hit out, or caused minor damage to things. Usually these episodes subsided in a few hours, but they could also continue for several days, with intermittent outbursts and provocations. At these times Jimmy also became much more tense and worried about school, fearing that he was "dumb" and that the others would not like him.

Jimmy's parents began to tell him that he tried to give them his conscience at these troubled times and wanted them to be angry at him and punish him, perhaps because he felt bad about himself. Would it not be better to be his own boss and let himself know what he felt he had done wrong? They added that then he would be able to get himself in control again, would not have to make others punish him at home or worry about not doing well at school. This helped Jimmy to cut short his "naughty" episodes. Closer observation showed that the incidents which precipitated his outbursts were either displacements from masturbatory concerns or "confessions" of masturbatory indulgence, but this was not discussed with him. In time he was able to cope better with his inner conflict and his behavioral disturbance subsided.

It is tempting for the environment to fall in with the child's defense, either by fulfilling the assigned superego role of harsh disapproval and punishment or by attempting to counteract it by lowered expectations and increased reassurances of love. Both approaches fail to help the child with his developmental struggle, both tend to perpetuate and intensify the use of the defense mechanism, and both may add further pathological elements, e.g., stimulation of regressive sadomasochistic strivings in the case of harsh punishments, and a failure to develop age-appropriate behavioral self-controls and skills in the case of permissiveness. In some instances these forms of environmental mishandling may constitute a developmental interference (Nagera, 1966a) and contribute to pathological exaggerations of developmental conflicts or to the establishment of maladaptive character traits. Anna Freud (1936) noted that identification with the aggressor can also lead to a specific characterological pathology if the use of this defense mechanism fails to be supplanted by a more mature internalization of the superego.

Pathological Formations Arising from Phase-Appropriate Conflicts

Pathological exaggerations of developmental conflicts are rarely explicable in simple terms. Internal and external, past and present factors interact in complex patterns. Of special significance in their onset and resolution are the child's general personality characteristics—mastery of anxiety, frustration tolerance, sublimation potential, and progressive versus regressive tendencies. Other important factors include developmental interferences such as specific stressful experiences, unhelpful educational handling, and lack of age-appropriate relationships with the parents—the role of the father in this developmental phase is of particular importance. In addition, conflicts resulting from the normal, partial libidinal regression may be complicated by fixation points at earlier levels, and, by the same token, earlier conflicts may cast their shadow on the child's management of the internal stresses of latency.

Whereas difficulties in this category may take many forms,

an example of pathological use of the defense of externalization may serve as an illustration and provide a comparison with the preceding case of Jimmy, in whom manifestations of the same defense were within the range of normality. With Steven, described below, the pathological exaggeration of his developmental conflict was not due to poor educational management; instead it resulted primarily from the child's failure to mediate pathologically harsh superego demands and to tolerate the resulting anxiety.

Case 2

Steven was a handsome boy of almost 6 when he entered Hanna Perkins Kindergarten. He had been well prepared for this new venture and had shown by his behavior during the previous year that he was emotionally and intellectually ready for it, with signs of beginning latency development. It was therefore quite disconcerting for everyone when Steven, almost from the first day, allied himself with the most aggressive and disobedient boy in the class; he followed the latter in disruptive behavior, initiated trouble on his own, and seduced others to join him. Impervious to the teachers' admonitions, he indulged in excited play and would not apply himself to learning tasks. His reply to reminders was, "There are no rules in kindergarten, and there are no rules inside me."

At home with his mother, however, Steven was well behaved and enjoyed many activities both with her and on his own. In treatment-via-the-parent interviews with Steven's mother it was learned that, during the summer, several experiences had served to heighten Steven's anxieties, culminating in a nightmare and a week of severe fears at bedtime just prior to his entry into kindergarten. When school began these worries disappeared, and his uncontrolled classroom behavior began. This behavior warded off the intolerable anxiety by externalizing his conflict and investing the teachers with his superego, which he could then defy or deny. Other defenses too played a part in his behavior—displacement, isolation, regression in relationships, turning passive into active, and, as we understood later, identification with the pathology of the paternal model. At first, however, Steven was helped to become aware of his defenses and to face his anxiety. As he improved at school, his night fears returned. His dictum of "no rules for me" could be related to his masturbation and oedipal fantasies; the fear of punishment was linked to his extremely harsh superego.

Steven's latency conflicts were greatly exacerbated by the fact that he had experienced his father's debilitating illness and subsequent death when Steven was 3 years old. He had mastered this major stress in relation to the conflicts of the earlier levels and had been able to progress in his development. During early latency the stressful experiences again represented a developmental interference in the form of a threatening superego introject. With his mother's help and that of the school, Steven could modify his inner turmoil and improve his outward adjustment.

Observers of Steven's school behavior at the start of kindergarten could have been easily misled into thinking that he either had not entered latency or had regressed from it instinctually and structurally. Indeed, children who use externalization to a pathological extent are often misdiagnosed as not having achieved latency and are treated as though they had as yet no superego. Actually, cases of complete arrest or structural regression are quite rare and usually manifest widespread, additional pathology. When a latency-age child exhibits apparently guiltless aggressive or sexual behavior, it is therefore quite likely that such difficulties are of a defensive nature. The consistent use of externalization brings about a measure of functional ego regression (e.g., in reality testing), of drive regression, and of regression in object relationships (e.g., direction of aggression outward rather than inward). These regressions, however, are of a secondary nature and differ from the more serious conditions of arrest or structural regression.

Steven's experiences with his father's illness, death, and consequent absence during early latency constituted a particularly stressful interference. It highlights the special importance of the father at this stage of development. His physical or emotional absence, his attitude to the child's growing up, the nature of his relationships, his personality as a model for identification—these and a myriad of other aspects deeply affect early latency in children of both sexes. The following case vignettes illustrate some of these vicissitudes.

Case 3

John had worked through many of his earlier difficulties during his attendance at the Hanna Perkins Nursery School and was anticipating kindergarten with a healthy mixture of pleasure and apprehension. He was keen to further his beginning knowledge of the 3 Rs, regaled his parents with accounts of "My teacher said . . . ," and, in line with his new superego development, took all the rules seriously and worried about being criticized for the least imperfection. After some time, however, John's eager work came to a halt and gave way to complaints that work was no fun and that he only wanted to play with nursery-school-type toys. His striving for success was replaced by an "I-don't-care" attitude to school activities. He told boastful stories of things he would do or own when he grew up. He often peppered these tales with items of exotic information he had picked up in reading adult science articles with his father and used them to convey an aura of supremacy vis-à-vis his peers. Increasingly his lowered self-esteem and guilt showed in berating other children and inviting the teachers' controls and their punishment of his unruly behavior.

In treatment-via-the-parent we explored several factors underlying his trouble; some were internal, e.g., his regression in the face of unattainable ego ideals; some were external, e.g., his mother's reluctance to relinquish the close prelatency relationship with her son. The most crucial aspect, however, proved to be the father's unconscious attitude to his firstborn's developmental step. The father was very fond and proud of John. He verbalized high hopes for his son's future and supported John's fantasies—for example, that he would become a millionaire if he wanted to. But the father was openly opposed to the mother's and the teachers' realistic demands for John in the present. "He is just a child. The hardship of the world comes all too soon. Let him play and dream and have fun." The father failed to see that grandiose fantasies did not bolster John's self-esteem and that neglect of the necessary ego skills jeopardized John's chances of age-adequate achievements. It was possible for the father to gain insight into the fact that, for John, this leniency represented a paternal prohibition against real competition: "You can pretend to be grown-up like me or even bigger than me, but in reality I want you to remain little and incompetent." With much honest and painful soul-searching the father changed his attitude, discussed it with John, and was able to enjoy his son's resumed application to the daily tasks of a schoolboy.

Case 4

Brian's early latency difficulties manifested themselves in apparent lack of ambition, an unwillingness to work at tasks in the Hanna Perkins Kindergarten, and indulgence in excited cops-and-robbers games with peers. Treatment-via-the-parent revealed Brian's underlying low self-esteem, expectation of scholastic failure, and distrust that anyone would appreciate him as a friend if he offered himself without seductive excitement. Intelligence tests had shown Brian to be of superior intellect, and our knowledge of him in the nursery years had proven his capabilities.

Brian's relationship with his father contained many positive elements but, already during the phallic and oedipal phases, had been weighted by the father's exhibitionistic qualities and tendency to intimidate. With the beginning of latency, Brian showed interest in the father's hobbies, which the father greatly welcomed. When Brian wanted to learn something about photography, the father bought him a rather complex camera; when Brian thought he would like to make music, he was given a violin. Brian's own unrealistic standards were thus fostered by what he perceived as the father's expectations for him. His dismal failures with the proffered equipment intensified his inner tensions to an intolerable extent and forced him to give up all attempts at mastery. In addition, and correctly so, Brian understood that his father's attitude represented an unconscious scathing mockery and condemnation to defeat: "So you think you can do as I do? Just look how inadequate you are at performing with adult equipment." Brian was greatly helped when the father could more appropriately ally himself with the boy's ego and support its attempts to mediate the internal demands, instead of reinforcing his harsh superego.

Case 5

Anne, a bright, pretty first grader, was a great source of annoyance to her teacher. Ironically, Anne's interest and fluency in reading were a major hurdle. Absorbed in books, she failed to attend to her other tasks, to hear instructions, or to respond to the requests of children and adults. As a result, she never knew what she should do in a given situation, created disruptions, and singled herself out by having to be told separately while everyone else waited and looked on. She made teacher and peers feel helpless, put upon, and exasperated, but she herself was unaware of her aggressive disregard for them. She met their reproaches and protests with feelings of deep hurt and privately took them as proof of her conviction that she was unloved and unlovable, which she voiced to her mother at home.

Among a number of factors contributing to Anne's difficulty, the most significant proved to be her current relationship with her father. During her earlier years he had maintained a stimulating interplay with her which, in spite of its complications, had made her feel loved and appreciated. With the passing of the oedipus complex this relationship largely ceased, but, unfortunately, nothing positive took its place. The father was unable to relate to Anne in a more neutral manner. Disinterested in her daily life and activities, his brief hours at home were increasingly filled with his work, and he ignored Anne's attempts to interrupt his reading and writing with her approaches. She interpreted his "rejection" of her as a punishment in line with her strict new conscience. Her guilt was further intensified by her anger at him and by her masturbatory activities and fantasies, which invaded her loneliness. Anne unconsciously dealt with her conflict by identifying with the father's attitude. With the aid of displacement and turning passive into active, she became the busy reader at school who made others feel helpless and unloved. At the same time she achieved the central position that eluded her at home.

Current stresses and phase-specific conflicts are frequently colored by those of earlier levels of development. With the children discussed above, for example, the father's role in early latency was intricately linked to his part in the child's oedipus complex. This, in turn, affected the form of its resolution and the nature of the superego internalizations.

The interaction of present and preceding phases is just as evident in phase-appropriate pathologies that stem from the partial instinctual regression of the postoedipal period. Fixation points appear to affect the extent of regression and the "choice" of level.

Regression to the anal-sadistic level is cited in the literature (Bornstein, 1951, 1953b; A. Freud, 1965) and linked to many normal phase-appropriate manifestations, as mentioned earlier. The case of Jeremy illustrates a pathological exaggeration and its relation to earlier difficulties.

Case 6

When Jeremy was almost 3 his mother sought help for his ongoing difficulty with toilet training. He had recently begun to smear his feces and provoked his mother with his unwillingness to cooperate with the cleanup.

A successful year of treatment-via-the-parent enabled us to learn of several underlying causes, among them Jeremy's reaction to the birth of a brother in his second year and, later, a regression from phallic competition with his father, with whom he shared the use of the bathroom. Jeremy then experienced a normal phallic and oedipal development and entered latency.

Around the age of 6, however, he found himself in considerable distress. He had trouble going to sleep and instituted a number of bedtime rituals. During the day he often ruminated about death and plagued his parents with questions about it which they could never answer to his satisfaction. His ambivalence conflict was heightened when his parents were absent for the evening or when he had managed to sleep over with relatives. He then spent much of the time feeling unloved or unlovable, accused himself of having neglected some task or other, or worried about everyone's safety. Illness in the family exacerbated Jeremy's concerns. With the help of maturation and his parents' educational support, his difficulties subsided in the later phase of latency.

As mentioned earlier, regression to the phallic-narcissistic phase is normally found in boys and girls, but it tends to be marked or pathologically exaggerated with children who have experienced earlier phallic-narcissistic difficulties. Some children's oedipal relationships are foreshortened by an extensive phallic-narcissistic phase. They enter latency almost directly from that level, which affects the nature of their superego and characterological development (R.A. Furman, 1976) and intensifies their regressive concerns.

Case 7

Beginning in the latter part of her third year, Linda suffered from severe evening fears and nightmares. In treatment-via-the-parent it was learned that Linda's symptoms were caused primarily by her reaction to the discovery of sexual differences, a discovery that occurred when she was with a babysitter shortly after her sister's birth. With her parents' help she gained better understanding and mastery and later formed a very close and exclusive oedipal relationship with her father. Her earlier phallic difficulties, however, seemed to heighten her hurt at his "rejection" of her infantile sexual wishes. They also contributed to a harsh superego and to an instinctual regression to the phallic-narcissistic level in early latency. In that period she sometimes looked dejected and withdrew into herself. She refused to wear feminine clothes and avoided girls' games. She followed the boys at school but felt disliked by them. Her interest in schoolwork diminished, and she put out little effort to achieve scholastically. Despite very good intelligence, she felt she was stupid. On a few occasions she stole small items from a boy's locker or the teacher's desk. She did not use them, stored them so as to be found out, and readily returned them. But even a gentle confrontation mortified her. Her family's understanding and helpful handling enabled Linda to overcome some of her difficulties, but her feeling of intellectual inadequacy improved only in late latency.

Pathological Formations That Are Not Phase-Appropriate

A latency child placed in this group has neurotic conflicts which, however, are not incapacitating to further development. In early latency it is sometimes difficult to differentiate between pathological phase-specific manifestations and isolated neurotic conflicts, because the normal libidinal regression in this phase may make a current conflict appear as though it belongs to an earlier level. Some neurotic symptoms are carried over from the preceding developmental levels; others originate during early latency. A very detailed history sometimes helps in determining the exact time of onset. In some cases isolated neurotic conflicts from earlier levels also interact with ongoing conflicts. Fixation points, arrests, and regressions play a part (Nagera, 1964). For example, Linda's previously described feeling of intellectual inadequacy in relation to schoolwork (Case 7) may be viewed as a neurotic symptom related to earlier phallic and oedipal conflicts rather than as a pathological manifestation of conflicts during early latency. Her apparently normal intervening oedipal period suggests that the latency conflicts were the primary cause of her learning difficulty. However, the symptom may represent an interaction of phallic and early latency conflicts. The following case illustrates more clearly how conflicts stemming from previous developmental levels may manifest themselves during early latency.

Case 8

Billy suffered from projectile vomiting as a baby. This was a stressful experience for him and for his mother. It necessitated his always being fed twice, as the first feed was always thrown up. Although this physical condition subsided without corrective surgery by the end of his first year, oral manifestations accompanied his subsequent development and, at each level, linked up with phase-specific conflicts. Billy was an unusually messy eater throughout his preschool years and maintained a very close link between food and his mother, so that his eating or not eating reflected his ambivalence. In early latency he felt very guilty about lapses in table manners and worried that his eating too much caused a slight overweight. From toddlerhood on he chewed at his clothes in anger and distress. This difficulty also became connected with his masturbation conflict: periodic recurrence of clothes chewing came to represent both confession of masturbation and its displacement. In his earlier years Billy always reacted to new situations, e.g., the start of nursery school, with episodes of vomiting. In kindergarten he suffered only slight stomachaches at such times, but his characterological equivalent of ejecting the first feeding and taking in the second was still marked: When faced with a new experience, he would always angrily berate and reject it and declare his total unwillingness to have any part of it; following such vehement protest he could then attempt to deal with it and usually achieved mastery. Billy's very loud voice and flow of angry verbal abuse could also be traced back to early oral elements. Whereas all these manifestations at times distressed Billy and others, they did not affect his overall progressive development.

Neurosis and Character Disorders as the Outcome of Rigidly Internalized Conflicts

Freud (1909b, 1918, 1923c, 1926a, 1939) considered latency the determining factor for the origin of the neuroses and linked the onset of obsessional neurosis in particular to early latency. Whereas neurotic disturbances occur frequently in preschoolers, and the crest of the infantile neurosis is associated with the oedipal phase, early latency is the time when childhood neuroses and character disorders can be seen to crystallize into lasting pathologies. In these cases a metapsychological assessment of all aspects of the child's personality (A. Freud, 1965) shows that the neurotic manifestations are not isolated areas in a maturing personality, but rather that the regression and fixation of the libido have become so widespread and so rigid as to preclude forward movement and that the compromise formations (symptoms and character traits) constitute the child's main instinctual gratification. Owing to the relative strength of the ego in latency and especially to its intense defensive measures, the child's manifest behavior may show less turmoil than during the earlier phases, and he may also suffer less as anxiety is warded off more effectively. However, since the conflicts within and between the different structures of the personality are now unconscious, they can no longer be modified either by the child's own endeavors or by environmental measures. There is always a chance that the pubertal upsurge of instinctual strivings may correct the inner balance and force libidinal progression (A. Freud, 1945), but even in such instances improvement may be only temporary and the pathological libidinal constellations may become reestablished after adolescence. For these reasons, and in contrast to the disturbances in the preceding diagnostic categories, with neuroses and character disorders in early latency therapeutic intervention is indicated, and psychoanalysis is the treatment of choice.

The psychoanalytic literature contains many accounts of the treatment of such cases, most of them focused on special technical or theoretical problems, but all of them illustrate various types and forms of neurotic and characterological disturbances. (The following is a sample of articles from the most readily available publications: Bornstein, 1946, 1953a; Hall, 1946; Daunton, 1967; Fraiberg, 1967; E. Furman, 1967; R. A. Furman, 1967; Hamm, 1967; Shane, 1967; Novick, 1970; Evans, 1975; Bernstein, 1976; Scharfman, 1976.)

Arrests and Regressions in Drives with Parallels in Ego and Superego Development

For present purposes I shall discuss the disturbances in this category under two headings: (1) delinquent or psychopathic pathology; (2) atypical disorders.

Delinquent or psychopathic pathology. When the child reaches early latency, he is expected to exercise a considerable amount of behavioral self-control within and without the family. It is assumed that he is capable of respecting the rules of his environment, not only with the help of a supervising adult but to an extent, through the guidance of his own conscience. When the child's development has failed in this respect or suffers internal interference, early latency is the time for these disturbances to become manifest.

Starting with Aichhorn (1925), psychoanalytic investigators of dissociality have stressed certain features of the antisocial character. According to Friedlander (1945, 1947), it "shows the structure of a mind where instinctive urges remain unmodified and therefore appear in great strength, [and] where the ego, still under the dominance of the pleasure-principle and not supported by an independent super-ego, is too weak to gain control over the onrush of demands arising in the id" (1947, p. 94). Internal and external factors in the earliest years of emotional development are responsible: A disturbance in the mother-child relationship during the first 5 years, particularly disruptions through separation, rejection, or inconsistency, interfere with the young child's developing ability to modify his instinctual urges, to fuse libidinal and aggressive drives, and to acquire the capacity for identification (Bowlby, 1944; A. Freud, 1949a, 1949b). Anna Freud (1965) also stresses quantitative factors, i.e., the variable relative strength of the ego vis-à-vis the id, and notes the causative connection between "failure in higher ego development . . . and . . . the large number of delinquents and criminals who . . . are found to be of primitive, infantile mentality, retarded, deficient, defective, with low intelligence quotients" (p. 178). All authors, in addition, stress the crucial role of both parents as models for identification: "dissociality and criminality on the part of the parents are incorporated into the child's superego" (A. Freud, 1965, p. 178).

With the beginning of latency, the potentially delinquent character formation becomes consolidated and "it will depend on the various factors exerting their influence in the latency period and puberty, whether delinquent behavior becomes manifest or not" (Friedlander, 1947, p. 94). Among these secondary factors Friedlander lists school, companionship, use of leisure, and poverty, but she stresses that these influences do not of themselves bring about dissocial behavior. Friedlander's case examples (1947) well illustrate these points.

Delinquent and psychopathic disorders of this characterological nature have to be distinguished from other disturbances with manifest dissocial behavior. Aichhorn (1925) points out that in early latency even children with a normal psychic apparatus, unimpaired relationships, and capacity for identifications can become delinquent when the superego takes over the parent's delinquent features. In early latency we see this quite often to a minor extent in otherwise well-developed children. They do not show delinquent behavior in prelatency and the parents' delinquencies are usually hidden from the view of those outside the family. Only close scrutiny reveals that the child's difficulties in early latency represent an identification.

Case 9

Danny is a case in point. He had been known to us since he was a toddler and had attended the Hanna Perkins Nursery School for two years. Although he exhibited a number of developmental difficulties at each stage, he progressed satisfactorily. Early superego precursors were noted to be rather harsh and contributed to Danny's low self-esteem. During early latency in the Hanna Perkins Kindergarten, Danny showed some new behavior patterns. He lied in order to cover up minor wrongdoings; he made up tall tales in order to impress his peers; he occasionally stole small objects from other children's lockers and disregarded school rules. He felt no guilt about these acts and resented reprimands, although at other times his superego was very much in evidence.

When, in treatment-via-the-parent, we explored possible reasons for his troubles, Danny himself drew his mother's attention to his father's almost identical delinquencies. The mother knew them well but had tried to ignore her husband's failings and hoped they went unnoticed by the children. Discussion with both parents brought the matter into the open. The father felt bad about his delinquencies. The parents from then on acknowledged the father's difficulties, and the father told Danny that he hoped his son would take on only his good qualities, not his troubles. This helped Danny a great deal in modifying his as yet fluid inner standards, and his dissocial episodes subsided.

Delinquent behavior stemming from a sense of guilt was referred to earlier in the context of the developmental conflicts and defenses of early latency. The difficulty in these cases is caused by a structural conflict within the personality and is therefore essentially of a neurotic nature. In latency it is particularly related to the child's masturbation conflict (A. Freud, 1965). It may manifest itself as a pathological exaggeration of a developmental conflict or form part of a neurosis or character disorder. As such, it has been discussed by several authors (Freud, 1916b; Aichhorn, 1925; Friedlander, 1947).

Anna Freud (1949b) described two particular types of dissocial behavior which not infrequently manifest themselves in early latency and result from a pathological resolution of the struggle against masturbation and its attendant oedipal and preoedipal fantasies. In the milder form of these maladjustments, the child may be "moody, anxious, resentful, inhibited, and apparently unresponsive" (p. 199). He may complain of being "picked on" by teachers and peers or withdraw into his own fantasy world and fail to avail himself of social and intellectual opportunities. In these cases the child's attitude to the school stems from his oedipal and preoedipal fantasies, which now distort his view of the teacher as earlier they colored his picture of the parents. His unhappy emotional life and maladaptive behavior at school represent both defensive and gratifying aspects of the transferred primitive fantasies.

A much more severe form of this type of social maladjustment results when the child's fantasies are not merely thought and felt but acted out. This happens when the child's struggle against the bodily act of masturbation and against the content of the attendant fantasies is too successful. Deprived of all bodily gratification, the full force of the masturbatory fantasy is displaced "from the realm of sex-life into the realm of ego-activities" (A. Freud, 1949b, p. 203) and leads to dissocial and psychopathic behavior. Its specific form depends on the nature of the masturbation fantasy it serves to dramatize: children with passive-feminine or masochistic fantasies succeed in getting bullied, attacked, and persecuted; sadistic fantasies tend to be acted out by torturing the helpless or by watching their maltreatment by others, if scopophilic fantasies play a part; exhibitionistic fantasies are gratified by means of compulsively taking center stage as hero or, negatively, as the fool. Particularly disruptive are those children whose fantasies derive from their having, at earlier levels of development, observed intercourse, which they had perceived in the light of their own crude pregenital urges. Such children revel in constant fights with peers, provocations of adults, and defiance of rules and are most successful in engaging adults and children alike in battles at their own level. Whatever the fantasy, "the monotony and repetetiveness of the child's behavior correspond to the endless monotony of the crude fantasies which accompany masturbatory acts; the compulsive and periodic character of the acting out corresponds to the periodic need for masturbation which arises from the id and appears in the child's ego as an unrelated foreign body" (p. 203).

These disturbances do not subside with maturation nor can they be alleviated by changes in the child's environment. Psychoanalysis is the treatment of choice.

Atypical disturbances. Anna Freud (1965) and Daunton (1969) use the terms "borderline" and "psychotic" in this diagnostic category.[2] I prefer the term "atypical" because I consider the other terms misleading in the context of childhood disorders—"borderline" because it cannot be clearly distinguished from "psychotic" (Pine, 1974) and "psychotic" because it suggests an identity with the quite dissimilar adult psychoses, which do not occur before prepuberty. Rosenfeld (1977) recently expressed a similar opinion. By any name, however, children in this diagnostic category show severe disturbances. In spite of extensive and intensive research, it is as yet not possible to define them fully in metapsychological terms. Since it is well beyond the scope of this chapter, I shall not cite any of the numerous contributions or discuss divergences in scientific opinion but limit the description to a few widely accepted factors.

Thus, Daunton (1969) notes that in addition to arrests and regression of drives, ego, and superego "children in this group show a lack of the usual progression in drive development (coexistence of all pregenital drives in almost equal measure). In the area of ego functioning they show particular impairment in the synthesizing and reality-testing functions and in the capacity for secondary-process thinking" (p. 214). Analysts are generally agreed that the genetic factors are to be found in the first 2 to 3 years of a child's life and that the disturbance, however varied in individual manifestations, causation, and severity, affects all parts of the personality.

[2] Daunton used the terms "borderline" and "psychotic" with the consent of the Hanna Perkins Nursery research group of which I am a member. None of us, however, felt satisfied with this terminology at the time, and our entire group has since then adopted the descriptive term "atypical."

It is not a disorder that originates in latency, nor do latency conflicts contribute to the basic nature of the disturbance. Early latency does, however, sometimes serve as a crucible in revealing more clearly some pathologies of personality functioning which may have been difficult to assess during the earlier years. This concerns particularly such areas as the capacity of the ego to neutralize energy for functional use, to sublimate, and to achieve secondary autonomy. In relation to the superego it concerns the capacity for advanced, as opposed to primitive, forms of internalization and the ego's capacity to mediate tensions vis-à-vis the new structure. These aspects are not the only ones, nor can they be isolated from other internal and external factors. However, latency development is characterized by so many ego tasks that failures and deficiencies stand out more starkly than in the preschool years, when the parental figure legitimately complemented the child's personality, when it was normal for some ego regression to occur, and when functions were still expected to be labile. Early latency becomes the period for differential diagnostic assessment, especially in the milder atypical cases and in those which have responded well to treatment during the earlier years and have shown improvement, as was the case with Vivienne, described below.

Case 10

Vivienne, whose birth her parents anticipated with pleasure, was good looking, physically well developed, and intellectually well endowed. She experienced, however, a great deal of difficulty at every emotional level and her mastery of developmental tasks was impaired.

The parents received professional help with Vivienne's upbringing from the time she was a toddler. With much effort, Vivienne's troubles with eating, sleeping, toileting, fears, aggressive behavior, etc. subsided sufficiently to allow progressive development, but the manifestations of earlier levels persisted along with new conflicts. Typically, anxiety situations of old retained their full force for her in the present and could never be overcome. Motility and speech, however, started somewhat early; she was quite adept at age-appropriate play and skills, and there were signs of special gifts, particularly in music. She always functioned much better when she could rely on the full attention of a loved adult. She could never bear to be alone and found the turmoil of a group of people equally distressing. At such times she would become uncontrollably excited or aggressive. Vivienne enrolled in a small, structured, and individually attuned kindergarten group in which she did quite well and showed signs of ego strength in better tolerating stimulation, frustration, and anxiety and in which she also made good strides in academic learning.

The following year Vivienne left this sheltered and supportive school environment to attend public school while coping internally with the beginnings of latency development. Within a short time the stress proved too much. She was beset by fears of imaginary attackers, fiercely criticized everyone, and could not tolerate or respond to reprimands, while her behavior constantly invited punishment. When these defensive measures failed to enable her to deal with her instinctualized and poorly integrated superego, she regressed structurally and instinctually. Reaction-formations of cleanliness, pity, and modesty gave way to messiness, sadistic attacks on others, and crudely exhibitionistic behavior. She ate greedily but was also finicky in her choice of foods and overwhelmed with disgust at times, as thinly disguised cannibalistic fantasies threatened to force their way into consciousness. Schoolwork lost interest for her. She tried to impress others and bolster her own self-esteem with items of pseudoknowledge, tall tales, and self-aggrandizing fantasies. She often had difficulty in knowing where her own person ended and that of others began, as when she barged or melted into people or confused what she or others did and said. Her speech was incorrect, indistinct at times, and full of mispronounced words and some neologisms. Reality testing became instinctualized, as she keenly observed selective aspects for sexual or aggressive gratification and shut out or altered anything that would have caused unpleasure. Similarly, all other ego functions lost secondary autonomy at times of stress, as did her many beginning sublimations; e.g., reading, which earlier she had enjoyed for ego gains, was now neglected or used for instinctual stimulation via certain comic strips.

Vivienne's personality could maintain itself in the earlier

years with the help of adult egos but proved unequal to the tasks of latency, which required more internal stability and independence.

There are three remaining diagnostic categories: psychosomatic disorders; primary organic deficiencies or very early deprivations leading to defective or retarded personalities; and destructive processes at work (organic, toxic, psychological, and so on) effecting a disruption of mental growth. None of these is related to the phase of latency or affected by it, except in the case of psychosomatic disorders, in which the nature of the psychic factors is individually so variable that generalizations are inevitably inaccurate.

Closing Statement

This detailed review of early latency conflicts and pathology may leave the reader with the impression that this developmental phase is particularly fraught with hazards and hardships and must be difficult for children to enjoy, not to mention the adults who by choice or necessity associate with them. Such assumptions would be quite erroneous. Latency is usually, and with justification, the part of childhood which is rather fondly remembered—though this is perhaps more true of middle and late latency than of the early period. It is a time of relative inner and outer mastery, with energy to spare for exploring the new horizons of reality and for playing, and with newly won ease with the derivatives of the inner world, which no longer threatens to take over. It is a time when a child can be an easy friend and congenial companion for peers and adults alike, with few of the heart-rending heights and depths of emotion which tend to accompany the earlier infantile and later adolescent relationships.

References

Aichhorn, A. (1925), *Wayward Youth*. New York: Viking, 1935.
Alpert, A. (1941), The latency period. *Amer. J. Orthopsychiat.*, 2:126–133.
Becker, T., rep. (1965), Panel: Latency. *J. Amer. Psychoanal. Assn.*, 13:584–590.

Bernstein, I. (1976), Masochistic reactions in a latency-age girl. *J. Amer. Psychoanal. Assn.*, 24:589–608.

Blanchard, P. (1946), Psychoanalytic contributions to the problems of reading disabilities. *The Psychoanalytic Study of the Child*, 2:163–187. New York: International Universities Press.

——— (1953), Masturbation fantasies of children and adolescents. *Bull. Phila. Assn. Psychoanal.*, 3:25–38.

Bornstein, B. (1946), Hysterical twilight states in an eight-year-old child. *The Psychoanalytic Study of the Child*, 2:229–240. New York: International Universities Press.

——— (1949), The analysis of a phobic child: Some problems of theory and technique in child analysis. *The Psychoanalytic Study of the Child*, 3/4:181–226. New York: International Universities Press.

——— (1951), On latency. *The Psychoanalytic Study of the Child*, 6:279–285. New York: International Universities Press.

——— (1953a), Fragment of an analysis of an obsessional child: The first six months of analysis. *The Psychoanalytic Study of the Child*, 8:313–332. New York: International Universities Press.

——— (1953b), Masturbation in the latency period. *The Psychoanalytic Study of the Child*, 8:65–71. New York: International Universities Press.

Bowlby, J. (1944), Forty-four juvenile thieves. *Internat. J. Psychiat.*, 25:19–53.

Brodey, W.M. (1965), On the dynamics of narcissism: I. Externalization and early ego development. *The Psychoanalytic Study of the Child*, 20:165–193. New York: International Universities Press.

Burlingham, D.T. (1945), The fantasy of having a twin. *The Psychoanalytic Study of the Child*, 1:205–210. New York: International Universities Press.

Clower, V.L. (1976), Theoretical implications in current views of masturbation in latency girls. *J. Amer. Psychoanal. Assn.*, 24(Suppl.):109–125.

Daunton, E. (1967), Some aspects of ego and super-ego resistance in the case of an asthmatic child. In: *The Child Analyst at Work*, ed. E.R. Geleerd. New York: International Universities Press, pp. 206–228.

——— (1969), Diagnosis. In: *The Therapeutic Nursery School*, ed. R.A. Furman & A. Katan. New York: International Universities Press, pp. 204–214.

Edgcumbe, R., & Burgner, M.A. (1975), Differentiation between preoedipal and oedipal aspects of phallic development. *The Psychoanalytic Study of the Child*, 30:161–180. New Haven: Yale University Press.

Evans, R. (1975), "Hysterical materialization" in the analysis of a latency girl. *The Psychoanalytic Study of the Child*, 30:307–340. New Haven: Yale University Press.

Ferenczi, S. (1913), Stages in the development of the sense of reality. In: *Sex in Psycho-Analysis*. New York: Basic Books, 1950, pp. 213–239.

Fraiberg, S. (1966), Further considerations of the role of transference in latency. *The Psychoanalytic Study of the Child*, 21:213–236. New York: International Universities Press.

——— (1967), The analysis of an eight-year-old girl with epilepsy. In: *The Child Analyst at Work*, ed. E.R. Geleerd. New York: International Universities Press, pp. 229–287.

——— (1972), Some characteristics of genital arousal and discharge in latency girls. *The Psychoanalytic Study of the Child*, 27:439–475. New York: Quadrangle.

Freud, A. (1922), Beating fantasies and daydreams. In: *The Writings of Anna Freud: Vol. 1*. New York: International Universities Press, 1974, pp. 137–157.

——— (1930), The latency period. Lecture 3 of 4 lectures on psychoanalysis for teachers and parents. In: *The Writings of Anna Freud: Vol. 1*. New York: International Universities Press, 1974, pp. 105–120.

——— (1936), *The Ego and the Mechanisms of Defense*. New York: International Universities Press, 1946.

——— (1945), Indications for child analysis. In: *The Writings of Anna Freud: Vol. 4*. New York: International Universities Press, 1968, pp. 3–38.

——— (1949a), Aggression in relation to emotional development: Normal and pathological. *The Psychoanalytic Study of the Child*, 3/4:37–42. New York: International Universities Press.

——— (1949b), Certain types and stages of social maladjustment. In: *Searchlights on Delinquency*, ed. K.R. Eissler. New York: International Universities Press, pp. 193–204.

——— (1965), *Normality and Pathology in Childhood*. New York: International Universities Press.

——— (1970), The symptomatology of childhood. *The Psychoanalytic Study of the Child*, 25:19–44. New York: International Universities Press.

Freud, S. (1905a), Fragment of an analysis of a case of hysteria. *Standard Edition*, 7:3–124. London: Hogarth Press, 1953.

——— (1905b), Three essays on the theory of sexuality. *Standard Edition*, 7:130–243. London: Hogarth Press, 1953.

——— (1908), Character and anal eroticism. *Standard Edition*, 9:167–176. London: Hogarth Press, 1959.

——— (1909a), Family romances. *Standard Edition*, 9:235–241. London: Hogarth Press, 1959.

——— (1909b), Notes upon a case of obsessional neurosis. *Standard Edition*, 10:153–250. London: Hogarth Press, 1955.

——— (1911), Formulations on the two principles of mental functioning. *Standard Edition*, 12:213–226. London: Hogarth Press, 1958.

——— (1914), Some reflections on schoolboy psychology. *Standard Edition*, 13:241–244. London: Hogarth Press, 1955.

——— (1916a), Introductory lecture 21. *Standard Edition*, 16:320–338. London: Hogarth Press, 1963.

——— (1916b), Some character-types met with in psycho-analytic work. *Standard Edition*, 14:311–333. London: Hogarth Press, 1957.

——— (1918), From the history of an infantile neurosis. *Standard Edition*, 17:3–122. London: Hogarth Press, 1955.

——— (1919), A child is being beaten: A contribution to the study of the origin of sexual perversions. *Standard Edition*, 17:175–204. London: Hogarth Press, 1955.

——— (1921), Group psychology and the analysis of the ego. *Standard Edition*, 18:67–144. London: Hogarth Press, 1955.

——— (1923a), The ego and the id. *Standard Edition*, 19:3–68. London: Hogarth Press, 1961.

——— (1923b), The infantile genital organization: An interpolation into the theory of sexuality. *Standard Edition*, 19:141–148. London: Hogarth Press, 1961.

——— (1923c), Two encyclopaedia articles. *Standard Edition*, 18:235–262. London: Hogarth Press, 1955.
——— (1924a), The dissolution of the Oedipus complex. *Standard Edition*, 19:173–182. London: Hogarth Press, 1961.
——— (1924b), A short account of psycho-analysis. *Standard Edition*, 19:191–212. London: Hogarth Press, 1961.
——— (1925), An autobiographical study. *Standard Edition*, 20:77–178. London: Hogarth Press, 1959.
——— (1926a), Inhibitions, symptoms and anxiety. *Standard Edition*, 20:77–178. London: Hogarth Press, 1959.
——— (1926b), Psycho-analysis. *Standard Edition*, 20:259–270. London: Hogarth Press, 1959.
——— (1926c), The question of lay analysis. *Standard Edition*, 20:179–258. London: Hogarth Press, 1959.
——— (1939), Moses and monotheism. *Standard Edition*, 23:3–140. London: Hogarth Press, 1964.
——— (1940), An outline of psycho-analysis. *Standard Edition*, 23:141–208. London: Hogarth Press, 1967.
Friedlander, K. (1942), Children's books and their function in latency and prepuberty. *American Imago*, 3:129–150.
——— (1945), The formation of the antisocial character. *The Psychoanalytic Study of the Child*, 1:189–204. New York: International Universities Press.
——— (1947), *The Psycho-Analytical Approach to Juvenile Delinquency*. New York: International Universities Press.
——— (1949), Latent delinquency and ego development. In: *Searchlights on Delinquency*, ed. K.R. Eissler. New York: International Universities Press, pp. 205–215.
Fries, M.E. (1959), Review of the literature of the latency period, with special emphasis on the so-called "normal case." In: *Readings in Psychoanalytic Psychology*, ed. M. Levitt. New York: Appleton-Century-Crofts, pp. 56–69.
Furman, E. (1967), The latency child as an active participant in the analytic work. In: *The Child Analyst at Work*, ed. E.R. Geleerd. New York: International Universities Press, pp. 142–184.
——— (1969), Treatment via the mother. In: *The Therapeutic Nursery School*, ed. R.A. Furman & A. Katan. New York: International Universities Press, pp. 64–123.
——— (1977), On readiness for school. *N. Amer. Montessori Teachers' Assn. Quart.*, 2(3):28–34.
——— (1980), Early latency—normal and pathological aspects. In: *The Course of Life: Psychoanalytic Contributions Toward Understanding Personality Development, Vol. II: Latency, Adolescence and Youth*, ed. S.I. Greenspan & G.H. Pollock. Washington, D.C.: National Institute of Mental Health, pp. 1–32.
——— ed. (1986), Readiness for kindergarten. In: *What Nursery School Teachers Ask Us About*. Madison, Conn.: International Universities Press, pp. 207–233.
Furman, R.A. (1967), A technical problem: The child who has difficulty in controlling his behavior in analytic sessions. In: *The Child Analyst at Work*, ed. E.R. Geleerd. New York: International Universities Press, pp. 59–84.
——— (1976), Personal communication.

——— & Katan, A., eds. (1969), *The Therapeutic Nursery School*. New York: International Universities Press, pp. 299–305.

Goldings, H.J. (1974), Jump-rope rhymes and the rhythm of latency development in girls. *The Psychoanalytic Study of the Child*, 29:431–450. New Haven: Yale University Press.

Hall, J.W. (1946), The analysis of a case of night terror. *The Psychoanalytic Study of the Child*, 2:189–227. New York: International Universities Press.

Hamm, M. (1967), Some aspects of a difficult therapeutic (working) alliance. In: *The Child Analyst at Work*, ed. E.R. Geleerd. New York: International Universities Press, pp. 185–205.

Harley, M. (1962), The role of the dream in the analysis of a latency child. *J. Amer. Psychoanal. Assn.*, 10:271–288.

Jacobson, E. (1954), The self and the object world: Vicissitudes of their infantile cathexes and their influence on ideational and affective development. *The Psychoanalytic Study of the Child*, 9:75–127. New York: International Universities Press.

Kaplan, E.B. (1965), Reflections regarding psychomotor activities during the latency period. *The Psychoanalytic Study of the Child*, 20:220–238. New York: International Universities Press.

Kaplan, S., rep. (1957), Panel: The latency period. *J. Amer. Psychoanal. Assn.*, 5:525–538.

Katan, A. (1978), Personal communication.

Kestenberg, J.S. (1975), *Children and Parents: Psychoanalytic Studies in Development*. New York: Aronson.

Klein, E. (1945), The reluctance to go to school. *The Psychoanalytic Study of the Child*, 1:263–279. New York: International Universities Press.

——— (1949), Psychoanalytic aspects of school problems. *The Psychoanalyic Study of the Child*, 3/4:369–390. New York: International Universities Press.

Kolansky, H. (1967), Some psychoanalytic considerations on speech in normal development and psychopathology. *The Psychoanalytic Study of the Child*, 22:274–295. New York: International Universities Press.

Kramer, E. (1971), *Art as Therapy with Children*. New York: Schocken.

Lampl, H. (1953), The influence of biological and psychological factors upon the development of the latency period. In: *Drives, Affects, Behavior*, ed. R.M. Loewenstein. New York: International Universities Press, pp. 380–387.

Lampl–de Groot, J. (1950), On masturbation and its influence on general development. *The Psychoanalytic Study of the Child*, 5:153–174. New York: International Universities Press.

Maenchen, A. (1970), On the technique of child analysis in relation to stages of development. *The Psychoanalytic Study of the Child*, 25:175–208. New York: International Universities Press.

Meers, D.R. (1966), A diagnostic profile of psychopathology in a latency child. *The Psychoanalytic Study of the Child*, 21:483–526. New York: International Universities Press.

Nagera, H. (1964), On arrest in development, fixation, and regression. *The Psychoanalytic Study of the Child*, 19:222–239. New York: International Universities Press.

——— (1966a), Early Childhood Disturbances, the Infantile Neurosis and the

Adulthood Disturbances. *The Psychoanalytic Study of the Child*, Monograph 2. New York: International Universities Press.
——— (1966b), Sleep and its disturbances approached developmentally (Sleeping disturbances of the latency period). *The Psychoanalytic Study of the Child*, 21:393–447. New York: International Universities Press.
Novick, J. (1970), The vicissitudes of the "working alliance" in the analysis of a latency girl. *The Psychoanalytic Study of the Child*, 25:231–256. New York: International Universities Press.
——— & Kelly, K, (1970), Projection and externalization. *The Psychoanalytic Study of the Child*, 25:69–95. New York: International Universities Press.
Pearson, G.H.J. (1952), A survey of learning difficulties in children. *The Psychoanalytic Study of the Child*, 7:322–386. New York: International Universities Press.
——— (1966), The importance of peer relationship in the latency period. *Bull. Phila. Assn. Psychoanal.*, 16:109–121.
Peller, L.E. (1954), Libidinal phases, ego development and play. *The Psychoanalytic Study of the Child*, 9:178–198. New York: International Universities Press.
——— (1959), Daydreams and children's favorite books. *The Psychoanalytic Study of the Child*, 14:414–436. New York: International Universities Press.
Pine, F. (1914), On the concept "borderline" in children: A clinical essay. *The Psychoanalytic Study of the Child*, 29:341–368. New Haven: Yale University Press.
Rosenfeld, S. (1977), *Beyond the Infantile Neurosis*. London: Sara Rosenfeld Research Fund, Hampstead Clinic.
Sandler, J. (1960), On the concept of superego. *The Psychoanalytic Study of the Child*, 15:128–162. New York: International Universities Press.
——— Kennedy, H., & Tyson, R.L. (1975), Discussions on transference: The treatment situation and technique in child psychoanalysis. *The Psychoanalytic Study of the Child*, 30:409–442. New Haven: Yale University Press.
Sarnoff, C. (1976), Latency. New York: Aronson.
Scharfman, M.A. (1976), Perverse development in a young boy. *J. Amer. Psychoanal. Assn.*, 24:499–524.
Shane, M. (1967), Encopresis in a latency boy: An arrest along a developmental line. *The Psychoanalytic Study of the Child*, 22:296–303. New York: International Universities Press.
Smith, R.P. (1957), *"Where Did You Go?" "Out" "What Did You Do?" "Nothing."* New York: Norton.
Sperling, M. (1967), School phobias: Classification, dynamics and treatment. *The Psychoanalytic Study of the Child*, 22:375–401. New York: International Universities Press.
Widzer, M.E. (1977), The comic book superhero: A study of the family romance fantasy. *The Psychoanalytic Study of the Child*, 32:565–603. New Haven: Yale University Press.
Williams, M. (1972), Problems of technique during latency. *The Psychoanalytic Study of the Child*, 27:598–620. New York: Quadrangle.

10

Some Vicissitudes of the Transition into Latency

ROBERT A. FURMAN, M.D.

Perhaps others may have a difficulty similar to mine in writing scientific papers. A new concept or a new way of thinking about an old concept is stimulated by a paper, by some research work with a group, or by a clinical case. An idea forces itself upon the mind until some degree of understanding and integration is possible and then seems to fade from conscious thought. Weeks, months, or years later the same concept seems to surface again to demand more thinking and more attention, after it has been unconsciously worked on, with questions and disparities better pinpointed for further mental work. When a concept finally seems fully integrated, it no longer demands the attention it does when it is not fully thought through. Many wait to write until the moment of apparent resolution and consolidation has been reached, their papers representing an end point in their thinking. For me the process can often be a bit different, in that writing may help to focus unresolved problems and to stimulate the thinking of others, seeking their aid in completing the mental work or in indicating where the thinking has gone astray. Writing often seems easiest when a concept has not yet fully found its place in an integrated fashion, the irritation of the incomplete nature providing the stimulus needed for writing. This chapter surely falls within this cate-

Some of the clinical work upon which this chapter is based comes from the project Children of Divorce, made possible by the support of the Cleveland Foundation and the Gund Foundation.

gory, its thinking not fully completed but perhaps far enough along to seek the responses of others.

In the mid-sixties I worked in a research group that was struggling with formulating diagnostic categories for prelatency children. As described by Daunton (1969b), the greatest difficulty was encountered with

> the children in our study whose disturbances did not appear age- or phase-appropriate, on the one hand, and did not fit into the category of neurosis or character disorder on the other. All of these children as we saw them at the nursery school showed partial arrests caused by pathological fixations. Some, in addition to these arrests, showed the beginnings of regression from phallic or oedipal stages. All had symptoms maintained by pathological defenses and, in most cases, there was secondary defensive interference with ego functioning.
>
> We reached the conclusion (formulated by Dr. Anny Katan) that there was an important difference between those children with the pathological formations described above, who had not yet completed the oedipal phase, and those who were already in latency or adolescence. In the former, the neurotic conflicts endangered the proper resolution of the oedipal conflict. [p. 212]

The concept of disorders, particularly in the phallic phase, precluding subsequent successful mastery of oedipal conflicts in a prelatency child who does not yet have a fully crystallized neurosis, has stood the test of time for our group. Although in essence a predictive diagnosis, it has pinpointed the significance of the pathology of a number of children seen at the Hanna Perkins Therapeutic Nursery School and Kindergarten. Given a mother who is able to work in treatment via the mother as utilized at the school (E. Furman, 1957), the children in this category have done extremely well, their improvement well maintained in follow-up studies (Daunton, 1969a). This diagnostic concept, once evolved, was readily assimilated. In addition, however, it focused clinical attention on the resolution of oedipal conflicts and the transition into latency.

Observation of the oedipal development of nursery school

and kindergarten children over the years has seemed to me to reveal in many an almost diphasic sequence. In nursery school there is often a period of quite open, intense feeling for the parent of the opposite sex, a yearning that seems to ignore the existence of the parent of the same sex. In kindergarten the situation is often quite different; the yearning for the parent of the opposite sex is less pronounced, and an ambivalence conflict regarding the parent of the same sex is clearly evident.

A nursery school girl I had in analysis many years ago may illustrate this point. At the outset of her treatment she had no difficulty in bringing into her analysis her longing for a close, affectionate, exclusive relationship in the transference and with her father in real life. Many efforts on my part to explore the fate such plans held for her mother or my wife fell on deaf ears. As I persisted, she became exasperated with me, finally declaring that her mother or my wife could serve in some grandmotherly sort of way. The puzzle of what to do with the parent of the same sex was a conflict avoided, to be sure, but was also something that was not of paramount concern to her at this juncture. A year or so later, when she was in kindergarten, the same constellation of feelings was revived, but this time with an entirely different focus. In dreams associated with her enuresis she clearly struggled with wishes for her father, and was enormously guilty over the accompanying aggression toward her mother. When this conflict was made conscious, there was no assuaging her distress. I can recall telling her one day that many girls, in fact I felt all girls, at some point wanted Mommy dead so they could have Daddy to themselves. She was adamant that I did not understand her: The other girls just wished it; she *really* wanted Mommy dead!

From this and many similar examples it was impossible to avoid the thought that oedipal wishes are very different at the beginning of the phallic-oedipal period from what they are at the end of this time; they are essentially dyadic in the phallic period, triadic in the oedipal period. The many other profound differences between 3- and 4-year-old nursery schoolers and 5- and 6-year-old kindergarten children led to the conclusion that the phallic-oedipal phase encompassed just too much to be considered a homogeneous whole; in fact, we deal with two phases, phallic and oedipal, not just two aspects of the same phase, with oedipal relationships characterizing the latter part.

Here thinking seemed to halt until the appearance of the Edgcumbe and Burgner (1975) contribution on the phallic-narcissistic phase, "a differentiation between the preoedipal and oedipal aspects of phallic development." In a carefully reasoned manner they began by distinguishing levels of object relations from phases of drive development and then moved on to describe the characteristics of drive derivatives and object relationships in the preoedipal phallic child.

> In the preoedipal phallic phase, exhibitionism and scoptophilia are the most pronounced drive components. In the child's object relationships, correspondingly, the real or fantasied use of the genital serves primarily exhibitionistic and narcissistic purposes, to gain the admiration of the object. In the preoedipal phallic phase, the one-to-one relationship is still dominant, since the rivalry of the triangular oedipal relationships has not yet developed. [p. 162]

They discussed the historical origin of the lack of division between the two phases, to which I shall return in a moment, and then introduced the phrase *phallic-narcissistic* to describe the earlier, preoedipal part of the phallic phase, a term for which Anna Freud was given credit. Their clinical examples highlighted the dyadic aspects of the phallic-narcissistic phase, a third party often just an "intruder" interfering with the child's attempt to obtain the praise of the object of his affection. Certainly in her response to my questions about her mother or my wife, the little girl I have described treated my queries as just that, intrusions. They also reported the oedipallike advances of this earlier period as precursors of true oedipal feelings and described the anxiety of this phase as a castration anxiety born of competitive wishes for the phallus rather than of wishes to replace the parent of the same sex.

Regarding the historical origin of the failure to distinguish the two phases, the phallic-narcissistic and the oedipal, from one another, yet another source of confusion might well be mentioned. It will always be quite easy to confuse the two clinically unless there is an awareness of the difference between them. A little nursery school girl some years ago was most fascinated by her father, most attentive to him, and eager to have a baby. Careful attention to her mood soon revealed the source of her interest—the phallus, whose absence the baby was to repair or replace. Likewise, a little boy attentive to his mother, eager to elicit her praise, resenting his father as an intruder, and fearing retaliation for envying the father's larger phallus, is easy to confuse with the oedipal boy, attentive to his mother as an object of his love, resenting his father as a rival, and fearing retaliation for his wishes to replace him in the relationship with the mother.

At the end of their paper, which had so well knit together so many clinical and theoretical points, Edgcumbe and Burgner discussed the role of phallic-narcissistic fixation in disturbances of adolescence and adulthood. "Indeed," they wrote, "we are struck, as we examined the level of object relationships of these patients, how many of them could be described as *hysterical characters,* and we would further suggest that in the hysteric the phallic-narcissistic level rather than the oedipal one is the nodal point of the regressive behavior" (p. 178). They felt it was possible in these patients to reconstruct the "regression from a brief and imperfectly resolved oedipal level of relationships" that had taken place in early childhood. This concluding section of their paper can only stimulate thinking to start anew. It relates a number of observations which have not previously lent themselves to easy assimilation to clinical observations of children in transition into latency.

In describing a case of treatment by way of the mother some time ago (R. Furman, 1969), I reported how Sally, a kindergarten girl, told her mother of her distress that George, a classmate and an object of her affection, as was I, seemed to her to love others but not her. It was for her a great and sad time. What was not reported at that time was the nature of Sally's relationship at age 5½ to George. Sally's father had left home when Sally was 2, following the onset of a character change, later to be identified as paranoia. This had presented many developmental and neurotic difficulties for Sally which her mother had been able to help her master. Sally had an adolescent brother whose name was also George and toward whom she directed her oedipal feelings. She also brought these to school in the very fond and intense relationship with her classmate George. Her teachers and I were struck by the intensity of her feelings, her wish to please and thoughtfully do things for George, who in fact reciprocated her affection. The feeling that emanated from their relationship was one of love and was described by the teachers as having all the components usually thought to characterize an early adolescent romance. The feelings soon succumbed to repression as Sally moved into latency and became a most effective schoolgirl.

Another child comes to mind in this regard, a 5-year-old named Tom who had started at the nursery school with great difficulties exercising self-control. The work via his mother had been quite successful, and at the onset of kindergarten he moved into a state of apparent good control, which was first accepted by the staff as representing only a tenuous adjustment, their memories clear of his earlier troubles. But something remarkable happened to Tom when he turned his affection toward a little classmate, Kathy, with whose mother I was working at the time. It was as if a brief romance flourished, with Tom a thoughtful and considerate swain. I remember my surprise at watching him hold Kathy's chair for her one day at lunch, going to the kitchen to get seconds for her almost before she had indicated her wish. This was true, vigorous masculine behavior which persisted for about 2 months before Tom became a latency schoolboy, his attention more directed to the learning process.

At the opposite end of the spectrum I think of a current kindergarten boy whose alternating passivity and exhibitionistic responses to me at lunchtime betray his difficulties with his phallic adjustment. Just recently he has calmed enormously and wants to tell me at the table of his progress with his reading, and of his morning's activities in the classroom. Although I know that oedipal material has appeared in the work by way of his mother, his appeal to her has been more of a passive, dependent kind, not a vigorous masculine one. He seems now to have moved into latency after perhaps the most brief of contacts with oedipal feelings.

Retrospectively, I was able to construct a similar transition into latency of a boy with whom an analysis was started at age 12. It seemed from his analytic material as if problems in controlling aggressive outbursts had barely been brought into order and an exhibitionistic tendency only partially controlled around 5½ before he moved into latency. This time was marked by the transient appearance of a school phobia in kindergarten which lasted but a few days. Early latency seemed most successful for him, with many scholastic, social, and athletic achievements before a parental divorce ensued and his adjustment failed, with the appearance of temper outbursts and the return of phobic symptoms.

With Sally and Tom, the first two children described above, the transition into latency came at the end of a period of oedipal feelings which were displaced to the school setting in what seemed to me a possible precursor of the object removal Katan (1951) has described as characteristic of successful adolescent development. With the two boys described above, their transition into latency seemed much more to come in the midst of phallic-narcissistic concerns, oedipal strivings much less in focus. Both boys had strong relationships with their mothers, but both were more of the dyadic, exhibitionistic nature that Edgcumbe and Burgner have described.

The thought occurs from these examples that it is possible for children to move into latency from many points along a continuum from the phallic-narcissistic phase through the oedipal phase. Castration anxiety to motivate this progression is available at both ends of this continuum: at the phallic-narcissistic, emerging from the envious aggression toward the father for his phallus, prized as a possession in itself; and at the oedipal, from an aggressive wish to replace the father in the relationship with the mother, the wish to acquire his phallus arising from the conviction that it is the phallus that gives him his preeminent status with the mother.

Describing this phenomenon in terms of a continuum may be inadequate and misleading. It is easier for me to conceptualize it in this fashion, but it might be equally well described in terms of an almost infinite variety of combinations of various aspects of the phallic-narcissistic and oedipal phases that can be operative at the time of transition into latency. For example, the two boys who seemed to move into latency from a predominantly phallic-narcissistic position were not without some true oedipal feelings and conflict. It is rather that these latter aspects had both in duration of time and quantity of feeling involved been much less dominant.

Certain factors can be identified that could be responsible for a transition into latency more from a phallic-narcissistic position. Temporary arrests of development at any preceding level could delay forward phase-by-phase progression so that quite simply not enough time would remain to deal adequately with oedipal conflicts before the curtain of repression descended. Katan has described (E. Furman, chapter 9, this volume) the situation that may exist with a parent absent during the oedipal phase. An oedipal development did ensue in proper time sequence with the parent absent, but on the parent's return the oedipal struggles were revived and repeated with greater intensity before latency was belatedly entered. This observation, of course, makes one wonder what happens in single-parent families in which the absent partner never returns or is present so intermittently as to preclude full availability as an object for complete maturational development. A third possible factor would be constitutional, one hard to evaluate beyond commenting on its possible existence. The main point to emphasize here would simply be that it is not just problems of the phallic-narcissistic phase alone that can cause a delay in development that leads to a transition into latency from this level.

Clinically and diagnostically it is difficult to distinguish between three groups of early latency children: those with a phase-appropriate regression to the phallic-narcissistic (E. Furman, chapter 9, this volume); those whose phallic-narcissistic posture represents a pathological fixation point, either as a neurotic conflict or as part of a crystallized neurosis; and those whose phallic narcissism represents the unfortunate outcome of a normal identification with a phallic-narcissistic parent in the resolution of the oedipal conflict. A transition into latency from the earlier phallic-narcissistic position will certainly make more difficult the proper mastery and integration of phase-appropriate regression. It will provide crucial or additional potential fixation points for neurotic disturbances. Early transition would not be a factor for those with an oedipally phase-appropriate identification with a parent with a phallic-narcissistic disturbance.

The phase-appropriate regression should in the course of latency evolve toward mastery, with, for example, the exhibitionistic and narcissistic gratifications becoming increasingly and progressively integrated through reality-based sublimations, even if the level of object relationship stays basically, though not rigidly, narcissistic. Progression and flexibility might be the diagnostic hallmarks here. Neurotic conflicts and a proper, crystallized neurosis will be more rigidly entrenched, and further regressions will probably accompany them. I do not know any way short of analytic work to select out those whose pathology represents an identification with a disturbed parent. An example of such work follows.

With the 12-year-old analysand mentioned above, his many areas of good functioning early in latency inclined me to think that the basic mechanism involved with the phallic-narcissistic aspects of his clinical picture was an identification with his father, who had a severe disturbance at this level. Only after intensive analytic work on this identification produced little modification in both his level of drive development and the regressed level of his ego functioning could I reluctantly conclude that his phallic-narcissistic fixation point was a primary and intrinsic one.

The question of identification leads to another aspect about a phallic-narcissistic dominance to the move into latency: the quality of the accompanying introjections. It would seem reasonable, for example, to assume that the representation of the father that is introjected by the son will be less reality-based, i.e., will be more the father as seen through the eyes of a 4-year-old rather than a 6-year-old. The introjection will be motivated more by fear and aggression, with little modulation by the conflict between love and aggression toward the father, than would be the case with the truly oedipal boy. As would perhaps be true of all earlier identifications, it might be expected that the introject would be less easy to integrate, less easy to modify or correct by reality exposure, than would be the case with a developmentally more mature identification.

I have introduced these thoughts about the nature of the introjection because of certain difficulties that characterized the analysis of the 12-year-old boy whose case I have discussed. His parents separated when he was 10 and divorced when he was 11; the divorce was apparently instrumental in causing the appearance of his neurotic disturbance. What was so difficult to understand and work with in his analysis concerned the nature of his identification with his father. His father was a seriously disturbed man, but not a man without some redeeming characterological features. His son was at first unable to identify selectively with any of his father's virtues. Erna Furman has reported the work one family did with an early latency boy who had identified with some delinquent aspects of his father's behavior. The father's discussion of this with his son, to whom he expressed the wish that he not use these attributes as a basis for identification, successfully modified the boy's behavior and personality. Granting that such a healthy attitude from the father was not available to my patient, still he was much older, an early adolescent, was in analysis, had a good therapeutic alliance, and the problem was openly available for observation and work. Modification of this identification, however, was very slow to evolve and it was only in the last year of six years of work that I had some hope that genuine progress had been made in this regard. I would like to summarize his analysis briefly in order to describe what I felt had transpired to give me this hope. My analysand's phobia and an intermittent enuresis came into his analysis first and yielded to understanding of what appeared at first to be negative oedipal wishes: his aggression toward his mother coupled with his passive, excited wishes toward his father. It seems important to interject here that the anger toward the mother, and the excited wishes toward the father, only *appeared* to represent a negative oedipus complex. In reality I believe his aggression toward his mother was a response from that phase of his life when he felt she had exposed him unsafely to what was perceived as a dangerous father. He projected his aggressive phallic wishes onto his father, feared him, and then, when the anxiety became too great, sexualized the aggression perceived in the father and became passively excited about him. This would be yet another example of apparently oedipal wishes revealing themselves on further examination to be primarily of phallic-narcissistic origin.

After two years of this work the focus moved to his temper outbursts and a new symptom, an inability to masturbate to emission. The outbursts he finally understood as an orgiastic substitute for his emissions and also as an identification with his father; the inhibition of his emissions was understood as a response to his great fear of his father. Work on his aggression, but basically his great fear of his dad, gradually restored his ability to have emissions.

He became more active in dating around this time, at 16, and about four years into the analysis, but was callous and selfish with his girlfriends. He thoughtlessly seemed to use them to enhance his own image and reputation with male and female peers. Work seemed to alternate between a focus on this part of his pathology and on his by now long-standing inability to use his intellect in his schoolwork.

As we reworked some of the material that had led to the restoration of his emissions, some of his intellect did start to become available to him. This work dealt with his fear and anger in relation to his father. At the start of the last year of our work new material appeared. He was seen at my home, early in the morning, and infrequently had the opportunity to catch a glimpse of my daughters. He vaguely knew of my younger daughter from some of his friends who had gone to elementary school with her. He knew they were about the same age. In the last year fantasies started to emerge about her. Between girlfriends and beginning to be able to be thoughtful and considerate to his dates, he began to wonder about trying to date my daughter. The wishes were relayed to me primarily from his dreams.

Concomitant with these wishes emerged an envious aggression toward me, my home, my career, and my long summer holidays, which he equated with having great wealth. His attention then focused on a true ambivalence conflict: he was aware of feeling toward me both a raw anger and a deeply affectionate fondness. He truly struggled with this conflict, which of course was interpreted in the transference. I must confess, however, that I wondered if the depth of his fondness for an envied male was of greater intensity than he had experienced before, and whether in effect he was completing a maturational process he had started earlier in life.

It was after this work seemed successfully mastered and he had decided to seek life's rewards from his own efforts rather than simply envying their possession by others that his mind truly became available to him for work. It was not just our impression that a true change had occurred. He had taken an extra physics course his last year and had done so poorly the first semester that he had changed it from a graded course to a pass-fail course and had barely passed. The second semester his performance was so improved that his teacher said to him, "What happened to you? You would have earned a low D the first semester, a strong A the second. It was as if you suddenly started to be able to think and use your mind." That was an accurate quotation that pleased us both.

My feeling was that he had at last had the opportunity to work through in the analysis, aided by the transference, the ambivalent aspect of his oedipal development that had so largely been bypassed in his growing up, and in his transition into latency.

Another characteristic of his analysis was an apparent intermittent availability of certain ego and superego attributes and the level and quality of his object relationships. Self-observation, reality testing, tolerance of anxiety, thoughtfulness, and a sense of responsibility could be present in most adequate strength at one phase of the work, only to seem totally absent a short time later. It was difficult to understand these fluctuations. On one hand, I felt they represented an identification with the inconsistency that was one aspect of the father's personality. On the other hand, it became clear that this was not all that was involved, as analysis of this factor was not fully helpful. Later in the work it became clear that he was apprehensive that any alteration of his identification with the father threatened the entire fabric of his sexual identity. The more intensely he was involved with his adolescent struggles, the more inflexible he seemed to become in terms of modifying his identification with the father.

I could understand the situation only in terms of an early introject that existed in such a fashion that it could not be well integrated with the rest of his personality, modifying and blending with his self-representation. As such, the introject could at times be dealt with only by total rejection, something done at great peril in early adolescence. Elsewhere (R. Furman, 1978), I have described a mechanism for the acquisition of autonomous functions of the conflict-free sphere of the ego through gradual identification with the caretaking parents, a process finalized by the introjection at the time of transition into latency. The thought occurs to me that among the multiplicity of factors that might have operated to produce this intermittency, perhaps my patient's ego functions never achieved autonomy through integration because the early quality of the introjection made them at times subject to a type of total rejection.

This quality of intermittency applied as well to levels of relationship and to superego functioning. This is to be distinguished from consistent but immature levels of functioning that may occur when regressions in the ego and superego accompany instinctual regressions. These two, intermittency and immaturity, may occur together in varying admixtures, to be sure, but ultimately are capable in an analysis of being distinguished one from another.

Another avenue for consideration made possible by this thinking concerns some of the developmental tasks of latency and adolescence. I am accustomed to thinking that in latency the superego slowly becomes more civilized and integrated within the personality functioning and that such ego functions as reality testing, integration, self-observation, and tolerance for anxiety and other unpleasant affects are slowly matured. I am used to thinking that in adolescence consolidation of a sexual identity, identification with the parent of the same sex as an active sexual being, and object removal occur as the basic maturational tasks. I still think in these ways but find myself adding a new dimension to this thinking. Many of these tasks may well be initiated by the time latency starts for some, but may not even have begun to be approached by others, the difference dependent on the point on the continuum of phallic and oedipal development that marked the step into latency.

Children who enter latency from a phallic-narcissistic position have much greater tasks ahead of them in both latency and adolescence. These tasks may of course prove insurmountable for many, and otherwise inexplicable deteriorations in functioning in response to external stress or the internal pressures of adolescence may betray a latency entered more from the phallic-narcissistic point of development. I do, however, have an impression that some children in latency and adolescence master these tasks belatedly if these periods of their lives are free from external stress. E. Furman (chapter 9, this volume) has emphasized the significance of the maturational progression possible during a thoughtfully managed latency. My thinking has been stimulated by observations of children of divorce. One stress of divorce for boys, for example, would be that it throws them back into dyadic relationships, providing regressive seductions that cannot be resisted. Simultaneously it may deprive them of their fathers as models for their sexual identity and as reality figures whose presence could allow modification and hence integration of earlier introjections. The more a child of divorce would have entered latency from an earlier phallic-narcissistic position, the more he would be at risk, and the more these factors would be operative.

In this context it seems possible that the good results so often obtained in treatment by way of the mother may in part result from the identification that parents make with the aim of the work (E. Furman, 1969), enabling them to provide for their children in latency and adolescence the milieu that favors mastery and consolidation of developmental tasks the children may have come to belatedly.

In this chapter I have tried to trace the evolution of the thinking that has led to the concept of latency being entered across a continuum that spans both the phallic-narcissistic and the oedipal phases. This concept may possibly contribute to the understanding of two attributes seen in certain analytic patients: an intermittent availability of some ego functions, and a difficulty in selective identification that may be particularly evident in adolescence. I have introduced the thought that the earlier, in a developmental as opposed to a chronological sense, some children make the transition into latency, the more vulnerable they may be to later difficulties and the more they may require an externally stressless latency and adolescence in order belatedly to complete maturational tasks.

Finally, I wish to emphasize that my thinking on this question is tentative and ongoing, and to mention that after so many years of working and thinking as part of a group of analysts it is impossible to tell which ideas have originated with which participant of this group.

References

Daunton, E. (1969a), Description, evaluation and follow-up of cases treated via the mother. In: *The Therapeutic Nursery School*, ed. R. Furman & A. Katan. New York: International Universities Press, pp. 215–230.

——— (1969b), Diagnosis. In: *The Therapeutic Nursery School*, ed. R. Furman & E. Katan. New York: International Universities Press, pp. 204–214.

Edgcumbe, R., & Burgner, M. (1975), The phallic narcissistic phase. *The Psychoanalytic Study of the Child*, 30:161–180. New Haven: Yale University Press.

Furman, E. (1957), Treatment of under fives by way of their parents. *The Psychoanalytic Study of the Child*, 12:250–262. New York: International Universities Press.

——— (1969), Treatment via the mother. In: *The Therapeutic Nursery School*, ed. R. Furman & A. Katan. New York: International Universities Press, pp. 64–123.

Furman, R. (1969), Case report. In: *The Therapeutic Nursery School*, ed. R. Furman & A. Katan. New York: International Universities Press.

——— (1978), Some developmental aspects of the verbalization of affects. *The Psychoanalytic Study of the Child*, 33:187–221. New Haven: Yale University Press.

Katan, A. (1951), The role of displacement in agoraphobia. *Internat. J. Psycho-Anal.*, 32:41–50.

11

The Father-Child Relationship

ROBERT A. FURMAN, M.D.

In the discussion to follow I have in mind the average devoted father who has entered the developmental phase of parenthood. Not all fathers, just as not all mothers, are successful in achieving this goal, but this need not deter us from delineating this role, to which we hope all fathers aspire and which many reach as they mature. I shall begin with some observations of Winnicott's, both because of their intrinsic importance and because they lead to some thoughts expressed by Erna Furman, whose work I draw on for much of what is presented here.

The Father's Role in Helping His Wife to Mother

Winncott (1964) says that with her newborn the mother should behave in a way which at other times in her life we would have to consider pathological. She should withdraw her investment from the reality world around her to invest herself primarily in the unit that she and her baby constitute. In this exclusive investment she will accommodate to the transition from the baby within her, a part of herself, to the baby without, still essentially a part of herself. She will use this unique closeness to get to know her own baby's particular cries and signals, what makes the baby comfortable or uncomfortable, and how to provide the responses from which the baby will learn to recognize her as the one who fulfills its needs and to experience her as the source of pleasure.

Winnicott defines clearly his view of the father's role at this phase of life, a role which in many ways is never to change—modify, yes, but never entirely to disappear. This role is that of protector of the mother-child unit and relationship, as if he were to encompass them in his arms, keeping them safe from outside interferences so that the mother can devote herself to establishing her relationship with the baby.

This primacy of the mother with the child is something some men, perhaps particularly men who work professionally with children, may have difficulty appreciating emotionally. We all know it intellectually, but I have worked with mothers, the wives of such professionals, who have felt that their husbands acted as if they knew better than they did and subtly, ever so subtly, undermined the primacy of the mother's caretaking role. I was no exception, but was helped very much with this by our pediatrician, whom I called when our first baby first became ill. He was an old and dear close friend of mine and so I elected to do the phoning as a kind of comrade-in-arms. His first words to me, when I paused long enough for him to say anything, were, "Please get off the phone and let me talk to the baby's mother."

The view of the father's initial role of protecting and supporting the primacy of the mother-child relationship may say something about my suspicions and reserve about those who see the father's early role as that of a mother substitute. If that is what the mother wants and needs at some moments to get some respite so that she can better return to her tasks as need-fulfiller, all fine and good. That would make him a mother substitute at her wish, at her beck and call, in response to her needs, not in response to his own. Some fathers may need to start their relationship with their child through feeding, diapering, doing some of the mother's tasks, and that is all right too, as long as it does not interfere with the mother's mothering. What I am addressing here primarily is how a father deals with his maternal side. All fathers have such a side, not just professionals who work with children. One hopes that early on in his parenting a father will learn to gratify this part of himself vicariously, through his pride in, support and protection of his wife's maternal role. In doing so he is of enormous help to the mother and to his child.

In addition to the first months of life, there are two other specific times when the father's relation to the mother may be crucial for the child's well-being: in the toddler phase and at all those times when a mother has to be there to be left (E. Furman, 1982). During the toddler phase, perhaps more than at any other time—though not exclusively then—a mother's adult personality makeup gets a severe test when she spends hour after hour, day after day, week after week with dirty diapers and bottoms, runny noses, food all over the floor and the child's face and clothes. It is difficult to confront constantly these early instinctual manifestations, and every woman will need an opportunity to have very civilized, very adult times with her husband to re-cement her adult personality. We often say that the best thing we could do for our nursery school teachers at the Hanna Perkins School would be to offer them a candlelight dinner each Friday night, complete with tablecloth, china, crystal, and wine. Similarly, the mother of a toddler periodically needs special civilized adult times, be they just simple times of adult conversation.

As for the times of being there to be left, some of these impinge primarily on the mother—for example, weaning and the start of nursery school. At those times a husband who understands and is there for the mother after she has been left by the child can be a big help. At later times—going away to college, living away from home, marriage—the being left is still hard, but it is more readily understood because it affects both parents more equally. It is shared and they can help one another.

The Father's Role in Loving His Child

I would like at this point to move to some of our experiences with children in single parent homes whom we have gotten to know at Hanna Perkins. The observation was first made in *A Child's Parent Dies* (E. Furman, 1974) that the loss of a parent denies to a child a source of love as well as a person to love. This deprivation is especially serious for children who lose a parent in their first two or three years. Even when these children receive the best of early help, it has been impressive to note the unfortunate aftermath of their having sorely missed the extra love from the absent parent. This is not always the case, but it is a frequent enough occurrence, well enough studied, to allow us to draw some fair inferences about the role a father's loving of his child plays in his child's development.

We have particularly observed the combination of lowered self-esteem, difficulty in mastering aggression, and difficulty in integrating a helpful conscience. Although each of these is a most complex issue, deriving from many sources, it is possible to see and perhaps understand how these problems relate to one another. The lowered self-esteem perhaps manifests itself earliest. We see it in a lack of adequate pleasure in accomplishments and in a tendency to have one's feelings hurt too easily. The difficulty in mastering aggression shows next, in the exaggerated anger that flares up in response to what otherwise might be experienced as minor hurts to the feelings. Then, as latency starts and a conscience begins to be integrated into the personality, we note a great many more of the externalizations that Erna Furman has described as appropriate to this age (see chapter 9, this volume). All children experience some difficulty in learning to listen to the "inner voice" of the new conscience, which tends to set higher standards than they can meet. Young schoolchildren often avoid this unfamiliar painful inner conflict by attributing the demands of conscience and its punitive role to the outside world, to the principal who is seen as an ogre or to the parents who are perceived as excessively strict. With the single parent child, however, these developmental manifestations are greatly exaggerated and not easily outgrown. There is an increased need to provoke punishment from without, because the child unconsciously prefers it to the threats, reproaches, and punishments meted out by a conscience which is much too harsh.

We hypothesize that the lowered self-esteem comes from inadequate supplies of love, from missing out on that extra source of love from without that may be available with two parents present. A deficiency of that love inside, a love that should be self-protecting, may mean a deficiency of the love that can tame the aggression all must struggle to master. If there is enough love it helps the toddler to fuse anger, to modulate and tone down its harsh destructiveness for the sake of loving. Likewise, it helps the preschooler neutralize aggression, transform its energy into zest, and invest it in constructive activities. When there is not enough inside love, we find that these important steps in personality development are impeded. We also feel that when this anger, which has remained too harsh and too unmodified, later fuels the developing conscience, it accounts in part for the child's trouble in integrating such a conscience and learning to live with it.

If we understand our experiences correctly and if our hypotheses are valid, it is clear that the loving of his children that a father does, contributes to a child's self-esteem, to the mastery of aggression, and to healthy conscience formation. These contributions, often so silently made, seem so significant that I mention them explicitly. It is true that some children with one parent escape these difficulties, but the risk of problems arising in these areas is much greater without a father's healthy contribution.

How can a mother help her child if a father is not available in the home? It is important to realize that a mother cannot be both a mother and a father, that there will be a void in the fatherless family. The child will know and feel this. The mother cannot fill this void, but if she can acknowledge it openly and sympathize with the child's feelings about it, she can preclude the development of a gulf between them which could interfere with what she has to offer as a mother.

This brings us to another area of relevance to our topic. I shall start with an observation from one of the classes in a high school that took our course in child development (E. Furman, 1981). The question always arises whether in a single parent family, say with the father absent, his role cannot be filled by an uncle, a grandfather, or a friend of the mother's? I was interested in the discussion of this question by the high school students. With surprising ease and unanimity, but not without careful deliberation and discussion, one group summed it up rather well by saying that unless the man was the child's father, married to the child's mother, he was just different. It just was not the same. They all agreed that something is better than nothing, but that did not change their feeling that for the healthiest and happiest resolution of early childhood there should be a family unit consisting of mother, father, and child.

What these students were addressing is that crucial period of life that marks the transition from preschool to school age, the period of life marked by what psychoanalysts call the resolution of the oedipal phase. It is difficult to discuss our research about this crucial period without becoming either too theoretical or else simplifying the essence out of our thinking. I hope you will bear with me as I try to skirt between these twin dangers.

Preschool teachers know well the struggles of their charges to keep instinctual feelings and thoughts out of their learning; when children have made the transition to becoming schoolchildren, their sexual wishes and strivings have become more quiescent or latent—hence our designation of the period as latency. One second grader in analytic treatment described this well for me when he said that he knew one day he would like girls, as his teenage brother now did, but for him this was hard to believe, as right now girls seemed so "yucky." Teachers know also that a great repression or forgetting of the earlier years ensues during this transition and that the teachers and experiences of the preschool years are apparently almost totally forgotten by most school-age boys and girls. Preschool teachers know also that conscience formation is something that ensues from the struggles that mark this transitional period. For example, kindergarten teachers cannot leave a class alone for a moment at the start of the year but may by its end have some children who can manage on their own to stay in control for brief periods. These children have become schoolchildren, latency children with consciences that can function adequately if demands are not too great.

These are the observable phenomena of this transition, well known to the observant educator of children of this age: instinctual wishes become latent; a repression sets in; and a functioning conscience now appears. How all this comes about is perhaps not so easy to describe, and we still struggle to understand all that goes into this transition, what motivates it and sustains it. It would appear as if the preschooler follows the dictum, "If you can't lick 'em, join 'em." For the little boy this means surrendering his competition with his father, giving up his instinctual wishes for his mother, and modeling himself on his father. All this somehow ends up with the boy taking into his personality an image of his father that becomes the focal point for his developing conscience.

What we have emphasized in our thinking has been the attempt to understand how some boys and girls come through this transitional period confident and content regarding their sexual identity and as kind, caring, considerate, and giving people with reasonable consciences, while others come through as if chronically discontent with themselves and as rather nasty and selfish human beings with great troubles with their consciences. We believe that fathers have a great deal to do with how this transition period is concluded regarding these vital characterological features.

When a father fulfills the "average expectable" role with his son, one of kindness, pride, and respect, he is experienced as a man who cannot be wished ill without great internal stress and pain. A most difficult conflict arises, an irresolvable one unless the boy decides to bow to his love for his father and to the reality of the impossibility of his wishes for his mother. As the oedipal father goes inside somehow to become the boy's conscience, it is more a loving father that is then taken in, and a conscience is thereby formed that has a good chance of becoming a helpful aid to growth and development, not just a punitive force and voice. This inside father also becomes a source of identification with the father, acquiring in this way his kind, affectionate, protective aspects. To the extent that reality plays its role in the boy who surrenders his wishes, there is less loss of self-esteem, less sense of being the vanquished in a vital struggle. All the years of the father's caring availability pay off for the son when he masters this transitional phase with a healthy identification with his father and thus acquires his positive attributes.

As regards daughters I would emphasize a father's ability to give and be given to. A little girl's ultimate wishes regarding her father in the transitional period revolve around giving and receiving, the wish to receive and in turn give a baby to the father being the unconscious core. It is easy to see how a father who enjoys his daughters, enjoys their femininity, enjoys supporting it with the gifts he gives them, is a great help to a little girl. He makes her femaleness something prized and respected. He helps further by accepting her gifts to him, by admiring and enjoying her efforts at sewing, cooking, and doing other jobs her mother has taught her. The girl's more instinctual wishes will of course be there in full force, but as these are met by the father with affection and not excitement, so he facilitates mastery of their instinctual base.

The Father's Role in Helping Children Develop Sensible Values and Attitudes

In considering the father's relationship with his school-age children from 6 until puberty, and his role in helping them with developmental tasks, it is not necessary to distinguish relationships with sons from relationships with daughters.

The school-age child must integrate into a developing personality the new conscience and new character attributes that are outcomes of the transition from being a preschool child. These new aspects at first seem a bit foreign to the child, the conscience sounding almost like the voice of another telling him what is right and wrong, and not to do the wrong. It takes a while before the conscience is truly his and assists him by having him know when something is wrong. Then there is no issue about doing or not doing it; since it is wrong, it won't be done. It takes a while also before this conscience is solidified, so much a part of him that it is immune to almost any stress or temptation. At this point it has achieved full autonomy.

But until then, the conscience will seem a bit like a foreign body. Initially the conscience is crude and harsh, rather like a caricature of angry parents as seen by a very young child. As latency unfolds, however, the child will see that when parents get angry they are not angry in the way the conscience is; with the help of these experiences the harsh voice of the conscience will come more into conformity with the real and more gentle voice of the parents.

In similar fashion a child can come to see that earlier impressions of the father as only intermittently kind may have been incorrect, and the reality of the father's consistently available kindness can buttress identification with this aspect of him. Some fathers can even discuss with their children aspects of their own behavior that they hope their children will not have to copy (see chapter 9, this volume). The father who is realistically and consistently available does much by his simple presence to enable his child to mature and to integrate both conscience and personality attributes.

School is another major developmental task for the child of this period and here again the father can be of great assistance. By his interest in school and schoolwork he tells his children of his attitude to work, and of his aspirations and hopes for them. A positive attitude in this regard may assuage any apprehensions the children may have about competition with their father and supports the maturation of the character attributes of perseverance and responsibility.

Throughout this period a very important factor is the father's protection of his children, both sons and daughters. I do not mean simply protection when they are ill, or keeping them safe from danger, but include also protection from demands that are too great, that are not age-appropriate, as well as from demands that are not strong enough. Such things as allowance management, job management, and responsibilities at home can be a part of the father's relationship with his school-age children. How he does his own jobs around the house certainly sets an example for them; equally important, he can make sure they have age-appropriate expectations set for them, ones he supports and assists. I used to concern myself mainly with fathers whose expectations exceeded what was appropriate, but lately I have encountered increasing numbers of fathers whose expectations of their children are too low, in this way subtly telling them not to compete with him or implying that their efforts are not worth the trouble.

In addition to supporting new steps in personality maturation, and to supporting school and work, the father retains his long-standing role in introducing aspects of the world that particularly appeal to him. He has the opportunity to share his own special interests in a way that shows his children how to play joyfully and work joyfully. The mother, of course, can show these capacities herself, but how much more meaningful it is when her example is repeated by the father.

I worry a bit that what I have said about the father's relationship with his school-age children might sound too much like a recommendation that he be a model to them during this period. I worry because I hear so much about "role modeling" that sounds superficial, as if the idea were to act in certain ways at certain times for the benefit of the children. Rather, what I am trying to point out is the flexibility of the healthy school-age child's personality, a flexibility that enables it to be modified with the help of the father's reality as a person. It matters what he is as a person, what his values are, and it matters particularly in this period in which the foundation for adolescent development is being completed. It matters in that it can provide a sensible reality that contrasts with and counteracts the child's unrealistic fantasies, born of his wishes and urges.

The Father with His Adolescent Children

In adolescence what I often call "due bills" are called in. The time for personality modification in some areas has passed with latency, and I hope this point will underscore what I have said about a father's relationship with his school-age children. (Modification in latency does, of course, have its own limitations, as we are all aware. I hope this highlights, in turn, the importance of the father's relationship with his preschool children.)

I am not implying that what a father does with his adolescent children is of no moment, as this is not the case. Because the adolescent suffers lapses in control, may in fact have to have such lapses, in order to see what that is all about, a father's consistency with his own control becomes all the more important. I know of one father who jokingly said to his adolescent daughter, "In our family there is no generation gap." He received the sharp rejoinder, "Oh yes, there is, and don't you forget it." Unruffled, persistent consistency—steadfastness—is what the adolescent boy or girl asks of a father. It is a tall order, one they cannot ask of themselves, but it is precisely because they cannot ask it of themselves that they so wish to find it in both their parents.

How Does One Become a Good Father?

In concluding this whirlwind tour of the father-child relationship from birth through adolescence, a few brief words seem in order about what may enable a man to father well. I believe a man learns to parent, to put another ahead of self, primarily from his mother; but he learns how to father from his father. He will succeed in his own fathering endeavors to the degree he is able to integrate these two examples within himself, aided by the marital relationship within which his fathering develops and unfolds.

By way of conclusion let me repeat that this was no attempt to be inclusive with the very vast topic of the father-child relationship. What I am struck with as I think back about the material, is how much my effort has been centered on elucidating the method of action of something so easily taken for granted—the quiet, loving role of the good enough father; his protection of the mother-child couplet, the role his loving plays in promoting mastery of aggression, successful conscience integration, development of adequate self-esteem, mastery of the oedipal phase, passage into schoolchild status with the acquisition of many character traits we so admire and cherish. We all know of the father's traditional roles of protecting and loving. I think what I have been doing is describing the mechanisms by which these roles are fulfilled and how they facilitate a child's emotional growth and maturation.

References

Furman, E. (1974), *A Child's Parent Dies*. New Haven: Yale University Press.

——— (1981), The high school course in child development. *Parent Education Newsletter of the Family Health Association of Cleveland*, 9(1):1, 4.

——— (1982), Mothers have to be there to be left. *The Psychoanalytic Study of the Child*, 37:15–28. New Haven: Yale University Press.

Winnicott, D.W. (1964), *The Child, the Family and the Outside World*. New York: Penguin Books.

12

A Developmental Approach to Systematic Personality Assessment

STANLEY I. GREENSPAN, M.D.
JAMES L. HATLEBERG, M.D.
CECIL C. H. CULLANDER, M.D.

While the importance of systematic personality assessment has been highlighted by a number of authors (A. Freud, 1962, 1965, 1969; A. Freud, Nagera, and E.W. Freud, 1965; Kohut, 1970; Greenspan and Cullander, 1973; Greenspan, Hatleberg, and Cullander, 1976), the extensive time and organization required for such an assessment have compromised their routine use. In order to facilitate a systematic approach to personality assessment, we have presented a profile structure (Greenspan and Cullander, 1973, 1975; Greenspan, Hatleberg, and Cullander, 1976) for both the initial assessment and the course of analytic treatments for children and adults. In this chapter we will present a refinement of our assessment profile for children (Greenspan, Hatleberg, and Cullander, 1976). Although this profile resembles the Freud-Nagera profile, it is different in several respects. This profile is constructed so as to provide a structure for assessment based on a limited number of interviews. It is oriented more toward the structural elements of personality functioning, while including specific content or fantasy considerations. It is somewhat shorter, and it is hoped that it can be completed within a limited number of interviews. Most important, it provides a scale by which the interviewer can assess and rate personality functions in order to compare an individual with himself at various points in time and compare one person to others rated reliably within the same scale.

The profile assesses personality functioning sequentially, going from a broad, encompassing perspective to specific evaluation in detail. The initial categories focus on the overall intactness and flexibility of the ego, while the later categories consider specific ego functions, superego, object relations, affects, defenses, and drives.

The profile is constructed to take into account the age of the individual. Impressions are based on a comparison between age-expected developmental accomplishments and observed level of development. In order to arrive at these determinations, a knowledge of developmental stages in the various categories is necessary. The theoretical structure of the profile will be presented, followed by a case illustration.

Introduction to the Profile

Narrative accounts of evaluation interviews, and auxiliary data such as psychological testing and school reports, should be followed by a metapsychological assessment of the person's functioning in the format presented here.

In this format the interviewer first describes the individual's functioning in each category. Following this, he is to rate his impressions from "good" to "inadequate." Whether ratings can be applied to the descriptions is an open question and should be attempted with this in mind. Ratings are indicated by a check in the appropriate box. If the area of functioning falls between two of the descriptions, e.g., fair to good, a check is placed on the line between the two relevant boxes. In addition, confidence in the accuracy of the rating is indicated on a scale of 1 to 3, with 3 indicating relative confidence and 1 indicating relative lack of confidence.

Systematic descriptions in each category have been developed to help orient the interviewer toward a systematic report of his impressions. The descriptions are not intended to be comprehensive but rather to give the flavor of those areas of functioning that are to be assessed. It should be emphasized that the style and structure of the session with the individual is to be one's own, independent of this outline. It is to be expected that it may not be possible to gain impressions of all the listed areas.

For ready reference and visibility a rating sheet appears as Figure 1.

Category 1: Ego Intactness (vs. Ego Defects)

Included in this category is the general basic integrity of the ego—an overall evaluation of ego apparatuses and functions.

a. Ego apparatus. This category includes the basic organic integrity of the ego: the perceptual, visual, auditory, and motor apparatuses; apparatuses that coordinate these (perceptual-motor); and other similar apparatuses, such as memory, that have to do with the integrity of the mental apparatus.

b. Basic ego functions. This category includes only the basic overall functions of the ego (e.g., reality testing, predominance of secondary process thinking, presence of ego boundaries). Special attention should be paid to the more subtle aspects of these functions that will give the interviewer clues about well-hidden borderline organizations, for example, the predominance of magical thinking, extreme impulsiveness, and avoidance and withdrawal covering up a subtle ego defect. In evaluating this category, attention must be paid to what would be considered age-appropriate levels of development in ego functioning. The relative attainment of reality testing, secondary process thinking, and ego boundaries must be evaluated in the context of the expectable developmental accomplishments, as follows:

1. *Good.* The organic ego apparatuses and ego functions are basically age-appropriate. Interference from neurotic formations, developmental lags, or organic dysfunctions are minimal to none.
2. *Fair.* Physical or psychological factors, e.g., neurological dysfunctions, ego defects, neurotic or characterological constrictions, moderately impair the ego's capacity for age-appropriate functioning.
3. *Marginal.* Same as above, only there is marked interference with the ego's age-appropriate capacities.

Figure 1. Metapsychological assessment profile.

Categories	Good	Fair	Marginal	Inadequate	Confidence of Rating 1–3 Scale
1. Ego Intactness a. Ego apparatus b. Basic ego functions					
2. Ego Flexibility a. Adaptive capacities (1) Relationships					
(2) Education; learning; work					
(3) Play					
b. Intrapsychic experience: Specific maladaptive tendencies (1) Organized disturbance					
(2) Relinquishing area of experience					
(3) Unmodified discharge					
(4) Tendency for fragmentation					
c. Overall ego flexibility					
3. Ego Functions Related to Autonomous and Conflict-free Spheres of the Ego					
4. Relationship Potential					
5. Superego Functioning					
6. Affects					
7. Defenses					
8. Drive Organization					
9. Reality Considerations					
10. Intuitive Impressions					
11. Capacities for Further Growth					
12. Recommendations					

4. *Inadequate*. Physical or psychological factors severely interfere with the ego's capacity, e.g., severe neurological dysfunction or ego defects result in psychotic processes.

Category 2: Ego Flexibility (Adaptive Capacities of the Personality)

Under this category is assessed the ego's flexibility—its capacity to utilize a variety of finely discriminated operations. At the lower end of this scale would be found a rigid ego with only a few poorly discriminated operations at its disposal. Included in this category are age-appropriate capacities to tolerate internal or external tension and to form and tolerate conflicts and a variety of affects. The presence of these capacities stands in contrast to signs of arrested ego development, severe ego constrictions, below age-appropriate externalizations of inner tensions, and altered or restricted modes of drive gratification. In addition, the individual's capacity to develop transient symptoms, affective states, or behaviors in response to internal or external stress, which do not interfere with developmentally relevant ego functioning, should be contrasted with the development of symptoms, affective states, or behaviors which compromise developmentally relevant ego functions and lead to restrictions in a capacity for further development (e.g., withdrawal).

In this category, behavior should be described and rated from two perspectives: (1) flexibility of adaptation to development and phase-expected tasks; and (2) flexibility of the ego in dealing with "intrapsychic" experience. Note: these capacities are separated here for purely conceptual and descriptive purposes.

a. Adaptive capacities. Under this heading is assessed the individual's ability to engage in a broad range of life experiences in the major arenas of relationships, work, learning, and play. These experiences may be scored quantitatively by considering the variety and richness of available choices; the depth of experience; and the degree of differentiation and appropriateness.

1. Relationships
   a. *Good.* Has full and satisfying age-appropriate relationships; e.g., has intimate continuing relationships with significant other persons; has friends; feels loved.
   b. *Fair.* Restricted in close relationships; e.g., relationships repeatedly get neurotically tangled and/or yield little satisfaction.
   c. *Marginal.* Severely restricted in close relationships; limited in capacity for maintaining relationships in general or deriving satisfaction from them.
   d. *Inadequate.* Incapable of relationships.
2. Work, Career, Education, or Learning Experiences
   a. *Good.* Works and/or learns at full creative, productive potential, with satisfaction.
   b. *Fair.* Productivity or satisfaction from work and/or learning limited or distorted.
   c. *Marginal.* Severely limited in learning activities and/or work; e.g., major characterological interferences result in frequent self-defeating behavior in home, school, or career; gets little satisfaction from above.
   d. *Inadequate.* Totally unable to maintain work or learning experience or to derive satisfaction from it.
3. Play
   a. *Good.* Has capacity to relax, experience pleasure, and enjoy a variety of age-appropriate experiences.
   b. *Fair.* Mild limitations in above; conflicted about having pleasure.
   c. *Marginal.* Moderate to severe limitations in capacity for relaxation and pleasure; e.g., must always be "serious" (studying or working) and, when not, is sleeping; other conflicts often interfere with pleasure.
   d. *Inadequate.* No capacity at all for play activities, due to inhibition or interference.

b. Intrapsychic experience. Here is assessed the capacity to form, perceive, and tolerate conflict and to remain in touch with thoughts and feelings (no matter how unpleasant or intense) concerning the important issues confronting the individual at the time. Implied is the ability to use these thoughts and feelings to work out adaptive life solutions. Deviations from this most desirable position may be represented by four tendencies:

1. *Tendency toward formation of an age- and phase-appropriate organized disturbance* in part of the ego, which condenses, with great economy many other conflicts and issues and allows the remainder of the ego to function normally. This includes many neurotic symptoms, a circumscribed compulsion, and short-term, temporary affective disturbances or other states, yet leaves the person still able to involve himself in most life endeavors and to experience a wide range of thought, feeling, or other age-appropriate internal experiences.
2. *Tendency to relinquish age- and phase-appropriate areas of experience* by walling off or preventing access to certain types of behaviors, thoughts, or affects, e.g., limited capacity to experience anger, love, sadness, anxiety, sexual feelings and fantasies, etc. The expectable range of thoughts and affects is limited by certain of these being walled off by the ego; the ego gives up flexibility through avoidance of the expectable range of inner experience. The ego may also relinquish areas of behavior to protect itself, e.g., avoidance of intimate heterosexual relationships or intimate friendships, avoidance of accomplishment in work, avoidance of all human relationships, etc. In this category the ego may be dominated by an overwhelming defensive operation. This would include many character disorders, chronic affective disorders, and developmental arrests.
3. *Tendency toward unmodified discharge* of drives or expression of affects, e.g., impulsive, aggressive, or sexual behaviors; extreme affect states (e.g., manic states); may include sexual perversions.
4. *Tendency toward fragmentation of age- and phase-expected levels* of ego organization under stress, e.g., in an older child or adult, compromise in basic ego functions such as reality testing, integration of thought and affect, cohesion of sense of self and sense of other (feelings of depersonalization, derealization), loss of attention to outer world (total withdrawal, acute psychotic phenomena). This fragmentation may be

encouraged by the use of primitive defenses, such as projection or denial.

Standards for rating each style of ego flexibility

1. *Tendency toward formation of an organized disturbance*
   a. *Good.* Tendency to form organized disturbance is transient, appearing when person is under stress (e.g., transient phobia).
   b. *Fair.* Organized disturbance is more continuous, appearing with only minor stress.
   c. *Marginal.* Organized disturbance is chronic and severe. While in part protecting the other areas of ego function, it is quite painful, e.g., severe obsessive-compulsive symptoms such as hand washing, chronic doubting, etc.
   d. *Inadequate.* Organized disturbance is chronic, painful, and potentially debilitating, e.g., severe obsession about own sexuality that keeps person awake at night. Compromises work performance and makes relationships extremely painful.
2. *Tendency to relinquish areas of experience*
   a. *Good.* Tendency to relinquish areas of feeling, thought, or experience is minor and transient and related to internal or external stress, e.g., mild withdrawal after a relationship breaks up.
   b. *Fair.* Tendency to relinquish areas of feeling, thought, or experience is more continuous, though only in very limited life areas, e.g., moderate, continuous avoidance of competition.
   c. *Marginal.* Tendency to relinquish areas of feeling, thought, or experience is chronic and shows itself in major life areas, e.g., avoidance of all intimacy.
   d. *Inadequate.* Tendency to relinquish areas of feeling, thought, or experience is chronic and shows itself in so many areas of life as to be debilitating, e.g., withdrawal from all human relationships.
3. *Tendency toward unmodified discharge*
   a. *Good.* Occasional—in relationship to stress.
   b. *Fair.* More continuous, but relatively minor incidents, e.g., regular mild temper tantrums.

   c. *Marginal.* Chronic and severe, e.g., sexual perversion.
   d. *Inadequate.* Chronic and severe, and evident in many areas, e.g., violence and sexual perversion, potentially debilitating.
4. *Tendency toward fragmentation*
   a. *Good.* Very occasional episodes of fragmentation under very extreme stress and of lowered capacity for integration, e.g., occasional depersonalization, when getting to sleep, working very hard, or under extreme psychological stress.
   b. *Fair.* Occasional episodes of fragmentation in the context of moderate internal or external stress, e.g., feelings of derealization when very angry.
   c. *Marginal.* Frequent episodes of fragmentation, e.g., frequently feeling unreal, illusionary experiences, misperception of reality, e.g., paranoid fantasies, dissociation of parts of self (object and self-object splitting), etc.
   d. *Inadequate.* Total experience of fragmentation, psychotic delusions, e.g., bodily delusions, hallucinations, persecutory delusions, total disintegration of affect regulation and/or tolerance (completely flat affect), etc.

c. Overall ego flexibility. This category includes both intrapsychic and reality-adaptive aspects of ego flexibility.

1. *Good.* The ego demonstrates age-appropriate flexibility in its response to internal or external stress. Developmental interferences and conflicts, neurotic conflicts, and neurotic formations only minimally interfere with this flexibility. Either no impairment or very mild impairment of ego's flexibility, e.g., a mild, organized disturbance such as some phobic tendencies.
2. *Fair.* The ego is somewhat rigid in terms of age-expected capacities, but along with this rigidity there is a capacity to tolerate internal or external stress of varying degrees without marked disruptions in age-appropriate ego functioning. May have #1 tendency to mild organized disturbance, e.g., phobia; may have some minor #2 tendency to relinquish areas, e.g., tends to deny anger at authority or to avoid competition

with authority; mild use of #3 unmodified discharge, e.g., mood swings under stress; very rare use of #4 fragmentation, and only under extreme stress, e.g., occasional depersonalization.

3. *Marginal.* The ego tends to be quite rigid in regard to age-expected capacities. Internal and/or external stress markedly intensifies this rigidity and/or leads to minimal breakdowns in age-appropriate ego functioning; e.g., in a latency child there are occasional losses of age-appropriate reality testing, severe states of inhibition, or markedly impaired impulse regulation. Moderate to severe use of #2 relinquishing areas, e.g., the very passive individual who avoids almost all experiences of rage, expression of anger, or assertion; or the narcissistic individual who avoids any intimacy and cannot experience balanced empathy; moderate use of #3 unmodified discharge, e.g., severe mood swings, some perversions, impulsiveness; moderate use of #4 fragmentation, e.g., loss of reality testing under stress, depersonalization, etc.
4. *Inadequate.* The ego is severely limited in its age-appropriate capacities and has only a few poorly discriminated operations (defenses) to cover more basic earlier structural defects (as is seen in psychotic or borderline organization). Where the ego is in its early formative stages, it is severely limited in its capacity to use the objects in its environment to further its own development. Severe use of #2 relinquishing areas, and of #3 unmodified discharge and/or fragmentation, e.g., psychotic character disorder, extreme lability of affect, perversions, and psychotic phenomena.

For a more differentiated assessment, the interviewer may also rate the person's ego flexibility for each style of ego inflexibility and for overall ego flexibility in each of these life areas:

1. *Relationships*
   a. *relationship* with one or a few individuals
   b. *friendship*—relationships in general
2. *Work*
3. *Play*

4. *Intrapsychic phenomena*

Category 3: Ego Functions Related to Autonomous and Conflict-Free Spheres of the Ego

This section of the profile, which is related to ego intactness and ego flexibility, should include a description of the individual's age-appropriate precursors or capacities for (a) self-observation; (b) regression in the service of the ego; (c) ability to learn; (d) intelligence; (e) creativity; (f) curiosity; and (g) synthesis and integration. In addition, describe any other assets or liabilities that would facilitate or hinder adaptation and the capacity for further differentiation.

These abilities or capacities are to be looked at from two points of view: their *potential* utility and their *current* functional utility (the degree to which current stress or conflict may or will continue to interfere with their functioning).

1. *Good.* Autonomous functions are age-appropriate and capable of being used to integrate new experiences and facilitate development.
2. *Fair.* Age-appropriate autonomous functions are slightly restricted by internal or external stress and/or are mildly impaired due to other factors (genetic endowment, cultural background).
3. *Marginal.* Age-appropriate autonomous functions are markedly restricted by developmental interferences, developmental or neurotic conflicts, neurosis, and ego constrictions, and/or are relatively deficient due to other factors.
4. *Inadequate.* Functions usually considered autonomous are not. Instead they are severely restricted, below age expectations, and used mainly in the service of developmentally early drive gratifications or to cover up early ego defects. Where the ego is still in its early formative stages, these functions are not used in the service of further ego development.

Category 4: Relationship Potential (Object Relationships)

This section should include an assessment of the individual's capacity for relationships with others. The history of early object relationships, growing relationship patterns, current patterns, and the quality of affect and relatedness in the assessment situation should be used as indicators. Predominant aspects of relationship patterns should be assessed: autistic, narcissistic, anaclitic, symbiotic, sadistic, masochistic, phallic, sharing, loving, etc. Special attention should be paid to age-expected accomplishments. For example, in a latency child attention should be paid to the degree to which relationships are based on pregenital dyadic patterns versus the degree to which they represent an integration and resolution of triangular oedipal patterns and movement on to age-expected peer relationships. In a preoedipal child of 2½, where one would expect predominantly dyadic patterns based on pregenital concerns, attention should be paid to the degree of internalization occurring. The relative attainment or movement toward object constancy in the context of age expectations should especially be noted (i.e., it should be achieved by 3 years of age).

1. *Good.* Relationship patterns reflect age-appropriate capacities for intimacy and stability as well as age-appropriate capacities for frustration and rage. Earlier than age-expected relationship patterns are capable of being integrated with current levels of relationship. For example, in the oedipal child there is a capacity for a full range of affective ties, e.g., sharing and loving as well as envy, jealousy, and anger. In the preadolescent there is a significant "chum" relationship.
2. *Fair.* Relationship patterns reflect age-appropriate capacities but are mildly compromised by earlier unresolved issues.
3. *Marginal.* There are relationships, but these are predominantly characterized by developmentally earlier patterns. For example, in a disturbed latency child, relationships may be markedly unstable and based on preoedipal concerns.
4. *Inadequate.* Relationships, if they occur, are markedly below age-appropriate expectations. For example, in a severely disturbed latency child, relationships either might not occur as such or would be based on anaclitic or symbiotic patterns. In a severely disturbed 2-year-old, autistic patterns might be prominent.

Category 5: Superego Functioning

This may be rewarding and productive of self-esteem, or punitive and productive of guilt and depression. This section should include an assessment of the degree to which the superego or its precursors have achieved and maintained an age-appropriate level of functioning: (1) Consider the degree of age-expected structuralization (e.g., in a late latency child the superego should be relatively internal and organized). (2) Consider the degree to which the age-appropriate superego processes or its precursors are smoothly integrated with ego and id and the degree to which there is finely discriminated regulation in the context of a relatively stable esteem system and capacity for pleasure. This would include an assessment of the character and consistency of either the figures for identification or established introjections and their relationship to the developing identity, sense of self, and attitudes toward predominant types of age-appropriate drive discharge expression.

At the other extreme, this category should include an assessment of (1) the degree to which the superego or its precursors are below age expectations and/or are experienced as separate and in conflict with the ego; (2) the degree of inconsistency in age-expected relation (e.g., in a latency child superego lacunae or overgeneralized strictness and punitiveness —everything is bad); and (3) the degree of instability in the age-expected esteem maintenance and capacity for age-appropriate pleasures. At this extreme, consider how the character and consistency of figures for identification or established introjects may interfere with identity formation, sense of self (e.g., incomplete or negative sense of self), and/or drive discharge expression (e.g., aberrant, inhibited).

Because the superego is continually forming during childhood and adolescence (and even to some degree in adulthood) and is only relatively organized with the oedipal resolution, knowledge of age expectations is particularly important in assessing this category. The two extremes presented above have definite implications for pathology only where a relatively complete superego organization is expected. In the preoedipal child, for example, inconsistency is to be expected. Assessment of the superego precursors of the very young child will of necessity be more speculative and depend in part on assessments of aspects of his early drive and ego organization and his family.

1. *Good.* The superego or its precursors are age-appropriate and in balance, and provide for a reasonable amount of age-appropriate drive gratification and self-esteem while exerting age-appropriate regulation.
2. *Fair.* The superego or its precursors are relatively age-appropriate, but there are mild compromises in age-appropriate drive gratification, self-esteem maintenance, and impulse regulation.
3. *Marginal.* The superego or its precursors are below age-appropriate expectations, resulting in a lack of regulation, overinhibition, or vacillations between the two. Age-appropriate drive gratification and self-esteem maintenance are markedly impaired.
4. *Inadequate.* The superego or its precursors are significantly below age-appropriate expectations. The structures dealing with age-appropriate impulse regulation, drive gratification, and self-esteem maintenance are either defective, developing improperly, or not developing at all.

Category 6: Affects

These may be multiple, flexible, and developmentally appropriate or few, rigid, and developmentally retarded. This section should include an assessment of:

1. The types of affects (those that predominate and those that emerge under stress).
2. Their developmental level in the context of the expected developmental level based on age and environment. For example, in a 5-year-old predominant affects of emotional hunger, fear, rage, jealousy, and envy may represent developmentally immature affects, while some capacities for sharing and loving together with the former may represent an age-appropriate pattern. For a 2-year-old, however, the former pattern would be age-appropriate.
3. Their flexibility and selectivity. For example, are there a

number of expected affects potentially available, some of which can be selectively called forth in the appropriate situation (fear and rage in one situation, love and concern in another)? Alternatively, there may be only a few, below age-expected affects (fear and rage or pseudowarmth) which are used in most situations.

Special attention should be paid to the type of anxiety manifested:

1. Is it related to integrated, internal structural conflict, i.e., is it signal anxiety?
2. Is it related to a combination of internal and external concerns, e.g., partial projection of fears onto the external world or poorly integrated internal conflicts, e.g., fear of the instincts?
3. Is it predominantly related to external concerns such as fear of castration, fear of punishment, fear of loss of love, fear of separation, fear of object loss, or fear of annihilation by the subject?

1. *Good.* There is an age-appropriate variety of affects which can be used selectively in response to external or internal stimuli as well as conflict. Anxiety is age-appropriate. For example, in the postoedipal child anxiety is related to internal, integrated structural conflict (signal anxiety), whereas, in the 3-year-old, anxiety is in part related to a fear of loss of love from the mothering figure.
2. *Fair.* There is a capacity for age-appropriate affects when not under stress. Anxiety is also age-appropriate, but regressions occur under stress.
3. *Marginal.* A few affects which are below age expectations predominate. For example, in a latency child there are predominantly feelings of emptiness, sadness, rage, envy, and pseudowarmth. Anxiety is below age expectations; for example, in the oedipal child the anxiety is predominantly related to fear of the instincts and/or concerns over separation and annihilation.
4. *Inadequate.* The affect system is significantly below age ex-

pectations, to a degree that it is either inappropriately or incompletely developed. This results in either flat or highly inappropriate affect. Anxiety is related to concerns which are significantly below age expectations to such a degree that the type of anxiety significantly interferes with age-appropriate ego development and functioning, e.g., intense fear of self- or object destruction.

Category 7: Defenses

These may be age-appropriate, stable, flexible, selective, and effective or developmentally retarded, unstable, rigid, overly generalized, and ineffective. This section should include an assessment of the general defensive styles and specific types of defenses or groups of defenses used both ordinarily and under stress. Included should be an assessment of:

1. Their age-expected developmental level (e.g., in a latency child, primitive defenses such as projection, denial, and introjection vs. developmentally more appropriate defenses such as repression, reaction-formation, sublimation, and beginning capacities for intellectualization).
2. Their stability (what happens under stress).
3. Their flexibility (how well they adapt to new situations).
4. Their selectivity (can the most effective defense be called forth in a given situation?).
5. Their effectiveness (do they protect vital, age-appropriate ego functions?).

Because this is an important category that often reflects general personality functioning, a number of defenses will be listed, and the rater is asked to evaluate the relative roles of these and others: avoidance, withdrawal, denial, blocking, projection, introjection, somatization, undoing, acting out, displacement, repression, identification, isolation, excessive use of affects (affectualization and magical thinking), the turning of emotions into their opposites, reaction-formation, sublimation, rationalization, intellectualization, and regression.

1. *Good.* Defenses are age-appropriate and organized. They

tend to protect the ego without significantly hampering age-appropriate functions. For example, in a latency child defenses only minimally interfere with memory (repressed memories), age-appropriate reality testing, and ego flexibility.

2. *Fair.* Defenses are mixtures of age-appropriate and immature defenses. The immature defenses are used mainly in response to stress. Age-appropriate ego functions are compromised only under stress.
3. *Marginal.* Defenses are below age expectation. They hamper age-appropriate ego functions markedly to moderately by constricting them (phobias), impairing their regulatory capacity (impulsive behaviors), leaving them open to severe ranges of affect (anxiety or depressive equivalents), or, in cases of unusual stress, allowing disruptions in age-appropriate reality testing.
4. *Inadequate.* Defenses are significantly below age expectations, e.g., the predominant use of incorporation, projection, and denial in a latency child. They are unselective, and severely hamper age-appropriate ego functions (reality testing). At best they serve as only a fragile defense against psychotic processes.

Category 8: Drive Organization

This section should include as complete a description as possible of the person's current level of drive organization. It should (1) assess the degree to which the drives (both libidinal and aggressive) are age-appropriately fused and have progressed to age-appropriate levels of organization (e.g., have the drives fused and progressed to a phallic-oedipal level of organization in a 5-year-old?); and (2) determine whether aspects of drive organization which are below age expectation tend to reflect major fixations or potential regressions to fixation points.

States intermediate between age-appropriate drive organizations and earlier levels of drive organization should be assessed in terms of (1) *quantity* (how much is still tied to the earlier position and how much has progressed to the age-appropriate position?) and (2) *quality* (how rigidly is it tied to earlier positions—secondary gains, severe conflicts at the next position?).

1. *Good.* Drive organization is predominantly age-appropriate. Regressions are temporary. If neurotic manifestations exist, they represent regressions to fixation points.
2. *Fair.* Drive organization represents a mixture of age-appropriate levels and earlier developmental levels.
3. *Marginal.* Drive organization is predominantly below age expectations. This is due to arrested development, major fixations, or marked regressions.
4. *Inadequate.* Drive organization is significantly below age expectations. Drives are primitive and disorganized to such a degree that activation of drive derivatives, even from routine stresses, results in states of panic, fear, and ego disorganization.

Category 9: Reality Considerations

Here should be assessed the reality circumstances of the individual and/or his family as these might effect the implementation of potential recommendations. Stability, economic status, and capacity to understand and fully support treatment and, in the case of a child, to establish a productive working relationship with a therapist should be considered. The reality situation may be regarded as

1. *Good*
2. *Fair*
3. *Marginal*
4. *Inadequate*

Category 10: Intuitive Impressions

Here may be included any impressions of the interviewer that are not captured by the preceding categories. Special assets, liabilities of the individual, or feelings about the individual, based on the interviewer's experience, although not easily formulated in metapsychological terms, should be described. This category is also to be rated "good" to "inadequate," based on the implications of these intuitive impressions for the individual's capacity for current coping and further growth.

1. *Good.* Special assets or liabilities and intuitive impressions considerably strengthen the estimate of the individual's potential for further growth.
2. *Fair.* Special assets and liabilities and intuitive impressions neither strengthen nor weaken the estimate of the individual's capacity for coping or further growth.
3. *Marginal.* Special liabilities and intuitive impressions weaken the estimation of the individual's capacity for coping and further growth.
4. *Inadequate.* Special liabilities and intuitive impressions weaken considerably the estimation of the individual's capacity for coping and further growth.

Category 11: Capacities for Further Growth and Development in an Average Expectable Environment or in the Current Environment

Include here a description of the capacities for further development in terms of the categories previously outlined (ego, superego functioning, drive organization, defenses, affects, etc.) and anticipated special problems. For example, does the current evaluation of the individual's ego structure forecast difficulties in schoolwork or peer relationships? Is treatment necessary or will it become necessary? If so, what kind? In this section it is especially important to present the interviewer's evaluations in narrative form so that the basis for these impressions will be clear.

1. *Good.* Capable of optimal development; should be a relatively well-integrated, happy person.
2. *Fair.* Capable of relatively healthy further development, but may encounter some difficulties of minor to moderate proportions and may need some therapeutic intervention.
3. *Marginal.* Does not appear to be capable of further healthy development without some major intervention. Without intervention it is expected he will have, or continue to have, significant problems in major life areas.

4. *Inadequate*. Expected to have or continues to have significant difficulties in most major life areas. Even with major interventions, development will likely be compromised.

Category 12: Recommendations

Justify recommendations in the context of the total assessment.

Assessment of a 6-Year-Old Boy

Sessions with Parents

Session 1: First parental visit. Bryan, 6 years old, was presented by his parents, an attractive couple in their mid-thirties, as having numerous problems. Among these was his refusal, from the time he was trained, to defecate regularly, sometimes withholding for as long as 2 weeks. Occasionally he would soil himself. He was stubborn, had temper tantrums, and was unable to make a choice and be happy with it. He would cry hysterically when his mother left him at school.

Bryan's playtimes with his parents would end disastrously. With his mother, the sessions would result in mutual irritation and bickering. With his father this was less likely. Rather, Bryan would jump and wrestle long after his father felt it was time to stop, and the play would come to an unhappy end with Bryan being scolded and pushed away, whereupon Bryan would sulk. Bryan, they both implied, never knew when enough was enough. At the same time, they were saying, he had "an extraordinary ability to get under your skin, and he also knows how far he can go."

The mother thought Bryan's problems stemmed from the time of his brother's birth. She had been hospitalized for 10 days, and Bryan had been cared for by a "witch" of a nurse, a rigid, depriving woman who was fired immediately upon the mother's return home. Up to that time Bryan, like his brother Robert now, was characterized as a happy-go-lucky child. As difficult as Bryan has been, he has apparently gotten on well with his younger brother, now 3. From the very beginning he wanted to see and hold the baby and was never hostile toward him. He pals with him sometimes, and although they fight occasionally, Bryan acts "maternally" toward him.

Their present housekeeper, an Italian woman of 27, gets on well with both children. Recently, when she was on vacation for 5 weeks, Bryan regressed markedly. He was temperamental, threw temper tantrums, would not move his bowels, and had a number of soiling accidents. Yet along with all this, he seemed very sad.

The parents described their family relationships as open and vocal with one another. The mother felt they might be too open about some things, such as nudity, for example. Only a month ago, Bryan and his father were still taking showers together. Recently, Bryan started to climb into bed with them, but the mother was firm about making him leave.

A bright, tense, clever woman, organized somewhat along hysterical lines, the mother saw herself as "up-tight, and unable to express love." She did not want Bryan to grow up similarly handicapped. At least on the surface, she scapegoated herself by attributing all the negative aspects of their family interactions to herself and all the positive ones to her husband. Her hidden agenda, however, seemed to be one of controlling what went on in the family while keeping her husband on the perimeter. She accomplished this through her family role of protecting her husband from family feuds.

The father seemed a likable, warm, and self-satisfied man who nonetheless conveyed an underlying sense of sadness and depression through the expression in his eyes. From him I learned that his business was a great source of pleasure, that he relished its success and gave it a great deal of his attention.

Session 2: Meeting with mother. Bryan's mother talked about her own earlier years as a schoolgirl, her meeting and marriage with Bryan's father when she was about 20, and her relationships with the family and with Bryan.

As a youngster, she had been uninhibited, skilled in music and dancing, and a good student. When she entered high school, however, the increased competition intimidated her, and her self-esteem diminished considerably. A series of psychosomatic complaints that never quite incapacitated her completely led her eventually to therapy, which terminated about the time she met her future husband on a blind date.

Her father, a physician, had been in the military. For the past 10 years he has been ill and partially paralyzed from a stroke. Bryan shows him much compassion, plays with him, and is able to touch him. The mother barely mentioned her own mother until asked, and then termed her "terrific." Her mother was described as gentle, her father as intimidating.

She described her relationship with her husband as good, except for her "sexual hang-ups." She added that her husband would "tune himself out" when a family flare-up occurred, and this frightened her.

Session 3: Meeting with father. The father explained that his main concerns centered around his work, that it consumed much of his time and brought him his enjoyment and fun. When he was 14, his own father, a dynamic trial lawyer, had died of a stroke. He had gone to work then and attempted to take his father's place at home. He was surprised and annoyed at his mother's remarriage when he was 16. Thereafter, he felt that he could depend only on himself, that he could look to no one else for comfort.

The father said that since coming to the last session he had begun to feel concern that Bryan, when angry, would sometimes threaten to kill himself, whereas he hadn't paid attention before. This was not pursued further. Instead, he went on to issues of competition. He viewed himself as a nonaggressive person who had avoided competition as far back as he could remember, in his family of birth, in school, in sports, and in business.

From talking about himself, he turned to his family relationships. He spoke of his inability to provide emotional support, shutting the family out instead. He mentioned that his wife would reject him sexually when she was angry. And he described Bryan's inability to set or accept limits to his physical activity when they were playing together.

The main theme that emerged was Bryan's absolute need to control, his use of passive and withdrawing mechanisms to feel in control, and his resentment at being regimented or controlled.

Session 4: Developmental history. Bryan's mother conceived easily and felt healthy throughout her pregnancy. Bryan was delivered by cesarean section. He was a "good baby," who slept a lot, cried little, and was easily pacified. His mother nursed him for about 8 months. She spoke again of her exhaustion and need to sleep, and her nervousness, acute stomachaches, and severe depression that first year ("All I could do was care for Bryan"). She felt her self-preoccupation must have interfered with her mothering of Bryan. Yet they did play and have good times together and enjoyed a one-on-one relationship. She said, "I was thrilled; I am still thrilled with infants." Her emphasis on the general phrase "with infants" was more narcissistic than a response to her son as an individual. The father's role in helping with Bryan seemed to be feeding him breakfast occasionally after the first few months.

When Bryan was 6 months old his parents distinctly recalled that he differentiated between them and others. When he was 8 months old his mother had to leave him for 3 days. On her return, she found Bryan covered with a rash from head to foot, and he was put on a soybean diet. Other than this, he seemed a happy baby that year. Speech developed early; he was walking by 11 months and appeared very coordinated. Bryan is smaller than most children his age and has frequently asked if he would be bigger when he grew up. The father said that he, too, had been a late starter in growing.

Bryan was extremely inquisitive and explorative, qualities he still retains. What he had never developed, according to his parents, was patience. He is extremely impatient, dislikes structured situations, and doesn't like to be shown how to do things.

From the time Bryan was 18 months old, his father's business had him traveling 2 or 3 days at a time, and the mother went with him. Frequently the parents took Bryan along; other times he was left with babysitters. All had gone well, apparently, until he was almost 2. From then on, he grew very stubborn. Between 2 and 2½, his negativism increased even further, and things really "started going downhill" after his brother's birth. Bryan was then 2 years and 3 months.

Toilet training Bryan was "not easy." He was about 2 when his mother decided to try, but he wanted no part of it. Her efforts were intermittent; sometimes a week would elapse between attempts, with the mother feeling extremely frustrated. Then one day he said, "Today I'll make you happy and go in the bathroom." This happened when he was 2 years and 9 months—just about the time he was to go to nursery school. Up to that moment, his mother had been sure she would not succeed and had about given up. She had tried bribes—reading to him, comparing him to his father, offering him candy—but nothing worked. Comparing Bryan with his brother Robert at this point, the mother related that the housekeeper had successfully trained Robert when he was 2, with only a few accidents occurring recently, when she had been on vacation. As for Bryan, his bowel movements had been regular for the past 12 days, ever since the housekeeper's return. Prior to that, almost from the time he was trained he would often hold back for as long as 2 weeks at a time. Bryan has always had to be reminded each day, whereupon he would complain and cry, saying he didn't like to go. During this entire recital, the father appeared to be keeping himself aloof.

While Bryan has had no serious medical illness, twice, between his first and second years, his temperature had risen to 105°. There had also been a fever of unknown origin just after his brother was born. He did frequently get sick when his father was away for more than a day or two. When this happened, there was much rectal temperature taking.

When Bryan was about 2 he joined a play group of four little boys on a regular twice-a-week basis and adjusted well to the change. When Bryan's friends came to his house he needed to be "king of the castle," whereas at other people's homes he apparently modified his behavior. At 3, he was enrolled in nursery school. Although hesitant and shy at first, he again did very well. As the youngest in the class, the teacher treated Bryan as special, often holding him on her lap.

Bryan has a few friends on the block and tends to get along well with them, but he doesn't seem to enjoy going out to play. The only friend Bryan is attached to is a child next door who seems retarded. Bryan seeks out nobody else, although sometimes he will play with his brother. Often his mother suggests other children to play with, but Bryan refuses.

Bryan seemed to withhold in other ways, too. If his father

suggested something they might do together, he would agree, only to change his mind and show disinterest. Neither parent ever felt effective with him, and both felt they were engaged in a perpetual power struggle with him. They often disagreed about Bryan, and both experienced a chronic sense of uncertainty in their dealings with him. The mother thought his problems were very serious and blamed herself, while the father thought they just didn't know how to handle him. Their self-doubts and conflicting opinions prevented them from pooling the information they obviously possessed to put together a consistent picture of their son. Instead, their differing points of view distorted their personal perceptions and undermined their individual efforts to set limits.

Toward the end of the session the parents added new information—that Bryan now insists that a light or the TV be on what he sleeps; otherwise he is frightened. His brother compares this to his own "security blanket." They agreed that Bryan's problems had magnified when he was to attend school all day, and they repeated that he had improved significantly since the housekeeper's return and the inception of these sessions.

In discussing Bryan's upcoming visit, they expressed concern with how he would react to a strange adult. His mother thought he would cry, and she would have to run off. His father thought he would have to be tricked into staying.

Playroom Sessions

Session 1. Bryan appeared as a very cute, small, somewhat shy and frightened 6-year-old, with big, bright eyes. He was sitting far back in the chair in the waiting room. When I motioned for him to come with me and offered him my hand in greeting, he came much more willingly than I had been led to anticipate. His walk was relaxed and coordinated. He entered the playroom readily and went first to the big bean bag and sat in it. He looked at me with his big, bright eyes, which seemed to be asking for something, then oriented himself with a series of "What's this? What's that?" questions, pointing to things from where he sat. He wanted to know who had drawn a certain picture, saying, "I could do better." He then took some paper and wrote his name.

Bryan was able to make eye contact with me almost from the first and continued to stay in warm and friendly eye and voice contact throughout. However, he did not come close physically, but seemed to keep his distance. His gross coordination appeared excellent, much better than his fine coordination (as when he tried to write his name). His speech was distinct and easy to understand.

After writing his name, he sat back as though waiting, quite firm in his passivity. He appeared reluctant to do anything further on his own initiative—draw, play, talk, etc. Instead, he wanted me to do the drawing and also wanted to direct me. When I asked him what he wished me to draw, he told me to draw a face. Only then did he take over and begin. I felt that had I not taken the lead he would have maintained a stubborn and negative attitude.

He began to draw a face. When prompted, he said it was a happy face. I was taking some notes, and immediately he inquired about this. I told him that I was writing down some of the things we were doing together and assured him that everything would be just between the two of us. I took this occasion to tell him about the rules of the playroom. Subsequently, he was able to walk around and explore. He took it all in, looking at all the toys and asking many questions. In looking at a particular box, he asked why there were two holes in it and then volunteered an answer—because someone had cut them out. I was feeling relaxed and comfortable with him at this point.

Bryan questioned me about a collage of butterflies that had caught his attention in the office, and when I asked him what he thought, he was again able to figure out the answer for himself. Right after this he began jumping on a footstool which he then placed on the bean bag. He appeared to be enjoying himself, jumping around and building things with blocks. Next he wanted some paper from a pad and asked, "Can I take the paper off?" He then moved to the blocks, picking out red and blue ones. When he heard a noise outside, he went quickly to the door, apparently very concerned that anyone would be doing anything close to our playroom. He did not explain the nature of his concern, but did show some annoyance and discomfort. I had some question about just how distracted he might be by a relatively minor sound outside.

After this interruption he returned to the blocks and began to construct a building. From here he went to a toy turtle whose neck had been stretched out of shape and tried to push it back in place. However, it ended up being stretched even further. Taking the turtle with him, he went to the play schoolroom and said, "Now this turtle can go to school." He toyed with the idea of the turtle blasting off. Then he took a pad and began showing me that he could add one and one, and two and two, putting in the proper signs and writing the answer. After this, he returned to the bean bag and jumped onto it. Next he showed me how he could jump off a platform onto the bean bag with "no hands."

During this time his activity level was well modulated, even, and rhythmical. He was reasonably well coordinated; his speech patterns remained clear throughout. There were no shifts in feeling tone, neither extreme happiness, extreme sadness, nor anger.

About this time he asked how much longer the interview would last. I wondered aloud what he was thinking about and why he had asked this, and he quickly changed the subject, saying that there were no more blocks and wanting to know "what got lost?"

Bryan now began to look into everything—in a cabinet—What's in there? and there? and there? He went back again to the blocks to build a very high tower and wondered, "Which way will it fall?" He picked up a rubber wolf, calling it a dinosaur and commenting on its big mouth and ears. Again he returned to the tower to add more blocks until it toppled. He quickly asked what time it was and said he was hungry. Now he built a corral and again asked the time and then began to laugh, claiming he did not know what he was building. Back to the wolf again, commenting that it was "scary."

While I sensed attachment and warmth from Bryan, I did not feel that he became more involved with me as the hour passed. Instead, just after he had finished expressing these last concerns, I could feel him beginning to pull away. At the same time, he was flitting from one thing to the next rather than developing a theme within one or a few play areas.

When I asked what his understanding was of why he had come to see me, he replied, "I forgot what my mommy said." Going back yet again to the blocks, he commented that his building would be really tall. I suggested that he didn't want to talk much about his reasons for coming to see me, and he then said, "You talk to kids," and knocked down the blocks, adding that he didn't wish to talk, he would rather play. My response was that I could understand that; sometimes it is hard to talk, but I wondered if it wouldn't be helpful if we talked about a few things. I asked him if he ever had any dreams. He was able to tell me somewhat shyly that he always had dreams about monsters, that he often dreams he is standing somewhere and the monster grabs him and he gets scared. Then he said, "I want to go home." I remarked that it was "scary" to talk about such "scary" dreams and he said "Yes," and again said he wanted to go home. Each time the anxiety level rose, he said he wanted to go home. It should be emphasized that there was no sense of disorganization or panic, or any attempt to go to the door. He was able to verbalize his feelings directly.

When Bryan picked up a little puppet and began to play with it, I tried to start a dialogue around it, but he became frightened of talking and said once again, "When can I go home?" He went to the blocks and then picked up the wolf and bit it. (This was one of only two overt acts of aggression during the interview.)

As we were cleaning up together, he became more openly aggressive toward the turtle, pulling off its neck and head and talking again about its blasting off. He clearly avoided participating in straightening up the room. At the end of the interview, when I explained that I would like to see him again, he looked scared, but immediately asked if we would be doing the same kinds of things. I responded that we would have a chance to play again and to talk about some things. At this time I also told him about psychological testing in the near future.

At the very end of the interview, I asked once more if he knew why he was here to see me, and he stated *very* quietly,

"To help me understand things." I said, "Yes," and there seemed to be a nod of understanding between us. When I opened the door, his mother came toward him giggling and while we were arranging for the next interview, said in front of him, "When do I find out what he did?"

A subjective feeling of caution on my part permeated the interview with Bryan. I found myself being more careful than usual about being intrusive. I was impressed with his initial negativism, his minimal-to-mild displays of aggression (a toy gun was left untouched by him), as well as the number of times he had said, "I want to go," in juxtaposition with his fear of talking about his dreams. Despite his fears, however, he did mention his dreams directly during this first interview.

While the play session was reasonably active, what impressed me more was Bryan's flitting from toy to toy and from theme to theme. Not only was there a lack of thematic development, but a richer sense of relatedness with the interviewer never emerged. Rather, communication was superficial and scattered. Both affect and activity were restricted yet well modulated. He did not show the characteristically rich fantasy production of the oedipal period, and I speculated that he had not yet moved fully into this phase of development.

Session 2. A week later Bryan came in with an eager look on his face and a rash on his cheek. He looked demure and shy, very appealing, almost seductive. Once again he sat on the bean bag, making himself quite comfortable. He smiled and made eye contact with me. From where he sat he examined the room and wanted to know where the paper was. He then proceeded to make a series of drawings, placing them in a makeshift album to which he then proudly attached his full name. For the first picture he drew a head, then two lines showing the unclothed body extending directly downward into the legs, with circles for the feet. This he labeled "big man." A square that he drew he called "the swimming pool." He labeled its different parts, drawing circles for stairs and other circles for himself and his brother. Another square represented a playground, again with circles to show different areas. A wishing well looked more like a rocket ship or a pencil; it had a cone-shaped head and a rectangular bottom. "You drop something in where the pointed head is and you look for things." He pointed out that water could be put in the bottom. He wished for a dog, a German shepherd, a watchdog to make sure nobody came when he was not ready. The need for protection was the theme that evolved.

Next he drew a picture of a house which looked more like a shoe, and then two faces, one of himself and one of Robert, with circles for the eyes and a line for the mouth. Then, in a scribble game, he drew a big man who, he said, was a nice man, again with circles for the head, lines for the body and legs, and circles for the feet. In a picture of his family, he placed himself next to his father, then his little brother, and then his mother. He and his brother were in the middle, his mother and father at each end. All of them were in a car. The only things he elaborated on in the drawings were the big men and, as he pointed out to me, that he always drew his brother Robert. He simply commented that he was interested in "big men."

Next he asked me to draw and do some things for him and that he would direct me. First he asked me to draw his family, guiding me. I tried to comply with his instructions. He was fussier about drawing his mother than the others. When I remarked that he liked me to do things for him, he agreed. He then told me he wasn't feeling well and showed me the rash, saying that it hurt.

Immediately after, he set up the bean bag and began jumping onto it. In an athletic exhibition, he kept moving the bean bag further and further from the platform he had made to show me just how far he could jump. Next he was jumping all around the room, at times making some motions toward me, but never quite jumping on me. He did come closer to me during this interview, however. After this he built an ingenious bridge to help him between the bean bag and the platform. It was apparent that he did not wish to stop what had become more zealous activity. I commented that he had said he felt sick, and yet he was being so active; he paid no attention. When it came time to stop, having spent most of his time jumping around the room and playing a variety of athletic games with the bean bag, he didn't wish to. He indicated that he wanted to continue and then showed some concern about locking away the things himself and making sure no one would have access to his drawings.

During this second interview there was again no development of thematic material except in the very early stages; when he was making the drawings. However, the contact with me remained; he stayed emotionally even; and his inclination to explore and his natural curiosity were intact.

Psychological Tests

Behavioral Observations

Bryan is a nice-looking, thin child who had a cold and was extremely nasal.[1] He left his mother immediately and took my hand, but looked at her sidewise. His hearing was not accurate, which may have been a function of both his cold and difficulties in attending. Toward the end of the three-fourths of an hour of testing, Bryan inquired, "Where's my mommy?" and "When can I go back home?" Bryan came into the room very quietly and was attracted to the toys at once. When I suggested we play later, he could not wait but immediately ran to grab the toys. I asked him to draw a picture, and he said he would draw a bag of candy, then decided he was going to trace his hand. He did so and then went on to draw a picture of a person. Everything took a very short time. He was more interested in playing with the Pick-Up Sticks, putting them into little holes in the box. Then he found a hammer and started hitting it against the table, against the test cards, and against a toy gorilla that he brought to the table. He could not sit still. He was constantly up and moving about. His high level of anxiety may have been caused by what I found out later. On the way into the Center, he slipped, fell on the ice, and had a big bump on his forehead, which he showed me. When questioned he would constantly say, "I don't know, I don't know," without trying. If he didn't say "I don't know," he would look at me and immediately say, "Tell me what it is." He did things very quickly; for example,

[1] Test results are reported by the clinical psychologist, Milton Shore, Ph.D.

when counting blocks (which he could do very easily), he threw the blocks vigorously at me from about 4 feet. He constantly scribbled and made marks on the cards, even though he had been told not to and paper was offered. He could not stop moving and constantly doing things. On the way out he remembered that there was a sign that we put up not to be interrupted. He asked to take it and gave it to the receptionist. As soon as he approached his mother, he put his coat on and started toward the door, although she was not yet ready to leave the room. He tried to turn the handle of the door leading outside but was unsuccessful. When his mother opened the door, he rapidly started on his way out, obviously very eager to leave.

Test Results at 5 Years 7 Months

On the Stanford-Binet Form L–M, Bryan obtained a mental age of 6–0, with an IQ of 112 (high-average). He passed all the items at a 6-year level and failed all the items at a 7-year level. There is very little to indicate that his abilities are higher than the high-average range. He demanded to do things he wanted to on the test. He would only do the things that he chose, carryng out my requests in a very resistant way. I was able, with a great deal of patience, to get him to complete the tests required for valid evidence of his intellectual ability. He made up some words and also heard words like "roar" as "war." When he said he didn't know something, he would anxiously say, "Tell me what it is." He constantly wanted to draw pictures, and it was very hard for him to accept limits. However, there was a very manipulative quality to everything he did, as if he wanted to get me involved in doing things he wanted to do, not wanting to respond to requests from me. In the completion of the man, he immediately translated it into damage, pointing out that the man had a cast on his leg before he had broken his leg. It was then that he pointed out to me how he had hurt his head on the way in.

On the projective techniques, Bryan constantly denied knowing what things were. There was an intense, anxious quality to what he said. He would vary between fantasies of omnipotence and tremendous fantasies of fear and annihilation. There was a constant feeling of being eaten up, devoured, and overwhelmed. Repeatedly asking me to tell him things seemed a way of establishing structure and order. For example, he recognized an animal, but couldn't figure out the name for it. He would keep asking for the name, making up names that he knew were quite inappropriate. Having gotten the correct word by himself, he then felt relieved. There is no evidence on the testing that Bryan has any basic reality difficulties, but there is clear evidence of the mixture of a great deal of lack of control with aggressiveness, with some rudiments of oedipal material. It appears that he has tried to reach the oedipal phase, but he easily regresses and cannot control himself. His fears are very great and his demands strong. He does not accept limits well and will not meet requests that are made. Anything that can be seen as damaged or being overwhelmed by powerful forces is picked up by him; in the Rorschach he sees huge dinosaurs.

In summary, from the psychological testing it seems that Bryan is a boy of high-average intellectual ability, who has not adequately been able to deal with the oedipal situation because of many preoedipal, particularly anal, issues that he has not adequately resolved. There are separation fears that he regresses to very rapidly, and strong feelings of annihilation. Any demands or requests by an authority figure are resisted, as he narcissistically wants to do what he wants, when he wants, and how he wants. His aggression is free floating, and he is unable to handle or control it. He becomes anxious when he feels he is not adequately dealing with reality, although basically his reality testing seems adequate for his age. Because of his fear of powerful forces, he cannot accept his dependency. Denial and avoidance are two of his major mechanisms for handling situations. I think Bryan is currently dealing with issues on a 2½- to 3-year-old level. The intensity of his uncontrolled activity and demands in the test situation may have been aggravated by his having hurt himself on his way in. On the basis of testing, he does need therapy, probably twice a week. I do not feel, however, that he could handle more frequent sessions.

Assessment Profile

Category 1: Ego Intactness

a. Ego apparatus: Good (2). The basic organic integrity of the ego (including perceptual, visual, motor, and auditory apparatuses), coordinating apparatuses (perceptual, motor), and other similar apparatuses such as memory appeared to be intact. However, early history revealed a delayed cesarean section and some early jaundice leading to questions of interference with optimal early maturation, although there is no present evidence of such. Fine motor coordination, as indicated in the playroom sessions, did not seem as well organized as gross motor coordination, but he demonstrated a capacity to write his name, to color, and to draw that appeared age-appropriate. The drawings were well done, indicating that while fine motor coordination is not as good as gross, it seems within the range of age-appropriate expectations. There were questions about his attention span. In the playroom sessions he flitted from one topic to another. Was this due to anxiety or to a difficulty in focusing and organizing attention on one task? Given these questions, which only further work would answer completely, the general feeling was that less than optimal performance in focusing attention was due more to functional issues and their concomitant anxiety than to a compromise in the basic organic integrity of the ego apparatus. The psychological tests appear to support this by the fact that his scores on all the tests were age-appropriate or slightly above level.

b. Basic ego functions: Fair (2). Overall, it was felt that basic ego functions were age-appropriate, but it was felt also that there was a proneness toward regression of certain ego functions in response to conflict greater than expected for a 6-year-old. For example, there seemed to be occasional compromises with reality testing when he was involved in a regressive, symbiotic pattern with his mother. Did he depend on her to define reality? When she was feeling good, he would feel good; but when she was feeling bad, did her bad or angry feelings so pervade his own reality that there was a compromise in his ability to perceive how things really were? The question centered on the degree of real resolution of the separation-individuation process. How vulnerable was his capacity to see the world accurately? There did not appear to be sufficient data to answer this question completely from the initial evaluation interview.

When he had his temper tantrums, it was learned in the history, particularly while the maid was away on vacation, he seemed to be completely out of control; here questions were raised about his capacity for regulation of motility. Was there a compromise in his ability to control his impulsiveness, or was this a conflict-generated, goal-directed, organized attack? There were some questions about his capacity to care for his own body. When he would become exhibitionistic, he seemed to take risks and was occasionally accident prone.

On the other hand, in his playroom sessions he showed a clear capacity to regulate his motor activity. He understood the rules of the playroom and seemed to have an internalized sense of what was expected, as he played within the boundaries of the situation. There was an even regulation of motoric activity and affect, and interpersonal contact was maintained. While there was not a rich thematic development, more a sense of flitting, the flitting themes seemed in themselves to put together a picture of his concerns. Thus, while he did not indicate his concerns as directly as some oedipal children might, he did communicate them during the course of the interviews. In addition, he could write his name. His pictorial representations were at an age-appropriate level. He had a clear perception of his family, knew his birth date, and so on.

Thus, in terms of certain structural properties of the ego when not under stress, he seemed to be at the age-expected level of a 6-year-old in terms of his ability to regulate wishes, impulses, affects, and motoric activity; to appreciate the situation he was in; and to regulate himself in a reasonably expectable way, organize his communications, and integrate (with thought and affect) a sense of relatedness. As indicated from the history, however, under certain conditions, particularly those that touched on unresolved symbiotic issues, there were questions of compromises in aspects of the basic ego functions of reality testing, impulse regulation, regulation of bodily function, and maintenance of a firm boundary between self- and object representations.

While this last statement is speculative and should be treated as such, the historical data are suggestive. When Bryan was 2 or 2½ (just prior to or just after the birth of his brother), his parents claim he went "downhill"; negativism and stubbornness began to emerge. There were extreme temper tantrums, particularly around issues of separation; an extreme reaction to separation from the maid when she was gone for 5 weeks; and a loss of certain regulatory functions, e.g., occasional soiling. Under stress, then, it appears that some of his basic ego functions are compromised.

Category 2: Ego Flexibility

a. Adaptive capacities

1. Relationships: Fair (2)
   Intimate relationships with family members, especially the mother, were markedly compromised, while relationships with friends and other adults were somewhat more age-appropriate.
2. Learning experiences: Fair to Marginal (2)
   From psychological reports and parents' description of Bryan's ability to concentrate, it appeared that learning experiences would be markedly compromised.
3. Play: Fair (2)
   From parents' descriptions and playroom interviews, it appeared that play activities were only mildly interfered with by low frustration tolerance and special conflicts with the mother.

b. Intrapsychic experience

1. Organized disturbance: Fair (2)
   Evidenced by transient symptom of withholding bowel movements.
2. Relinquishing areas of experience: Fair to Marginal (2)
   Evidenced by fixed character traits to be described below as part of overall ego flexibility.

3. Unmodified discharge: Fair (2)
   Evidenced by current impulsiveness.
4. Fragmentation: Good to Fair (2)
   Evidenced by occasional "out of control behavior"; at other times characterological restrictions are used to deal with anxiety.

c. Overall ego flexibility: Fair to Marginal (2). Ego flexibility appears to be compromised by stereotyped patterns of feeling and behaving. There appear to be constrictions in the ego's capacity for dealing with internal or external stress. For example, in the psychologicals, there was an extreme amount of negativism. In the history, the parents indicated that the negativism began around age 2 and increased dramatically after the birth of Bryan's brother. This seems to be a chronic pattern, implying a fixation, and therefore an early constriction in the ego's flexibility in tolerating a wide variety of internal drive derivatives, feeling states, and external stressful situations.

In addition, there appeared to be another constriction in Bryan's ego, one which seemed somewhat more fluid and more under the influence of present internal or external stimulation: that was his flitting and motoric activity. In the playroom interviews he did not develop organized, rich thematic material around any issue or within the context of one or another play area, but instead flitted from one thing to the next, occasionally appearing to be out of control, with phallic exhibitionist activity. In these activities he did not always demonstrate expected concern for his own body, as when he jumped from a platform into the bean bag, and there were times when he might have hurt himself. This would appear to be a fixed and stereotypical pattern of response to internal or external stress (in the context of age-appropriate, expectable patterns, as a "hypertrophy" of phallic issues and a defensive constellation to deal with implied castration anxiety from multiple sources of development).

Along with the negativism, there was a general pattern of withholding. This was supported by the symptomatic withholding of feces upon the departure of the maid and his chronic pattern of uncomfortable defecation and withholding. In this context it is interesting to note that when confronted with the two diagnostic playroom interviews and the psychological testing, the negativism increased dramatically as the interviews became more structured and demanding. For instance, there was a decided increase in negativism in the psychological testing situation, a more demanding situation than the playroom, which allowed him more leeway in his course of action.

In addition, there seemed to be a compromise in ego flexibility in being able to tolerate and form internal conflict. At times he dealt with internal stress through unmodulated discharge of activity. Historically this occurred with his temper tantrums, for example, when he would strip his bed and seemingly be out of control. This was suggested in the interview, when he became hyperactive after expressing some anxiety-laden curiosity about the "two holes" in the box. As indicated in the unstructured interviews, he flitted from one thing to another, probably under the pressure of anxiety.

There appeared to be another compromise in the general flexibility of the ego in forming age-expected, thematic expressions of feelings and thoughts—the rich thematic development that might be expected in a 6-year-old.

Questions should be raised about the level of thematic development a 6-year-old should optimally be capable of. Although we find this capacity well-developed in some children, it may be related more to precocious cognitive development, which serves as a considerable asset in organizing drive derivatives and affect states, and is not necessarily to be expected of all 6-year-olds.

On the positive side, it should be emphasized that Bryan's ego did show flexibility in being able to adhere to the basic structure of the playroom. He was able to regulate his motoric activity even under situations of stress. For example, when he was dealing with destruction around the dinosaur and the wolf, he wanted very much to leave the playroom, yet he was able to stay and return to the theme, indicating some ability to contain and deal with uncomfortable affects. There was also a rather significant moment when he showed a capacity for self-observation by acknowledging that he had come to get "better understanding." There also appeared to be an implied awareness of some unhappiness in his life.

It should also be added that there was some question about a compromise in his curiosity and capacity to learn, indicated by both historical and playroom material. It was speculated that this might be due to his bathroom behaviors and the potential overstimulation of seeing both mother and father nude. This would have to be watched for more closely, if treatment were undertaken. Along the lines already suggested around anxiety about "knowing," there is some question about the type of defensive pattern he employs to handle this anxiety. He gave some indication of trying to pretend he knows everything. It was shown in the psychologicals that when he did not know an answer, he either tried to get one quickly or demanded that the psychologist give him the answer at once, indicating a general lack of tolerance for being in the nonknowing state.

In summary, then, there appeared to be considerable compromises in optimal flexibility, with fixations around stereotypical patterns; negativism; withholding; diffuse discharge of aggressive impulses; occasional regressions in reality testing; together with more developmentally appropriate types of increased activity around expectable stress points in the phallic-oedipal stage of development and age-appropriate capacities for dealing with painful affects and self-observation.

Category 3: Ego Functions Related to Autonomous and Conflict-Free Spheres of the Ego

Fair (2). From this evaluation, it was hard to assess Bryan's capacity for self-observation, regression in the service of the ego, synthesis and integration, creativity, and curiosity and new learning. However, it did seem he had some capacity for self-observation, since at the end of the first playroom session he was able to say, with some prodding from the interviewer, "I've come here to try and understand." This suggests that the capacity was there, but his negativism often kept him from exercising it. He did show some capacity to regress, as he let himself go in the playroom and was able to reorganize himself at the end and leave in a contained state. He has not yet tried real academic work at school, and his ability to learn really cannot be estimated at this time. His psychological tests show his intelligence to be in the high-average range. Not much can be said about his creativity. He did convey to the interviewer a sense of curiosity. A very intuitive impression is that he has a fairly good capacity for integration.

There appear to be age-appropriate, autonomous functions somewhat restricted by internal and external stress. His genetic endowment and cultural background seem sufficient to support further development of these functions.

Category 4: Relationship Potential

Fair (2). Bryan seems to have attained the phase of triangularity as evidenced by the definite capacity he shows to separate from the maternal figure, both from the way he enters the playroom and engages with a new person, and his ability to go to school, play with peers, and generally to feel safe and secure when his mother is away. In each case he is able to call on a relatively constant internal representation of the nurturing figure, suggesting resolution of aspects of separation-individuation, the attainment of object constancy, and implying movement into a triangular period of relationships. This is further supported by clear-cut phallic-oedipal concerns demonstrated in the playroom. He is plainly manifesting competitiveness when the first thing he says in the playroom is that he can draw a picture better than someone else. He also builds towers and shows off in a phallic, aggressive way. When he plays cards, he tries to beat the interviewer, and there are indications that he wishes to rob his father.

At the same time that he appears to have moved into the phallic-oedipal stage in terms of object relationships, there is some interference in the earlier stages. He does not appear to have consolidated a firm sense of object constancy, that is, a firm internalized representation of himself and the significant other. This is indicated historically by the amount of separation anxiety he experienced and the symptoms he developed when the maid was away. The strong negativistic battles with mother imply regression to dyadic patterns of relatedness and to anal concerns.

In his play with other children, the level of expected peer relationships is somewhat constricted. Bryan does not eagerly look forward to playing with them for the fun of it. As his parents said, he does not seem to really want to go out and play with other youngsters on the block, yet he does engage actively once involved. His capacity for empathy could be questioned at this point in terms of appreciating the rights of other children, although not a great deal is to be expected at this age level. There are some indications of empathy and concern for his brother, however.

In summary, Bryan's relationship potential reflects age-appropriate capacities that are compromised by earlier unresolved issues. He seems to have moved into triangular relationship patterns which are vulnerable to regressions, reflecting difficulties in earlier dyadic patterns. The relationships, however, are not predominantly characterized by these developmentally earlier patterns.

Category 5: Superego Functioning

Fair (2). The superego shows age-appropriate structuralization. For example, Bryan was able to stay within the rules of the playroom during his sessions there—not to break anything or hurt either of us. He was explorative and took it all in, yet stayed within the boundaries of the rules both stated and implied. Recall that at one point he was able to ask for permission to open something, again showing an appropriate capacity for regulation. Since the interviewer was always present, the degree of internalized regulation may be questioned. Nevertheless, from history, the presence of this capacity is supported by the fact that when away from his parents and with friends and peers, both in school and out of the sight of adults, his behavior seems to be within the range of expectable limits. There are, however, the periodic temper tantrums which do show a compromise in age-expected structuralization of the superego. Under general stress or, as related in the recent historical material, under stress stemming from separation anxiety around the maid's absence, or from interaction with the mother colored by an aggressive power struggle, temper tantrums are likely. It is difficult to assess whether this represents an impairment in age-appropriate structuralization or more of a regressive movement.

In summary, age-expected structuralization appears to be

present. There is some internalization appropriate for an oedipal-age child, but it seems to be open to regressive movements under stress.

The superego processes and precursors to later superego organization do not appear to be smoothly integrated with ego and id so as to bring about finely discriminated regulation in the context of a stable esteem system and capacity for pleasure.

The capacity for regulation did not appear to be finely discriminated. In the playroom there seemed to be a general inhibition in the development of richly detailed themes characteristic of his developmental stage. There was a skipping from theme to theme. At home the temper tantrums, negativism, and belligerence and, in the office, the defensively used counterphobic behavior indicate that while regulation is present, it is not finely discriminated, but rather is at times tenuous and compromised by internal and external stress.

There was a sad quality to Bryan which was present throughout the initial playroom session. His explorations and curiosity did not seem to bring pleasure. While esteem appeared to be stable, there was little variation and almost no internally rewarding sense of goodness, even when he performed something that he felt was a complicated feat. For example, in the second interview, when he drew pictures, there was no sense of real internal pride. He showed them to the interviewer but did not appear pleased with himself. Historical material revealed that he was rarely able to give pleasure to his father in play, nor did his father feel that Bryan experienced much pleasure when they interacted. The occasional comments he made to his father—"I want to kill myself"—show that the esteem system is highly vulnerable to primitive feelings of aggression and guilt.

The character and consistency of his present figures for identification (his parents), and the already existing introjections, lead to questions regarding difficulty for his developing identity, sense of self, and attitudes toward predominant types of age-appropriate discharge expression. There seemed to be a great deal of inconsistency in the parents' view of Bryan. They could not get together on discipline—the father feeling that the mother was too harsh, she vacillating between an intrusive, at times seductively sadomasochistic relatedness to Bryan and a firm, limit-setting posture. The father, on the other hand, enjoyed playful, seductive, warm activity but would withdraw as soon as it got too aggressive. Mother and father continually undermined each other. He would tell her to let Bryan be, while she felt that he always avoided the tough times by coming home late from work. From the degree of negativism already existing in Bryan and his concern with diffuse angry feelings, both his own and those externalized upon others, one could already see a part of the maternal introject and its projection onto the world. The father's fear of aggression, it would seem, would cause Bryan to have a hard time working out his current oedipal situation. Difficulties could be expected due both to the dyadic sadomasochistic issues he seems involved in with his mother (which have already formed part of an introjective pattern) and to the father's inability to fully engage Bryan in warm, loving, and competitive play.

It could be observed in Bryan's tendency to externalize interpersonal conflicts, i.e., maintaining his negative position in the sadomasochistic power struggle with the mother, that some early introjects at the base of the superego may be laden with punitive and hostile affects. His disinclination to help clean up the mess in the playroom shows a lack of internalized regulation in this area. It was noted, too, that when playing with other children he often likes the parents of one of the other youngsters to be present, indicating that he wants external support and lacks trust in his own internalized system. His feelings toward his brother are not clear from the initial data. What is clear, however, is that he does find beginning identifications with more adult versions of his mother and father somewhat painful, and this is making it hard for him to form a more oedipally oriented superego system which will help him resolve this phase of development. The pain seems to have to do with issues of closeness with his father and hostile sadomasochistic interactions with his mother.

In summary, the superego system is partially at age-appropriate levels and partially below. Unresolved sadomasochistic struggles in the maternal introject and an inability to fully engage the father in a balanced relationship are compromising the development of age-appropriate capacities.

Category 6: Affects

Fair (3). Affects appeared to be developmentally appropriate. For example, he showed a capacity for warmth with the interviewer, with friends and peers at school, with the teacher. He also showed an intermittent capacity for this kind of engagement at home, with the maid and the family. There was some capacity indicated for compassion with an ill grandfather, although the accuracy of the mother's report must be questioned. There was some selectivity of affects in the playroom in terms of concerns with anger on some occasions, and warm engagement of the interviewer at other times. Aggressive, phallic affects seemed developmentally appropriate, as did the increased activity that emerged around the anxiety generated by these affects.

On the other hand, developmentally immature affect states seemed to be prominent, especially his precipitous discharge of angry feelings through action. As was noted, whenever the play reached a certain level, there occurred a diffuse and unmodulated discharge of aggressive behavior. Within the demanding situation of the psychologicals, he threw blocks at the psychologist, despite the psychologist's attempts to structure the situation and contain him; he insisted on leaving the psychological testing session early. Thus there seemed to be a predominance of primitive angry concerns. The extreme amount of negativism and stubbornness suggests an extraordinary amount of anger from these preoedipal, prephallic levels.

His anxiety seemed to demonstrate itself on all developmental levels. There was some capacity for signal anxiety, as shown in the playroom by his ability to switch themes when he came upon anxiety-provoking material. For example, he was involved in elaborating themes of destruction, talking about the dinosaur and the wolf, and then said he wanted to leave, clearly responding to a signal or internal danger. However, he did not dart for the door but was able in a moment to switch to phallic exhibitionistic concerns in the service of defense (against these earlier, perhaps oral, destructive issues). This "counterphobic" defense did not always work for him, as it brought forth a new kind of anxiety, namely, developmentally appropriate castration anxiety, manifested in his occasional concern with loss of body parts and the general theme of something being missing.

While Bryan showed concern on the psychological tests about being devoured, and showed developmentally appropriate castration anxiety, his most prominent anxiety was related to separation. It seems that there are fixation points here to which he regresses under stress. This was historically documented in terms of his temper tantrums when the maid left, his difficulty in separating from his mother to go to school, and in other ways which will be mentioned later on.

There is some question as to whether he evinced anxiety related to fears of his own instincts, particularly in terms of his wish to approach and perhaps even reunite with the mother. This is speculative at this point. Historically, it is suggested by his vacillating interaction pattern with the mother, from closeness to distance, and in the interviewer's feeling that he should avoid being intrusive with this youngster. Similarly, the mother's greeting to her son as the interviewer opened the door, and her wanting to know immediately what the boy had talked about, clearly showed her own tendency toward intrusiveness. Anxiety around such concerns might be elaborated should treatment occur.

In summary, this category would be rated Fair. While Bryan demonstrates a number of developmentally appropriate affects and shows some selectivity and flexibility under internal conflictual pressure or external stimulation, often in the presence of his mother, he also demonstrates developmentally immature, stereotyped affects around anger and negativism and occasionally a hypertrophied, phallic exhibitionism. Also present is a high degree of castration anxiety around issues of separation.

Category 7: Defenses

Fair to Marginal (2). A mixture of both age-appropriate and developmentally immature defenses was present. Although it appeared to be relatively stable, at times there seemed to be a breakdown in defenses and in capacity for internal regulation, e.g., a diffuse impulsivity and discharge of motor activity. The defensive structure appeared to be rigid in that there was no capacity to use flexible, age-appropriate defenses to meet the situation, but rather a predominant use of certain groups of stereotyped defenses.

The major defensive constellation emerging from history and playroom behavior was a passive, negativistic stance. This stubborn negativism seemed to be Bryan's way of dealing with angry feelings. Recall that in his first play session he entered the room and sat in the center as if to issue orders from an omnipotent position, and then demanded that the interviewer draw first. On the psychological testing, the negativism predominated, as he refused to comply with even minimal requests from the examiner. His parents, as related in the history, complained of stubornness and negativism as "his major problems at home." In addition to the negativism in his playroom behavior, he also used what appeared to be counterphobic defensive mechanisms. For example, during his second assessment, immediately after reporting that he did not feel well and showing the interviewer the rash on his cheek, he began exhibiting his power and strength in daredevil fashion by moving farther and farther away from the platform he had built. Use of identification with the aggressor seemed predominant also, as shown when he began talking about the wolf and the dinosaur, and themes of destruction emerged. Suddenly a shift occurred, and he became the aggressor, jumping around, showing off, and doing the biting himself. Bryan seemed to use increased but diffuse motor activity in the service of dealing with anxiety. He also appeared to use denial in his general refusal to want to talk about things, e.g., his frightening dream. Along these same lines there appeared to be some use of avoidance. While there was no direct use of projection, it was implied by how scared he became when he heard a noise from outside the playroom door, and in the historical material, e.g., his extreme degree of separation anxiety, which suggested that at times he saw the world as a dangerous place.

With the limited data, it was difficult to determine if a reaction-formation defense was being used. If so, it would be in relation to his brother. When Bryan spoke of Robert he showed no angry feelings, yet neither did he talk very much about him. Now did his parents indicate any rivalrous or aggressive behaviors or feelings toward the brother.

In terms of expected, age-appropriate defenses, there seems to be some compromise in age-expected capacities for beginning sublimation. There seem to be compromises in age-expected initial use of some obsessive-compulsive defenses to contain and handle some of his anxiety. There also seem to be limitations in his capacity to identify with certain positive aspects of his parents in order to help better resolve oedipal and preoedipal issues.

In summary, there appears to be a mixture of some developmentally immature defenses such as negativism, denial, avoidance, and projection, along with some age-appropriate defenses such as the counterphobic defenses, identification with the aggressor, and some sublimations. However, the immature defenses seem to be used excessively and the particular defense of negativism to an extraordinary degree. While most of the defenses are stable and work to protect the ego, they are extremely rigid, not permitting the ego the experience of a wide range of thought or affect. They hamper ego functions moderately by constricting the ego, as in the case of the negativism, and by impairing its regulatory capacity through impulsive, counterphobic behaviors. They do not, however, leave the ego open to disruptions in age-appropriate reality testing.

Category 8: Drive Organization

Fair (1). Trying to determine Bryan's level of drive organization in an initial evaluation would be highly speculative. However, the history and playroom data do suggest some facts about his drive organization. During the playroom sessions there was one short shift in movement between phallic-oedipal concerns and oral and anal concerns. In Session 1 he began by sitting expectantly, showing a controlling, narcissistic attitude. He then shifted to a competitive stance ("I can do it better"); then to explorative concerns; he saw two holes, wondered about this, became anxious, and started jumping around. He then became extremely scared by a noise and built higher and higher buildings; became sadistic toward a turtle, concerned with blasting it off; showed the therapist school skills; became frightened and then concerned with destruction around the dinosaur and wolf, with themes of "what was missing." In this session he also spoke about tall buildings, how he didn't want to talk, dreams of monsters, and how he wanted to go home. Thus, the negativistic starting position is seen; the base of security, the return to that position near the end (when he wouldn't help clean up), and in between, the movement from only a hint of curiosity about the two holes, to then what appeared to be a lot of defensive, phallic-aggressive activity, and much anxiety at the oral level and at the phallic, castration level. Session 2, in which he was more relaxed and drew a great deal, was consistent with this material in terms of thematic development. In his psychologicals, there was much stronger emphasis on the negativistic or anal aspect of his drive organization, which seemed to show up in relation to the increased demands put on him. Thus, he would seem to have advanced to the level of curiosity about holes only to defensively activate the aggressive components of his phallic-oedipal drive organization in terms of exhibitionistic derivatives, and then regressing further to show his concerns with basic hunger and the more intense fears of destruction at oral and anal levels. In summary, although he seems to have advanced to a phallic-oedipal level, there are strong fixation points to which he regresses, especially at the anal level.

It should be added that in the second session Bryan exuded a very appealing, seductive quality, suggesting there may be some fixation points at the negative oedipal position. It may also indicate some of his unresolved symbiotic concerns.

In summary, drives are somewhat fused and partially at age-appropriate levels. There appear to be major fixation points at the anal level which are quite rigid. Fixation points at the oral and phallic levels seem to be more mobile.

Category 9: Reality Considerations

Good (3). The parents showed a capacity to understand their child's situation and indicated support of treatment if it were recommended. Both parents seemed to have enough observing ego to establish a working relationship with the interviewer.

Category 10: Intuitive Impressions

Good (3). The sense of curiosity, interest, activity, relatedness to the interviewer, and the way in which the patient entered the playroom and seemed to make use of the time to communicate the wide range of his concerns led to an optimistic impression about his ability to use therapeutic involvement to facilitate development.

Category 11: Capacities for Further Growth and Development in an Average Expectable Environment or in the Current Environment

Marginal (2). This child did not appear capable of optimal age-appropriate psychological development without major intervention. Without intervention, it was expected that he would encounter continued problems in major life areas. For example, it was felt that while his basic ego functions were intact, there were severe compromises in the flexibility of the ego, highlighted by his already existing constrictions around the pattern of negativism and the likelihood that there would be further constrictions with occasional impulsive and counterphobic activity. Similarly, without intervention the superego would continue to be organized around rather punitive, unintegrated introjects. Most of the drives would remain fixated mainly at an anal level, with some at the oedipal level, and there would be little oedipal resolution, leaving the drives predominantly organized in oedipal and preoedipal structures. He would continue to use a variety of developmentally appropriate defenses, but a number of developmentally immature defenses and affects that would pervade his personality organization. Without intervention, there would likely be interferences in the ability to learn, in peer relationships, and, later, in the capacity for intimacy.

In general, it was felt that without intervention this youngster would most likely have a rather marked character disorder, highlighted by his anal fixations and unmet earlier needs. Passive negativistic, impulsive, and counterphobic behavior would predominate. Counterphobic behavior would tend to defend against fears associated with needs from all three levels of psychosexual development—oral, anal, and phallic. His character structure would probably appear immature, with negativism, impulsivity, and depressive features predominating. While during latency he might be capable of some relationships with peers, impulsive, counterphobic, and negativistic patterns would interfere with learning, and unresolved oedipal and preoedipal issues would compromise new identifications, limiting further ego and superego development. Puberty and the new demands of adolescence, it may be speculated, would tax unresolved issues sufficiently to lead to the possible primitive character structure outlined above.

Category 12: Recommendations

Because of the depth and internalized nature of the difficulties, the clear strengths in terms of the attainment of age-expected capacities in ego development and drive organization, and the clear capacity to communicate, regress, and reorganize in the playroom sessions, psychoanalysis was recommended. Questions regarding his occasional soiling, withholding, and other characteristics which might indicate severe fixations and difficulty in using the analytic process were viewed in light of his capacity to function at age-appropriate levels when not under stress, the goal-directed quality of his maladaptive patterns, particularly as they related to conflicts with the mother, and his capacities to use the initial sessions to establish a working relationship with the interviewer.

References

Freud, A. (1962), Assessment of childhood disturbances. *The Psychoanalytic Study of the Child*, 17:149–152. New York: International Universities Press.

——— (1965), *Normality and pathology in childhood.* New York: International Universities Press.

——— (1969), Difficulties in the path of psychoanalysis: A confrontation of past with present viewpoints. In: *The Writings of Anna Freud: Vol. 7.* New York: International Universities Press, pp. 153–156.

——— Nagera, H., & Freud, W. E. (1965), Metapsychological assessment of the adult personality: The adult profile. *The Psychoanalytic Study of the Child*, 20:9–14. New York: International Universities Press.

Greenspan, S.I., & Cullander, C.C.H. (1973), A systematic metapsychological assessment of the personality: Its application to the problem of analyzability. *J. Amer. Psychoanal. Assn.*, 21:303–327.

——— ——— (1975), A systematic metapsychological assessment of the course of an analysis. *J. Amer. Psychoanal. Assn.*, 23:107–138.

——— Hatleberg, J.L., & Cullander, C.C.H. (1976), A systematic metapsychological assessment of the personality in childhood. *J. Amer. Psychoanal. Assn.*, 24:875–903.

Kohut, H. (1970), Scientific activities of the American Psychoanalytic Association: An inquiry. *J. Amer. Psychoanal. Assn.*, 18:462–484.

13

The Normal Development of the Seven-to-Ten-Year-Old Child

MARSHALL D. SCHECHTER, M.D.
LEE COMBRINCK-GRAHAM, M.D.

Developmental propositions go far beyond the discovery and isolation of the childhood prototypes of reaction tendencies. Psychoanalysis interests itself in the nature of the problem, why it was not solved in childhood (a question that requires specification of what phase the child was in), why it was solved in a particular manner, and how this solution affected later development. A complete answer to such questions requires knowledge of what problem-solving and adaptive functions were available and how the environment responded to the problem—i.e., to the nature of the experience (Weiner, 1965).

In truth, of course, the infant is neither a "homunculus nor a tabula rasa," either in his psychological or biological development. The influence of the infant's biochemical and physiological characteristics, temperamental traits, and cognitive and perceptual attributes is determined by the opportunities, constraints, and demands of the family and society. Conversely and simultaneously, the influence of the family and society is shaped by the quality and degree of its consonance or dissonance with the infant's capacities in style of functioning. Furthermore, this reciprocal interaction is not a static process. It is a constantly evolving dynamic, as the child and family and society change over time (Thomas and Chess, 1977, p. 68).

I

The beginning school years have traditionally been termed by psychoanalysts the "latency" period. Throughout the writings of Freud, he referred to this chronological phase as the quiet interlude between the conflict-prone preoedipal and oedipal periods and the tumultuous period of adolescence. Latency was the lull after the resolution of the oedipal conflict and the establishment of the superego. It was the period during which the intrapsychic and physical forces gathered strength for that final adult personality configuration which would take shape in the crucible of adolescence. Latency was the period when major psychiatric symptoms would not likely appear unless the oedipal conflicts were unresolved or unless some specific trauma occurred causing regression to a state of conflict between instinctual forces and the tenuously established superego. The latency period was seen to be dominated by reaction-formation, identifications, and sublimations of instinctual drive forces, and curiosity about sexual matters was viewed as channeled into formal academic learning.

In "Three Essays on the Theory of Sexuality" Freud (1905), spoke of the biphasic quality of the sexual instincts, with one peak during the preoedipal period and the second during adolescence. He suggested both a physiological shift (Freud, 1905) and possible cultural or social shifts as well (Freud, 1923b). In "The Dissolution of the Oedipus Complex" (Freud, 1924b) he wove together physiological and cultural viewpoints. But in "An Autobiographical Study" (Freud, 1924a) he indicated that he thought that the phasic physiological aspect of the sexual drives dominated the advent of the prelatency period and that social forces merely capitalized on the repression of the instinctual drives by introducing schooling, with its pressure for the development of an internal ethic.

Freud noted that the child enters the school-age period after the dissolution of the oedipus complex. It is, he said, the threat of castration and the experience of disappointing nonfulfillments of fantasies, along with maturational development (i.e., genetically determined timing), that forces the child into latency. Freud (1905) viewed latency as a period of diminished sexual activity that begins at the end of the fifth year and continues to puberty, around the eleventh year. It occurs after the passage of the oedipus complex and the establishment of the superego, when the infantile sexual impulses are handled mainly by suppression. The chief task, according to Freud (1926), was to avoid the pressures for masturbation. He indicated (Freud, 1905) that the period of latency was a physiological phenomenon influenced by education. In a 1935 footnote to "An Autobiographical Study" (Freud, 1924a), he stated, "It can, however, only give rise to a complete interruption of sexual life in cultural organizations which have made the suppression of infantile sexuality a part of their system" (p. 37). During the latency period libidinal impulses are partially repressed, partially desexualized and sublimated, and in part inhibited in aim. From these mutations and modifications of instinctual drives derive the beginnings of morality, social order, and religious attitudes (1923a), as well as creative writing, which can represent sublimations of repressed infantile wishes (1924c).

It is striking to note the paucity of literature on this period despite the fact that the greatest numbers of referrals to child psychoanalysts, child psychiatrists, and child mental health clinics are in the 7–11 age range. With a few notable exceptions, little work has been done to integrate the findings from other theoretical perspectives on development with the psychoanalytic understanding of this time frame. Only recently, for example, have some of the constructs of Piaget and his coworkers been related to psychoanalytic understanding of the school-age child (Sarnoff, 1976).

In this chapter we will attempt to disturb the quietude of the latency period by recognizing that critical developmental issues for the child in this period do not simply rest with the intrapsychic processes of integration of the active sexualized experiences of the prelatency years; rather, the school-age years are characterized by an extremely active exchange between the child's inner world and the world around him, expanding now, for the first time, beyond the bounds of the family. We will comment, too, on the complex ecological forces affecting physiological and psychological outcomes—forces which begin exerting themselves well before birth and which determine the way a child enters the school years—and will describe the specific effects of these forces in the school years, demonstrating the vitality, beauty, and poignancy of our school-age youngsters.

We will cite a number of approaches to describing development in order to elucidate some processes with which to frame our discussion. We will show how each of these approaches attempts to integrate environmental and organismic factors in its account of development, and how each characterizes the accomplishments of youngsters entering the school years. We hope to enrich the psychoanalytic view of these years by a review of biological, ego psychological, temperamental, cognitive, and cultural methods of describing development and the issues relevant to the school-age child.

It is our purpose to describe contributions, analytic and nonanalytic, that can broaden the understanding of the normal in this timespan and thereby allow both an appraisal of the deviations which can occur and a consideration of treatment potentials and approaches for these deviations. After presenting some of the precursors of normal development leading up to ages 7 to 10, we will illustrate the features of this age in developmental terms, including psychoanalytic concepts. Specifically, we will touch on present-day contributions related to temperament; psychobiological givens; gender identity; cognitive development; cultural influences; coping and adaptive styles; physical development; and psychoanalytic understanding.

II

Temperament. As is now understood, the healthy newborn comes into the world with not only preformed ego structures, e.g., the five senses and motility (Hartmann, Kris, and Loewenstein, 1946; Piaget, 1951; Mittelmann, 1954) but the capacity to respond, react, and initiate interactions with animate and inanimate elements within his context (Klaus, Hand, and Kennel, 1976). Many have recognized the fact that infants differ. Thomas and Chess (1977), who have described the characteristics of these different temperamental styles, have observed the interaction of these styles with the child's environment and have been able to trace the continuity of some of these characteristics over time. These authors selected the following nine categories to characterize temperamental style: activity level, rhythmicity, approach or withdrawal, adaptability, threshold of responsiveness, intensity of reaction, quality of mood, distractibility, and attention span and persistence. It is in reference to the first item that parents will speak of the child who is either hypo- or hyperactive *in utero* and whose activity level persists similarly after birth. This activity level can be interpreted idiosyncratically, as in the following vignette.

Kathy was 2½ years of age when referred because of hyperactivity. The referring pediatrician said that he had tried medication and behavior modification, but to no avail. Giving her daughter's history, the mother related that Kathy was hyperactive before she was born, came out running, and had been running ever since. Yet, when seen in the five diagnostic interviews, Kathy seemed only slightly above normal in her activity level (with no driven quality). But her parents, who were present throughout the sessions, sat there rigidly, moving nothing but their heads the entire hour.

A child's normal behavioral patterns may be identified as pathological if for any reason there isn't a good match or fit between the child's and the parents' behavioral styles. By contrast, if a pattern of behavior is outside the norm but the child fits into a familial style (e.g., a hyperactive child in a hyperactive family), or if the parents learn early to accommodate and not label these behaviors pathological, they can be fitted into a normal conflict-free sphere of development. As Thomas and Chess (1977) state:

> Goodness of fit results when the properties of the environment and its expectations and demands are in accord with the organism's own capacities, characteristics, and style of behaving. When the "consonance" between organism and environment is present, optimal development in a positive direction is possible. Conversely, poorness of fit involves discrepancies and "dissonances" between environmental opportunities and demands in the capacities and characteristics of the organism, so that distorted development and maladaptive functioning occurs. [p. 11]

These authors group youngsters into three constellations: the easy child, the difficult child, and the slow-to-warm-up child.

The easy child is characterized by regularity in sleeping and eating schedules, positive responses to new stimuli, mild or moderately intense moods which are mainly positive, and high adaptability to changes. The difficult child is characterized by negative withdrawal in response to stimuli, irregularity in biological functioning, intense mood responses which are mainly negative, and wide swings in moods so that frustrations usually produce tantrum behaviors. The slow-to-warm-up child has mild mood reactions and slow adaptability to new stimuli, mild to moderate irregularities in biological functions, but with repeated exposures to new situations; these children tend to quietly and positively respond with interest and involvement. Thus one principle of development attends to the fit between the individual's particular attributes and the response of the environment.

Psychobiological givens. A vast number of biological processes govern the evolution of the individual. If we look at a few—physiological growth, endocrine systems, and neuroanatomical developments—we can see an unfolding process occurring as if a time schedule were built into the human genetic system. Yet each area of development is highly sensitive to the environment. A dramatic example of this is found in the work of Powell, Brasel, and Blizzard (1967a, 1967b) on failure to thrive due to maternal deprivation. Infants fitting this description were not gaining height or weight and on close study were found to have a growth hormone deficiency. In a hospital where attention was focused on adequate nutrition and affective bonding, and without any injection of growth hormone, the children began to grow and to produce increased levels of the hormone. However, when the children were returned home, having attained nearly normal height and weight, they again stopped growing and growth hormone levels dropped. A return to the hospital environment with its affectional warmth and individual stimulation resulted in a return of normal patterns of growth and normal levels of the hormone. This experiment in nature, akin to a demonstration of Koch's postulates, gives evidence of the intimate relationship between the child and the environment, one capable of affecting the most delicate neurochemical mechanisms. It shows that, even with normally functioning anatomical structures, the child still needs the right kind of external stimuli to trigger the production of biological substrates necessary for development.

Gender identity. Studies by Money (1968), Stoller (1968), and Green (1974) bear upon the important interaction between biological and environmental influences in the formation of gender identity and sexual expression. Gender identity refers to the sense of being male or female and the behaviors corresponding to this internal self-percept. Children become aware of genital differences often as early as 18 months, and their own self-concept within a male or female sex role is quite well established by age 5. There are suggestions that having male and female adult figures to relate to enhances and insures normal gender identifications. Within the first few hours of life—even when there may be genital ambiguity—the child is usually related to by parents with their own expectations of gender-appropriate behavior. In this fashion, boys are often handled more roughly (e.g., the father buys a football and helmet within the first year of life), and girls are talked to more than male babies are. Greater roughness in the handling of boys may encourage male aggressiveness later, while the greater verbal interaction between girls and mothers may stimulate earlier verbalization in females. Although there is some question about prenatal hormonal influences determining gender identity, it is clear that the environment plays an enormous part in solidifying this aspect of personality development. The wish to be a mother or father remains stable from earliest verbal productions on, and while the vocational role assumed at any given phase of development may change, it too has the cast of a sex-role function as children fantasize themselves as acting as adults. Playing house, playing doctor, cops and robbers, etc. are all preparatory activities for gender-related adult functions. Even the toys that adults give to children unconsciously tend to funnel children into specific sex role–related functions (i.e., giving girls dolls and boys toy cars and guns). The anthropologists Whiting and Edwards (1973) note that all behavior characteristic of males and females seem remarkably malleable under the impact of socialization pressures, which appear remarkably consistent from one society to another.

The father's role in a family has become the focus of a number of studies. Lynn (1974) states:

> The unfavorable consequences of father-absence may manifest themselves at an earlier age in boys than in girls. Father-absence may cause problems in the young boy's masculine identification; the girl, having to execute no shift in sex-role identification, may not manifest problems until later, when she lacks an adult male with whom to relate as she matures. Her problems in relating to males might be expected to surface during adolescence when her interest in the opposite sex heightens. [pp. 255–256]

Cognitive development. The work of Piaget (1952, 1954) in Europe and Werner (1948) in the United States yields another important developmental principle. Looking at cognitive development, Piaget described a process by which the individual, building first on inherent abilities, and later on acquired ones, assimilates new experiences and accommodates to his environment in a stepwise process that leads to the development of mature cognitive processes. The processes described in this model demonstrate that the individual's rate and kind of development depend on the abilities already achieved and the opportunities in the individual's environment—again, an exquisite relationship between constitution and environment as the important factor in development.

Cultural influences. Freud, himself, as noted above, was cognizant of the relationship between the social and cultural issues affecting development, but the specific nature of these effects is more clearly investigated in cross-cultural anthropological studies and in later contributions to the psychoanalytic movement, including those of Anna Freud (1937, 1951, 1965), and Mahler, Pine, and Bergman (1975).

Assuming that individuals have relatively similar fundamental schedules of development, cross-cultural studies help to delineate which developmental principles are invariable in an average expectable environment and which are highly subject to the issues of a particular culture. For example, Thomas and Chess (1977) compare their temperament scores from the New York Longitudinal Study (NYLS) with an African sample from the Kikuyu, Digo, and Masai tribes to find that threshold was the only category in which there was congruence: "In every other category there were significant differences between the African and American sample, as well as among the three tribes. The cross-cultural data indicate that temperament must be interpreted within a cultural context" (p. 151). These authors also note that in comparing the NYLS sample with a sample from a Puerto Rican working class parent group (PRWC), sleep problems occurred less frequently in the ages 5 to 9 NYLS sample because from early on in life the parents did not tolerate irregular sleeping patterns. By contrast, the ages 5 to 9 PRWC sample had frequent sleep problems emanating from a laxness in parental insistence on regular sleep habits in the preschool period.

Coping and adaptive styles. Neo-Freudians (e.g., Horney, 1939; Sullivan, 1953; Erikson, 1968) focus particularly on the nature of the interaction of the environment and the individual's intrapsychic development. Murphy and Moriarity (1976) present a model for this which details children's coping mechanisms. The authors indicate that styles of coping need to be seen in relation to the situation as experienced by the child and that coping styles and techniques shift and modify over time. This idea is similar to Anna Freud's considerations regarding defense mechanisms (1937). So another principle of development is conceptualized which relates the individual's particular experience in his context with intrapsychic mechanisms of adaptation, coping, and defense. During the preschool period, vulnerabilities were noted with regard to disorganization, deterioration, and inhibition of affective, cognitive, motor, or integrative functioning. Coping styles included gating excessive stimulation and restructuring the environment; acceptance of people; the ability to differentiate reality from fantasy. Murphy and Moriarity (1976) noted that the mother's respect for natural pace and rhythms and her acceptance of the child's autonomy consistently supported the child's vegetative, integrative functioning, thereby decidedly increasing coping capabilities. They suggest that "the mother's adjustment may be facilitated by the compatibility, but the mother's adjustment has little relation to the infant's activity level and sensory reactivity: the latter seems to be determined by constitutional dispositions. However, there is a reciprocal relationship between the infant's drive level and mother's responses through speech and facial expressions. The evocative, responsive baby draws responses from the mother that in turn stimulate that baby" (p. 339).

Murphy and Moriarity have noted that the capacity for self-regulation of sensations varies for different infants and within each individual along a number of dimensions. Self-regulatory mechanisms include the use of rest and of active behaviors in response to intense stimuli, as well as the tempo of mastery and integration achieved by each individual. If helped to overcome successfully the stresses to which they are exposed, infants can develop a resilience to overwhelming stress in the future. "It is not surprising, then," write Murphy and Moriarity, "that we found continuity in some motor and cognitive zones of the personality consistent with plasticity in the child's overall adaptational pattern: a stable core permits flexibility of response to change in pressures. But also variability, imbalances, moderate early instabilities and difficulties are balanced by coping efforts leading to creative integrations, reflectiveness and insight. *Mild vulnerabilities stimulate coping efforts*" (p. 343; italics ours).

Physical development. Exemplifying the above is the physical development of the child as he enters the 7–10 period. After a period of rapid growth up to age 2, there is a slower increase in total body size until the growth spurt before puberty. The volume of the brain at birth is 10 percent that of the adult volume and climbs to 90 percent by 5 years of age. The remaining 10 percent of brain growth occurs gradually over the next 9 years. So by age 7 the individual has acquired over 90 percent of his brain volume.

Normal physical development takes the child from complete dependency for physical and emotional care at birth to, at age 7, (1) an ability in the gross motor area to walk, run, jump, skip, ride a bike, balance, hop, catch, throw, somersault, etc.; (2) an ability in the fine motor as well as visual-auditory motor areas to use pincer's grasp, imitate geometric figures, draw a six-part person, develop printing and even elementary cursive writing skills, follow visual and auditory cues, etc.); (3)

an ability in the language sphere to track auditory stimuli, imitate speech, define words, identify bodily parts, express ideas, differentiate between make-believe and reality with an ability to convey these differences verbally (primary process vs. secondary process), count, differentiate colors, begin punning and enjoy verbally expressed humor besides scatological physical clowning behavior, etc.; (4) an ability in the personal-social spheres to separate from parents for considerable periods, dress self, i.e. shoes, relate with peers, express needs and desires verbally, participate in group activities, e.g., "Simon Says," "Put Your Little Foot Out," "Follow the Leader," etc.

As anatomical development of the central nervous system proceeds—perhaps measured and judged by myelinization—the cellular structures become more refined for specific functions (consider language development and the difference between childhood and adult aphasias, with the latter's reliance on the function of Broca's area); simultaneously these same tissues become less sensitive to infection and toxins. This is seen, for example, in the effect of phenylalanine in children deficient in phenylalanine hydroxylase, an inborn error of metabolism which inhibits the breakdown of phenylalanine into its normal amino acid byproduct, tyrosine. In these cases, phenylalanine becomes toxic to the brain, and unless there is a limitation in intake very soon after birth, the child can become severely retarded mentally. However, if phenylketonuria (PKU) is detected early and a low phenylalanine diet is instituted, chances are that normal intellect will be preserved as long as the diet can be maintained through age 6. The suggestion from this research is that, concomitantly with the shift to the Piagetian phase of concrete operations and to resolution of the oedipus complex, we see an increase in alpha activity on the electroencephalogram from 8 cycles per second to about 11 cycles per second, probably representing a greater specificity in utilization and localization of central nervous system function. Is it possible that the infantile amnesia may truly be a combination of psychological events being played out against the background of normal central nervous system maturational processes?

The normal 7-year-old has developed adequate visual motor and auditory motor control which help him stop reversing letters, numbers, or words, thereby bringing reading, spelling, and mathematics within his reach. There is some evidence that just about this time there is a major growth in the frontal areas of the brain, those areas most associated with socialization. The 7-year-old is therefore well prepared physically for the tasks which psychoanalytic theory has described and which society designates for him.

Psychoanalytic understanding. The contributions of psychoanalysis offer major insights into the interaction between individual and environment and how this interaction contributes to development. Mahler, Pine, and Bergman (1975) have made a most significant contribution in observing the nature of the infant's interaction with his mother, for example, demonstrating on the one hand the invariant stages of development—autistic, symbiotic, and separation-individuation, and, on the other, the fact that the outcome of these stages is entirely dependent on the nature of the infant-mother interaction, which is in turn dependent on the particular attributes of both infant and mother. In her highly focused work on infants and young children and their mothers, Mahler has specified the processes alluded to theoretically in the work of Hartmann, Kris, and Loewenstein (1946), who discuss the unfolding and development of ego functions as the environment provides opportunities.

Psychoanalytic theory describes, as occurring just prior to the school-age period, a phase in which a primacy of interest in the genital area and a simultaneous attachment to the parent of the opposite sex give rise to the oedipus complex. The increased libidinal tie to the opposite-sex parent—and a concurrently increased aggressive-destructive drive toward the parent of the same sex—creates an intolerable psychic bind. As a result of the negative thoughts and feelings toward the same-sex parent, who must be destroyed if the positive libidinal attachment to the opposite-sex parent is to be fulfilled, the child becomes fearful of retaliation by the same-sex parent, who, being bigger and stronger, must be more damaging to the child than the child can be to the parent. Out of this conflict a solution is evolved along the lines of the notion, "If you can't lick 'em, join 'em." Three outcomes help the child unravel the oedipal dilemma and move on into "latency." The first is that of identification (with the perceived aggressor), which has clear implications for how the child fits into the social world (of parents, peers, teachers, and other relevant persons) and also how the child perceives himself functioning both at present and in the future. (From these identifications the ego ideal is drawn.)

The second outcome is that of superego formation, which goes beyond the mere capacity to judge right from wrong to include the development of ethics, morality, guilt, anxiety, depression, altruism, social conscience, and the ability to put oneself in another's place.

The third outcome is the loosening of bonds to the family—in effect removing oneself from the combat zone—with the resulting opportunity to experience the values and judgments of those outside the family. Psychoanalytic theory of development, then, bestows on our ideal 7-year-old an emerging sense of who he is and who he wants to be, a conscience by which he can manage himself in the larger world, and enough comfort about his relationship with his parents that he can begin to form significant relationships with people outside his family.

Anna Freud (1965), in describing the child's steps toward independence along developmental lines regarding object relationships, characterizes the latency period as "the post-Oedipal lessening of drive-urgency and the transfer of libido from the parental figures to contemporaries, community groups, teachers, leaders, impersonal ideals and aim-inhibited, sublimated interests, with fantasy manifestations giving evidence of disillusionment with and denigration of the parents ('family romance,' twin fantasies, etc.)" (p. 66). In the same volume she notes the following developmental lines from play to work, so cogent to the school-age child: "Ability to play changes into ability to work when a number of additional faculties are acquired, such as the following: (a) to control, inhibit, or modify the impulses to use given materials aggressively and destructively (not to throw, to take apart, to mess, to hoard), and to use them positively and constructively instead (to build, to plan, to learn, and—in communal life—to share); (b) to carry out preconceived plans with a minimum regard for the lack of pleasure yield, intervening frustrations, etc., and the maximum regard for the pleasure in the ultimate outcome; (c) to achieve thereby not only the transition from primitive, instinctual to sublimated pleasure, together with a high grade of neutralization of the energy employed, but equally the transition from the pleasure principle to the reality principle, a development which is essential for success in work during latency, adolescence, and in maturity" (p. 82).

III

What happens during this period from ages 7 to 10—the "middle years of childhood"? What developmental tasks are to be tackled during this period, and what issues will be addressed? And when the child has finished his tenth year, what will he have accomplished in order to move on to the next phase of development?

As we have noted before, classical psychoanalytic theory describes the beginning of this period as occurring when the oedipus complex is resolved, thus setting the youngster free to move outside the family into a larger society of peers and adults. In the process of resolution of the oedipus complex the superego is formed, and this enables the child to deal with his newly expanded society with an accommodation that allows him to function more effectively without the protection of his family. Though in actuality both the resolution of the oedipus complex and the formation of the superego are gradual processes and extend well into the middle years of childhood, there does seem to be an almost discrete jump at around age 7.

Shapiro and Perry (1976) examine latency in its classical and psychobiological connotations and make a number of important observations. They note the historical importance of age 7 as a turning point in child development. In the Middle Ages children began formal training for adulthood as apprentices or as pages at court; upper-class children in present-day England are often sent to boarding school at this age; children in our own society begin grammar school around this age; and in the Roman Catholic Church children of 7 are considered to have reached the "age of reason" and receive their First Communion. Erikson (1950) observes the importance of this age in a number of societies. Because of the frequency with which societies identify this age as a turning point, we must consider the possibility that something built into the psychological template of the individual enables him to make these shifts at this age.

What are the shifts that must occur if the child is to adapt to a situation of new social demands? The child must be ready to move from an egocentric view to one in which he perceives himself as part of a complex ecological system in which he can function competently. An historical analogy to this shift of perspective is the shift from the geocentric view of Ptolemaic astronomy to the heliocentric view of Copernicus, the latter recognizing that the earth is only one of several planets orbiting the sun. At a greater level of complexity is the recognition that this solar system is only a minute part of an enormous universe.

Using this analogy, then, if all the tasks of the middle years of childhood could be summarized into one important one, it would be the child's realization of himself in larger contexts. If successful, the child would also have a perception of how he needs to function in these varied contexts and some of the rules that govern his participation—just as the Copernicans understood elliptical orbits and the forces which held the planets in their orbits.

The child in the middle years has developed a personal competence in language, motor, and ego functioning which allows him to present himself to society like a butterfly emerging from the chrysalis—sticky, shaky, unpracticed, but equipped to try himself in a larger world—to be introduced, as Erikson puts it, to the "technology of this society." The timing of this introduction appears to be related to the development of the brain at this time (refinement of motor skills, inhibitory feedback systems allowing for longer attention span, and frontal lobe development which seems related to socialization). It also seems to be related to a stability regarding the parental introjects, the formation of the superego, and an ability to repress, suppress, or sublimate instinctual drives, with a subsequent increase in the capacity to concentrate and to order thoughts and a consequent increase in fantasy. We realize that in the United States there are children in the middle years of childhood for whom environmental emphases differ from the mode, and the outcome differs because societal expectations are different. These children at the extreme ends of population distribution—inner city and rural—may need to mobilize psychic energies to properly adapt to their environment and may emphasize some areas of ego function at the expense of others. For example, the farm child will need to master a different technology—animal husbandry, driving a tractor, etc.—and his social contacts with peers may be more limited, even though attendance at school is mandatory. By contrast, the inner city child from a chaotic neighborhood may have important concerns with survival which take priority over concerns for formal learning. Clearly there are common denominators among these children, but the differences relate more to the pressure of parents, teachers, and social mores rather than to the presence of intrapsychic conflict states.

Sullivan (1953) characterizes this period and its vicissitudes thus: "This is the first developmental stage in which the limitations and peculiarities of the home as a socializing influence begin to be open to remedy. The juvenile era has to remedy a good many of the cultural idiosyncrasies, eccentricities of value, etc., that have been picked up in the childhood socialization; if it does not, they are apt to surive and color, or warp, the course of development through subsequent periods" (p. 227). According to Sullivan, the child in this era, the "juvenile era," now entering a broader interpersonal context, becomes subject to a variety of new experiences which he must learn to handle. Primarily these are related to exposure to a group of peers who are not his siblings and therefore bring with them customs different from those of his family, and to a group of adults who will evaluate him and, through him, his family. In order to adapt to the requirements of these new situations the child must learn certain things which Sullivan characterizes as follows. First there is "social subordination," through which the child recognizes a more general and impersonal adult authority, for example, the authority of policemen and crossing guards. And through the recognition of their authority over himself and his peers, he also learns a way of evaluating his peers—in effect, by how they are treated by these adults. In so doing, of course, he learns at first to evaluate his own behavior. "Social accommodation" refers to the process of grasping how many different ways of living there are. The child starts out with little sensitivity to others' feelings of worth, and for this reason juvenile society tends to be rigid and cruel, and the participation of the individual in it is at first compliant. As the child moves further into the period he begins to "differentiate authority figures," and this allows him for the first time to reflect critically about his own parents and to begin to evaluate them. The pressure of society then forces the child to give up many of the egocentric ideas of the childhood era and to focus more on the reality of his existence in society; this is called "control of focal awareness." These social pressures are internalized in the individual in "sublimatory reformulations," orientation of focal awareness according to group-approved behavior, and the development of "supervisory patterns," reflecting an awareness of one's own effect on others or in groups. The "supervisory patterns" become monitors which help the individual evaluate the effect of his behavior, not only during and after it, but in advance. Sullivan takes the view, then, that the pressure of social experience forces the development of self-evaluation, social awareness, and conformity, traits crucial to the individual's survival in society. That the child in this period does in fact develop these skills is confirmed by a number of psychological studies, even though the forces determining this development may be conceived as very different from those postulated by Sullivan.

As regards observational material relating to development in the "juvenile" era, psychological studies in two areas seem relevant. One is the child's perception of self and others, and the other is the child's sense of responsibility in society—his sense of morality. Both are central issues of development for the child between 7 and 10 years of age.

In her excellent review, *The Middle Years of Childhood*, Minuchin (1977) describes many studies that illustrate the movement of social and personal awareness in the child during this period. In the area of personal awareness, for example, children are described as moving from an egocentric view of themselves to a more differentiated, more objective position of self-description. By 9 or 10 children are able to put themselves in another's shoes. As we shall see later, this ability is intimately connected with the development of the ability to perform logical operations. Perception from another's position will clearly allow the youngster to see himself from another's point of view.

Evident also in this period is an increase in objectivity in the child's description of others. Minuchin cites a number of studies which present evidence of a shift in the child's descriptions of others and of the social situation away from an egocentric position. This ability to objectively evaluate others and oneself as seen by others undergoes significant development in the middle years, but, as with the evaluation of the self, critical evaluation of others becomes a major issue in adolescence.

The growing capacity to evaluate self, others, and the social situation is intimately connected with the child's moral development during these years. Both Piaget (1932) and Kohlberg (1967) describe the gradual growth of morality as maturational processes combine with social experience. Piaget's classic study of boys playing at marbles shows how children of different ages deal with rules. Children at ages 7 and 8 have very rigid respect for the rules, though they may argue vehemently about what the rules are. Toward the end of the middle years, children begin to understand the "spirit" rather than the "letter" of the rules, and negotiations about the rules often hold more interest than the game itself. In one of Piaget's experiments (1932), a child's understanding of intention and transgression is tested. Piaget presented two stories to the children, one in which a youngster breaks a cup trying to get a cookie he has been told not to take, and another in which the youngster breaks fifteen cups while running to get something for his mother. Each child is then asked which of the two should be punished more, and why. By 9, according to Piaget, most children can grasp the idea of being wrong by intention.

Kohlberg's study, a standard work on moral development, posits three stages—preconventional, conventional, and postconventional, each divided into two substages. Although Kohlberg, like Piaget, is loath to associate specific chronological ages with stages of development, the years between 7 and 10 are usually the period in which children pass through the conventional stage of moral development. Kohlberg's view is that each stage builds on the prior one and occurs in invariant sequence. Both maturation and experience are necessary to this development. Kohlberg does, however, maintain that people do not inevitably go through all the stages; depending on cultural norms and expectations as well as other factors, individuals may not reach the postconventional stage at all, but may still be well-functioning members of society.

The conventional stage of moral development, as one can imagine, is the first stage in which the individual registers in his moral reasoning the effect of his relationship with a society. In the first substage, the individual is concerned with the approval of others and defines his behavior as good or bad accordingly. One earns approval by being a "nice" person. In the second substage, the individual responds to the "law and order" of the society, has a fixed interpretation of the rules, and is interested in maintaining the social order for its own sake. As concrete as even the second of these substages is, one can see what an immense change there is from the morality of the preschool child, who measures good and bad in terms of the punishment he will receive.

Another major contribution to modern psychoanalytic theory is that of Erikson (1950), who characterizes the middle years of childhood as the stage in which the child deals with the issues of "industry versus inferiority." Discussing the psychosocial issues of this period, Erikson refers to it as the "time to go to school." The child leaves the family for the wider society, for the first time really, in order to learn the industry of his society, in order to become an adult. He focuses on the issue of personal competence in the activities of the adult society. "Children at this age," writes Erikson (1959), "*do* like to be mildly but firmly coerced into the adventure of finding out that one can learn to accomplish things which one would never have thought of by oneself, things which owe their attractiveness to the very fact that they are *not* the product of play and fantasy but the product of reality, practicality, and logic; things which thus provide a token sense of participation in the real world of adults" (p. 84). In this sentence Erikson characterizes what he perceives to be the important transitional nature of the middle years; the youngster with one foot in childhood and the play activities which have allowed him to master conflicts, and the other foot in the work of adulthood, mixing seriousness and play.

In chapter 6 of *Childhood and Society* (1950) Erikson reacquaints us with Tom Sawyer's chum, Ben Rogers, who is described as he appears just before Tom bamboozles him into whitewashing Aunt Polly's fence. Of Ben, Erikson says:

> My clinical impression of Ben Rogers is a most favorable one, and this on all three counts: organism, ego, and society. For he takes care of the body by munching an apple; he simultaneously enjoys imaginary control over a number of highly conflicting items (being a steamboat and parts thereof, as well as being the captain of said steamboat, and the crew obeying said captain); while he loses not a moment in sizing up social reality when, on navigating a corner, he sees Tom at work. By no means reacting as a steamboat would, he knows immediately how to pretend sympathy though he undoubtedly finds his own freedom enhanced by Tom's predicament. [p. 210]

Thus do Mark Twain and Erik Erikson characterize the child in the middle years—actively developing mastery and independence in his relationship with himself and with the social world around him.

To a large extent the success of this psychosocial stage depends on the youngster's sense of competence and mastery regarding the learning tasks placed before him. The child's thrust in learning is backed by his sense of competence (White, 1960). For Erikson, the child's accomplishments in this period depend often on how successfully the oedipus complex has been resolved, for if the child is still wrapped up in issues of the family he is not free to learn to read, for example. Current observations of the struggles of youngsters in this period add two other factors which determine how the child succeeds at these tasks—temperament and physiological development. The tasks themselves, for this society, involve first learning to read, spell, and calculate, and then learning simple facts—about history, for example—which can be recombined by the child into his own understanding in a rather concrete way. Let us examine some deviations in temperament and physiological development, turning to a consideration of the cognitive approaches that develop in this period.

In their book on temperament, Thomas and Chess (1977) present evidence from several studies that strongly suggests that temperament has a strong influence on the child's achievement in the middle years, both academically and socially. In one study they cite, there was a significant correlation between low academic achievement scores and the temperamental characteristics of nonadaptability and withdrawal—characteristics of the slow-to-warm-up child. In predicting children's IQs, teachers tended most often to underestimate the intelligence of children with these characteristics. Children with the temperamental characteristic of low persistence have difficulty establishing appropriate amounts of attention for mastering academic tasks or for moving from one task to the next.

When a child cannot master the fundamentals of reading, writing, spelling, and mathematics because of a specific learning disability, or cannot be a part of the peer group because of awkwardness in coordination and confused laterality, as seen in minimal cerebral dysfunction, he will develop a sense of inferiority and low self-esteem. Organic central nervous system dysfunctions can disrupt academic performance and peer interrelations—two of the major tasks of this phase of development. These areas of dysfunction first come to light in the beginning school years, with exposure to academic tasks and the interpersonal interactions they entail.

The cognitive tasks of the child between 7 and 10 are some of the most exciting of this period and provide the tools for the adjustments necessary for socialization and academic mastery. Piaget (1954) and his colleagues have described the major movement in cognitive development: from preoperational, associative, egocentric "rules" of "logic" to the concrete operational stage, with its logic bound to objects and situations but nonetheless transferable from one situation to another. Though some children develop more sophisticated concepts earlier than others, there is no doubt that most of the development of concrete operations occurs between 7 and 10.

The two major cognitive accomplishments of concrete operations are classification and conservation. Very simply, classification is the ability to form categories, conservation the ability to conceive sameness in the face of apparent differences. Realizing that the child starts with an idiosyncratic associative form of thinking, one can see that the development of these skills is a gradual process. In conservation, for example, the child starts from a position of "concentration," the ability to focus on only one property at a time. For example, if the child looks at the density of a group of objects, he cannot also take into consideration the length of the space occupied by them. In a transitional period, the child may alternately consider density and length but be unable to put the two together simultaneously. Only when he has achieved conservation of the particular property in question can he simultaneously consider two factors and see that changes in one may be compensated for by changes in the other.

It is worth considering for a moment how essential these abilities are to the academic tasks of the middle years. Consider the practice in first grade reading of classifying words by a particular sound (e.g., cat, mat, pat, rat, sat, etc.). The preoperational child is quite likely to become interested in "patting the cat" or having the "cat chase the rat." In fact, it is often helpful to the beginning reader to connect like-sounding words (categories) into stories, as the Dr. Seuss books do. But the later school-age child is expected to learn how to connect *things,* using dimensions other than the story connecting them. In first and second grade the student learns to subtract, and this, though at first it is often done by memorization, later involves a familiarity with reversibility. How much easier it is for the child, having learned that 6 (of anything) combined with 7 (of anything) always yields a total of 13, to simply know that if the operation is reversed two groups result—one of 6 and one of 7—than to have to memorize that 13 minus 6 equals 7. It is possible to teach a child by rote to spell words and to read a particular book, as well as to add, subtract, and multiply. But for the child to be able to use these skills and apply them in situations different from those in which he has learned them, he must know *how* to do these things, and knowing how in this period requires the operations we have described. Thus the child's success in school in the latter part of the middle years requires the appropriate cognitive development. By 10 years of age many children are ready to begin formal operations —building operations on operations (instead of on objects). An early example cited by Minuchin (1977) is the capacity to consider alternatives, even to consider that several solutions might be equally valid.

We alluded earlier to the intimate connection of cognitive development in these years to socialization and the ability to participate thoughtfully and responsibly in interpersonal contexts. Thus, the middle years of childhood normally present the child the task of becoming competent in society, separate from one's family, and of trying out intimate relationships with others. In this period, though children do travel in groups, achievement is essentially individual, as a basis is developed for self-esteem and a sense of competence. The child measures himself against others and competes for himself. It is only in the next stage of development that children begin to form teams and can be truly gratified by the achievements of important others.

Cultural factors always impinge on and influence the middle-years child, since the educational system carries with it the structure and mores of the society it serves. It is the school which promotes the language of the elders, permitting through the teaching of social studies the transmission of the myths of the society, or of a section thereof. It is the specific culture which dictates the spoken and written language, its idioms, and its accents. It is expected that the child after a few years of schooling will reflect the attitude and idiosyncratic emphases of the culture and of the individual's family. It is differences in systems of education—formal and informal—that account for the different languages in the world, and for the differences in religion, philosophy, and character inherent in each community. The normal child in the first few years of schooling is exposed to the pressure of emotionally charged music carrying the message of the culture. Sayings and customs are transmitted from class to class, e.g., "Step on a crack, break your mother's back," which fit well with the obsessive-compulsive defenses erected during this period. The indoctrination of children into their society is expected to be accomplished during the first few years of school.

Generally by age 7 sexual identity has been adequately established in boys and girls. Identification with the same-sex parent has been built up through innumerable societal attitudes and overt and covert messages from family, adults, and older siblings. Tasks lacking any natural link to sex-specific attributes are assigned according to gender: girls wash dishes and clean house, while boys take out the garbage and mow the lawn. Girls take babysitting jobs, and boys deliver papers. Until very recently, boys were encouraged to engage in contact sports, while girls were not, instead playing games like jump rope, hopscotch, and jacks. Cleanliness, neatness, and interest in clothing are valued in girls, while the typical boy of this age is characterized as having tousled hair and soiled clothes.

Fathers who have a significant position in the home offer models for identification for the male and aid the female child in asserting a feminine role. In families in which dynamics lead to the development of feminine traits in boys, the boys are presented for consultation around the age of 7 (see Green, 1974, p. 241).

In girls at about the same age there may be a beginning increase in estrogenization, which gradually reaches adult levels during adolescence (Kestenberg, 1967a, 1967b, 1968). This increase in female hormone secretion results by age 9 in the flaring of the alae of the hips and in the budding of the nipples. In similar fashion, rising androgen levels in boys of about 10 lead to increased testicular size. These physical changes usually drive the developing self-image toward a much more defined gender concept. Sexual identifications are made more secure by the influence of peer groups and of support systems provided by society—Little League, Scouts, Blue Birds, ballet class, and so forth.

During ages 7 to 10 the normally utilized defense mechanisms—obsessive-compulsion, reaction-formation, sublimations, repressions, and fantasy—are developed and strengthened. These can best be observed in the unconscious derivatives seen in fantasies, dreams, and play. The superego is most often represented by monsters, who in dreams early on in this period are pictured as chasing the dreamer until the dreamer reaches a place of safety. As the dreamer shuts the door to the protected area, the monster has its hand (or claw) on the doorknob; the dreamer awakens in a state of anxiety, as the question is posed in the dream as to whether the monster (or monstrous human) can open the door before the dreamer throws the bolt. This symbolic representation of superego formation indicates the severity and brutality of the internal representations that are erected to punish the child for unacceptable wishes derived from libidinal and aggressive drives. The child at this time of life is preoccupied during play with violent sadomasochistic activities, as well as with concerns about ultimate vocational and procreative goals. Movies and television programs often serve as the stimulus for manifest dream contents and play.

In a most erudite and valuable theoretical and clinical study of this period, Sarnoff (1976) notes that "psychoanalytic symbol formation constitutes a primary pathway for drive discharge in the state of latency, allowing for indirect drive discharge if the internalized demands of society block the direct discharge of drives" (p. 92). He goes on to note that fantasies leading to masturbation, which are generally more inhibited during the earlier phases of this period, due to fears of parental reaction and the internalized affects of shame and guilt, tend to relax in the later stages. Interest in bodily differences and changes, their own and others', is seen in sublimated doctor play and in more overt expressions such as looking at pictures of nudes, looking up salacious words in the dictionary, and voyeuristic peeking at members of the opposite sex. The conflict between consciously and unconsciously derived ideas of parental ethics, on the one hand, and a developing knowledge of peer group ethics, on the other, is joined with the ego of the child, who is forced to make a series of compromises. These compromises are the resultant of a series of forces: the maturation of the child, increased cognitive and verbal abilities, greater awareness of the surrounding environment, and modifying attachments to parents, peers, and other adults.

Regarding superego contributions to this conflict Sarnoff (1976) says:

> Cognitive maturation, psychosexual development, and social expectations contribute to superego changes throughout this period. The popular concept of the superego—that the superego forms only at age six with the internalization of parental imagoes that accompanies the passing of the Oedipus complex and is enforced through the negative influences of the affect of guilt—*is far too limited*. We present the view here that the superego is a product of a *multitude of influences*. [p. 131; italics ours]

Early in this time frame fantasies are often fragmented, so that only parts of drive, control, and defense can be seen. Later on these fragments, displaced onto symbolic representations, are elaborated and synthesized into a series of conscious visual and verbal images incorporating real people and real circumstances. Sarnoff (1976) explains this function thus: "These fantasies discharge the drives and protect the mental equilibrium of the latency state" (p. 31). It is through this fantasy life that we can see how conflicts may be dealt with first in thought rather than in reality, leading later to specific goal-directed activities as the result of more reality-oriented fantasies during adolescence.

During the middle years aggressive drives are observable not only in fantasies and play but also in curiosity in learning (in the broadest sense), in competitiveness, and in regressive phenomena such as self-injury, nailbiting, self-blame, and self-doubts. These later expressions of the turning of aggression inward can be evidenced by depressions, by projective mechanisms giving an almost paranoid quality to some children, and by phobic reactions to the responses expected from the environment with regard to the child's destructive impulses.

Masturbatory activity occurs in both sexes, often accompanied by psychologically similar fantasies. Sensitive genital areas are identified early in life in both males and females. Spontaneous erections in males are observable from birth on, during periods of both sleep and wakefulness. Similar clitoral responses can be assumed with the stimulation attendant on diapering, bathing, etc. In general, in either sex, compulsive masturbation during the years from 7 to 10 most likely reflects disturbed mother-child relationships. Orgastic potential during this period seems debatable, but retrospectively in adult analyses a number of patients, of both sexes, have described orgasms before puberty (Sarnoff, 1976, p. 49). Whereas Freud (1905) originally considered the early life events reported in females as actual seductions, he later considered them oedipal fantasies. Today there is increasing evidence that many of these early memories are not mere fantasies but in fact represent incestuous relationships with adult members of their family (see Schechter and Roberge, 1976). This suggests the possibility that females can have an awareness of their genitalia from early childhood experiences, and that these may color and modify subsequent masturbatory thoughts and activities. Many girls between 7 and 10 have difficulty in conceptualizing the vaginal area and its uterine connections, which remain cognitively amorphous. Kestenberg (1967a, 1967b, 1968) notes that the estrogenic increase occurring in girls at around age 7 occasions stimulation that may lead to what Sarnoff calls "masked masturbation."

The exposed nature of the penis and scrotum in males, the occurrence of erections associated with urinary urgency, friction, and Rapid Eye Movement sleep, and the visual and manual availability of the male genitals permit boys of this age to be very specific in their localization of erotic sensations. Although ejaculation does not occur until adolescence, orgastic responses do occur frequently during this time (Sarnoff, 1976, p. 54). In the later stages of this period, masturbation becomes less indirect, and many boys enter adolescence with a well-established pattern of genital stimulation that leads eventually to ejaculation.

In both sexes the primary love object in masturbatory fantasies is a disguised parental figure. With very little pressure the camouflage is uncovered.

Uncertainties about identifications frequently occur in the child between 7 and 10, accompanied by a recrudescence of bisexual conflicts. Boys will envy the adult female role, as will girls envy the adult male role. Cross dressing and cross play are frequently seen. The occurrence of menarche in girls and ejaculation in boys ultimately serves as an organizing influence toward biologically defined sex-role identifications, with the objects of masturbatory fantasies shifting from preoedipal and oedipal figures to more current, reality-based contacts. The severe castration fears so evident at the beginning of this time period gradually diminish with the development of a greater capacity to identify with the same-sex parent in their relationship with the opposite sex. At the end of this period, usually by age 10, both boys and girls can distance themselves from the primitive superego, permitting them to see movies and TV programs, and to read books, without these serving as a stimulus for the manifest contents of dreams—especially anxiety dreams.

IV

What follows are brief paradigms which demonstrate the intertwining of the various factors involved in development. Awareness of their various contributions is crucial in determining normality or pathology and the most effective intervention for deviations from the norm.

As noted at the outset, differences between the child's activity level and that of the parents can in effect create symptoms from what are normal temperamental and constitutional givens. Any lack of congruence between parents and child can enforce an underlying feeling in the child that he is a bad person, who causes difficulties for his family, for others, and for himself. This attitude can be reinforced during ages 7 to 10, when guilt is so likely to be stimulated by the primitive aspects of internalized parental imagos. This is also true if the child is one of those difficult children whose rhythms, avoidance behaviors, intensity of reactions, quality of mood, and lack of adaptability are antagonistic to familial styles of reacting. These children have problems with academic learning and peer relationships that affect their cognitive abilities and coping mechanisms. Their object relationships are constantly exerting internal pressures that result in chaotic behaviors. Interventive modes which do not include involvement with the family, psychoanalytic psychotherapy, and consultation with the school are bound to end in treatment failure.

Physical and mental retardation can be the result of insufficient nutrition—emotional or alimentary. This can occur at any phase of development, but the earlier it takes place, the more devastating its effects. When it happens during the child's middle years, one can see a stunting in the growth pattern, low self-esteem, fragility in object relationships, depressions, poor impulse control, and self-destructive behavior. Such children may have normal or above normal intellect but do badly in school; their dreams and daydreams reveal a preponderance of oral regressive features with the frequent theme of lack of fulfillment. Again, involvement with the family is required plus intensive psychoanalytic work aimed at getting at the aggression that is turned against the self.

Children who demonstrate a confusion in gender identity between 7 to 10 are similar to borderline adults with poor ego boundaries and sexual confusion. When these symptoms are combined with fire-setting, enuresis, and injury to animals (showing poorly established empathic capacities), what might be called the Lee Harvey Oswald syndrome may be said to exist *in statu nascendi*. Some of these children are impulse-ridden and represent a realistic threat of violent outbursts, especially during and after puberty. In males with confused gender identity, there is a great increase in passivity creating a resistance of significance. Often in such cases we find a passive or absent father and a powerful mother, both of whom support the gender confusion. In females with sexual identity conflicts there may be a similar family setting or one that is just the reverse. Although truly there are no absolute formulae regarding family dynamics in these cases, it is generally apparent that some of these dynamics—some conscious, many unconscious—play a considerable role in the evolution and perpetuation of this symptom. Since parental compliance in this picture is generally quite evident, the parents' motivation for treatment is minimal. At times it is the child who asks for help, usually because of peer pressure for clear-cut, unambiguous sex-role performance. When presented for treatment between ages 7 and 10, the symptoms may be so relatively fixed that major change may be difficult to effect, even with the cooperation of the parents. Undertaking psychoanalysis at this time along with family therapy should be considered. Treatment in these cases should continue well into adolescence, so that the powerful physiological spurt of puberty may be engaged as a positive force for psychological awareness and change. In boys with sexual confusion and the added features of the Lee Harvey Oswald syndrome, a thorough neurological workup should be done and the use of anticonvulsive or psychotropic medication considered.

Deficits in cognitive development can involve relatively discrete areas of functioning or can be diffuse and generalized. Neuropsychological and emotional factors are of particular importance in children of this age, since it is during these years that the fundamentals of all subsequent academic learning are acquired. With minimal cerebral dysfunction, an object inconstancy may be present as regards printed letters or numbers, but there may also be an object inconstancy regarding the introjection of stable parental imagos. This, and other symptoms make this type of child difficult to live with, as very realistic difficulties in impulse control are created by superego lacunae. These are the children of whom it is said that they are like the girl with the curl in the middle of her forehead: "When she was good, she was very, very good, but when she was bad, she was horrid." With difficulty in auditory and visual sequencing and problems with attention and concentration, interpretations given in psychoanalysis—even when timed and dosed correctly—are forgotten or distorted. Problems in passing from one Piagetian phase to another have the effect of restricting development, interfering with peer relationships, disrupting scholastic progress, effectively diminishing self-esteem, and limiting the child's capacity to feel productive at a period where productivity is the key word for this age. Ego functions can also be limited so that memory and judgment are affected, interfering even more with the verbal exchanges so essential to the psychotherapeutic process. Transference reactions are as unstable as the relationships with the parents. Treatment approaches need to deal continuously with the fragmented levels of psychosexual development and the tenuous object ties so characteristic of this condition. The family and the school (including tutors) must be included in the treatment process. Since delayed maturational processes are significant factors in this deficit, and since there is no guarantee that development will permit this child to attain age-appropriate behaviors and reactions, the psychoanalyst must use the positive transference to get the child to solve problems using his intellect.

A lack of knowledge of the social mores of the family of origin and of the culture within which children live is antithetical to proper treatment. Various cultures emphasize different aspects of psychosocial and psychosexual development, and the meaning of idioms and metaphors must be understood as originating from that cultural base. If a child is chronically hungry, if violence or sexual exploitation is an integral part of family interactions, if there is little help for the child in focusing in on the differences between figure and background, or if the parents have abdicated their authority, various symptom patterns can develop which require specific interventions by the psychoanalyst. These societal influences can have a negative effect on physical growth, coping mechanisms, cognitive development, and object ties.

Interferences in psychoanalytic developmental lines can present themselves as fixation points or as regressions. In the former, not only are there areas of delayed development in ego functions and psychosexual stages, but the magnetic pull of these fixations attracts to their nuclear core all aspects of emotional, cognitive, and behavioral disabilities. The possibility that these fixations may represent an organic or constitutional anlage is present and tends to determine the parameters of psychoanalytic treatment. In the case of regressions, treatment can be focused much more toward the traumatic incidents which have occasioned the developmental interruptions and subsequent slipback. Clearly, since the regressive pull takes the child of 7 to 10 to earlier stages of relationships and accomplishments, normal attainments leading to feelings of esteem are not possible. Even with successful psychoanalytic treatment of the child presenting with regressive phenomena, even after symptom removal, tutorial help and family therapy may be required to reintegrate back into the family with new, more age-appropriate behavior and feelings.

V

We have attempted to demonstrate how knowledge of normal development is needed in order to understand the children of 7 to 10 who are referred to psychoanalysts, child psychiatrists, mental health workers, and psychiatric clinics. An awareness of developmental precursors and of the accomplishments of this period bears out the prevailing psychoanalytic opinion that children of this age are not at all in a phase that could be characterized as "latent."

What is clear is that this period is one of growing self-esteem, a capacity to separate from family and interact with peers and other adults, a shift from primary process to secondary process thinking, an ability to undertake formal schooling, a greater joy in bodily control, the development of sexual identity, the control of primitive impulses leading to sublimated pleasures and gratification in learning, a growing sense of humor, and a sense of mastery and competence that permits the child for the first time to conceive of himself as a functioning adult. As psychobiological development proceeds, there is an increasing feeling of an internalized locus of control within the individual. Aggressive and sexual feelings and fantasies begin to separate from earlier primitive and preoedipal objects and attach to people outside the family.

The mutual interaction of inherent constitutional forces, developmental factors, and environmental influences (family, society, culture) goes on continuously, tending to positive, reality-oriented changes. Interruptions in the normal progressions can occur with various psychological or physical traumata or with the time-bomb effect of a constitutional defect. Familial influences, of major importance at the beginning of this period, diminish as it draws to a close.

The child from 7 to 10 is growing in a physical and mental sense, emphasizing the continuous active exchange between the child's inner world and the world around him. The psychoanalyic understanding of this age child is enriched by developmental concepts from the biological, ego psychological, temperamental, cognitive, and cultural points of view. All of these facets of development add to our understanding and are necessary to properly evaluate and treat the child who may show deviations from the norm.

References

Erikson, E.H. (1950), *Childhood and Society*. Rev. ed. New York: Norton, 1963.

——— (1959), *Identity and the Life Cycle*. Psychological Issues Monograph 1. New York: International Universities Press.

——— (1968), *Identity, Youth and Crisis*. New York: Norton.

Freud, A. (1937), *The Ego and the Mechanisms of Defense*. Rev. ed. New York: International Universities Press, 1966.

——— (1951), Observations on child development. *The Psychoanalytic Study of the Child*, 6:18–30. New York: International Universities Press.

——— (1954), Psychoanalysis and education. *The Psychoanalytic Study of the Child*, 9:9–15. New York: International Universities Press.

——— (1965), *Normality and Pathology in Childhood*. New York: International Universities Press.

Freud, S. (1905), Three essays on the theory of sexuality. *Standard Edition*, 7:125–245. London: Hogarth Press, 1953.

——— (1923a), The ego and the id. *Standard Edition*, 19:3–63. London: Hogarth Press, 1961.

——— (1923b), Two encyclopedia articles. *Standard Edition*, 18:235–259. London: Hogarth Press, 1955.

——— (1924a), An autobiographical study. *Standard Edition*, 20:7–74. London: Hogarth Press, 1959.

——— (1924b), The dissolution of the Oedipus complex. *Standard Edition*, 19:173–179. London: Hogarth Press, 1961.

——— (1924c), A short account of psycho-analysis. *Standard Edition*, 19:191–209. London: Hogarth Press, 1961.

——— (1926), Inhibitions, symptoms and anxiety. *Standard Edition*, 20:77–175. London: Hogarth Press, 1959.

Green, R. (1974), *Sexual Identity Conflict in Children and Adults*. New York: Basic Books.

Hartmann, H., Kris, E., & Loewenstein, R. (1946), Comments on the formation of psychic structure. *The Psychoanalytic Study of the Child*, 2:11–38. New York: International Universities Press.

Horney, K. (1939), *New Ways in Psychoanalysis*. New York: Norton.

Kestenberg, J. (1967a), Phases of adolescence, with suggestions for a correlation of psychic and hormonal organization: Part I. Antecedents of adolescent organization in childhood. *J. Amer. Acad. Child Psychiat.*, 6:426–463.

——— (1967b), Phases of adolescence, with suggestions for a correlation of psychic and hormonal organization: Part II. Pre-puberty diffusion and reintegration. *J. Amer. Acad. Child Psychiat.*, 6:577–614.

——— (1968), Phases of adolescence, with suggestions for a correlation of psychic and hormonal organization: Part III. Puberty, growth, differentiation and consolidation. *J. Amer. Acad. Child Psychiat.*, 7:108–151.

Klaus, M., Hand, J., & Kennel, C. (1976), *Maternal-Infant Bonding*. St. Louis: Mosby.

Kohlberg, L. (1967), Moral education, religious education and the public schools: A developmental view. In: *Religion and Public Education*, ed. T. Sizen. Boston: Houghton-Mifflin.

Lynn, D. (1974), *The Father: His Role in Child Development*. Monterey, Calif.: Brooks/Cole.

Mahler, M., Pine, F., & Bergman, A. (1975), *The Psychological Birth of the Human Infant.* New York: Basic Books.
Minuchin, P. (1977), *The Middle Years of Childhood.* Palo Alto, Calif.: Brooks/Cole.
Mittelmann, B. (1954), Motility in infants, children and adults: Patterning and psychodynamics. *The Psychoanalytic Study of the Child,* 9:142–177. New York: International Universities Press.
Money, J. (1968), *Sex Errors of the Body.* Baltimore: Johns Hopkins University Press.
Murphy, L., & Moriarity, A. (1976), *Vulnerability, Coping and Growth.* New Haven: Yale University Press.
Piaget, J. (1932), *The Moral Judgment of the Child.* New York: Free Press.
——— (1951), *The Child's Conception of Physical Causality.* London: Routledge & Kegan Paul, 1951.
——— (1952), *The Origins of Intelligence in Children.* New York: International Universities Press.
——— (1954), *The Construction of Reality in the Child.* New York: Basic Books.
Powell, G., Brasel, J., & Blizzard, R. (1967a), Emotional deprivation and growth retardation simulating idiopathic hypopituitarism: I. *N. Engl. J. Med.,* 276:1271–1278.
——— ——— Raiti, S., & Blizzard, R. (1967b), Emotional deprivation and growth retardation simulating idiopathic hypopituitarism. II. *N. Engl. J. Med.,* 276:1279–1283.
Sarnoff, C. (1976), *Latency.* New York: Aronson.
Schechter, M., & Roberge, L. (1976), Sexual exploitation. In: *Child Abuse and Neglect,* ed. R. Helfer & C. Kempe. Cambridge, Mass.: Ballinger.
Shapiro, T., & Perry, R. (1976), Latency revisited: The age of 7 plus or minus 1. *The Psychoanalytic Study of the Child,* 31:79–105. New Haven: Yale University Press.
Stoller, R. (1968), *Sex and Gender: On the Development of Masculinity and Femininity.* New York: Science House.
Sullivan, H. S. (1953), *The Interpersonal Theory of Psychiatry.* New York: Norton.
Thomas, A., & Chess, S. (1977), *Temperament and Development.* New York: Brunner-Mazel.
Weiner, H. (1965), Psychoanalysis as a biological science. In: *Psychoanalysis and Current Biological Thought,* ed. N. Greenfield & W. Lewis. Madison: University of Wisconsin Press, pp. 11–33.
Werner, H. (1948), *Comparative Psychology of Mental Development.* New York: International Universities Press.
White, R. (1960), Competence and the psychosocial stages of development. In: *Nebraska Symposium on Motivation,* ed. J. Cole. Omaha: University of Nebraska Press.
Whiting, B., & Edwards, C. (1973), A cross cultural analysis of sex differences in the behavior of children age three to eleven. *J. Social Psychol.,* 91:171–188.

14

The Latency Stage

SELMA KRAMER, M.D.
JOSEPH RUDOLPH, M.D.

In the course of normal development latency appears to the observer to be a delightful productive phase, one full of movement (Kaplan, 1965), curiosity, and intellectual striving under the aegis of the ego. During latency the ego becomes resilient, malleable, and educable, but this state is not reached without a struggle. The emerging superego, which itself is in the process of integration and organization, comes to the aid of the ego. At times, especially in early latency, this help is a bit heavy-handed, but more of that later. Latency can be viewed and described descriptively or dynamically, or, better, by combining the two perspectives.

Latency: A Combined View

Physical growth proceeds at an even pace, without the rapid increments in height and weight seen in the previous 6 years. Familial physical characteristics and activity types become more evident. The child becomes more adept in both fine and gross muscle coordination. Throughout latency, at each step in development girls tend to mature earlier than boys. However, the development of each youngster is individual; it is not only difficult but impossible and unfair to make comparisons with other children of the same age. Parents and their children should be made aware that there are differences in patterns and rate of growth of the various body parts.

The brain grows very rapidly at first, especially during

infancy, as would be expected by the rapidity of the development of cognitive and sensory functions and motor skills. The growth of the brain slows by age 6, and is almost complete by 12. Development of the lymphatic system is very pronounced during latency, but gradually decreases thereafter. The genital organs grow relatively little until the end of latency, when growth is more rapid.

Sexual development will be described separately for the boy and for the girl. In the latter, the genitalia are less accessible to sight and touch. As a consequence, except for the clitoris and labia, the genitalia generally remain a relative mystery to the latency age girl. Masturbation in latency usually does not involve the use of foreign objects in the vagina. There is a continuum of activities which serve to discharge sexual excitation as well as aggression.

At one end of the spectrum, activities which discharge sexual pressure combine with whole body movements, as in jumping rope, gymnastics, dodgeball, riding, and dancing. At the other end is the more direct stimulation of the clitoris, as by sliding down banisters, rubbing against hard objects, and, less often, manual stimulation of the clitoris, causing excitation and orgasm, even in young girls (Kestenberg, 1957).

Several factors tend to diminish masturbation in girls or even to stop it altogether. For some the intensity of orgastic experience, with its transient loss of ego boundaries, is so frightening that inhibition of masturbation results; in others, especially in girls who perceive their genitalia as a cloaca, the affect of disgust inhibits masturbation. Guilt arising from sadomasochistic masturbation fantasies or erotically tinged fantasies also limits masturbation. Of course, both sexes are influenced by actual parental attitudes. Both sexes fear punishment, e.g., castration in the boy, or guilt. The girl, in particular, fears loss of approval, loss of love, and of self-esteem.

In contrast to girls, boys encounter more situations which promote manual masturbation, largely because of the visual and tactile availability of the penis. They show the same spectrum of masturbatory activity as do girls, from whole body movements to symbolic fantasies, including erotic and sadomasochistic ones. Recent studies challenge the supposition that boys indulge more frequently in genital masturbation than do girls. As with girls, boys too may be disturbed by the intensity of the orgastic phenomenon; masturbation is then inhibited. Because of the magnitude of the narcissistic investment in the penis, castration anxiety itself, together with direct or subtle castration threats by adults, stifles masturbation. Alternative pathways of drive discharge are similar for boys and girls: regression to more infantile modes of gratification. Total inhibition is pathogenic (A. Freud, 1948).

A distinct shift in cognitive development occurs in latency. Piaget's studies (1936) show that beginning at about 7 years of age preoperational processes are gradually replaced by concrete operational ones. In the preoperational mode of functioning, the youngster (2 to 7) tends to focus on a limited view or single dimension of a given situation. This Piaget calls "centration." The concrete operational child (7 to 11) decentrates; that is, he takes into account several factors or dimensions of a problem before arriving at a conclusion. The preoperational child concentrates on the static aspect of a situation rather than on the dynamic transformation. The concrete operational child can form images of the changes in matter. While the preoperational child's thinking lacks reversibility, the concrete operational child can reverse processes in his mind. Piaget conceives of three aspects of thought as different in the preoperational and concrete operational child, respectively: centration-decentration, static-dynamic, irreversibility-reversibility.

Piaget posits that cognitive growth is a result of two processes: development and learning. Of the two, he feels the more important is development, which depends on maturation, experience, social transmission, and equilibration (the child's self-regulatory processes). Through equilibration the child forms a new structure of mental operations, a form of learning which is stable and lasting. Piaget thinks that learning in the narrow sense (responses restricted to a specific situation) does not appreciably enhance development, that such learning is too unstable, impermanent, and unlikely to lead to generalization.

Sarnoff (1976) divides cognitive development of latency into early, middle, and late stages. He holds that latency as a state is characterized by calmness, pliability, and educability, and is reached when the demands and prohibitions of society are internalized through identification (introjection) with the parents (as they are and as they are perceived by the child).

The first stage of cognitive development, according to Sarnoff, extends from ages 6 to 7. To attain this first level of functioning, the child must have achieved the capacity to symbolize and to repress, must have a highly developed verbal conceptual memory organization, and must have achieved behavioral constancy.

Sarnoff's next cognitive organizing period extends from age 7 to almost 8. It is during this period that the shift from preoperational to concrete operational thinking occurs and, with it, the development of abstract conceptual memory organization. Thought content shifts from fantasy objects to real objects. The primitive, harsh preoedipal superego, based on early parental introjects, gradually changes to a superego more closely related to reality. This change is aided by the child's increased exposure to peers and other new experiences outside the home.

The last of Sarnoff's organizing periods extends from ages 8 to 10, and is characterized by increased conflict with parents, as the standards of peers are increasingly used as criteria for behavior. Masturbation increases. Night fears change from fear of fantasy objects to fear of reality objects. Some youngsters manifest an increase in compulsive symptoms, such as rituals or counting; in others, phobias may increase. These defensive and regressive activities are related to conflicts secondary to forbidden wishes. Preadolescence follows.

Latency: A Dynamic View

Massive repression of infantile sexuality, the replacement of object cathexis by identifications with the parents, and the introjection of parental authority in the organization of the superego pave the way toward latency. Freud (1905) gave the name *latency* to the life cycle phase between 6 and 10 years of age, and described its psychodynamics. Later contributors to the theory of latency include Bornstein (1951), Blos (1962), and

Anna Freud (1965), all of whom focused on organization of structures and functions in latency.

Bornstein divided latency into at least two major phases: from about 5 to 8 years, and from 8 to 10. In the early phase the superego is strict and harsh, the result of introjection of true parental authority, the perception by the child (or rather, the misperception) of that authority, together with the projection of the child's own hostility onto them and its reintrojection. The ego is under pressure from both the drives and the superego. The main defense against genital impulses is regression to less threatening pregenitality. This regression causes conflicts; therefore, other defenses come into play. They include reaction-formation, denial, and identification with the aggressor. This last serves a dual role; by allying the child's superego with that of the parents, it increases control over the impulses.

In the second phase of latency the superego is less strict, for it has been modified through experience and by the more complete resolution of the oedipus complex. The ego becomes more involved in coping with reality, so that sublimation takes place in play and games, and through learning. Thus play and school add impetus to development; they foster physical and emotional separation from the parents as the maturing child begins to see the parents in a new light. Friendships with the peer group become increasingly important, adding new structure to the child's ego and superego by introducing learning and mastery within the concept of "fairness," nonfamilial competition, and appropriate rules and regulations. The parents cease to be paragons of all virtue and the source of all rules. The inability to use the peer group by middle or late latency must be considered pathognomonic of difficulty. The latency child's activity has many functions. While competitiveness and aggression are expressed in very active games, every nuance of aggression is controlled by strict rules. Younger children play Red Light and Giant Steps, games in which permission to move must be given by the leader. Older children, especially boys, engage in contact sports, partly in imitation of older male friends and siblings, and partly as an expression of their own controlled aggression and need for body contact.

Latency boys and girls play separately and differently.

Girls' active games are rhythmic, often involving jumping, skipping, and hopping; strict rules limit physical aggression but permit verbal aggression, which is frequently aimed at the mother, e.g., "Step on a crack, break your mother's back." Girls' games also include none-too-deeply-hidden sexual allusions (Goldings, 1974).

Both sexes show interest in organizing clubs; these serve to increase the distance from the family and also strengthen the nonparental superego. Often a club is organized, rules established, officers chosen, and then the club disbands. This repeats itself many times. Formal organizations, such as Cub Scouts and Brownies, offer greater stability and longevity in latency.

Just as peer friendships aid separation from primary love objects, so too does the growing importance of adults from outside the family. As children begin to relate to and become attached to teachers, relatives, parents of friends, and club leaders, they take their first steps in comparing and contrasting their parents with other adults; they increasingly realize with both pleasure and loss that their parents are imperfect. Although this realization will be worked through with greater resolution in adolescence, younger children begin to challenge their parents' authority with, "My teacher says . . . ," thus diminishing the rigidity and harshness of the parentally derived superego. Concurrent with the realization of parental imperfection, the "family romance" appears. The child has fantasies that he is the offspring of noble parents (royalty at least), and that he is being reared by ordinary people who are not his biological parents.

Latency is also the time of life when active superheroes, such as Superman, make their appearance in fantasy life. Identification with such figures of "good" who overcome "evil" serves several purposes: to strengthen the superego; to increase the distance between parent and child; and to defend against feelings of powerlessness.

Throughout latency, children struggle against the breakthrough of incestuous fantasies and the temptation to masturbate. They do not succeed, nor would it be advantageous to completely stop masturbating. Total suppression of masturbation blocks the discharge of libido and aggressive energy which then flows back onto ego functions and interferes with the child's relationship with the environment (A. Freud, 1948). Severe repression would also indicate the persistence of a harsh and primitive superego in an overly passive, compliant child.

Latency has been viewed by some as a period of relative sexual quiescence between two peaks of sexual activity, i.e., between the oedipal and the adolescent psychosexual stages of development, or between the resolution of the oedipus complex and the onset of puberty. Whether the latency period is biologically determined is a moot question, for a decrease in sexual activity between 6 and 10 is not universal. In some primitive cultures overt sexual activity continues unabated. In more advanced cultures, however, direct expression of the drives is curbed and modified, and the energy of the drives serves to augment the energy available to the ego for further development, particularly in the cognitive sphere. In most civilized cultures, the impulses are modulated and directed as a result of more sophisticated ego defenses, with the help of the superego, into acceptable channels for gratification. As a consequence, there are changes in the child's relationships with other members of the family, together with increased interest in peers and their values, and sublimation of sexual curiosity into intellectual curiosity and formal learning. The child becomes "calm, pliable, and educable" (Sarnoff, 1976).

This shift in mode of expression of the drives is a result of increased complexity and efficiency of the ego in its adaptive and organizing functions. At first the latter is relatively weak, but with the replacement of splitting by repression (Mahler, Pine, and Bergman, 1975) and other higher level defenses it gains in strength. With progress in organization, a more harmonious relationship is established among the three mental structures, id, ego, and superego, as well as with the environment. This is the essence of normality.

Constitutional and experiential variations in the ego's capacity to integrate and organize result in children who constitutionally are more aggressive and, at the same time, show decreased tolerance for frustration and anxiety. These children have a greater than average probability of failing to experience the relative calm of latency. Failure to reach this level has dire consequences in adolescence (Blos, 1962). The possibility of failure is increased for children whose life experiences have been so traumatic, so devoid of the tempering influence of love, that their destructive aggression toward others and themselves is abnormally increased. When aggression has not been modulated by libido, there is an interference with the development of the state of latency (Sarnoff, 1976).

A major task of the latency age child is to learn and master the skills which are necessary if the child is to become a happy, loving, creative, and productive member of society. The most basic skill in our culture is literacy: one must read and write in order to acquire and dispense information. Failure to achieve this skill may be caused by one or more factors: organic, emotional, or cultural. The organic factors include gross or subtle cognitive impairments caused by damage to the brain, genetic processes such as dyslexia or strephosymbolia, etc.

Learning requires freedom from the imperative impulses and strains of the oedipal period. It requires also that the child be able to separate physically and emotionally from the parents and to learn from people other than the parents. Emotional privations, defects, or conflicts in early phases of development may prevent the child from mastering the oedipal conflicts and entering latency. Regression caused by emotional turmoil after entering latency, or by cultural deprivation (including the exclusive use of language appropriate only to a minority culture), may result in the failure to attain necessary abstract concepts and nuances of the primary language and, in the extreme, even appropriate language for conversation. Overstimulation or negative attitudes on the part of family or peers toward education may cause shame rather than pleasure in school achievement. Family secrets or distortion of reality by parents may also inhibit learning.

Mastery of basic skills provides the child a sense of accomplishment which is usually confirmed by the attitude of the important people in the environment. This mastery results in greater independence from drives and objects and in constancy of behavior and elevated self-esteem. Failure to master the needed skills results in lowered self-esteem and behavioral difficulties. Or, as Erikson (1950) emphasizes that success produces the ego quality of industry, whereas failure produces that of inferiority.

Precursors of Psychopathology in Latency

Many authors, in agreement with Waelder (1936), have stressed the concept of multiple determinants in psychic development. The ego, the organ of adaptation, integrates and organizes separate and yet interdependent elements including the interactions of a multiplicity of constitutional, experiential, developmental, and maturational factors. If these factors are "average" and do not overwhelm the ego's capacity to adapt, development proceeds normally; if too many are pathogenic, development will probably be stressed and may be abnormal or atypical. Even in the best of circumstances, development does not proceed in a straight line; it can best be described as series of phases, marked predominantly by progression, but also by some regression from time to time, especially at times of stress, which every child must encounter.

Categories of Psychopathology in Latency

Descriptively, the latency child may manifest any one of the following disturbances (International Classification of Diseases, 8):

1. Reactive disorders
2. Specific developmental disorders
3. Neurotic disorders
4. Personality character disorders
5. Psychotic disorders
6. Disorders directly due to acute or chronic brain condition
7. Somatic disorders
8. Mental disorders
9. Antisocial behavior not classifiable elsewhere
10. Disorders not classifiable under 0–9

Many times in attempting to ascribe a diagnosis in any one of the above categories to a youngster we very much feel as if we are trying to fit a square peg into a round hole. This difficulty is most apparent in the younger child. Mahler (1945) states that because of the weakly organized personality of the child we usually meet with diffuse disturbances which are impossible to classify in terms of adult psychiatry. She adds that, even in a relatively normal environment, due to stress the child will in the course of his development show temporary symptoms which are difficult to distinguish from those indicating pathology. It is important to recognize and treat developmental arrest, fixation, and regression. The magnitude and persistence of the symptoms, their tendency to increase rather than subside, and the degree to which they interfere with normal ego development must be assessed in order to determine pathology.

To be able to distinguish normal from abnormal development requires a sound knowledge of psychoanalytic concepts of development. Among the titans who have contributed to this understanding are Anna Freud (1949), Erikson (1950), Spitz (1965), Winnicott (1965), and Mahler, Pine, and Bergman (1975). They have pointed out that early precursors of pathology may be caused by deviations in the development of the drives, object relations, or the ego. Such deviations frequently cause abnormalities in the areas of cognitive, emotional, and social functioning, or in a combination of them. Dissemination of our knowledge of early precursors of pathology could be used both for prevention and for early intervention in childhood disturbances.

Transient symptoms of stress are encountered in normal development. There are typical fears, normal conflicts, and characteristic symptoms which child developmentalists have come to expect. The oedipal phase child is often beset by phobias; the latency child may show ritualistic behavior and "school phobia," which really derives from unresolved separation problems. In the healthy child these symptoms are related to anxiety, which is soon mastered by the ego.

Genetically determined bases for problems in latency age children have been the subject of increasing interest. Prenatal, neonatal, and postnatal traumata may cause minimal cerebral dysfunction occasioning hyperactivity, learning difficulties, and behavior problems. The same symptoms may arise from tension, anxiety, depression, or phobia caused by loss of important love objects due to serious accident, illness, or surgery. Adoption poses its own problems.

Psychotherapy During Latency

The subject of psychopathology in latency leads naturally to a discussion of therapeutic modalities appropriate for the latency age child. With a few subtractions and additions, these are similar to those used in adult therapy. Chess and Hassibi (1978) list behavior therapy, eclectic psychotherapy, group therapy, family therapy, compensatory education, institutionalization, and drug therapy. One other effective and powerful form of therapy, child analysis, must be added to the list.

The choice of therapy should be based on a thorough history and evaluation of the child and his environment, both familial and extrafamilial. The latter includes school and neighborhood. Intrapsychic factors included in the evaluation are specific ego structures and functions (Beres, 1956) and dynamics, i.e., the forces in conflict both within the child and between the child and his environment. Evaluation of dynamics should attempt to determine the degree to which conflicts are internalized. The younger the child, the less likely this is to be an issue. However, with preoedipal children, superego precursors may give rise to intrapsychic conflict.

A family diagnosis is of great importance in estimating the relative health or disturbance of parents and siblings, the stability of the family, and the parents' attitude concerning treatment. Unless the parents support therapy, emotionally as well as financially, unless they can tolerate the regression and progression that inevitably accompany psychotherapy, and unless they can handle their fears that the therapist may be a better parent than they are, psychotherapy will be seriously compromised.

As child analysts we feel it is appropriate to discuss child analysis as a therapeutic modality. Where it is indicated, that is, for neurosis, analysis is the treatment of choice, as it is in the adult. Latency, especially early latency, is regarded as the optimal time to conduct child analysis. Instead of using the patient's free associations, the child analyst understands and uses the child's affects together with play and verbalizations.

The latency child's ability to distance himself from the parents "provides the potential for transference in analysis," state Kramer and Byerly (1978, p. 206). Other reasons that make latency an optimal time for analysis are the ego's increased capacity to cope with reality due to improved cognitive development; its capacity to delay gratification; and the fact that the defenses of early latency are not yet consolidated and that therefore "the psychic structure is modifiable" (Becker, 1974, pp. 4–5).

Conclusion

Latency is the phase of development during which there is a consolidation of superego and a strengthening of ego structure and function. We believe, as does Blos (1962), that what happens to and with the ego in latency determines how well the adolescent passage will fare. The consolidation of the ego serves as the bedrock, the foundation, during the disequilibrium of psychic structure in adolescence.

Normal development in latency, as in other phases, unfolds as a result of good enough endowment, good enough parenting, and experiences at each stage of development that the ego can assimilate and master. Fortunate is the child who experiences all three. Knowledge of the possible dangers at various stages of development, and its dissemination, should help prevent serious pathology. Where pathology exists, this same knowledge enables the therapist to select the most effective therapy.

References

Becker, T.E. (1974), On latency. *The Psychoanalytic Study of the Child*, 29:3–11. New Haven: Yale University Press.

Beres, D. (1956), Ego deviation and concept of schizophrenia. *The Psychoan-*

alytic Study of the Child, 11:164–225. New York: International Universities Press.

Blos, P. (1962), *On Adolescence*. New York: Free Press.

Bornstein, B. (1951), On latency. *The Psychoanalytic Study of the Child*, 6:279–285. New York: International Universities Press.

Chess, S., & Hassibi, M. (1978), *Principles and Practice of Child Psychiatry*. New York: Plenum.

Erikson, E. (1950), *Childhood and Society*. 2nd ed. New York: Norton, 1963.

Freud, A. (1948), Certain types and stages of social maladjustment. In: *Searchlight on Delinquency*. New York: International Universities Press, 1949, pp. 193–204.

——— (1965), *Normality and Pathology in Childhood*. New York: International Universities Press.

Freud, S. (1905), Three essays on the theory of sexuality. *Standard Edition*, 7:125–245. London: Hogarth Press, 1953.

Goldings, H.J. (1974), Jump-rope rhythms and the rhythm of latency development in girls. *The Psychoanalytic Study of the Child*, 29:431–450. New Haven: Yale University Press.

Kaplan, E.B. (1965), Reflections regarding psychomotor activities during the latency period. *The Psychoanalytic Study of the Child*, 20:220–238. New York: International Universities Press.

Kestenberg, J.S. (1957), Vicissitudes of female sexuality. *J. Amer. Psychoanal. Assn.*, 4:453–476.

Kramer, S., & Byerly, L.J. (1978), Technique of psychoanalysis of the latency child. In: *Child Analysis and Therapy*, ed. J. Glenn. New York: Aronson, 1978, pp.205–236.

Mahler, M.S. (1945), Child analysis. In: *Modern Trends in Child Psychiatry*, ed. N.D.C. Lewis and B.L. Pacella. New York: International Universities Press.

——— Pine, F., & Bergman, A. (1975), *The Psychological Birth of the Human Infant*. New York: Basic Books.

Piaget, J. (1936), *The Origins of Intelligence in Children*. New York: International Universities Press, 1952.

Sarnoff, C. (1976), *Latency*. New York: Aronson.

Spitz, R. (1965), *The First Year of Life*. New York: International Universities Press.

Waelder, R. (1936), The principle of multiple function. *Psychoanal. Quart.*, 5:45–62.

Winnicott, D.W. (1965), *Maturational Processes and the Facilitating Environment*. New York: International Universities Press.

15

Between the Oedipus Complex and Adolescence: The "Quiet" Time

EDITH BUXBAUM, PH.D.

Freud's Concept of Latency

The period between the seventh and tenth years covers approximately what Freud (1905, p. 178) called the period of sexual latency, a term he "once again" borrowed from his friend Wilhelm Fliess. In the "Three Essays" Freud discussed for the first time the existence and importance of infantile sexuality and "the period of sexual latency in childhood and its interruptions" (p. 178), that is, the manifestations of sexuality in a supposedly asexual period, and how only in adolescence sexuality continues uninterrupted into adulthood.

In 1920 (1905) Freud writes in an addendum: "Those authorities who regard the interstitial portion of the sex-gland as the organ that determines sex have on their side been led by anatomical researches to speak of infantile sexuality and a period of sexual latency" (p. 177). This was important confirmation for Freud, who always strove to find a physiological basis for his ideas. But he added cautiously: "Since a period of latency in the psychological sense does not occur in animals, it would be very interesting to know whether the anatomical findings which have led these writers to assume the occurrence of two peaks in sexual development are also demonstrable in the higher animals" (p. 177). He describes how during the latency period feelings of disgust and shame are developed, as well as aesthetic and moral ideals, which seem to be a product of education, though in reality they are fixed by heredity. The period of latency "appears to be one of the necessary conditions of the aptitude of men for developing a higher civilization" (1905, p. 234). "It would seem that the origin of this peculiarity of man must be looked for in the prehistory of the human species." Following Ferenczi's ideas (1913), he ventures to say (1923, p. 35), "According to one psychoanalytic hypothesis the . . . diphasic onset of man's sexual life . . . is a heritage of the cultural development necessitated by the glacial epoch." Ferenczi (1913), in *Developmental Phases of the Sense of Reality,* says, "May it be permitted to be so daring as to suggest that the geological changes of the surface of the earth with their catastrophic consequences forced the predecessors of mankind to the repression of their fondest habits and forced them to 'development.' " He continued: "Let us not shy away from the last analogy to connect the great phase of repression of the individual, the latency period, with the greatest catastrophe that struck our forebears, i.e., with the misery of the glacial periods, which we still repeat in our individual lives". Freud liked the idea, which fit with his biological concepts, that ontogeny is a repetition of phylogeny, that certain characteristics and habits of the individual are precipitates of the experiences of the species in the past, according to Darwin. However tentatively Freud and Ferenczi proposed these ideas, their idea of the importance of latency as a period of hominization in the past, as acculturation and civilization in the present, still stands. Education itself, which was somewhat deemphasized by Freud, keeps its place in this scheme, facilitating adaptation to culture and thereby taking the place of necessity "that forced our predecessors to give up and change their ways of life."

Educators found by experience that the age of 6 years (plus or minus 1) is in fact the time when children can be taught; their abilities to concentrate, to think abstractly, and to reason have greatly increased in comparison to the preceding years. Anna Freud (1965) quotes her father's explanation of this development as the "biologically determined lessening of drive activity". He says (Freud, 1905), "In so far as educators pay any attention at all to infantile sexuality, they behave exactly as though they shared our views as to the construction of the moral defensive forces at the cost of sexuality, and as though they knew that sexual activity makes a child ineducable: for they stigmatize every sexual manifestation by children as a vice . . ." (p. 179).

Maturation and Ego Development

In "Latency Revisited" Shapiro and Perry (1976) bring together research in the areas of brain development, behavior, and maturation, which seem to converge around the age of 7 years. Rapid integrative growth of auditory-visual functioning coincides with maturing spatiotemporal orientation around the same age. Cognitive development is found to be involved in the development of moral thinking and socialization. Shapiro and Perry argue

> that processes within the central nervous system and cognitive strategies derived from maturation may provide latency with its biological clock. . . . The greater stability and invariance of mental process and the new cognitive structure at seven also permit the inhibition and control of drives and the postponement of action. . . . These confluences in development are not fortuitous but are part of the design feature of the human organism and this design feature permits higher level organization and, therefore, latency.

Their paper supplies the physiological basis for the development of ego functions in the latency period, whereas Freud looked on the same period from the point of view of drive development. Hartmann (1952) argues that the "consideration of maturational processes also on the side of ego development seems natural enough if we keep in mind that the ego aspect of development is no less biological than its id aspect" (p. 19). He adds the remark that "it is particularly the study of the ego-functions which might facilitate a meeting between the psychoanalytic and the physiological, especially the brain-physiological, approach. . . . As to the physiological aspect of the problem, Freud always maintained that in some future time physiological data and concepts would be substituted for the psychological ones, referring to all mental functions and not only to those of the id" (p. 19). Shapiro and Perry make us aware, by compiling the physiological and brain-physiological data for the development of ego functions, that that "future time" has come. Hartmann (1952) pointed out that factors in the nonconflictual sphere codetermine the ways of conflict solution and are in turn influenced by the latter. In the case of the decline of the oedipus complex the consolidated ego functions may facilitate the inhibition and control of drives, whereas the biologically diminished drive may allow the consolidation of ego functions. It is not a question of priority, but a question of mutual influences.

The Decline of the Oedipus Complex

It is the consensus of educators, researchers in the natural sciences, and psychoanalysts that the period between approximately 6 and 10 years is of great importance for the development of the child into a member of society. We might say that the period before this time ideally allows the child to develop his body and his functions to the point of independence from the mother. His libidinal drives as well as his aggression are still dependent on guidance by another person. He needs somebody to be his supplementary superego; somebody has to tell him what is right and wrong, or he may forget it when that person is not around.

The mother satisfies all the needs of the young child and is his first love object. He wants her all to himself. The mother is for a long time not seen as a person separate from himself; he learns to recognize their separateness only gradually. The world interferes in this unity, even while it reveals itself to him. He turns his affection to other people in addition to the mother. In the schematic model we see the dyad between mother and child disturbed but also enlarged into a triad which includes the father. The child cannot have his mother all to himself any more, but ideally has gained another love object. This first restriction of the baby's all-consuming desires forces his first important adaptation to the world at large, because it demands of him the recognition of a person outside of his unity with the mother. His sexual feelings are directed toward her, as all his needs are. But while she has satisfied all his previous demands to a great extent, his genital needs are not accepted and not gratified. He is excluded from sleeping with her, while the third person in the triangle can do so. This frustration heightens his desire for her and arouses his aggression against the rival. He would want to eliminate him if he would not thereby risk losing him.

The Role of Narcissism and Object Loss

His aggression against the father—his wanting to kill him and to take his penis away—flounders at his fear of retaliation (really his fear of talion). He fears that what he wants to do to the other will be done to him; and since the other is stronger, he capitulates. This conflict between his love and his hate for the father, but also his instinct for self-preservation, is the bulwark which forces him to relinquish his wishes for the mother; he solves his rivalry with the father by identifying with him. This is one model for the decline of the oedipus complex.

It is different for the girl. Things are essentially the same for her as for the boy, until she becomes aware of her father. She too wants the mother all to herself, wants to sleep with her, and sees the father as her rival. But her aggressive wishes against him are not as strong as those of the boy, because her loving feelings are stronger, fortified by the sexual attraction she feels toward the father. Her jealousy turns her against the mother. However, her dependency and love for her curb her aggression. Her feelings toward both parents are ambivalent, but less threatening than those of the boy. Under normal circumstances her feelings toward both parents continue; she has no penis to lose but is concerned that she might lose their love. The decline of the female counterpart of the oedipus complex, the electra complex, is not as violent as that of the boy. Despite the decline, the mother remains the prime love object for both the boy and the girl; the girl's love for the father remains intact, while the boy identifies with his rival. The passions are calmed. The decline of the oedipus complex is crucial for the development of drive control.

Sexual Feeling

Yet sexual feelings continue; the children masturbate but are more discreet about it. They do not express their sexual wishes as blatantly as before; they keep them to themselves in their fantasies. Sexual play between children is to some extent exploratory and experimental; their attempts at intercourse are unsatisfactory because of their immaturity. They usually do not spend an excessive amount of time and interest on these activities. If they do so to the exclusion of other play and interests, it is usually the reaction of being exposed to a great deal of sexual stimulation, either by witnessing nudity and sexual relations between adults or having been seduced by a person who is older and sexually mature. Such experiences are traumatic to children, who feel overwhelmed by the other person as well as by their own feelings. They may react by repeating, in an active way, either with other children or by themselves in excessive masturbatory activities, the traumatic experience to which they were passively exposed. Alternatively, they may react by total repression of all sexual feelings. Fraiberg (1972) has discussed this outcome and connects it in girls with frigidity in adult women.

Aggression

Aggression in the latency period comes from different sources, as it does in other phases of development. The child uses phase-specific tools in libidinal, functional, and aggressive ways. The baby, who learns to put something in his mouth and develops this important function, practices the function, enjoys it, and uses it aggressively; the modes of the activity will be determined to a large degree by the handling and reaction of the caretaking person to the child. An observation comes to mind. A boy baby of about 12 to 13 months, sitting on his mother's lap next to a curtained window, pulled the curtain because it was there to be pulled; the mother disagreed and said 'no.' The child did it again; the mother slapped his hand. He persisted, and so did she. The interaction became a battle of wills which the child lost with crying and tears. Pulling the curtain, which had started as a joyful activity, became an aggressive one in response to the mother's aggression. Part of the aggressive feelings in the latency period are displaced sexual feelings. Children's fantasies are full of aggressions; they fantasy that they are stronger and smarter than anybody, that they will conquer the world. They have displaced their aggression to some extent from the oedipal rival to other objects. They act out these rivalries in their more or less serious fighting with other children, in their competitive strivings in learning situations, and to a great degree in organized games. In learning and organization, in making rules and regulations for themselves, both libido and aggression are sublimated. Running, jumping, and climbing are necessary activities for healthy children. When they are restrained for a while, as happens in varying degrees, e.g., in the schools, they practically burst out in recess or when school is out. They run, yell, throw balls, jackets, or stones, and roughhouse with each other. While children of a younger age act out these needs more or less at random, after age 6 or 7 they have a tendency to organize in groups and play games.

Kaplan (1976), in a paper read at a panel on female sexuality, pointed out that girls have a proclivity for rhythmic movement, which she views as biologically and hormonally determined. Girls' liking for horseback riding is partly related to this; in addition, it satisfies their tomboyish and masturbatory needs. Rhythmic games like jump rope and jacks, with accompanying jingles and songs, are played by girls in all countries. These rhythms and verses give the aggression form and organization; the organized games of boys, from cowboys and Indians to baseball and football, serve the same purpose. Aggression is expressed but is organized and restricted by rules and regulations.

Superego Development

The ability to formulate rules and follow them, even if they should result in one's own defeat in a game, is not easy to come by. Children go through different phases. They make the rules, but they also change them and break them, while they do not allow others to do so. Sometimes they are quite strict with others in observing rules in games or behavior, but not with themselves. Tattletaling is one of the side effects of this struggle, because it is a struggle with themselves about obeying rules, only at the time being it is projected onto others. Eventually they accept the rules for themselves as well, except when they cheat. There is a difference between breaking rules and cheating. The one who breaks the rule feels in his right and does it openly—like certain delinquents or psychopaths who act as if they had the right to make their own rules. When the child cheats, he does so secretly, knowing that he does something wrong. By accepting rules for himself, the child shows that he has arrived at certain concepts of right and wrong, that he is in control of his aggression, and that he has developed a superego. "Play is to the child what thinking, planning and blueprinting are to the adult, a trial universe in which conditions are simplified and methods exploratory, so that past failures can be thought through, expectations tested" (Erikson, 1973).

Sarnoff (1976) lists the cognitive skills which mature and develop during the years 7½ to 8½ that produce the shift to late latency:

> 1. Concrete operational thinking. This is a term used by Piaget to describe cognitive improvement in reality testing.
>
> 2. Abstract conceptual memory organization. This is a skill which relates to the ability to recall on an abstract rather than a rote level.
>
> 3. A shift in fantasy contents from thoughts about fantasy objects to thoughts about reality objects.
>
> 4. Reorganization of superego contents in the direction of the child's own ethical individuation of motives and away from motivational contents derived from parental demands.

The latency child who renounces his openly sexual demands and his open aggression toward his parents is more reality oriented. He has lost his belief in his omnipotence (pp. 115–116).

The Decline of the Oedipus Complex as an Organizing Agent

Children who grow up with a single parent and whose sexual drives remain relatively unrestricted may be retarded in their development of morality and socialization; their ability to sublimate and to concentrate may be poor. The case of a girl of 9 may illustrate. Mary grew up with her mother without a permanent man in the house. She stole, had no friends, and was a bed wetter. Frequently she went to bed with her mother, wetted, and then returned to her own bed. She fantasied when urinating that she was her mother's lover who ejaculated, but also that she was her mother's baby. She was intelligent but behind in her schoolwork because she didn't pay attention and didn't do her homework. At one point in her treatment she decided that she wanted to become a good student, that she wanted to do her homework, but that she needed her mother's help. She practically forced her mother to help, keeping her and herself up at all hours of the night and incidentally out of bed. She achieved what she wanted in school, stopped stealing, and stopped wetting, in chronological order. Her ego functions developed before she achieved instinct control. She structured it so that her mother helped her to accomplish age-appropriate tasks; she had to help her daughter replace instinctual-regressive satisfactions with age-appropriate achievements.

An experience to the contrary happened in a classroom of 6-year-olds. These children had a great time playing in their dollhouse, where they acted out all their fantasies, including mutual explorations. The teacher complained that they were not learning the three Rs because they were not interested. When the time for playing was restricted and attention and work demanded before they were allowed to play, the result was immediate. They learned, and the intensity of their dollhouse play diminished. After a short time they were not even interested in it any more. Too much drive discharge and gratification prevented or made it unnecessary to sublimate, although the children had the ability to do so and had matured to that point.

Reality-Oriented Fantasies

The reduction of instinctual demands and the maturing of ego functions seem to occur nearly at the same time. The child finds abilities in himself which give him satisfactions in reality and make it easier to renounce the incomplete satisfactions of his immature sexuality. Id forces, diverted from the sexual struggle, supply the ego functions with energy, while the superego, expressed in moral thinking and socialization, regulates id discharges and aggression. The decline of the oedipus complex acts as an organizing agent around which a number of changes occur. The integrative growth in auditory-visual functioning enhances memory and conceptualization. The heard and remembered word becomes internalized as part of the inner voice, that is, the voice of the superego; the superego, however, is the precipitate of the oedipus complex. The child changes from acting out his oedipal wishes to fantasizing. His increased ability to think logically makes his fantasies less magical and more reality-oriented. Instead of fighting monsters, he fights burglars in his fantasies; instead of moving his magic wand, he fantasies flying an airplane. Then again, it might be interesting to build an airplane instead of only imagining one in fantasy, and fantasy is being changed into activity. Concrete operational thinking is at his disposal. The fantasies may become continued daydreams which are changed many times, less fleeting and more complex than the short ones of earlier times. Sometimes they are written up or drawn in pictures. The sublimation which was already present in the first change from acting to fantasizing becomes more strongly developed and requires the learning of certain skills. The ability of the child to recognize spatial relations enables him to construct, build, and draw. A similar development takes place in girls. Their doll play and playing house provide many opportunities to implement their fantasied, dramatic role playing with making things, from making dolls and their dresses, to cleaning, cooking, making furniture, and building houses. Their mothers, who may or may not work outside the home (they may be both homemakers and breadwinners), influence the roles which they take in their play and eventually in their planning for the future.

For fantasies may become daydreams of the future and the beginning of planning. The ability to think and distinguish past, present, and future is due to the child's newly developed sense of time, his remembering, conceptualizing, and distinguishing past experiences from fantasy.

The Sense of Self- and Object Constancy

The continuity of his fantasies is parallel with his sense of self; he is today what he was yesterday and what he will be tomorrow. He is not as much under the sway of his changing identifications. When he gets into a different environment, he is not as confused as he used to be: he can more or less maintain his ego functions—he can speak, eat, sleep, and use the toilet in most environments. He can tolerate separations from his parents more easily than before. Partly because he can function by himself, he remembers longer and feels less insecure in the absence of the parent, less angry at being left, less anxious because his death wishes against the parent are weakened, and therefore less vulnerable. However, his security and self-assuredness do not last indefinitely. There comes a time when he cannot stand the strain of being alone, on his own without his parents.

Two Novels

Two novels whose protagonists are latency children are apposite here; through some accident the children become separated from their parents without knowing when, if ever, they will be reunited with them. One is *High Wind in Jamaica* by Richard Hughes; the other is *Lord of the Flies* by William Golding. In both novels the authors sensitively describe the anxiety of the children, who feel unprotected against the unpredictable and possibly dangerous external situation and the precariously civilized self within themselves, and how they defend against the latter with denial and bravado. In the course of these struggles they regress to their more primitive selves and their superegos dissolve; they become the murderers they had been afraid of and fantasied about. Then, as unexpectedly as they were removed from their civilization, they are returned to it, and with it to their civilized selves. The memory of the time they have experienced in that other world fades into a dream. They are, however, left vulnerable for the future: some of the children are afraid it could happen again, and others remain susceptible to breaking the law should the occasion present itself. Both authors catch the essence of the latency child, who stands on the brink of becoming a responsible member of his society or falling back partly or entirely into the lawless self-indulgence of the prelatency child. In both books the catastrophes of the outside world can be interpreted as symbolic representations of the inner storms of the children. However, we are reminded of the effects of wars and revolutions, which are man-made catastrophes, on adults and children. The horrors of My-Lai were perpetrated by people whose consciences had been rendered nonfunctional by legalized acts of destruction ordered by their superiors. Freud and Burlingham (1943) described how the children in London enjoyed using the bomb craters of the Blitz in their games, adding their own destruction and making it their own.

The cataclysms in these stories are real and symbolic, and act as catalysts to unleash the only tenuously tamed jungle instincts of the children. Being children of latency age, they have only just started to have a conscience of their own, independent of their parents; it is still not well enough established, is as weak as they are themselves in the face of threats and bribes; they are still in need of the presence of their ideals in order to identify with them. The plight of the children in these novels is similar to that of children left on their own through any circumstance—death, the illness of a parent, marital discord, psychiatric illness, or natural catastrophes like floods or airplane crashes. Delinquent behavior, stealing, breaking into houses, destructiveness, and overt sexual behavior frequently occur in the wake of such events, indicative of the breakdown of the only recently established superego. The children's anger and disappointment in their parents play an important part. They blame them for having left them, regardless of the reason. The parents are deemed to have failed them by not being omnipotent; or if they are considered omnipotent, the children blame them for wanting to destroy them. They see their parents as evil and become so themselves. They need the image of the ideal parents to follow their example; if that image is destroyed, the ego ideal and the superego may become destroyed with it.

Splitting and Projecting

During their separation from their parents, the children in the two novels are exposed to evil authority figures, while the parents are left as the representatives of all that is good. The parental images are then split into good and bad. This is a device to which children often resort. It helps them distance themselves from their parents in order to achieve the independence and autonomy they need; by splitting the parental image and projecting one part onto another person, they preserve the ideal parent they need. The ideal they choose to identify with is not necessarily the socially desirable one. Their choice will again depend on the outcome of the oedipal solution and on the superego of the parents. There are parents who are part of a criminal society. Their relations to their children may be nurturing and protective and at the same time so threatening that the children have no choice but to adapt to them for self-preservation. They may see the persecutors of their parents in the people outside their immediate family, become identified with the criminal parents, and become their defenders.

Regressions and Reaction-Formations

Bornstein (1951) divides the latency period into two phases. In the first one, which she sets from 5½ to 8, the child's superego is not yet sufficiently consolidated, and the child frequently regresses; his ability to sublimate is easily disturbed. The regressions that occur in this period consist of giving up reaction-formations. Cleanliness, orderliness, and modesty are reaction-formations to the younger child's lack of concern for dirt, disorder, and exhibitionism. In the course of learning how to take care of himself, he identifies with the caretakers' demands and frequently overdoes them in order to fight his own desires to the contrary. When he gets tired at the end of the day or when he is under stress, he gives up the fight and regresses to being a dirty, disorderly little kid. Usually he recovers again after such letdowns; when he is under too much stress, however, the regression may become permanent and is then a sign of pathology.

Guilt Feelings and Projections

The second period, from 8 to 10, Bornstein characterizes as one in which guilt feelings appear and are defended against with projections. The splitting of the parent image into a good and a bad part allows for projection of the child's own forbidden impulses onto the bad parent and spares him feeling guilty. Frequently the child projects his forbidden impulses onto a playmate or sibling. It is the well-known syndrome of saying he or she did it, not I. Sometimes this is a blatant lie, but at other times the child honestly thinks it is the truth. He attributes his forbidden wishes to the other child and feels himself free of guilt. Sometimes two or three children plan to do something, like stealing or running away. One of them might come to a parent or teacher and tell about the other's plans in order to prevent them (and himself) from carrying them out. Not only does he split his wishes from himself and project them onto the others, but he also calls upon the help of the adult to become his supplementary superego because his own superego is not strong enough. He is oscillating between good and bad, between identifying with those representing his id and those representing his superego.

Identification and Its Uses

Identification is an important mechanism that continues through much of the child's life and serves different functions.

By making the parents' demands his own he identifies with the parents in his superego. By acting like his parents, he identifies with them in his ego. In the oedipal triangle, the child acts like the father in order to be loved by the mother; he acts like the mother in order to be liked by the father. But the child also identifies with parental characteristics of which he is afraid. He tells himself to brush his teeth like his father does and has told him to do, but he also hits his little brother like his father hit him. To identify with a parent is also a way to become independent of his presence; if he is like his father himself, he can do without him. The identification allows the child to feel safe when he is away from home; being identified with the caretaking parent, he can take care of himself. Having achieved control of his body and its functions, his ties to his parents are loosened, and he is free to some degree to enter new relationships. The child is ready to learn, due to his matured skills.

Acculturation and Self-Esteem

Most cultures offer their children instructions in the skills they consider important at this age, i.e., beginning at about 6. They are initiated into their society. In some cultures there are schools; in others the boys are taken from their mothers and live with the men and learn their ways, while the girls help their mothers and take care of the younger children. But for all the children it is a time to learn the ways of adults, to take on duties and responsibilities. Failing to do so, they feel inferior to their peers and compensate with antisocial acting out or withdrawal. The child defines himself in doing things; he is what he does and what he can do. He "shows and tells" what he has achieved—his picture, his story, the stones he has collected, or how high he can jump. He needs the approval and disapproval of parents and teachers, but peer judgment becomes increasingly more important. Both are necessary if he is to be proud of what he can do and what he has achieved. His self-esteem, which has suffered in the defeat of the oedipal crisis, needs to be restored. The child who has not gone through this crisis, who has not given up his incestuous strivings, to some extent does not accept the judgment of others on what he does, his own judgment of his achievements, however, is unrealistic. He thinks he can do anything; he thinks of himself as omnipotent. He does not learn because in fantasy he already knows and can do, even if in reality he fails. His fantasies of being an adult are sometimes reinforced by the parent who participates in them, while in reality he does not learn what is necessary for him to become an adult.

A 6-year-old boy of normal intelligence did not learn in school. He talked and acted like an adult; he pretended to know more than the other children, but they found out he didn't and made fun of him. His father had been a pilot and was killed in the war. The mother said in an interview that when the father died she told her boy, who was then 5 years old, that he would have to take his father's place and be the man of the house. She let him sit at the head of the table and push her chair in when she was sitting down. He was her companion when she went out to restaurants or shows. But she also complained that he misbehaved and was not a gentleman when she had a male visitor or when she went out with a man. Obviously, the little boy was confused by her demands to behave like a man in some situations and in others to behave like the child he was. However, to be his age deprived him of both his privileged position and his mother; he was then left without either parent. He could not admit his helplessness. In school he had to pretend to know and to be able to do, as he had to pretend to be an adult with his mother. To learn to read and write like the other children meant to admit that he didn't know, that he was not an adult, that he could not in reality take the father's place with the mother. Normally children at this age develop friendships and enter peer groups; these children do not. They remain outsiders and feel excluded.

The ability to learn and to do things for himself leads to self-esteem and increased autonomy. If a child has achieved autonomy in his body functions in early childhood, he is now learning to use his brain, his hands, and his body for doing things. Visual-motoral and auditory-visual integration and spatiotemporal orientation have matured around the age of 7 (Shapiro and Perry, 1976). He can concentrate and be attentive for longer periods. He can plan to do things that will not be finished the same day. He can set a timetable for himself so he will know what he will do first and what next. He wants to decide on his own what he will do, when, and how. The 6- or 7-year-old may be able to plan two or three things to do in sequence. When it gets to be more, he will get confused and forget. As he gets older, he is able to plan for longer periods, but characteristically he wants to do things on his own and wants to decide on his own. He resents the helpful interference of parents and teachers. He wants to make his own mistakes and correct them. As his superego gets stronger, he becomes more reliable; he can perform certain tasks and take on obligations. He is pleased with himself that he can do so, but he is also sensitive and angry when interfered with. When he plans to take out the garbage and the parent reminds him to take it out, he becomes angry and may not do it. This is comparable to a younger child who wants to do something himself and gets angry at his mother when she helps him. In both cases the parent interferes in a developing ego function. The prelatency child is in the process of mastering a function. The parent interferes in his blossoming autonomy, holding him back in dependence when he struggles for independence. He reacts with anger because his development in being able to live separately from the parent is threatened. The latency child is in the process of becoming his own master, of internalizing certain demands and developing an autonomous superego. He feels interfered with in this learning process by the parents' reminders. It is a difficult task for the educator to steer a course between allowing too much autonomy where the child does not have the tools to do something and letting him make his decisions and plans when he is able to do so. Robert Hall Smith caught the flavor of the stubborn 6-year-old perfectly in the title of his book about adolescents: *"Where Did You Go?" "Out" "What Did You Do?" "Nothing"* (1958). It is part of this striving for autonomy to have and keep secrets; of course, at times it is to avoid confrontation and punishment, but to have secrets by oneself or with peers, to form secret clubs, is part of growing up.

The Group

The peer group becomes increasingly more important for the child. He feels alone and unhappy if he doesn't have friends. The group serves a number of functions for the latency child. The school group, which is the choice of the parents and licensed, i.e., sanctioned by the state, is supposed to introduce the child into the knowledge and mores of his society. The knowledge he is taught is censored, i.e., it is selected by educators who decide what he should and should not learn. The child is being indoctrinated. That word is usually reserved for regimes who teach children an ideology which may or may not be in agreement with that of the parents. If it is different from that of the parents, it may bring the children into conflict with teachers or parents. Yet teaching with the system or against the system has in common that in either case it is an authority figure who imposes ideas on the child. However, the child uses the group in ways which do not serve that purpose alone. By joining or making a children's group within the school or outside it, he gets into a group which has a life of its own, unsupervised by adults. In such a subgroup he may re-create the world as he sees it: play house, or school, or church, but also form a gang, roam the streets, break into houses, or terrorize younger children. In either case, the children devise their own rules and organization, decide what is or is not permissible within the group. It is the subgroup which allows the child to think differently from his parents; the subgroup's judgment may supersede the parents' judgment and strengthen his own. Depending on his own strength or weakness, he may go from being dependent on his parents to being dependent on the group or to making himself independent of both. The authority-directed group will help the child to move away from the parents by accepting the authority of persons other than the parents; the subgroup may help in the transition from dependency to independence. Through the group the children may learn from others what the parents cannot teach them—and eventually surpass them. The latency child is exquisitely malleable, and it is to a certain degree in the power of the educator to adapt him to society in one way or another. Bernfeld, making

Machiavelli his spokesman, calls the educator the servant of society (Bernfeld, 1925). The Russians call their dissidents mentally disturbed and force them to undergo psychiatric treatment. When Sarnoff (1976) says, "The healthier the structure of latency the more closely does the content [of fantasies] hew to the patterns of the culture" (p. 162), he agrees with the Russians by calling the well-adapted child healthy and, by inference, the child who is less adapted, sick. In this way the psychiatrist joins the educator who considers it his task to adapt the child to the society as it is. The latency child has a wealth of fantasy and is creative with all kinds of material in arts, crafts, writings, and dramatic play. Most frequently these creative abilities disappear in the latter part of the latency period or in early adolescence. Logical thinking and verbal communication take their place.

The Outsider

However, there are some talented children who continue to be creative later on as well. They may not be as well adjusted as the others and have difficulties with both peers and teachers. Yet they produce something which may eventually bring them recognition. Such a child was a boy who lived in a world of his own, in fantasies which he continued and represented in innumerable drawings. He fantasied how he would free his mother, who was locked up in a dungeon. It was true that she was hospitalized off and on. He also fantasied and drew complicated machines, and played and worked with electronics. His relationships with other children were nonexistent. He only waited to visit his mother when she was well enough to see him, either in the hospital or at home. He was attached to his therapist, who helped him disentangle himself from the frightening identification with his mother. The father was a mad scientist who had committed suicide when the boy was 2½ years old. The boy was drawn to identify with the father but afraid that he might go mad and kill himself, too. The therapist helped him to follow the father in what was viable and to stay away from his self-destructiveness. Identification with the therapist was one way to achieve this. He eventually went to college to study physics and mathematics. The child had therapy and was able to use it. He never really adjusted to the children's group in which he grew up, but he gained their respect with his skill in electronics. He was able to continue to be creative because he had a talent; but he also learned to accept his position as an outsider without becoming paranoid like his mother or suicidal like his father. He developed the ego strength to live in society as an outsider.

The child may become well adapted to society but at the cost of his creativity. Maybe this is one of the reasons there are so many interesting, creative children and so few interesting creative adults. Also we may be aware that people who remain creative as adults are rarely well-adjusted people. Margaret Mead (1970) talks about the allowance for the occurrence of genius that is necessary for new cultural forms to be created "by a vision—or a dream." The outsider may have a talent, even if he is short of being a genius. Nonconformity is not necessarily maladaptive or sick. Psychoanalytic psychology is developmental psychology. The people who are working within this theory feel committed to allow and encourage the child to develop his faculties and to allow him to establish his way of dealing with himself and the world and with himself in the world. This will be his character, which will determine his development in adolescence, which in turn will determine his adult person. However, we have to recognize that our theory is shot through with value judgments which are the values of our society, by which we decide which faculties to promote and which ones to suppress. By calling somebody healthy or unhealthy, normal or abnormal, we are giving good and evil other names.

Summary

The latency period is a time of great importance in the child's life. It is a period of relative quietude between anxiety-ridden early childhood and stormy adolescence. When the task of being physically independent from a caretaking person is sufficiently accomplished, when separateness is comfortably established and maturation has occurred as far as it will go, the child is ready to acquire what he can of the knowledge of his society and to adapt to its mores. He is being less forced into the mold than he was at an earlier age, when he was entirely dependent on the parent and when he had to submit passively to what was being done to him. Although still dependent in many ways, he has more choice of action. He adapts to the demands made upon him by making compromises between inner and outer world. But the balance between the two will be relative to their respective strength. A child with strong drives will deal differently with outside demands than will a child with weak drives; object relations and identifications will help or disturb in establishing the balance. The more self-assured and self-sufficient he is, the better established his superego, the better able he will be to deal with the assault of adolescent drive increase; the more he can do, the better able he will be to deal with reality and to use fantasy in the service of the ego. His ability to learn, to fantasize, and to play is the foundation on which his ability to work creatively as an adult is based. His relations to others determine his future ability to love others and himself.

References

Bernfeld, S. (1925), *Sisyphos, oder Die Grenzen der Erziehung* (*Sisyphos, or the Limits of Education*). Leipzig: Internationale Psychoanalytische Verlag.

Bornstein, B. (1951), On latency. *The Psychoanalytic Study of the Child*, 6:279–285. New York: International Universities Press.

Buxbaum, E. (1970), *Troubled Children in a Troubled World*. New York: International Universities Press.

Erikson, E.H. (1973), Dimensions of a new identity: Jefferson Lectures. New York: Norton.

Ferenczi, S. (1913), *Developmental Phases of the Sense of Reality*. Leipzig: Internationale Psychoanalytische Verlag, 1927.

Fraiberg, S. (1972), Genital arousal in girls. *The Psychoanalytic Study of the Child*, 27:439–475. New York: Quadrangle.

Freud, A. (1965), *Normality and Pathology in Childhood*. New York: International Universities Press.

——— & Burlingham, D. (1943), *War and Children*. London: Medical War Books.

Freud, S. (1905), Three essays on the theory of sexuality. *Standard Edition*, 7:130–243. London: Hogarth Press, 1953.

——— (1923), The ego and the id. *Standard Edition*, 19:12–66. London: Hogarth Press, 1961.

Golding, W. (1959), *Lord of the Flies*. New York: Putnam.

Hartmann, H. (1952), The mutual influences in development of ego and id. *The Psychonalytic Study of the Child*, 7:9–68. New York: International Universities Press.

Hughes, R. (1957), *High Wind in Jamaica*. New York: Harper.

Kaplan, E. (1976), Manifestations of aggression in latency and preadolescent girls. *The Psychoanalytic Study of the Child*, 31:63–78. New Haven: Yale University Press.

Mead, M. (1970), *Culture and Commitment*. American Museum of Natural History.

Sarnoff, C. (1976), *Latency*. New York: Aronson.

Shapiro, T., & Perry, R. (1976), Latency revisited: The age 7 plus or minus 1. *The Psychoanalytic Study of the Child*, 31:39–106. New Haven: Yale University Press.

Smith, R.H. (1958), *"Where Did You Go?" "Out" "What Did You Do?" "Nothing."* New York: Norton.

16

The Eye of the Hurricane: From Seven to Ten

RONALD M. BENSON, M.D.
SAUL I. HARRISON, M.D.

Idealized or stereotyped images of the golden age of childhood often focus on the typical grade school child who is the subject of this chapter. Notwithstanding inevitable changes over time within this age range, children from 7 to 10 are characterized by their stable educability, pliability, and adaptability to external demands, and by relative calmness (Sarnoff, 1976). Although a modification of psychological organization from action in favor of ideation characterizes all child development, this shift is particularly evident in the latency phase of development.

As a discrete developmental phase, latency is well demarcated from the developmental phase that precedes it as well as from the one that follows it. Descriptively, these children are differentiated from the preschooler in several ways. For example, the latency-age child's needs and desires seem much less preemptive and undisguised. While the preschooler appears to change physically and psychologically at a rapid pace, the grade school child changes and grows emotionally, cognitively, and physically in a seemingly more slow and steady fashion. Dramatic spurts are rarely obvious in this phase of development.

Similarly, these school-age children are in marked contrast to preadolescents and adolescents. Latency-age children's interests seem much more directed toward mastery of external challenges, and their attention is focused more on acquiring new skills than on their inner lives or on rapidly changing body images in a swiftly altering "self." Characteristically, latency-age children seem relatively uninterested and untroubled as regards their "inner life." This maturational turn away from internal feelings and undisguised concern with impulses makes it easier for learning to be a highly valued activity. Children's knowledge of the world around them increases notably during this time, as attested by the vast educational, psychological, and anthropological literature devoted to the cognitive development of the child in this phase of life.

During the years 7 to 10, the locus of children's activity shifts from the home as the almost exclusive center of life to the official "dual headquarters" of home and school. In addition, other community-based loci assume expanding importance, e.g., the playing field, the church or synagogue, the site of special activities such as music lessons, the swimming pool or gym, the place where Cub Scouts, Brownies, or self-generated clubs meet.

By the same token, the important people in the child's life become more diverse. Although parents remain uppermost in importance, it is evident that teachers and friends play an ever increasing role in the child's life and thoughts.

During this period both boys and girls become "joiners" and begin to belong to organizations such as Cub Scouts, Brownies, Camp Fire Girls, Little League, and so forth. The trend is that each sex seems to avoid and depreciate the other. Sometimes less formal clubs and cliques are formed. Again, these are generally unisexual. Elaborate rules are quite frequent, especially with 7- or 8-year-olds.

Boys seem to retain friendships more constantly during these years than girls, who appear more fickle and seem to form very intense but relatively short-lived relationships.

As a group, girls seem to do better in school than boys during this period, although both sexes may enjoy and like school. Girls probably are more open in their fondness for school and teachers, most of whom are female. The enforced quiet and lack of motor discharge and the "feminine" characteristics of school seem to impose a greater burden on boys than on girls. In addition, girls are superior in language skills at this age.

Some parents welcome these years in their children. Fathers finally can play a sport with their sons. Mothers often characterize this phase as a relief from the unceasing demands of earlier years. Parents who have experienced their children's adolescence often speak longingly of the latency years as a breathing spell for parents in the course of their children's development.

On the other hand, there are parents who regret their children's decreased dependence on them as school and friends become more important. The end of the exclusivity of the parent-child pair may pose a threat for some parents. Mothers without an outside career may in particular find a troubling void in their lives, one requiring an adaptive response.

Metapsychology

To this eye in the hurricane of development Freud gave the name "latency" (1905), referring to the seeming quiescence of the libidinal drives following the resolution of the oedipal complex and extending to prepuberty. Freud (1923) pointed out that massive repression and subsequent amnesia regarding infantile sexuality, the withdrawal of object cathexis from the primary objects, identification with these objects, and the internalization of their prohibitions may be said to begin the latency period. As this process occurs over time, so does the onset of latency occur gradually.

In many ways the designation "latency" has proved an unfortunate choice, as it is so often misunderstood and misapplied. To many, it implies that sexual interests come to an abrupt halt, both consciously and, by implication, unconsciously. As a matter of fact, sexual interests persist during latency. Too often manifestations of sexual interest and occasional breakthroughs of direct sexual activity such as masturbation have been inappropriately assessed as pathological. Indications that sexual interests and activity may be in evidence during nonpathological latency does not alter the fact that impulse life is certainly much less directly expressed during latency than in the infantile phases of development preceding it.

Reviewing Freud's views on latency, Sarnoff (1976) notes that at times Freud attributed latency to a primary diminution of the drives, while at other times he supported the theory that latency resulted from an initial increase in defenses damming up the drives secondarily. Controversy regarding these two perspectives has continued in the literature that followed Freud. Both viewpoints have found eloquent adherents. Some writers assert that a biological change associated with a biphasic sexual drive results in diminished drive pressure accounting for the principal manifest features of the latency period. Other observers maintain that it is the maturation and development of ego functioning and coping mechanisms that facilitate a more sophisticated range of adaptations permitting less direct expression of the drives, which nevertheless are basically undiminished.

Notable among those pointing to a decrease of drive pressure in the postoedipal period as primary are Bornstein (1951) and Anna Freud (1965). Drawing on data from disciplines outside psychoanalysis, Shapiro and Perry (1976) assert that there is indeed a significant discontinuity in development occurring in the vicinity of the seventh year of life. They assume that since this is demonstrably cross-cultural, it must be biologically determined. But they argue that it is not the libidinal drive demonstrating the long-assumed classical sequence of preoedipal growth, succeeded by diminution of the drive, to be followed by a new upsurge in adolescence, that is "the significant substratum" on which latency is based. Instead they cite exhaustive neurobiological and cognitive data pointing to the conclusion that "processes within the CNS and cognitive strategies derived from maturation . . . provide latency with its biological clock." In metapsychological terms, they attribute latency to maturation and increasing structuralization of the ego. Sarnoff also takes issue with primary drive reduction as the core concept of latency. Employing rich clinical observations, he demonstrates convincingly that drive pressure continues unabated during the middle-grade school years. But regardless of whether drive reduction or increased coping mechanisms are credited as the relevant factor, there is unanimity that the relative balance between id and ego is shifted to the latter during latency.

In a comprehensive review of the psychoanalytic literature on latency, Fries (1958) noted that in addition to repression, which Freud focused on, other defenses have been identified as common in latency, e.g., temporary regressions to pregenitality, reaction-formation, and sublimation. Sarnoff (1976, p. 31) has schematically summarized the characteristic mechanisms of defense that contribute to the maintenance of latency. As forbidden genital impulses threaten to become conscious and manifest, the child regresses to an anal sadistic drive organization. Repression is increased, and a turn toward reality and away from inner life takes place. To then deal with the anality to which the child has regressed, the defenses of sublimation, doing and undoing, reaction-formation, and repression tend to be used. Once the latency state has been achieved, breakthroughs of anal, genital, and oedipal conflicts tend to be dealt with via repression, fragmentation, displacement, symbol formation, synthesis, and secondary elaboration in fantasy formation. Sarnoff refers to this third group of defenses and maneuvers as the structure of latency.

Thus, while the preschool child prefers to gratify impulses directly with primary objects, and adolescents by preference are moving toward nonincestuous heterosexual objects to satisfy their sexual and competitive needs, neither of these solutions is open to the latency child. These unavailabilities stem from both internal and cultural prohibitions, as well as from the child's immaturity. Yet the most compelling evidence suggests persistence of considerable drive pressure demanding adaptive management from the latency child. In latency, the preferred and normative means of discharge, albeit partial, is through fantasy.

Two phases of latency generally are recognized (Alpert, 1941; Bornstein, 1951; Sarnoff, 1976), with 8 years considered to be the usual transition point. Early latency is characterized by the child's preoccupation with self. The superego is very strict. Fantasies, often of amorphous monsters, serve simultaneously as a means both of defense and of partial discharge of genital and pregenital aims. Ambivalence is marked. In later latency, real objects and sublimations are more available and permitted. The early latency child represents the archetypical model whose sexuality is manifestly less visible. As latency continues, however, sexual curiosity becomes more directed. Objects and activities in the external world play a more significant role. As the maturing latency child returns toward objects and away from fantasy as the preferred route of drive discharge, the latency phase is approaching its end, and preadolescence assumes greater importance. Presumably this stems from a combination of the maturation of ego functions and the biologically derived increase of drive pressure associated with puberty.

The ego during normal latency is developing, establishing strong defenses, increasing the strength of secondary processes, acting more and more in accord with the reality principle, and establishing positive object relations (Fries, 1958).

In most areas of functioning, the self-representation of a latency child is quite well demarcated from the object representation. An age-appropriate exception to this involves those developmental lines in which the latency child still experiences the parents' capacities as his own and vice versa. For example, latency children usually act as if they have little responsibility for their own health and hygiene, fully expecting this area of their lives to be properly managed by their parents. Anna Freud (1965, p. 77) points to this as a residue of the original symbiosis between mother and child.

In contrast to the situation prevailing in the preschooler, self-esteem regulation and self-regard in the latency child are based to a far greater degree on real accomplishments in relation to internalized standards and goals (Benson, 1974). Doing well in school, at games, and in other social situations enhances self-esteem. The fact that the standard accomplishment is becoming less dependent on external authorities and more on the child's internalized standards and values represents, in structural terms, the increasing dependence of the child's self-esteem regulation on his performance being consonant with his ego ideal and superego.

The typical latency-age child has progressed a long way in relinquishing infantile omnipotence and grandiosity. Nevertheless, on occasion he will boastfully overestimate his own capabilities. Often this has a much more defensive quality than was formerly the case. Now the youngster remains relatively aware that he is small, limited in capacity, and in need of help from parents and teachers.

The infantile idealization of parents diminishes manifestly during latency, although the infantile parental images remain the unconscious objects of the drives. Latency children will idealize and identify with teachers, sports heroes, and TV stars. From the point of view of self-esteem maintenance, these identifications serve as attempts to regain some of the infantile omnipotence that has otherwise been relinquished. In addition, these objects of idealization are more distant than the parents; the absence of physical availability makes them more suitable and less threatening objects for the partial discharge of libidinal and aggressive drives in disguised derivative form.

Typically, the latency child develops a particular kind of fantasy to aid in this process of continuing separation from the early narcissistic involvement with the primary parental objects. Simultaneously, these fantasies deal with conflicts and guilt stemming from the fact that the parents continue to serve unconsciously as objects of the drives, oedipal wishes in particular. This fantasy, which has been designated the family romance, is characterized by two central themes (Moore and Fine, 1968). In the first the child typically imagines himself as not the biological offspring of his parents but as adopted. He fantasies that he is descended instead from exalted, often noble parentage. The second theme entails the child's imagining himself as accomplishing the dramatic rescue of someone important. Both the narcissistic aggrandizement and the relief from unacceptable oedipal wishes are quite transparent in such fantasies. The specific variations on these themes elaborated by a particular child are revealing clues to the details of that child's state of development and conflict. Therefore, these fantasies are not only developmentally useful for the child, but have great diagnostic significance and psychotherapeutic potential as well.

Despite the use of fantasy, the channels for sublimation, and other defensive maneuvers, direct breakthroughs of impulse do occur, even in latency children whose ego development is adequate and who are sufficiently gratified by a good enough environment. Usually this takes the form of direct or masked masturbation or outbursts of temper. Though typical, such behavior tends to be quite guilt-provoking for latency-age children and often leads to punishment-seeking activity. This conflict over the direct emergence of impulse in such relatively undisguised forms as masturbation has been termed the central conflict of this phase of development.

As noted above, the characteristic manifestations of the latency phase depend on an optimal balance between drive pressure and ego development. Further, the typical resolution of the pregenital and oedipal phases should have occurred, entailing identifications and introjections contributing to consolidation and structuralization of superego functioning. But in addition to these vital developmental strides derived from the vicissitudes of the drives, from the resolution of conflict, and from object relations, the maturation of autonomous ego functions is a necessary precondition for the characteristic state of latency to develop. In Piaget's formulation (Piaget and Inhelder, 1969), the child must pass from preoperational (prelogical) thought to the kind of cognitive processes characterized as concrete operational thought. The attainment of a certain degree of rationality and conceptual constancy is integral to latency. The child's knowledge, perception, and memory all increase dramatically to usher in this phase of development and to maintain it, and they continue to expand throughout this period. The world of objects (in the Piagetian sense) around the child becomes stable and orderly. Physical quantities, such as volume and weight, become constant, despite changes in size or shape. The capacity for symbol formation and attendant advances in language function are also important. Failure in the appropriate development of these cognitive capacities will handicap the child's efforts to deal with impulses in ways other than direct gratification with primary objects.

If ego development has not proceeded adequately up to the latency period and/or does not continue to progress once that period is under way, the typical pathological result is a habit or impulse disorder. However, the psychopathology par excellence of latency is the learning difficulty, in which the capacity of the child to sublimate is interfered with, either secondarily, through conflict, or primarily, through the failure to develop requisite ego functions. The latter can stem from either endowment, internalized conflict, or environmental interference.

Treatment of the latency child depends, as it does with all other age groups, on determining the appropriate interventions based on a diagnostic understanding of the youngster. In some cases, ego-building skills must be taught through an educative approach. In others, intervening in the child's environment through special programs or parental guidance may be most helpful. Although the number of children for whom medication is indicated is a controversial subject, there is general agreement that for some children psychotropic medications, such as stimulants and occasionally tranquilizers, aid in organizing the child's mental functioning, e.g., the capacity to focus attention, or in the reduction of anxiety. For a large group of children, intervening in a way designed to reduce internal conflicts based on inadequate resolution of oedipal and earlier neurotic solutions impresses psychoanalytic observers as most helpful. This might be accomplished in individual psychotherapy accompanied by parental guidance, in systems-oriented family therapy, or in group therapy. Child psychoanalysis might be the treatment of choice for well-entrenched neurotic processes already firmly established by latency age.

Many of the deviations occurring at this phase of development are often quite responsive to appropriate intervention; however, impairments of development at this age may lead to severe consequences in later life. For example, obsessional neuroses and childhood schizophrenia may become manifest at this phase of development. In addition, any set of circumstances interfering with the attainment of the state of latency will very likely result, if untreated, in the reduction of sublimatory channels throughout life, resulting in an adult who lacks certain capacities and skills; e.g., intellectual functioning could be interfered with on a permanent basis.

It has long been assumed on the basis of uncontrolled clinical observations that failure in the establishment of the state of latency would render it impossible for preadolescence and adolescence to take their typical form (Blos, 1962). This might, in consequence, lead to significant problems in object relations, sexuality, and independent functioning.

References

Alpert, A. (1941), The latency period. *Amer. J. Orthopsychiat.*, 11:126–144.

Benson, R. (1974), The psychoanalytic assessment. In: *A Practical Handbook of Psychiatry*, ed. J. Novello. Springfield, Ill.: Charles C Thomas, pp. 71–86.

Blos, P. (1962), *On Adolescence*. New York: Macmillan.

Bornstein, B. (1951), On latency. *The Psychoanalytic Study of the Child*, 6:279–285. New York: International Universities Press.

Freud, A. (1965), *Normality and Pathology in Childhood*. New York: International Universities Press.

Freud, S. (1905), Three essays on the theory of sexuality. *Standard Edition*, 7:123–234. London: Hogarth Press, 1953.

——— (1923), The ego and the id. *Standard Edition*, 19:3–68. London: Hogarth Press, 1961.

Fries, M. (1958), Review of the literature on the latency period. *J. Hillside Hosp.*, 7:3–16.

Moore, B., & Fine, B., eds. (1968), *A Glossary of Psychoanalytic Terms and Concepts*. 2nd ed. New York: American Psychoanalytic Association.

Piaget, J., & Inhelder, B. (1969), *The Psychology of the Child*. New York: Basic Books.

Sarnoff, C. (1976), *Latency*. New York: Aronson.

Shapiro, T., & Perry, R. (1976), Latency revisited: The age 7 plus or minus 1. *The Psychoanalytic Study of the Child*, 31:79–105. New Haven: Yale University Press.

17

The Child Analyst and the Prediction of Psychopathology Based on the Study of Behavior in Young Children

SERGE LEBOVICI, M.D.

There are many works which define mental disorder as a continual process whose diverse manifestations depend on the social and cultural milieu, the circumstances, and especially the age of the patient. Such is the tendency still expressed by traditional psychiatry.

Nonetheless, since Freud took infantile neurosis as his model to define the transference neurosis, and also to reconstitute it within the psychoanalytic cure of adults (Freud, 1918), we have been able to study the pathological value and the evolutive potential of neurotic symptoms in children. With the Little Hans case Freud showed that neurotic symptoms could disappear spontaneously, but that it was impossible to know what scars they would leave on vanishing (Freud, 1909).

Since the psychopathological manifestations and behavior disturbances of the child are of an aleatory nature, we believe that some of them belong to normal developmental relations (A. Freud, 1965; Lebovici and Sadoun, 1968) and that still others constitute the precursors of eventual mental disorders.

As an example, it would be of interest to show briefly that we can venture imagining an ulterior pathology, not yet expressed, based on the study of another child in the same family (in this case a brother). An 8-year-old boy presents sleep and eating disorders. He is perturbed by an intrusive phobic system;

Translated by Frances N. Dropkin.

among other things he is in the habit of keeping his food in his mouth a very long time. He is part of a family of Portuguese immigrants who live in Paris. His mother complains of being tired by the constant presence of her small daughter, who is with her all the time.

During the session, the boy draws an automobile which falls into a pool. For diverse reasons which are unnecessary to enumerate here, this shows the meaning of his rumination and of his phobic inhibition.

When invited to talk with the consultant, the mother has great difficulty in separating herself from her daughter, who is constipated because she is afraid of "falling into the hole of the W.C." She evokes her past, her childhood in Portugal, the surveillance her mother kept over her, the depression she went through when she arrived in Paris (in order to join her future husband) because of "the air pollution." When the mother is told that she does not want to be separated from her daughter, just as her mother had not wanted to be separated from her—in order to protect her against sexual impulses—and that her daughter keeps her inside of herself by being constipated and her son by keeping his food in his mouth, she accepts leaving her daughter.

She is surprised that her daughter accepts this separation, but she fears an accident. She might fall down the stairs, which is what happened to her son, who was pushed by a cousin and fell. She adds that her father brought her up without accidents and that she wants to do as much for her children. Of course, she is evoking here a moral education which preserved her from "falls," that is, moral offenses. Finally she refuses all psychotherapeutic approaches and explains her son's difficulties by the existence of mental disorders in two of her father's brothers. The therapeutic space which is proposed to her is thus peopled with seductive men who provoke a fall, like that which menaces her daughter.

It must be mentioned that the receptionist in charge of watching what happens in the waiting room had to intervene in order to prevent this little girl from rushing down the emergency stairs, whose use can be learned only from the sign which indicates their existence behind a door. In short, the hole—a space inhabited by a dangerous sexuality—becomes both provocation and danger, both organized by the mother's fantasies. The boy uses holes for fighting against his aggressive sexuality and manifests obviously phobic behavior concerning swallowing. The little girl might fall into the hole. One might imagine that later this hole/space will be represented by the road which separates home from school and that we are in the presence of a case which might lead to a school phobia.

This example, of metaphorical value, would show that the constipation of a little girl expresses the fantasies of her mother. It also allows us to imagine the organization of a constraining symptom which took another form in her older brother. In this chapter I particularly intend to study the conditions for such prediction based on the study of the child's development and on knowledge of the parents' fantasies. To begin with, it is probably necessary to review the way in which the child psychoanalyst sees the impact of development on the child's mental functioning and its normal and pathological variations.

Psychoanalytic Considerations on the Relationship Between Child Development and Psychopathology in Children

We have already mentioned the difficulty encountered in evaluating the appearance and disappearance of neurotic symptoms in children. The presence of phobic symptoms in the nonconsulting population of children in the latency period presents the problem of the utility of the concept of normality (Lebovici and Diatkine, 1974). We know that these neurotic symptoms do not tend to persist into adulthood. They are of a composite form, and they may be linked to various behavior disorders (Lebovici and Braunschweig, 1967). Neurotic disorders in adults organize themselves on the basis of ego-syntonic symptoms which often appear in a brutal manner, at least on the surface. Through anamnestic study of the childhoods of these subjects, we recognize diverse disturbances; often we learn that these were turbulent children in whom diverse manifestations of anxiety were hidden under the agitation. The specificity of the infantile neurosis can be reconstructed through the psychoanalytic treatment of the adult, without, however, being able to attain, through this work, a precise dating of the event or situation, which had been a potential organizer. Reconstructions or constructions in psychoanalysis (Freud, 1937) have a meaning very different from recollection, as shown by M. Kris (1956).

Inversely, certain serious character neuroses of adults seem to constitute the latest phase in childhood disorders which are difficult to classify, but which seem to be part of a psychotic potential. It is for this reason that certain child analysts, belonging to what one may call the Parisian school, have proposed the notion of *prepsychosis* (Lebovici, 1963; Chiland and Lebovici, 1977). It is a question of dysharmonic evolution which is translated by diverse clinical particularities on the behavioral and verbal level, but in which one does not find neurotic symptoms. Such children express their fantasies in a raw state, and organization of reaction-formations and defensive systems is very fragmentary. Their mental functioning remains largely impregnated with primary mechanisms.

We have briefly recalled these considerations (which are frequent for child psychoanalysts, who have occasion to deal with the problem of continuity in the disorders they observe, and especially to ask about the relationships between infantile psychopathology and that of adults) in order to study the limits of the field of neurotic symptoms and the different modes of organization of infantile psychosis with respect to the child's development. Several theoretical trends come into conflict precisely over this matter.

The genetic point of view is amply represented in the Anna Freud school as well as in numerous psychoanalytic schools in the United States. All of Anna Freud's work aims at introducing the child and its environment, his dependency on his family throughout the vicissitudes of his development, into psychoanalytic thought. We read about this particularly in *Normality and Pathology in Childhood* (A. Freud, 1965). "The real child," who can be observed directly, must be taken into consideration in order to understand his development and his pathology (A. Freud, 1963).

Given this point of view, Nagera (1966) is justified in differentiating neurotic conflicts and neurotic symptoms described as such only after the postoedipal period, when the psychic agencies, differentiated according to the tripartite structure defined by Freud, are functioning. As we know, Nagera distinguishes between reactions and intrusion, defined in other terms as internalization, neurotic conflicts, and actual neurotic symptoms. They suppose the reinvasion of reaction-formations by more or less displaced instincts or their substitutes.

Such a description implies a knowledge of the child's development, that is, the interaction between the effects of maturation and of environmental intervention. The longitudinal study carried out at Yale first by E. Kris (1950) and continued after his death by his followers (in particular, M. Kris, 1957) showed the utility of understanding those errors in prediction which are particularly linked to the reciprocal interaction between mother and child.

This interaction defines, according to many authors, the developmental lines, thus assuming that a certain number of conditions are fulfilled which constitute, as it were, prerequisites. For example, Spitz (1965) underlines that this development cannot be assured unless (1) there exists an adequate progression of libidinal cathexes; (2) the maturation of the child's perceptual-motor apparatus allows him to take an interest in his environment; and (3) his mother invests her libido in him sufficiently for him to obtain reassurance and satisfaction.

One could cite many other authors who have concerned themselves with these basic prerequisites. We will mention only two of them here to show that these prerequisites have been described in different terms by different authors. Mahler in her numerous works has studied the separation-individuation process and has shown that the differentiation between object representation and self-representation necessitates a sufficient motility maturation, certain epistemophilic ego functions, and a basic confidence which allows for object constancy. In order to ensure this, the mother must, on her side, find pleasure in the child's autonomy (Mahler, 1968). Winnicott (1971), for his part, described certain varieties of what he called maternal holding that are indescribable in words but whose accidents can provoke "catastrophes which never happened." They must be reconstructed or even "predicted" in adulthood, because of their influence on development (Winnicott, 1971, p. 38).

These authors' works show that any modern genetic study of the development of the young child and the prediction of consequences pass through the knowledge of the interactions between a mother and her child. This is a fundamental point of view, one we will come back to. Nevertheless, the concept of maturation, which is invoked in these studies, implies that the development timetable in particular of nervous system functions, can be taken into consideration independently of interaction with the environment.

It seems to me that this can be done when it is a question of studying the consequences of aptitudes and inaptitudes. Anna Freud (1977) shows, for instance, that in blind children the attachment to the object world is retarded and often expresses itself in a primitive way. Freud (1913) has shown that the predisposition to obsessional neurosis rests in particular on hypermaturation of the ego with respect to libidinal development, which observers of children confirm in connection with the premonitory signs of this pathology. For instance, when tics are manifested, toilet training is often found to have been intense and precocious. The maturity of language often observed in so-called prepsychotic discordance leads to hypercontrol of an obsessional character type, that is, a neurotic outcome of hypermaturation. I have observed this development also in boys who either are precociously preoccupied with their sexual identity or who refuse their sex (Lebovici and Kreisler, 1965).

By contrast, in a study devoted to hysteria in young children I thought it a relevant hypothesis in such cases that libidinal maturity might be precocious with respect to ego development (Lebovici, 1974). This idea would lead to the answer that the expression of symptoms would depend on the developmental status of the ego. That is, hysteria would correspond to the first manifestations of anxiety and would be followed by phobias and obsessions. This is a classical theory which has been validated by Rivto's study (1966) of a patient seen during his childhood by Bornstein. This phobic child became obsessional as an adult.

But this perspective is not the only one which has led me to propose the idea of libidinal prematurity in infantile hysteria. I saw in it the possibility of defining a particular predisposition at the origin of these disorders. Also, considering the range of early pathology (characterized by an opposition between externalized cases and internalized cases), I judged hysteria to be situated among the former. It may lead eventually to the organization of phobo-obsessional symptoms; hysterical character traits, with or without the formation of conversion symptoms; prepsychotic discordance; etc.

Thus, rather than considering only the effects of maturation, I propose to study the potential of morbid "prestructures" and their eventual sequences.

The Point of View of the Kleinians

Apparently, psychoanalysts who consider themselves followers of Melanie Klein separate themselves completely from those who take maturation and development into account. In fact, they consider that object relations are organized from the beginning, since instinct implies an object that is cathected by it. The well-known aphorism is formulated as follows: The oral instinct supposes a breast to be sucked or devoured.

The sequence leading from needs to desires, which will be considered later on and which is fundamental in the metapsychological study of the genesis of object relations, is absolutely neglected by Klein. However, a genetic perspective is not entirely foreign to this author, whose ideas on the central psychotic position organized on the basis of a splitting into good and bad objects are familiar enough. Thus it will suffice to say that, according to her, neurotic symptoms are an elaboration of the central depressive position, which she places in the second half of the first year of life, after the necessary reparation of the object, now perceived as a whole. From this point of view, we will now see that it is not impossible to find the importance of the depressive position within a coherent metapsychological study of development.

On the Necessity for a Metapsychological Point of View on the Precocious Development of Object Relations

Freud (1905) did not neglect direct observation in order to propose his theory of infantile sexual development. He made use of it as well in studying his grandson's game with the spool in the theoretical essay "Beyond the Pleasure Principle" (1920).

Genetic studies of the object relation are numerous. Spitz (1965), and Lebovici (1960), and Lebovici and Soule, (1977), in particular, have shown that on the road that leads from an undifferentiated stage to differentiation and object constancy one must take into account the initial cathexes of the object before it is perceived as such. Taking this point of view, I described, probably more systematically than others, the narcissistic stage, and the preobject stage previous to the organization of the object relationship.

Nonetheless, I have remained faithful to the fundamental hypothesis of Freudian metapsychology in explaining the origin of desires by their being rooted in the hallucination of pleasure. This hypothesis has been formulated by Freud in diverse ways, of which the most categorical is to be found in chapter 7 of *The Interpretation of Dreams* (1900). I present it here in an intentionally schematic manner. The memory traces of pleasurable experience are reactivated and hallucinated in a state of need that provokes an interoceptive excitation. For example, pleasure accompanying ingestion and swallowing of milk leads to the hallucination of this satisfaction. Soon the sucking becomes independent of the need and its satisfaction. The hallucination of pleasure through these activities independent of the feeding rhythm leads to a first fantasy, the hallucination of the breast. It is therefore the autoerogenous buccal zone that creates the internal object, the breast (Freud, 1905).

Confrontation between metapsychology and direct observation is doubtless a necessity, but semantic and conceptual difficulties intervene here and render the debate unclear. The problem is to describe the evolution of the object relationship, on the one hand by taking into account the evolution of relationships with external reality and, on the other, by describing the process of creation of the internal object—internalization, which implies incorporation, introjection, and identification, three terms meant to designate different effects of the same work.

From the undifferentiated stage to the stage of a differentiation and object constancy, it is sufficient to remember that the newborn, who is protected from intero- and exteroceptive excitations, lives in a state in which he cannot distinguish between himself and the environment. To a certain extent this is what we would call narcissism. However, one can note that on the level of the most primitive automatism the influence from what goes on outside is undeniable. For instance, the archaic buccolingual orientation reflex is reinforced when mealtime is far off and tends to fade once the infant is satiated (Ajuriaguerra and Diatkine, 1956). As we have observed, everything shows that the child has cathected the object before perceiving it as such. Evolution toward the preobject relationship is made because fortunately the child, whose life rhythms become more precise, learns to distinguish external from internal. According to the Freudian hypothesis of the initial unity of the infant and the mother's care, he escapes mental death through the constant satisfaction of his needs, which he obtains through his dependency on this care, which he does not distinguish from himself.

Spitz (1965) has shown how the first smile specific to the approach of the mother's face from the front constitutes a first organizing element in the preobject mental life constructed on the basis of peribuccal reflex movements. After a phase of several months during which the relationship between mother and child is reciprocally organized on the basis of situations that set positive and negative affects, the phobia of a stranger's face sets in around 6 months of age and testifies to the differentiation of a permanent object. To a certain extent it is an actual phobia, as the mother's absence is equivalent in that moment to danger, new experiences, and strangers, which awaken all the negative affects. It is also this period that inaugurates fantasy life in the usual sense of the word; it is a time when the infant dispenses with a mother image with which he can identify inside himself.

I will go no further into the description of how recognition of the object leads to the permanence of its image, that is, to the object relation, which assumes representation of the self.

The genesis of object relations depends largely on the specifics defining the interaction between infant and mother. Various events can have cataclysmic influences on it. Such is obviously the case when a child is separated from his mother, once he recognizes her, particularly during the second half of the first year of life. But even the simplest events can intervene in this dual and direct relationship and have unforeseen effects. This was the perspective which allowed Spitz (1965) to link a range of functional disorders of newborns to their relationships with their mothers.

This description of the origin of object relations is based on the dependency in which the newborn finds himself; it is genetic and tends to integrate all knowledge of the child's development, be it neurobiological or even cultural. This would not be as true of another description, which would in fact be closer to Freudian metapsychology and would aim at a definition of the process of organizing an internal object.

The Metapsychological Status of the Internal Object

The emergence of desires on the basis of the experience of need satisfaction, according to the Freudian hypothesis I have already mentioned, is understood as belonging to the hallucination of pleasure.

Precociously differentiated erogenous zones, such as the buccal zone, define orality by means of their very functioning, organize the hallucination of the object of pleasure, and thus create the object, which is thereby incorporated. The initial undifferentiated state leads, in this description of autoerotism, to both narcissism and the creation of the object, in an interplay of successive and reciprocal investments.

This description is genetic in the sense that it implies that pleasure experiences and their memory traces lead first to the hallucination of the pleasure and then to the object. But it is ahistoric, since finally the creation of the object, the first fantasy, does not depend on its specificity.

The reading of countless works on the origin of object relations and the particularities of the first phantasmic organizations permits—through the opposition between the two approaches I have just outlined—an evaluation of the excesses of certain theses.

Numerous works attempt to specify the embryology of neonate behavior. From animal ethology we have gone on to that of babies. One line of investigation describes very early infant behavior which bears witness to a surprising interaction with certain kinds of maternal behavior—dialogue with the eyes, for example, and vocal dialogue. Certain experiments recently conducted have shown that the infant from the fourth week on reacts specifically to the voice of its mother, who is hidden behind a screen. Other investigations show that from the very first days after birth mothers have differentiated reactions toward boys and girls in their ways of feeding them (Lezine, Robin, and Cortial, 1975).

Two distinct theoretical trends emerge from this area of study. The first aims at specifying the precocious aspects of development, but at the same time at limiting the theoretical hypotheses as to the mother's role, reducing it to a presence whose particularities intervene but little in programs of behavior development. The second, essentially represented by Bowlby (1969), defines the nature of mother-child relations on the basis of a series of mechanisms, such as have been described by ethologists. Harlow's experiments in the United States (Harlow and Harlow, 1965) justify beyond doubt the importance of this point of view, as do other ethological studies on imprinting mechanisms. But the description of attachment behavior and its vicissitudes eliminates the understanding of mental fantasy life and any consideration of its psychoanalytic economic aspects. To take an example of some practical import, one would no longer speak of the consequences of separation of mother and child. Anaclitic depression such as Spitz (1965) described would become simply a rupture of attachment ties.

Thus, one would tend less to protect children from these separations and educate mothers to avoid them than to create replacement institutions which furnish rich experiments for the purpose of furthering progress in programmed behavior. This theory would deprive psychoanalytic theory of the study of the specific ties between mothers and children and emphasizes the creation of social institutions for warding off difficulties and compensating for lacks in maternal care.

This approach has the same practical consequences as have those proceeding from ahistorical perspectives. We have seen why we can include Kleinian analysts in this category, at least to a certain extent. According to them, fantasies express, in effect, the contradiction between life and death instincts; thus the internal object exists from birth and is at once split into good and bad objects.

Another school of psychoanalysts—for the most part French—tend to deny the importance of the genetic and historical point of view. They reject diachronic studies and identify themselves more or less clearly with structuralist theories.[1] Viderman (1970), for example, considers historically marked conflicts as belonging to a sphere not properly the object of psychoanalytic investigation. Unconscious fantasies lie dormant—repressed—elsewhere in the primary process and come to light via the creation of the psychoanalyst, who actually invents them to give them life and meaning. This primary repressed material is independent of all actual experience and constitutes the "structure" of the unconscious.

From this perspective, a patient's personal history must be constructed and created by the psychoanalyst in order to take on its full meaning. The unfolding of time is not a history of events. At bottom, knowledge of mother-child relations —particularly that which is gathered through direct observation—is of no interest to the psychoanalyst, whose role is to decode or give life to the primary repressed material.

I have compared these two theoretical approaches, the one directed toward ethological studies, the other ignoring direct observation. In spite of their absolutely different points of view, they end in the same result, which is to say, they prevent us from using our knowledge of child development for diagnostic and prognostic purposes. As a corrective I would like to consider some theoretical and clinical data that lend consistency to

[1] These theories have a connotation quite different from that evoked by Anglophone psychoanalysts who speak of a structuralist point of view when referring to the Freudian tripartite agencies of the psychic apparatus.

our knowledge of the infant's mental life. The reconstruction of the past must provide a history of the child and his family. Past events may be known from screen memories or worked through from their repetition in the transference neurosis. When they are known directly, for instance through the psychoanalytic observation of early interactions between the baby and its mother (or other parenting figures), and then are repeated during a therapeutic consultation, it appears that such events are playing their role by means of an "after-effect."[2] The events become part of a probabilistic epigenesis (Lebovici, 1982).

In conducting research on the early interactions between mothers and infants conceived after the sudden death of a baby born earlier, we have consistently seen that these mothers consider as a causative factor insignificant events which, had the death not occurred, would hardly have been remembered. For instance, such a mother might feel herself guilty of her child's death and accuse herself of having inadequately monitored her baby's sleep after a party celebrating her wedding anniversary. This view of their history is of course quite different from what is described as "life events" in some empirical researches.

Predictive approaches, enriched by videotaped material, confirm the importance of very early interactional pathology. Psychoanalysts must observe and try to avoid any intrusion. But they may also use their understanding of the baby's place in the psychic life of the mother and of her husband or companion. We have described two babies different from the actual infant in the mother's arms.

(1) The "imaginary baby" is the product of preconscious work by the mother. She has wanted to be pregnant; in our society, she has programmed this baby, who is a gift to the husband. She sees the baby, as it were, guessing something of this future child thanks to sonograms and the like. She gives this baby a name, often one that has some meaning as regards "intergenerational transmission" (Lebovici, 1988).

(2) The "fantasmatic baby" (Lebovici, 1983) is the product

[2] This word is directly translated from the French *après-coup*. Strachey's English translation uses the expression "deferred action" (Freud, 1900).

of the mother's oedipal wishes. When she was a girl, she wanted to become a mother and receive a baby from her father. The actual baby is fantasied to be the child of the maternal grandfather. For him, the mother owes a debt to the maternal grandmother.

From his side, the baby is acting on his parents and contributes to their parental status. The infant, with his performances and eventual defects, reinforces the parents' ambivalence. As mentioned earlier, I have written (Lebovici, 1960) that the baby cathects the mother before perceiving her. Today I would add: "He is the best to proclaim that this mother is now *a mother*."

In other words, it seems clear that any prediction about the future psychic life of the child, and his eventual mental or psychosomatic pathology, might use the psychoanalytic study of early interactions, which must include the three babies described (real, imaginary, and fantasmatic), the baby's performances and way of acting on his parents, and his use of parental ambivalence and of such eventual parental difficulties as depressive and anxious reactions. These considerations impel us to consider the preventive value of therapeutic consultations in which psychoanalysts succeed in curing such difficulties in the neonate as sleeping or eating troubles.

From the Behavior of the Infant and His Parents to the Prediction of His Mental Disorders

The preceding discussion has focused on the study of genetic theories of the object relationship and on the necessity of recourse to Freudian metapsychology for the understanding of this organization.

The very young infant's evolution can in fact be reconstructed from the psychoanalytic treatments of adults and children. Nevertheless, one must be on guard against making naive judgments on the regressive positions observed in them. Their depth does not allow for a judgment on the precociousness of their organization. The predominance of raw fantasies expressing themselves through pregenital fixations, both oral and anal, does not allow us to conclude the existence of simple sequences—first preoedipal, then oedipal. Primitive mechanisms can persist within the organization and vicissitudes of oedipal conflicts. Avoidance of these conflicts can obviously reactivate them as well.

In any event, it is a matter here of judging the developmental potential of the behavior observed in infants and of determining which mental mechanisms aid us in the understanding of conflicts. This is possible only by taking into account interpersonal and intrafamilial interaction, knowledge regarding the mother's mental life, and also the derivatives of her unconscious.

We have seen schematically how this interaction organizes itself through a development leading to the differentiation of a whole object and also to the re-creation of the object; the imago is the fruit of its internalization. In the course of this progress, good enough mothering, to use Winnicott's expression, must be combined with other concerns. The child's capacity to hallucinate pleasure he has procured organizes not only the object, but also the continuity of lived experience, the self.

The mother functions in the first place as a stimulus barrier and protects the budding psyche of the child by virtue of her own narcissism. Weaknesses on this level may cause her to be overbearing in her care, thereby leading the child to develop a false self. To the mother-nurse corresponds the baby who uses his energy to repair the mother (Winnicott, 1958) and who himself will become narcissistically fragile. This shows that the study of early behavior may lead to a prediction concerning not only modes of organization of unconscious conflicts, but also flaws in narcissism.

During the course of such a development, the mother's concern for the child tends to diminish; her relation to her husband, the father of her child, and to her own fantasy life with her parents increases. Braunschweig and Fain (1971) have shown how the "shattering" reality of the mother is mediated by the fact that she puts the child to sleep, both because she is able to calm his excitation and because she would think of her "lover." Such mediation plays a fundamental role in the evolution of neurotic conflicts. According to the expression of Castoriadis-Aulagnier (1975), the mother is the "spokeswoman" of the father, an arrangement which allows the child to interpret reality and not have to face parents as reproductions of their imagos, as is the case, we shall see, in psychosis. These considerations show that predictions at the level of observed behavior cannot be validated unless one includes parental fantasies in the data.

The child, for his part, even full and satisfied, lives through moments of angry excitation which, according to Winnicott (1958), can only worry him. His concern for reparation makes him go through depressive phases rich in incorporative and introjective work, in comparison to which external reality is as yet lacking in structure. Here we must again look at the Kleinian theories in a larger sense and recognize that mourning for the object is the source of identification and introjective processes, the primary origin of external reality on a mental level, as Freud in fact repeatedly observed.

All during this process the mother gives meaning only to what is observable. A very eloquent expression, used often in France, is that *her anticipations are creative*. This is obvious in the first smile of her baby and also in his cries, since this latter manifestation, which is purely an expression of excitation and discomfort, is understood by the mother as a call. It becomes in fact a summons, because the mother considers it such; when it occurs, she takes care of her baby, either by comforting him or by reprimanding him.

Nonetheless, it would be advisable for a mother to leave a certain margin of explained mystery in her baby's behavior. Complete understanding would deprive the infant of all exploratory interest in the outer world and all possibility for action.

These introductory remarks on the interaction between mother and child indicate the path leading from observable behavior to the interpretation of behavior through the study of neurotic conflicts and their elaboration. I will give two examples in order to propose some hypotheses which go beyond the mere confrontation between the developmental point of view and the exploration of fantasy life.

The Interaction Between a Baby and His Mother and a Prediction Concerning Previous Sleep Disorders

Here is a baby seen at 6 months of age because of an insomnia described as almost total. Suffice it to say that this was a little boy, the only child of a young couple of high economic and cultural level, adamantly in favor of modern education. In keeping with "enlightened" principles, the mother, who worked during the day and took care of him in the evenings, undressed for these tasks in order to favor "skin to skin" contact. After a long interview, about which I will say more later, calm returned to the baby, who for the first time fell asleep in his mother's arms. First of all, her behavior was rectified. Initially in the interview she had taken her little boy on her forearm and sitting, rocked him against her. In this position, he had his head above her shoulder and, though rocked, could see only the wall behind her. Second, this mother was told that holding the baby differently allowed him to see in her eyes the effect he had on her as her baby; that is, he conferred on her the status of mother. It is a fact that the sleeping disorders stopped that very day, during this interview.

Three months after this first contact, mother and child were seen again. One might describe his behavior as both agitated and rather advanced, in particular on the level of overall and specific motor functioning. However, his exploratory tendencies were constantly frustrated by the mother, who was quick to anticipate them. For example, whenever the baby looked for a hidden object, she gave it to him immediately. While viewing the video recording of this examination, she was able to accept the idea that no desire could emerge in her child, since she tried to satisfy the desire even before it could be expressed.

This young woman refused on several different accounts diverse forms of help that were proposed to her, that is, psychotherapy based on observation of her relations with the child, participation in groups of young mothers, etc. She made a short attempt at psychoanalytic psychotherapy, quickly interrupted on the pretext of her professional duties.

Two years after the first interview, the mother asked for psychiatric help once again. Her son, almost 3 years old, was dangerously agitated and almost mute, and banged his head incessantly. Briefly, it was a clinical picture more or less approximating that of autism.

The scope of this chapter does not allow me to go into great detail about the mother's mental life. I will merely indicate that she had married in order to collaborate in the rather important business of her husband. When they had nearly died in the Sahara as a result of some imprudence, they recounted, they were then prepared to die, happy with what they had experienced. The couple decided to have a child several years later. Shortly after his birth, the child was moved out of the mother's bedroom so that she could resume intimate relations with her husband; at the same time, as we remember, she undressed when giving her infant maternal care. She also knew that her husband could very well feel jealous of his son.

In short, this little clinical vignette shows the genesis of a psychosis. Without doubt, the early insomnia was the first of the symptoms. Pathogenic factors included the situation in which the child found himself, the impossibility of conferring maternal status upon his mother. Here observation of behavior shows inconsistencies in the support given the baby, but it also testifies to the lack of eye-to-eye dialogue that prevented this baby from seeing his mother looking at him. In other words, it is not simply a matter of noticing educational errors, but also of giving them meaning, by taking into account both our knowledge of child development and our observations of the influence the baby exercised on his mother. The mother's fantasies made her unable to divide herself between her status as mother, as woman, and, above all, as "therapist" to her baby, for whom she wanted to facilitate the realization of any exploratory project. As additional factors, one might also invoke the sociocultural conditions that favor maternal activism and the interpersonal relationship of the couple, in which a very dependent husband exhibits his search for a second mother in his wife.

I shall simply underline that what one might have considered elements of hypermaturation and rapid development, ended up—in the circumstances I have described, which obviously can be considered only as an etiologically closed constellation—with difficulties raising the possibility of psychosis.

In such cases, it is the understanding of the child's behavior through the interaction he manifests with his mother, understood by way of both her behavior and her fantasy life, which allows for the prediction of mental disorders such as those which finally surfaced.

The Choice of First Names as an Expression of Phantasmic Familial Interrelations over Several Generations

This is the case of a 4-year-old child, a little girl who was adopted rather late—at 9 months of age. She is an autistic child. This case is interesting if only because of recent studies focusing on psychoses in adopted children, as compared to psychotic evolution in those who themselves have psychotic parents.

I shall present only a few aspects of the adopting family. The wife declared right off that the adoption was due to her husband's sterility; she soon forgot this declaration and explained that her ovarian tubes were blocked, but that her husband was depressed because he couldn't have children with his wife.

The adoption came late. The little girl was living with a foster family and was named Christiane. The mother changed the child's name to Helene, a name to which the child became "accustomed" within two weeks. The choice of this name is interesting. According to the mother, it is linked to the circumstances of her own life. The daughter of an unwed mother, a piano teacher, she was taken in after her mother's death when she was about 10 by her father, who was married and himself a musician. The choice of "Helene" is linked to the fact that it is the name of the patron saint of music; it signifies to her that her parents "are united in heaven."

Helene played with a doll from which she never wanted to be separated. From snippets of language it was learned that the doll was named Marie, a name chosen by the mother because "the Virgin Mary didn't need a man in order to have the baby Jesus."

These notes illustrate a most particular aspect of the mother's relationship with her husband and her underlying fantasies, which refer to a denial of the primal scene. Her parents are united in heaven. Her husand is sterile. The parthenogenetic line that denies the sexual role of men thus begins with the maternal grandmother, continues through the adopting mother, and ends with Helene and her doll, daughter of Helene and also the husbandless mother of a child without a father.

The weight of the maternal fantasies might be expressed in numerous ways. But I have often had the impression that the choice of the children's first names, which is obviously linked to many factors—often to traditions or to passing fashions—is a significant factor in the intrafamilial organization of psychotic or (as in this case) prepsychotic children.

These observations, whose very reduced presentation has had a demonstrative aim, concern two cases of this type. It is not surprising that prediction based on observation of the behavior of young children and their parents, along with the study of the mental life of the latter, allows for the understanding of the risk of eventual psychosis.

Psychosis expresses, among other factors, a nonmediated relationship between child and parents. Mental elaboration does not evince the adaptive functions of the ego. Fantasies are raw, charged with fragmented meanings testifying to the failure of the introjective process, which, as we have seen, contributes in normal development to the establishment of a sense of continuous external reality. In other words, external reality conforms to the child's fantasies, which it has helped organize under the weight of the mother's fantasies, which generate the psychosis. To be schematic, I would use the following formula: the child's imagos are strengthened by the weight of the external object's reality. In children in whom neurotic elaboration can be expected, however, the imagos are constructed on the basis of a deformation of reality in the course of the incorporative and introjective work, within identificatory and therefore conflictual perspectives.

The prediction I have tried to describe here constitutes a kind of work which aims at foretelling healthy developmental potential or neurotic elaboration when the clinician is restricted to (1) observing types of behavior; (2) hearing about functional disorders; (3) understanding interactions between mother and child, perhaps with the introduction of the father, especially if the observation takes place in the family setting; (4) exploring the mother's fantasy life, and (5) exploring the larger intrafamilial interaction.

The practice of long-term observations, which tends to develop with the creation of community psychiatric services, obviously gives meaning to these attempts at prediction and to the work of prevention they may justify. I myself have followed up some cases of infantile psychosis for over 25 years. The outcome of child psychosis is far from being clearly known: one does not find traditional schizophrenia appearing in adults who as children were treated for infantile psychosis and followed up (Lebovici and Kestemberg, 1978).

As far as this chapter is concerned, I wish simply to indicate that in the latency period there is an absence of solid defenses and flexible neurotic mechanisms. In the best of evolutions, behavior is hypercontrolled by tight pseudoobsessional systems, which could develop into character neurosis.

During the years preceding latency, examination can include children's games, which facilitate exploration of fantasy life, providing certain methodological precautions are respected. Understanding gleaned from such exploration is of two sorts, since, on the one hand, play in an adult's presence contains a reactional aspect tied to this very situation and, on the other, it allows penetration in depth of the themes evoked.

In any case, what I wish to indicate in this respect is that between the period when one is reduced to predicting mental function on the basis of behavioral observation and the period when one can study mental function directly there is a lapse of several years during which behavior remains the essential means of approach for the psychiatrist. As development continues, the study of the internalization process constitutes the essential approach. Starting from the moment at which the elaboration of detailed neurotic mechanisms allows for a differentiation among cases which risk entering the psychotic register, a range of possible outcomes must be considered. Obviously, outcome depends on diverse factors either hindering or promoting the development of various nervous system functions; these factors express themselves in variations in learning capacity. But clinical judgment may also take into account the retroactive value of what one has learned about the mother-child interaction. For example, lack of fear at the appearance of a stranger's face would seem to herald the direct utilization of the body for the expression of conflicts (Kreisler, Fain, and Soule, 1974). The organization of neurotic conflicts during prelatency often grows out of a very ordinary hysteria (Lebovici, 1974). One may also judge in retrospect two closely linked operational concepts: the narcissistic deficiencies of the mother and the difficulties encountered in the child's organization of the self and the ego ideal. The deficiencies observed lead to a narcissistic pathology involving the ego ideal, suggesting, in addition, the notion of depression in the young child. Instability of behavior and states of excitation are sometimes a maniclike reaction to difficulty in object introjection and also to a failure in the development of the depressive phase necessary for reparation of the object. From this point of view there is, it seems to me, some connection between these states of excitement and those which might be identified as prepsychopathic.

These considerations, despite their brevity, introduce group values, by way of what Freud referred to as the ego ideal (Freud, 1921). Familial relations define a group in which social and cultural values are expressed as well. Indeed, it is necessary to distinguish expressions of *intra*personal relations—the parent's fantasy life—from *inter*personal relations. In the latter, fantasies are also expressed, but the sociocultural environment intervenes. As we have seen in studies of communication within the family, the import of verbal exchange, its richness and coherence, simultaneously admits the elaboration of conflicts.

The contemporary family is without a doubt going through a crisis leading to incertitude as to values to be transmitted and to challenge to the ego ideal. This is particularly evident in so-called multiple-problem families. Help, if offered them, may be given in a somewhat disjointed fashion and may include access to the services of a psychiatrist who may be inept at appreciating their style of life and the values underlying the behavior observed in it. The lifestyle of these families is not ours, and prevailing ideals and mainstream values, conversely, are not theirs. Conflicts are constantly acted out and therefore are not elaborated mentally. The therapeutic or preventive strategy chosen in such cases should not entail a psychotherapeutic relationship in which the verbalization of conflicts and affects allows for interpretive activity. Nothing but the study and rectification of their behavior will answer to the case. Psychoanalysts, if they accept the full implications of their knowledge about the origins of behavior, must accept acting directly on the behavior of young children and their parents; the great risk such families run demands it. Here we have to decide between two approaches: that of the behaviorists, which aims at the simple rectification of behavior, and one that tries to assign a meaning to this behavior which might be comprehensible to the parents, not only through the dialogue in which one often tries to engage—often in vain—but also through gestures they can learn and use to express themselves. For example, such parents might grasp the value of eye-to-eye dialogue between mother and child, or might see the connection between the cries and the colics of a baby whose abdomen is racked by waves of intestinal peristalsis.

In other words, the extension of psychoanalytic understanding to sociocultural levels of people generally unconcerned leads inevitably to explorations centered increasingly on the behavior of young children and their parents. The aim is the prevention of mental health risks, among them the tendency toward psychopathy and mental retardation.

Conclusions and Summary

The study of behavior in young children has generally been considered by psychoanalysts to be a means of minimizing the dangers of extrapolation from the constructions that the psychoanalytic treatment of adults and children has allowed.

An emphasis on maturational potential tends to favor a contrast between the reconstructed child and the so-called real child. There is some difficulty, however, in admitting that there can be as developed a fantasy life as that described by Kleinians. In addition, neurobiological data and metapsychology have to be taken into account, and genetic studies of the object relationship must be corrected and supplemented by cognitive studies on mental representations of the object, based on the fundamental hypothesis of the unity between the child and maternal care. Conversely, through behavioral studies resembling those of animal ethology, one highlights very refined programs testifying to the precociousness of the mother-child interaction.

These perspectives must be recognized by psychoanalysts, who must not content themselves with the comparison of the real child with the reconstructed child. In other words, the observed child is in addition the product of maternal fantasies. Such phenomena must be included when one wants to predict inherent mental health risks on the basis of behavioral observations, the only material available when it is a question of very young children.

I have attempted to indicate in a concrete way how one might evaluate the risk of psychosis or prepsychosis during this period, in the sense accepted at present in France. Continuous studies of children over long periods of time demonstrate the importance of the findings of such evaluations, which may then be reintegrated into the study of children before latency, at a time when neurotic conflicts do not yet have the value of neurotic symptoms.

Maternal fantasies play a role in the care and education given to children. They involve both the relationships with their husbands and their oedipal fantasies. The mother's behavior thus plays a role in the introjective process which establishes external reality and allows the child to perceive a differentiated and "whole" mother, thereby overcoming what might be called the depressive position and thus achieving the first neurotic mechanism, that is, the fear of a stranger's face, which implies projection and displacement.

The direct study of behavior and mother-child interaction in the very young child allows us, therefore, to specify psychotic potential. Later, taking this into account authorizes the study of pathological preorganizations which necessarily are composite and fluid. The importance of the mother's narcissistic deficiencies must not be forgotten in attempting to understand the weight of the young child's depression and antidepressive struggle, which manifests itself both in manifold states of excitation and their immediate consequences—learning difficulties—and in risks down the line at the crossroads of acting out against the body (the psychosomatic realm) or of acting out against the family (the psychopathic realm).

I have tried to show how the family approach necessarily implies the study of parental fantasies and their consequences. But this approach must be enlarged so as to include both specific and nonspecific difficulties of communication in present-day society and at various levels of sociocultural deprivation.

It may be that psychoanalysts from now on will be led to accept the behavioral study of those who have not yet learned to verbally express themselves, not in order to modify anything through the pressure of reconditioning, but rather to understand in effect those who do not know how to speak or elaborate, and to allow them to feel the meaning and weight of their acts. This might be a relevant means to develop a truly preventive approach to the considerable dangers many children face, those of perpetual acting out or of mental impoverishment.

References

Ajuriaguerra, J. de, & Diatkine, R. (1956), Psychanalyse et neurobiologie (Psychoanalysis and neurobiology). In: *La Psychoanalyse d'aujourd'hui*, ed. S. Nacht. 2 vols. Paris: Presses Universitaires de France.

Bowlby, J. (1969), *Attachment and Loss: Vol. 1. Attachment*. New York: Basic Books.

——— (1973), *Attachment and Loss: Vol. 2. Separation, Anxiety*. London: Hogarth Press.

Braunschweig, D., & Fain, M. (1971), *Eros et Anteros* (*Eros and Anteros*). Paris: Payot.

Castoriadis-Aulagnier, P. (1975), *La violence et l'interpretation* (*The Violence of Interpretation*). Paris: Presses Universitaires de France.

Chiland, C., & Lebovici, S. (1977), Borderline or prepsychotic conditions in childhood: A French point of view. In: *Borderline Personality Disorders*, ed. P. Hartocollis. New York: International Universities Press, pp. 143–154.

Coleman, R.W., Kris, E., & Provence, S. (1953), The study of variations of early parental attitudes. *The Psychoanalytic Study of the Child*, 8:20–47. New York: International Universities Press.

Freud, A. (1963), The concept of developmental lines. *The Psychoanalytic Study of the Child*, 18:262–265. New York: International Universities Press.

——— (1965), *Normality and Pathology in Childhood*. New York: International Universities Press.

——— (1977), From normal development to psychopathology. *Revue Francaise de Psychoanalyse*, 16:429–438.

Freud, S. (1900), The interpretation of dreams. *Standard Edition*, 4/5. London: Hogarth Press, 1953.

——— (1905), Three essays on the theory of sexuality. *Standard Edition*, 7:130–243. London: Hogarth Press, 1953.

——— (1909), Analysis of a phobia in a five-year-old boy. *Standard Edition*, 10:5–147. London: Hogarth Press, 1955.

——— (1913), The disposition to obsessional neurosis. *Standard Edition*, 12:317–326. London: Hogarth Press, 1958.

——— (1918), From the history of an infantile neurosis. *Standard Edition*, 17:7–122. London: Hogarth Press, 1955.

——— (1920), Beyond the pleasure principle. *Standard Edition*, 18:7–64. London: Hogarth Press, 1955.

——— (1921), Group psychology and analysis of the ego. *Standard Edition*, 18:69–143. London: Hogarth Press, 1955.

——— (1937), Constructions in analysis. *Standard Edition*, 23:257–269. London: Hogarth Press, 1964.

Harlow, H.F., & Harlow, M.K. (1965), The affectional systems. In: *Behavior of Nonhuman Primates*, ed. A.M. Schrier, H.F. Harlow, & F. Stolinitz. 2 vols. New York: Academic Press, pp. 287–334.

Kreisler, L., Fain, M., & Soule, M. (1974), *L'enfant et son corps* (*The Child and His Body*). Paris: Presses Universitaires de France.

Kris, E. (1950), Notes on the development and on some current problems of psychoanalytic child psychology. *The Psychoanalytic Study of the Child*, 5:24–46. New York: International Universities Press.

Kris, M. (1956), The recovery of childhood memories in psychoanalysis: Problems of genetic interpretations. *The Psychoanalytic Study of the Child*, 11:65–78. New York: International Universities Press.

——— (1957), The use of prediction in a longitudinal study. *The Psychoanalytic Study of the Child*, 12:175–189. New York: International Universities Press.

Lebovici, S. (1960), La relation objectale chez l'enfant (The object relationships in children). *La psychiatrie de l'enfant*, 3:147–226.

——— (1963), La notion de prepsychose chez l'enfant (The notion of infantile prepsychosis). *Bulletin de psychologie*, 17:224–228.

——— (1974), A propos de l'hysterie chez l'enfant (On hysteria in children). *La psychiatrie de l'enfant*, 17:5–52.

——— (1982), L'apes-coup dans l'organisation de la névrose infantile (Aftereffect in the organization of infantile neurosis). In: *Quinze Etudes psychoanalytiques sur le temps*, ed. J.Guillaumin. Toulouse: Privat.

——— (1983), *Le nourrisson, la mère et le psychoanalyste* (*The Infant, the Mother and the Psychoanalyst*). Paris: Le Centurion.

——— (1988), Fantasmatic interactions and intergenerational transmission. *Infant Mental Health J.*, 6(1):10.

——— & Braunschweig, D. (1967), A propos de la névrose infantile (On infantile neurosis). *La psychiatrie de l'enfant*, 10:43–142.

——— & Diatkine, R. (1974), Normality as a concept of limited usefulness in the assessment of psychiatric risk. In: *The Child in His Family: Children at Psychiatric Risk*, ed. E. J. Anthony & C. Koupernik. Vol. 3. New York: Wiley, pp. 29–44.

——— & Kestemberg, E. (1978), *Le devenir de la psychose de l'enfant* (*The Future of Childhood Psychosis*). Paris: Presses Universitaires de France.

——— & Kreisler, L. (1965), L'homosexualite chez l'enfant (Homosexuality in children and adolescents). *La psychiatrie de l'enfant*, 8:57–134.

——— & Sadoun, R. (1968), L'enregistrement du diagnostic au Centre Alfred Binet (Recording of diagnosis at the Alfred Binet Center). *La psychiatrie de l'enfant*, 11:533–550.

——— & Soule, M. (1977), *La connaissance de l'enfant par la psychanalyse* (*Knowing the Child through Psychoanalysis*). 3rd ed. Paris: Presses Universitaires de France.

Lezine, L., Robin, M., & Cortial, C. (1975), Observation sur le couple mere-enfant durant les premieres experiences d'alimentation (Observation of the mother-child couple during the first feeding experience). *La psychiatrie de l'enfant*, 18:75–146.

Mahler, M. (1968), *On Human Symbiosis and the Vicissitudes of Individuation: Vol. 1. Infantile Psychosis*. New York: International Universities Press.

Nagera, H. (1966), *Early Childhood Disturbance: The Infantile Neurosis and Adult Disturbances*. New York: International Universities Press.

Ritvo, S. (1966), Correlation of a childhood and adult neurosis. *Internat. J. Psycho-Anal.*, 47:2–3, 130–132.

Spitz, R. (1965), *The First Year of Life*. New York: International Universities Press.

Viderman, S. (1970), *La construction de l'espace analytique* (*The construction of the psychoanalytic space*). Paris: Denoel.

Winnicott, D.W. (1958), *Collected Papers: Through Paediatrics to Psycho-Analysis*. New York: Basic Books.

——— (1971), *Playing and Reality*. London: Tavistock.

18

On Phase-Characteristic Pathology of the School-Age Child: Disturbances of Personality Development and Organization (Borderline Conditions), of Learning, and of Behavior

FRED PINE, PH.D.

In this chapter I shall describe some of the characteristic psychopathology of school-age children, in particular borderline disturbances, behavior disturbances, and disturbances of learning. The period I have in mind is the one that Bornstein (1951) called the second period of latency, roughly the years from 7 or 8 to 10 or 11, following the early latency period in which the child is still very much involved in residual oedipal issues. By way of introduction I shall describe the age period in overview and give a rationale for the selection of the three specific areas of psychopathology.

What is that age period like? Let me contrast it to the surrounding developmental periods and, additionally, look at some of its internal features. By age 7 or 8 the child is normally solidly involved in the world of school and peer relations. The contrast to the preschool years is striking (though, of course, not absolute). At home, in early childhood, the preschooler is ordinarily in close proximity to the mother and other family members for much of his day; the sights, sounds, smells, and feel of family members are at all times the background, and

This chapter appears in somewhat altered form in *Developmental Theory and Clinical Process* by Fred Pine, Yale University Press, 1985.

often the foreground, of life, and contribute percepts and memories to the thought processes from which fantasy and wish are formed. The learning that takes place is in considerable measure learning on and about one's own body and the bodies of others. From early self-other bodily differentiation (Mahler, Pine, and Bergman, 1975) through the learning of self-feeding, bowel and bladder control, self-toileting, and self-dressing, important episodes of learning have an intimate relation to body and mother. Additionally, family members in general have no peer in their significance as external others in the life of the child.

But the entry into school brings major changes. While family members remain central figures in the psychic life of the child, teachers and peers begin to assume importance as representatives of a wider world—affectively a bit more neutral, less intimate, and providing new avenues of identification and attachment. Learning, too, changes. While motor skills continue to develop, learning linked to the body itself is less intimate and less central. And nonbodily learning assumes enormous importance—reading, writing, arithmetic, and social studies (the world of school), and chants, games, tricks, and rules (the world of childhood) (Stone and Church, 1973). The learning process is itself less tied to the parents; not only are they not always the teachers, but things may be learned (formally, from the teacher; informally, by observation of others) that the parents do not know or do not do. Importantly, the child's physical proximity to the mother is less, as he spends time in school, and after school has the skills and inner achievements to go out of the house without her to play with peers.

The contrast to the subsequent adolescent period is equally sharp, but I need only touch on it. In adolescence, once again, intimate bodily learning (newfound sexuality) becomes central; old family relationships and infantile fantasy are reactivated and achieve renewed force (Freud, 1905; Spiegel, 1951; Blos, 1962); and the child's task of defining his position vis-à-vis learning and same-sex peers, ordinarily accomplished reasonably well (for good or ill) in the school years, gradually becomes secondary to the task of defining his position vis-à-vis sexual development, heterosexual relationships, and the anticipation of full independence from the parents and physical separation from their home. For the child we will be discussing, all of this lies in the future.

The contrast of the school-age years to the preschool and adolescent periods helps bring out the internal features of the period. It is a time of entry into the wider, nonfamilial world—typified by peer relations and school. The formation of new relationships (with the opportunities they provide for displacement and reworking of old familial relationships) and new learning are major psychological tasks of the period. Character formation (the establishment of a reliable personal style of thought, relatedness, impulse expression, and defense), while inevitably beginning earlier, continues in this period; and its *external* accompaniment—socialization to the nonfamilial world—is of increased importance. While many of the indicators of such socialization are quite visible (play, relationships, school behavior and attitude), the more subtle ones (modes of thinking, feeling, and doing) are also being shaped. Certain kinds of disturbances in this age period—including the ones I shall be discussing—can at the descriptive level be viewed against this age backdrop as failures to accomplish the tasks of the age. From a more interior or clinical viewpoint, they may be looked at in terms of their intrapsychic specificity and developmental implications.

To repeat, the three areas of psychopathology I shall discuss are borderline disturbances, behavior disturbances, and learning disturbances. The three are not really parallel with one another; nor is any one of them a unified entity. But I select them because they are common, because they can be viewed as failures in the adaptational tasks of the school-age years, and because light can be shed on them by taking a depth-oriented, interior view.

These three forms of disturbance do not *begin* in the school-age period, but they are often first identified as problematic in that age period. Working clinically, one is deluged with complaints regarding learning or behavior and with diagnoses of "borderline" in this age group. And this is the clinical reason why, when asked to write about phase-specific disorders of the school-age period, my thoughts went immediately to them. It should be noted, however, that this chapter's title speaks of phase-characteristic (not phase-specific) pathology. The difference is by no means trivial for a developmentally oriented approach. For, though these three disturbances are common in, and thus *characteristic* of, the school-age period, they are by no means *specific* to it—having roots earlier (even being full-blown earlier), and certainly also continuing or even first clearly emerging later on. But at the age we are talking about they often are first identified or at least first begin to clash with social expectations regarding the child; hence they come to the clinician's attention.

We might suspect that any referral complaint we encounter with great frequency is being overused, in overextended or vague ways. And such is indeed the case, I believe, with the three areas to be discussed. A depth-oriented psychoanalytic view can lead to some clarification, however. The approach taken here will be consistent with the one Anna Freud (1970) espoused in her paper on the symptomatology of childhood—that is, to specify *common* genetic and structural features that underlie *divergent* surface pathologies and (more to the point for this paper) to specify *varying* genetic and structural features that underlie superficially *similar* presenting pictures.

In addition to their frequent appearance in current clinical work, their relation to the age period at hand, and my belief that an analytic approach will shed light on them, there is one other reason—an exclusionary one this time—for my choosing to discuss these three areas of disturbance. That is, at least two other areas—psychoneuroses and psychoses—are probably best discussed in terms of ages other than the ones I am focusing on here. The psychoses are best discussed in terms of very early formative (and genetic) conditions insofar as the infantile psychoses are concerned, and in terms of both infantile and post-childhood periods where what is at issue are psychotic conditions that ordinarily become apparent only in adolescence or later. And what can be said about the classical psychoneuroses in the school-age period is not distinctively different from what can be said about them (in terms of dynamics, psychic structure, and symptom formation) at other ages.

I have already indicated that these three areas of pathology are not parallel. Disturbances of behavior or of learning, as varied as each area may be regarding appearance or cause, at least have in common a more or less definitive sign: a child is not learning, or a child presents a behavior problem. The same cannot be said of borderline disturbances. At best, the common surface sign here is that these children are in some way "peculiar"—hardly an adequate clinical formulation. And, at that, it may at times be that they are peculiar only to those who have sufficient familiarity with the quality, the "feel," of normal children of this age.

In addition, the three areas are not strictly parallel in their relatedness to failures in the adaptive tasks of the school-age years, and again the borderline disturbance is the conceptual oddball. The identification of behavior problems and learning problems is clearly connected to school entry and the requirements of school performance, and many a child is first referred at the initiative of the school for one or a number of these complaints. Behavior problems are additionally linked to issues of the age because of their impact on peer relations and because of the increasing strength and opportunities for independent action in children of this age—making problems in the behavior domain much more worrisome. But borderline pathology is not related to anything as explicit in its age-linkage as school entry or school requirements. Yet I think there are important ways in which it is age-linked—specifically, reasons why the "peculiarities" (to be specified later, when I turn to this area in detail) are identified at this age. This is reflected in this chapter's title. The phrase "disturbances of personality development and organization (borderline conditions)" alludes to the greater degree of character stability, of socialization, and of peer and teacher relatedness that is normally expectable at this age; the "peculiarities" of these children are often violations of these age-linked, normally fulfilled expectations. When the major relationships are solely within the family, peculiarities of object relation or of ego function may go unnoticed by equally peculiar family members or may be compensated by them in the mix of habitual family interrelatedness. Teachers and peers may not be so generous.

So the three areas of disturbance are not truly parallel.

Indeed, I have elected to discuss them not because they are parallel, but because they are common in clinical practice, characteristic of the age, and in need of greater specification. In addition, they profit from being looked at in terms of the adaptational expectations of the school-age child and, from an interior developmental perspective, in terms of the child's progress along a number of developmental lines. I shall discuss these in detail, below.

In what follows, then, I shall discuss borderline disturbances, learning disturbances, and behavior disturbances (in that order), attempting, in each case, to specify the disturbance by taking an in-depth view of the developmental, dynamic, and structural contexts in which they are set. Each will be approached somewhat differently, in ways tailored to the issues in each area; but each will include a discussion of (a) distinctions within the general area of disturbance, (b) treatment implications following from these distinctions, and (c) the achievements and failures on normal developmental lines that underlie problems in each of these areas.

Borderline Disturbances

In recent clinical practice, the flow of children who are given the diagnosis "borderline" has reached flood proportions. Whence this flood? I believe one source is the decreasing frequency with which the classical, symptom-focused psychoneuroses are seen, in childhood as in adulthood, a trend causing clinicians to be alerted instead to issues of character pathology, a form of pathology which though essentially neurotic in structure shades into more serious conditions at its more disturbed extreme. Additionally, the post–World War II growth of the child guidance movement, as well as of research utilizing direct child observation, has brought to clinicians an acute awareness of the flagrant "psychopathology of everyday childhood." Third, the rapid extension of clinical services to poverty and ghetto populations following the civil rights battles of the 1960s brought us into greater contact with children whose lives are blighted by social pathology (crime, addiction, prostitution, violence, hunger, abandonment, etc.) as well as psychopathology, and whose overall functioning shows the toll taken by such massive pathological intrusions upon development. And fourth, the writings of a number of individuals (to be noted below) who have tried to isolate and define the key intrapsychic mechanisms or failures in what they call borderline children (or related entities) have given a sophisticated clinical-intellectual context for formulations in this area.

Whether these be all or any of the sources of the flood, the phenomenon is clear: the high frequency with which children are labeled "borderline," and an associated looseness in the meanings attached to the term. A multitude of phenomena—including isolation from others or indiscriminate relationships, nonavailability of stable defenses or rigid reliance on pathological defenses, panic states or affectlessness, hollow pseudomaturity or infantile behavior, and an assortment of peculiarities in social behavior, thought and language, or motor style—are used to produce the umbrella diagnosis: borderline. Is there something real here that clinicians are grasping at? Can the morass be sorted out? In an earlier work (Pine, 1974a), I have tried to answer these questions, as have a number of other writers on child psychopathology (Weil, 1953, 1956; Ekstein and Wallerstein, 1954; A. Freud, 1956; Rosenfeld and Sprince, 1963, 1965). I should like to review some of that work here, and in addition attempt to formulate some of the broad developmental lines that have gone awry in borderline patients, to draw distinctions within the broad borderline domain, and to specify at least some implications of these distinctions for the treatment process.

Some years ago a group of colleagues and I agreed to meet regularly in a small clinical study group to discuss issues in child psychopathology. Our ready consensus, for reasons apparent in what I have already said, was to begin with a look at the borderline child. Influenced by the writers we had studied, we kept certain concepts in mind when we looked at children who had been (or could easily be) diagnosed borderline: the absence of phase dominance and regression to primary identification (Rosenfeld and Sprince, 1963), the tendency toward panic anxiety (Weil, 1953), fluidity of psychic organization (Ekstein and

Wallerstein, 1954), heavy reliance on splitting mechanisms (Kernberg, 1967, 1968), and, from the point of view of Mahler's concept of the separation-individuation process (Mahler et al., 1975), early failures in that process (Masterson, 1972). While our group creative imagination could press clinical and metapsychological constructs into forms that would subsume most of the cases we examined, my own sense was that in so doing we were engaging in a rather forced exercise.

But shortly thereafter an enormous freeing of thought occurred with our abandonment of the word "the" in the phrase "the borderline child" and its replacement by the term "borderline children." That is, we gave up the self-imposed demand to find a single unifying mechanism and considered instead that we were dealing with an array of phenomena, having some larger developmental and pathological commonalities perhaps, but also having specific variant forms. In this it would be similar to psychoneurosis, with its commonalities and variant forms. In back of this change also was the idea, still very clear to me, that borderline is a *concept*—one we can *decide* how to use—and that our job is to specify the phenomena to which we will apply it. This rephrasing of our key term also set another aspect of our task: to identify the larger developmental and pathological commonalities that make this a reasonable, if not tight, conceptual grouping, and then to describe its specific variant forms.

In other words, children described as borderline are first defined by a dual negation: they are not merely neurotic, but neither are they clearly psychotic. What they *are* remains to be stated. In still other words, while we might have managed to subsume many children labeled borderline under one or another clinical construct (e.g., fluidity), we came to see this not as a *gain* in clinical generalization, but as a *loss* in clinical specificity. In short, we felt we could do better with the joint conceptual tools of (1) *broadly defined commonalities* and (2) *specific variants* in these children than we could do with any single concept, mechanism, or process alone.

What is the *general commonality*? I believe that all of the children who come to be considered borderline show failures in one or another of the developmental lines associated with the development of major ego functions or central aspects of object relationship; the failures may be in the form of developmental arrest, aberrant development, or both. Normally, by the ages of 7 or 8 to 10 or 11 that we are considering here, ego development has proceeded to the point where secondary process thinking and reality testing are well established and where some capacity for delay and at least some reliable and well-structured defenses have been attained. In addition, object relations have developed more or less normally through the early autistic (objectless) and symbiotic (undifferentiated) stages (Mahler, 1968); some degree of libidinal object constancy (Hartmann, 1939; Pine 1974b) and of specificity of object attachment have been achieved; and object relations have been subjected to the shaping influences of the drives at each of the psychosexual stages of development. Furthermore, the triadic relations of the oedipal period have been experienced and dealt with in some manner. Superego development, additionally, has proceeded to the point of at least some degree of internalization of standards—that is, with some experience of guilt for transgression and with some internally powered efforts at control and delay of impulses.

By contrast, the group of children who are generally considered borderline or severely disturbed do not show this context of normal development of ego function and of object relationship. In particular, ego malfunction in them may include disturbances in the sense of reality and at times in reality testing, as well as a failure in the development of signal anxiety so that unpleasant affect readily escalates to panic instead of triggering reliably available defenses. Object relations may be characterized by their shifting levels, by too great a dependence of ego structure on the object contact (Ekstein, 1966), and by regression to primary identification (Rosenfeld and Sprince, 1963). While superego forerunners are also likely to be impaired, these are not in fact readily separable in their impact from failures of judgment and affectional attachment that are already implied by pointing to failures in ego function and object relationship. Final superego formation is likely to be secondarily interfered with by prior developmental failures. The precise developmental failures, and their breadth and severity, may vary from one child to another.

These basic failures in the normal developmental progression of ego functioning and object relationship are what differentiates borderline children from neurotic children. For, though we may define the classical psychoneuroses as involving an unsuccessfully resolved conflict between drive and opposing forces (superego and defense), unsuccessfully resolved in that it culminates in anxiety and/or formation of compromise symptoms and/or neurotic character traits, we also assume that these features exist in the context of more or less normal ego function and object relationship, at least outside the area of focal conflict. That is why, though they involve personal suffering and, at times, impairment of functioning, we generally consider the neuroses to be relatively "healthy" conditions.

In passing, I should say a bit also regarding the distinction of borderline from psychotic conditions. I have discussed this more fully elsewhere (Pine, 1974a), and shall do no more here than to assert what was discussed there, in the interest of saving space and avoiding repetition. In brief, then, I believe that there are some psychotic conditions of childhood—notably, infantile autism (Kanner, 1942, 1949), symbiotic psychosis (Mahler, 1952, 1968), some organic conditions, and (though rarely) adultlike schizophrenias involving apparently adequate functioning followed by regressive disorganization—which can be fairly clearly differentiated from borderline conditions. But, for the rest, I do not believe a sharp line divides borderline and psychotic conditions; each of the borderline conditions I shall describe below shade into what can be called psychosis at the more severe end of its particular spectrum.

What are some of the specific developmental failures in borderline children? One frequently mentioned (Weil, 1953; Rosenfeld and Sprince, 1963) is the failure to achieve the signal function of anxiety (S. Freud, 1933). That is, even rather early on in development, the normal child begins to anticipate when an anxiety-inducing situation is imminent (based on memory of previous experience). Such anticipation is accompanied by mild anxiety which sets defensive operations into motion, be these flight, a turn to the mother, or (later) intrapsychic defense. But the capacity for this (both to anticipate and to have modes of defense available) is a developmental achievement of great moment. For the infant cannot do this and is instead helpless in the face of anxiety (unless the other intervenes), and the intensity of this anxiety can rise to traumatic proportions, i.e., well beyond the organism's capacity to master or discharge. For certain children, the failure to develop the capacity to use the anxiety signal to set a reliable array of defenses into operation is both an indicator of past developmental failure and a source of continuing inability to develop mastery. For, if anxiety rapidly escalates to panic, the kinds of new learning, new attempts at mastery, that can come at moments of delay in the face of danger, will not be able to take place.

Early failures in the process of separation-individuation (Mahler, Pine, and Bergman, 1975) also have consequences for the later stability of ego boundaries and of object attachment under stress. Rosenfeld and Sprince (1963), acknowledging their debt to Anna Freud, find a regression to primary identification to be a characteristic phenomenon in their severely disturbed children. That is, quite the reverse of those later identifications which are basic to the growth of individuality and are a prime form of "adding something" to ourselves, some severely ill children begin to lose their sense of self as they merge into an undifferentiated self-other duo. Masterson's work on borderline adolescents (1972) also draws heavily on concepts of failure in the process of separation-individuation.

Ekstein and Wallerstein (1954; see also Ekstein, 1966) describe the unstable, fluid ego organization characteristic of some severely disturbed children. These are children in whom the developmental achievement of stable personality organization has not taken place but in whom, instead, personality organization varies with changes in affect level and object attachment, having not achieved autonomy from them. Weil (1953, 1956) describes the pervasive unevenness of development in these children, and the equally pervasive oddness that follows from it. Kernberg (1967, 1968), working mostly with adult patients, focuses on the pathological consequences of excessive reliance on certain primitive defenses, most notably "splitting," i.e., the developmental failure of, or the regressive interference with, the integration of representations of good and bad (both self and other) into more realistic whole images. As I have noted elsewhere (Pine, 1974b), such integration can be conceptualized as fostering a toning down of idealization (via the effect of the "bad" on the "good" images) and a tempering of rage (via the effect of the "good" on the "bad").

All of these mechanisms, and others, are found in borderline children—that is, in children who show the broad defining attributes of developmental failure or aberration in major aspects of ego function and object relationship. In many ways, the persons whose work most nearly accords with my own views are Knight (1953a, 1953b), writing on borderline adults, and Redl (1951), writing on ego disturbances in children. For Knight emphasizes not single mechanisms but a general tendency to ego regression in borderline adults; in any particular instance, the specific nature of the regression would have to be identified. With a shift in emphasis from regression to primary developmental failure, that approach is essentially my own as well. And an argument for the value of specificity of identification of pathology within any broad domain is given by Redl in his paper on ego disturbances. There he indicates that generalized "support" for an ill-defined "weak ego" leaves us high and dry when it comes to choices regarding technique. Rather, careful specification of particular areas of ego pathology permits tailoring of technical interventions to those weaknesses. That clinical philosophy underlies my approach to the specification of particular psychopathological phenomena in the borderline domain as well (Pine, 1976).

Let me turn now to some of the observable clinical entities, the *variant forms,* with which child clinicians are familiar. These entities can be viewed as subtypes within the borderline domain, in part defined by the ways in which the mechanisms already described, among others, appear in them. Since I have given case examples of these subtypes elsewhere (Pine, 1974a), I shall, in the interest of avoiding repetition, not give them here. What I shall describe may alternatively be considered *variations in the phenomena* (rather than *subtypes*); by this I mean to suggest that more than one kind of "borderline phenomenon" can be found in any particular "borderline child."

Shifting Levels of Ego Organization

Some children show remarkable variation in the degree of pathology of their overall mode of functioning; I try to capture this phenomenon by the term *shifting levels of ego organization.* At one moment sensitively, often painfully, in touch with their thoughts and feelings, expressed in the context of a stable alliance with a trusted therapist, or, alternatively, simply playing-thinking-behaving in age-appropriate ways in the context of that same alliance and sense of therapeutic presence, these children may at another moment, often suddenly within a single session, become peculiar, voice odd ideas, lose the more mature relatedness to the therapist, and instead speak illogically, and uncommunicatively, and affectively withdraw. But, in the instances to which I refer, there is no apparent panic; rather, there is a sense of familiarity, of ego syntonicity in the child's move into peculiar functioning.

Ekstein and Wallerstein (1954; Ekstein, 1966) have written on such children, emphasizing how critical are the loss of contact and the return to contact with the therapist in setting off or terminating such states. The absence of panic in the "peculiar" state is, I believe, an important key to understanding what is going on. Such children have not simply "broken down"; rather, they have regressively moved to a more primitive level of ego organization and object relation. In the face of some disturbing stimulus, inner or outer, anxiety arises and culminates not in the triggering of a set of more or less adaptive defenses but in the onset of this single, massive, regressive, maladaptive defense. But maladaptive how? Only to the outside; only for social adaptation. For internally it is highly adaptive; that is, it terminates the anxiety; it truly "works" for the child (hence I refer to it as an ego organization), though it works at a substantial price.

My understanding is that such children have achieved two quite different levels of ego organization. But both are *organizations;* they include means of thinking, relating, and handling anxiety. The "higher" level is vulnerable, however, and too easily slips away. In terms of mechanisms described by other writers (reviewed earlier), these children show marked fluidity of functioning and a pervasive oddness when in their more primitive mode of functioning; though they do not demonstrate panic anxiety, they avoid it at a major adaptive price, by massive ego regression.

In terms of treatment, it is my impression that it is critical to recognize the anxiety-binding functions of the more primitive ego organization. Hence, while work with such children (and all severely disturbed children) must include a very real sense of the benign qualities of the therapist conveyed gently and unobtrusively to the child, a good deal of exploratory, interpretive work is also required. The work is not simply a matter of educatively making up for deficits, of supportively seeing the child through panic, or of developmentally fostering delayed growth. While, as any therapist knows, these may all come into play at times, work with these children includes exploration and insight into the source of the anxiety, the function of the regression, the secondary gains it offers, and the historical basis for its use.

Internal Disorganization in Response to External Disorganizers

In contrast in many ways to the children just described are those who evidence *internal disorganization in response to external disorganizers.* These are children whose lower-level functioning is not *their* achievement—it is not an "achievement" at all; it does not "work" for them but instead reflects a true incursion upon their functioning, the result of an invasion that disrupted it. Hence the descriptive name: *internal disorganization in response to external disorganizers.*

It is my impression that such children are most commonly the product of rearing environments where a high level of social pathology (addiction, criminality, prostitution, violence, etc.) are part and parcel of everyday family life. In the children's psychiatric ward of a big-city municipal hospital where I have seen them, they are often from ghetto or other poverty areas, though I see no reason to believe that the same disorganizing result cannot be brought about in other settings in which the child's functioning is subject to intense psychological barrage. In any event, observation of such children in the ward setting teaches something about the "clinical course" of the illness and in turn permits inferences about its structure. These children arrive in the emergency room, sometimes with reported hallucinations or delusions, often with confusion in speech and relatedness, and frequently with reports of recent suicidal or homicidal behavior. On the ward they rapidly pull themselves together and indeed often come to be seen as more or less normal children. What are we to make of this?

I believe that the rapid recovery in the benign setting of the ward (where they are shielded from their disorganizing environment) suggests that the basic developmental tools of ego function (here reality testing, reliable intrapsychic defense, and secondary process thinking) and of nondestructive, trusting object relationship had indeed been formed, but that they were fragile, unable to withstand the disintegrating effect of chaotic life circumstances. In a benign setting integration can take place. From a purely descriptive point of view, these children can also be seen as fluid, i.e., as functioning at different levels at different times; but the "fluidity" is very different here, and is captured better, I believe, by words like "breakdown" or "collapse" than by a phrase like "shift to a different level of functional ego organization."

From the point of view of treatment, there are important things to be said. I believe the first line of treatment is rescue. First-line rescue in this instance is not a fantasy of the therapist but a need of the child. It is essentially the benign setting, including a caring adult, that fosters integration and the use of capacities that are germinally present. At this stage exploration and insight are unnecessary. But it would indeed be a rescue fantasy if we were to believe that work is done at this point. First and most obvious, of course, is the issue of return to the offending environment; either extensive family work (often impossible to accomplish), placement, or long-term help for the child in withstanding the barrage is required. But second—and this is a more subtle issue—the child's tendency to repeat actively what he has experienced passively, both as a form of mastery and as an expression of his continuing love-hate attachment to his parents, can be forestalled only through long-term treatment that both supports and interprets, to the extent that is necessary and possible for a particular patient. Obviously such long-term treatment is often more an ideal than a possibility, and the generational repetition remains with us.

Chronic Ego Deviance

The group of children who show what I call *chronic ego deviance* are not really a group at all, since there is no underlying structural or developmental feature by which all may be characterized. So this is a loose array, perhaps waiting for distinctions within it to be described as our clinical knowledge advances. Described by Weil (1953, 1956) some time ago, these are children who show one or more of an assortment of aberrations of logical thought, reality testing, defense, or object relation. Panic anxiety, failure to achieve phase dominance in the course of psychosexual development, and unreliability of object attachment, of self- and object differentiation, and of stable defense may, in any one child, be characteristic. I emphasize the word *chronic* in describing their ego deviance to emphasize that the impairment is part of the child, not reactive, as in the group who respond to disorganizing environments, and also to emphasize that the instability of their functioning can be expected to continue; their instability is stably present.

In my own experience I have discovered one phenomenon in treatment that differentiates these children sharply from the preceding group. Children disorganized in response to external disorganizers tend to heal rapidly in the setting of a benign environment and a trusting relationship with the therapist; soon, from the point of view of basic ego intactness at least, they appear more or less normal. But some chronically ego-deviant children show a quite opposite phenomenon. That is, as the trusting relationship with the therapist develops, they permit themselves to reveal, perhaps for the first time, isolated bits of bizarre thought or behavior that previously they have concealed.

Treatment for these children must vary according to the specific failure or aberration of ego development (set, of course, in the context of the patient's whole life). It was Redl (1951) who first argued compellingly that indiscriminate support for a vaguely defined weak ego would get the clinician nowhere; instead the area of deficit must be specified and intervention techniques tailored accordingly. In an earlier paper (Pine, 1976), I tried to demonstrate instances of such work in the context of the implicit parenting function served by the therapist of the ego-deviant patient. Indeed, the present chapter, on specific variants among borderline children (and also among learning-disturbed and behavior-problem children), has the same intent: to specify pathological conditions more precisely so as to enable us to adapt a psychoanalytically informed treatment approach to the particular patient.

Incomplete Internalization of Psychosis

Of the borderline children I have thus far described, two of the groups (shifting levels of ego organization and chronic ego deviance) carry their pathology within, the former as a pathological defense organization and the latter as the result of developmental failure of various sorts; in both, the current *reactive* component in the pathology is relatively small. By contrast, the reactive component is more substantial in children whose internal disorganization is responsive to external disorganizers. Another group of children, those in whom may be seen *incomplete internalization of psychosis*, also shows an important reactive component. In this group, however, the reactive component does not simply reflect a destructive intrusion upon the child's functioning but is a core part of the child's attachment to the primary love object, usually the mother (see Anthony, 1971).

I am referring to children, generally of a psychotic mother, who assimilate parts of the mother's psychosis as a way of being close to her and of having her within them. This involves more than conscious mimicry and hence is pathological. But the internalization of the mother's psychosis is still incomplete; hence I call these children borderline rather than psychotic. The incompleteness of the internalization is made clear by the relative speed with which some of the more obvious indicator behaviors drop away when the children are separated from their mothers and other love objects become available (again see Anthony, 1971). At the descriptive level, fluidity of functioning is again apparent; but as the child moves toward merger with the mother, failures in the separation-individuation process (Mahler, Pine, and Bergman, 1975) can be inferred, as can the child's reliance on regression to primitive forms of incorporation for defense. There is no question but that treatment is a long and complex process, notwithstanding the gains the child may make if separated from the mother (e.g., by the hospitalization of either). For, like the other reactive group of borderline children (internal disorganization in response to external disorganizers), a large residue remains even when the obvious "reaction" terminates. With these children, extended work is required to relive (in the transference), to understand (through exploration), and to work through the relation with the primary love object. Within the essentially analytic and exploratory content of the sessions, the benign presence of the therapist—a differentiated other who allows individuality and who does not require sharing of pathology as a condition for relatedness—will (whatever his theoretical orientation) inevitably provide corrective emotional experience (Alexander, 1956).

Ego Limitation

There are other children who, though they vary in the precise area and quality of their pathology of ego function and object relationship, show enough similarity in the developmental route to that pathology to warrant grouping them for purposes of conceptualization and discussion of treatment. I call them children with *ego limitation*. This term may be used to refer to inhibited children, dull children, culturally deprived children, or whatever. But let me describe the children for whom I intend to use it.

Sometimes, for inner and familial reasons, a child "happens upon" an early adaptive-defensive mode that markedly curtails large areas of subsequent development. If this happens, and if at the same time the defense is "successful" in inner terms (i.e., by lessening anxiety, allowing gratification, or fitting with the family), it may be retained for a long time, with increasing damage to the developmental process. Thus, a pseudoimbecilic child (Mahler, 1942; Pine, 1974a), whose inner psychological requirements are not to learn, will show effects of that learning stoppage in formal school learning, peer relations, social sense, and everywhere else. Or, to take another example, Youngerman (1979) reports on a child, electively mute fairly continuously since age 3, the development of whose entire thought process was impaired as a consequence of the refusal to speak. Speech externalizes inner fantasies and permits their correction against the response of others; by verbalizing certain ideas and seeing that wishes do not always produce effects, the child learns to abanbon ideas of the omnipotence of thought; and of course speech is the instrumentality of relationships at a distance—permitting distal connection and not requiring highly charged body contact and affect and gesture as continuing modes of communication.

It is my experience that children showing this early and severe ego limitation bring a wide range of serious failings in ego function and object relation into their later treatment. It is also my impression, however, that a defensive-adaptive style of such long duration and, though pathological, such great intrapsychic "success" is not readily renounced. Not only does work with such children require sustained and sophisticated interpretive work to penetrate heavily relied-upon defense organizations but, and this is critical, once it is penetrated we are still left with a child with substantial deficits. That is, the years of nonlearning have taken their toll. Interpretation (of, for example, the basis for the pseudoimbecility or the mutism) may lead to lesser reliance on the defense but does not create what has been missed in development. For this, an extensive educative process is required, along with continuing therapeutic work. But two cautions are in order. First, the educative process cannot be undertaken until the defense barrier is more or less abandoned, until the child understands it and is trying to give it up, or else the "education" will be greeted with that very same defensive style and be cast away; second, optimism about making up for the lost development of years, even after the defense is penetrated and educational supplementation is begun (either within or outside of the therapy), is hardly warranted in such cases, where, in my experience at least, the child remains with considerable deficit.

Schizoid Personality

Schizoid personality in childhood, exactly parallel to its adult form, seems to warrant inclusion in the broader group of borderline children. Such personalities, characterized by a sharply constricted and undeveloped affective life, with emotional distance in human relationships and preoccupation with their own peculiar fantasy life (often quite rich), can be seen quite clearly already in childhood. The peculiarities of thought and severe limitations of object relationship reflect the developmental aberrations or failures of the general borderline domain.

Like children with shifting levels of ego organization, whose shift to a more primitive organization successfully wards off anxiety (even at the price of often severe disturbance of function), the preoccupation with fantasy in these schizoid children also will often serve well to avoid anxiety (or indeed any affect). Treatment is therefore difficult. Since fantasizing works well for the children, it will not easily be given up; relationships with others are quite cut off, and so the therapist cannot easily become important to the child. And, since the child does not shift between in-touch and fantasizing states, but rather stays safely shielded from others by affective distance and fantasy preoccupation, the therapist does not see the variability that allows for even periodic contact or interpretive inroads. Once again a long-sustained treatment seems necessary, with all the patience, restraint, and interpretive skill that is part and parcel of any full treatment, and all of which can lead to the slow growth of a therapeutic alliance.

Splitting of Good and Bad Images of Self and Other

I should like to describe a subgroup of borderline children that did not appear in my earlier paper (Pine, 1974a). Alerted by Kernberg's writings on adult borderline patients (1967, 1968), I became attuned to certain children who show an omnipresent splitting of good and bad images of self and other. Such children, often "sweet" or "good" on the surface, will in treatment reveal an absorbing inner preoccupation with hate and violence, often with homicidal or world-destruction fantasies, equally often with scant and precarious control over them. The splitting is evidenced in the lack of connection between the "good" and the "bad" self and other. Hate, unmodified by affectionate images, becomes icy or fiery, devouring of the self or the other (in mental life), and frightening—both to the patient and to the therapist who learns about it.

I first became aware of this as a phenomenon in childhood from an adult patient, suffering from irreconcilable love-hate images toward her adoptive parents, who was able to recall the phenomenon vividly from her childhood. The "teacher's pet" in school, the good girl, she nonetheless recalls sitting in class absorbed with violent and destructive fantasy. Hearing this, I was reminded of recurrent newspaper accounts of mass murderers who, as the history unfolds, were "good" children, generally quiet and not too well known to anyone, but well behaved, disciplined. And then I was reminded of the comment, often heard among educators, that troublesome (noisy, school-failing) children come to the attention of the school, but that quiet children who may also be in trouble may not be noticed. Might not these quiet children be "in trouble" not only as nonlearners but also as instances of the kind of child of which I am now speaking? Not all of them, by any means! But here and there.

Such were my thoughts at the time, listening to my adult patient speak. Since then, more alert to the issue, I have come across the phenomenon three or four times in a few years through supervision of the work of others or through direct consultation or treatment myself. There is no question but that the phenomenon exists in childhood. Its attendant disturbances in thought processes and object relations warrant its being considered another form of the borderline disturbance. Just beginning to work in the area, I do not yet feel comfortable commenting on any repeated issues in the treatment of such children; my impression is, however, that the work is exceedingly difficult, that the "split" modifies only slowly if at all, and that the primitive rage and violence are constantly in danger of either erupting or succumbing to repression rather than undergoing modification.

In this section on borderline disturbances I have advanced the idea that a loose but defensible category of "borderline children" can be defined in terms of central developmental failures or aberrations in ego development and object relationship. These disturbances are identifiable in the school-age period because, by that age, one ordinarily expects to see some degree of stability of character and socialization in the child; the "peculiarities" of the borderline child generally violate that expectation. Within the broad borderline domain, there is a distinct clinical gain from seeking not a single mechanism that is shared by all such patients but individualized descriptions of subtypes of borderline phenomena—subtypes which *do* have essential commonalities of etiology or structure and which can lead us to individualized treatment.

About treatment, I have made along the way a number of specific comments regarding each subgroup. I would like to make, in concluding this section, one final point. Once recently, when I was discussing an earlier version of the ideas presented here with a rather unsophisticated group of beginning therapists, the discussion began to turn around the question: should we or should we not make interpretations to borderline patients? Referring to Knight (1953b) in excessively simplistic form, one person concluded that we were not supposed to make interpretations. Another, referring to Kernberg (1968), concluded, equally simplistically, that indeed we were supposed to interpret. What, they asked, did I think they were "supposed" to do?

I assume by now my answer to that question is clear. With fuller understanding of the range of pathology subsumed under the concept "borderline," one cannot avoid the responsibility of creating an answer tailored not only to the events of the moment (as in all dynamic psychotherapy) but also to the specific form of the pathology. Sometimes we do one thing, and sometimes another. I can only say: It all depends. On what? That is what I have tried to spell out, at least in part, herein.

Learning Disturbances

A second characteristic area of disturbance in the school-age period is the broad one of learning. It is an area where concerns of parents, educators, child clinicians, and the children themselves often come together.

It is not surprising that this should be so. As discussed earlier, one of the basic tasks of the age is the establishment of the learning process as a sufficiently neutralized and automatic one such that new learning can be accumulated. Such learning, especially in school, is ordinarily different from earlier, preschool learning in that it is less intimately tied to the body (that is, it is unlike learning about dressing, toileting, eating) and is received from relatively more impersonal sources (teacher, not parents). Peer group learning is also prominent (games, rules, rhymes, tricks), but it is principally disturbances of school learning that lead parents to seek help for their children, and it is this on which I shall concentrate. While it has often been said that failures in love and work are central in adults' seeking of treatment, we can readily recognize how central learning is to the "work" of the school-age child. Love, in this case especially "self-love" (self-esteem), is also centrally involved with success or failure in learning, as is one's esteem in the eyes of peers, teachers, and parents. Problems of learning are important not only because of the disturbances they reflect and the suffering that may accompany them, but because they obviously have real consequences for the paths open to a child as he grows into later life.

In my discussion of borderline disturbances I tried to show the clinical value of recognizing the similarities and differences among borderline children. I suggested that core failures in the development of ego functions and object relations conceptually unite the group, but that the specific nature of the failures vary. I further suggested that, while ordinarily showing one or another form of oddness in their functioning and thus again similar (even if only vaguely so), they can be importantly differentiated from one another in terms of organizational and etiological features of their pathology—the subtypes that I described. Related considerations apply to disturbances of learning. There is no question but that a wide array of routes to learning disturbances exists and that this variation speaks to a nonunified set of pathological entities in the area of learning failure. But in various secondary, though still highly important ways, these conditions have much in common. Descriptively, the presenting symptoms are of course learning difficulties; functionally, they all have major implications for school success; and as a consequence of their presence, they often have an impact on self-esteem. Additionally, they all reflect failures in what I will formulate as one or more of three broad developmental lines on which the child must have progressed in order for learning to take place. Before turning to the description of specific forms of learning disturbance, let me describe the three developmental lines. These are, of course, abstractions from the developmental process. I shall give them a form that is helpful in highlighting the disturbances I shall later describe.

To begin, then, for learning to take place the basic tools for the process must be biologically and psychologically intact and must have developed in age-appropriate ways. First and foremost, it is obvious that learning capacity will vary with general intelligence; indeed, one definition of general intelligence is precisely in terms of the capacity to learn. Beyond that, specific tools are needed for one or another kind of learning, tools such as capacity for intake of information through visual, auditory, and tactile channels (and output through all channels as well), perceptual discrimination, visual organization, visual and auditory short- and long-term memory, sequencing of concepts, sustained attention, and the like. The last-listed, sustained attention, should alert us especially to the psychological-developmental achievements underlying some of these basic tools. The capacity to attend and, even more, the emotional investment in learning (i.e., so that learning matters and gives pleasure) are achievements forged in the developmental mix of object relatedness, drive-defense arrangements, and inborn capacities, and are core tools (capacities) for the learning process.

For school learning to take place the child must also have developed to the point where there is a reasonable inner harnessing of those affect states and behavioral expressions which, when present in unharnessed form, would readily upset the delicate balance of receptivity, sustained attention, and interest outside oneself that is necessary for optimal learning. If the child is still subject to affect storms (for example, of panic anxiety, of needy longing) and developmental-defensive modulation of these has not taken place, learning will ordinarily suffer. Similarly, if impulses and affects readily spill over into gross motor activity, the state of receptivity for learning will have suffered. I recognize, of course, that much learning is enhanced by affective involvement and even motor behavior. This is no contradiction. The "harnessing" of affect and motor behavior in development does not refer to their elimination but rather to their coordination with other aims of the individual.

And third, for learning to take place the learning process

must have a reasonable degree of autonomy (Hartmann, 1939; Rapaport, 1967) from a person's major urges and the fantasies connected with them. There are changing currents in the relation of fantasy to function in the course of development. Very early on, for example, eating (sucking) is clearly a biological, life-sustaining process. That it remains so goes without saying, but the presence in childhood of food fads, of disgust reactions, and of food avoidances reflect the intrusion of fantasy (anal, cannibalistic, etc.) into the biologically based process. Still later, with the attainment of "rational eating" (A. Freud, 1965), these fantasies have been more or less tamed in relation to the act of eating. Again this does not mean that they are eliminated. The relativity of autonomy from drives implies two things. (1) An ego function or a process (such as learning) is relatively autonomous from drives in that it can always be reinvaded, reinterfered with; it is not impervious; the autonomy is not absolute. And (2), especially relevant right now, it is relatively autonomous in the sense not that drive components are totally eliminated but that they are united with the function or process in nonconflictual ways; thus learning can be enhanced by the fantasy of becoming "just like Mommy or Daddy" and not only interfered with by such an idea.

So then, from the point of view of development, learning requires (1) the availability of basic tools; (2) the harnessing of potential interferences with the learning process, such as too intense affect or too impulsive behavior, that can disrupt attention and intake; and (3) the achievement and maintenance of a secondary autonomy from drives and their attendant fantasies (this is akin to but differentiable from the second tool). In addition, with reference to developmental lines, and though it is not as widespread in its relation to the normal range of the psychopathology of learning, I shall have to introduce issues in the development of self-other differentiation, object constancy, and object relations in order to clarify one particular area of learning disturbance.

Let us turn now to an examination of some clinical material to see how differentiations among the disturbances of learning can be made with these developmental lines as background. I shall include instances with problems of a built-in nature and of a psychogenic nature, as well as various distinctions within and mixes between the two. I shall organize the illustrations under eight headings: problems of general intelligence; specific cognitive deficits; interrelation of specific cognitive deficits and broader psychological functioning; learning problems secondary to other psychological conditions; learning failure as a specific symptom; learning failure as part of a general character trait; learning failure as a reflection of disturbance in object relations; and family-based disinterest in learning. "Learning" is of course not a unity in itself; I shall be drawing on interferences with various aspects of that process and with various areas of information intake that may be disturbed.

Problems of General Intelligence

Allow me, simplistically and briefly, to state the obvious: sometimes a reported learning "problem" is simply a reflection of the fact that the child has a lower level of general intelligence than is imputed to him by parents or teachers. I mention this not only for the sake of completeness but because it comes up as a problem in clinical work. It may become a problem for the child, but it starts as a problem for parents or educators in their role of goal-setters.

Some children, because their eyes are bright and their facial expressions winning, or because their social grace is captivating, or because they are very verbal (though not necessarily complexly so), or because their parents are quite successful, or for none of these reasons but because of parental hopes, are taken to be brighter than they are. This can be at any level: children whose work is fair rather than excellent, or poor rather than adequate. When the clinician accepts the problem as defined by the parents, perhaps finding a rationale in the perennial intelligence test conclusion that "this score does not represent the child's true optimal level of functioning" (a phrase often accurate but also often misused), and thus finds no need to make an adequate intellectual assessment at all, choosing instead to work with the child around his so-called "learning failure," then the problem becomes compounded.

No need to beat a dead horse. Such problems exist. I have more than once encountered resistance to the conclusion "low intelligence" in clinical or private work. The diagnostic task is adequate assessment; the therapeutic one is work with parents and school toward a realistic view of the child in order to avoid creating secondary problems for the child. Easily said, but not easily done. We well know that, especially in some families and in most schools, intelligence is intensely, often irrationally, valued. To help parents to develop a realistic view, without the consequence of the child's being viewed as debased, without provoking irrational feelings of guilt or failure in the parents, is a consultative task of no small delicacy and magnitude, one sometimes requiring extended therapeutic work.

Specific Cognitive Deficits

Specific cognitive disabilities (as well as problems of general intelligence) are discussed here in order to correct the psychoanalytic (or psychodynamic) contribution in this area, which has for the most part been a negative one. That is, it has been all too easy to find psychodynamic "reasons" for any learning failure, especially since fantasies are bound to get attached to any significant failure and the clinical method provides the clinician no good basis for distinguishing fantasy as "cause" from fantasy as secondary consequence. I discuss cognitive disabilities here for other reasons as well: for the sake of completeness; because the working clinician should have knowledge of his full range of diagnostic options; and because these disabilities exist in people who also "have psychodynamics," and almost inevitably they become interlaced with the individual's defense system, wishes, self-esteem, and object relations.

Following are two brief illustrations of the phenomenon of specific disabilities. Some years ago I consulted with a father and his young daughter about her problems in learning to read. Tutoring had not helped; the school regularly threatened failure and urged therapy. The girl seemed to function rather well in most areas, to relate adequately to her environment, and to express and control herself appropriately. Numerous test findings, however, suggested a deficit in the capacity for organization of the visual field; though the negative cannot be proved, nothing in the test or consultation findings suggested a specific psychological "meaning" for this failing. The problem slowed her enormously in her comprehension of that complex visual field, the printed page. Interestingly, just at the time of this consultation, this preadolescent girl had become fascinated with photography and taken it up as a hobby. That fact fit. My impression was that she inarticulately sensed her disability and that photography was a kind of mastery, a turning of passive to active—it organized the visual field for her. I had an opportunity for follow-up many years later. She had never had therapy; her reading never did more than inch along; and she had become a professional photographer.

A second child, presenting with pervasive and crippling pseudoimbecility (Pine, 1974a), gradually (and only partially) gave that up during a long period of intensive psychotherapy. His intelligence blossomed, however, in social perceptivity and language use. Many gaps remained in his school learning, though some areas saw slow improvement over time. Mathematical skills, however, were never more than abysmally poor. While again the negative cannot be proved, my impression was (and I knew this child well) that his failure in mathematics reflected specific disabilities in various aspects of number concepts that would not show improvement with the general freeing of intelligence. Thus, even after therapy had begun to have its impact, this specific cognitive deficit revealed itself as residual. Just as a depressed paraplegic who recovers from his depression will show livelier facial movement but still will not walk, so, too, work on psychological aspects of learning will not automatically reverse certain specific disabilities.

Recent attention to minimal cerebral dysfunction has highlighted problems such as those described but has also obscured the issue and exaggerated its importance where the uninformed are concerned. What I am describing here is not a single syndrome, not necessarily a syndrome at all (a connected set of signs such as hyperactivity or poor attention span, which, by the way, neither of these two children showed), but specific failings in special areas. As people vary in height and eye color, and in visual acuity and general intelligence, so too do they vary (presumably on neurological bases) in specific cognitive capacities. Benjamin (1971; Benjamin and Green, 1968; Benjamin and Finkel, 1969) has done considerable work in the assessment and individualized treatment of such specific disabilities. These children show a deficit in the basic tools for specific kinds of learning. While work with them might at times involve major dynamic therapeutic issues (see below), and may involve sensitive work with parents (as discussed above), much of the work is of necessity remedial and supportive in relation to their real difficulties in the educational environment.

Interrelations of Specific Cognitive Deficits and Broader Psychological Functioning

Though the distinction is necessarily arbitrary, I discuss these phenomena separately, for the sake of expository clarity, from those just described. I am still focusing on specific deficits, presumably with a neurological basis, that affect learning; but here I focus on their secondary effects in interplay with the child's intrapsychic life. I will describe two types of phenomena: reactions to the deficit and deficits as nodal points for further symptom formation.

An illustration of the former is provided by the case of a child brought to me for psychological assessment. The symptom picture (which included failures in writing and drawing) and a previous assessment were highly suggestive of specific problems in visual-motor coordination; he could spell well orally, but not in writing. The father's instruction to me was, however, "Don't tell me he's brain-damaged, I've already been told that." Indeed, the data again suggested visual-motor coordination problems. One especially revealing moment was the boy's attempt to draw a rocket. He could not get his hand to turn the pencil to make the angles go in the direction he wished; yet his eye could easily see that his final drawing was grossly distorted in its angles. The capacity for visual-motor coordination was flawed, but the negative visual feedback was received. The boy, pervasively anxious and embarrassed with regard to his deficit, wishing to please a father who refused to acknowledge the deficit, and trying to turn passive failure into active success (a process not too far from his conscious awareness), announced to me with feigned enthusiasm that he was going to be a blueprint designer when he grew up. To my response (once our work was nearly completed) that he had real skills but that those necessary for that job were not among them, that I thought he knew that from his rocket drawing, and that he was intelligent and could do many other things successfully, he responded with enormous relief and the touching exclamation: "This has been the best day of my life!" I believe the failure (which he was aware of but could not understand), plus the paternal denial, pushed the boy into a brittle denial of a reality he experienced every day (his failures) and left him preoccupied, on the edge of humiliation, and vulnerable (in self-esteem and in reality testing) to each new failure.

Such secondary reactions to deficit are not rare. Though "secondary" in a causal sense, they can have major impact on the child's functioning. (I am reminded also of children with depressed mood and low self-esteem secondary to reading problems or to problems in the acquisition of other skills, also on a neurological basis.) The therapeutic problem here is not minor. These children, and their parents, have to be helped to understand the reality of the deficit, including its specificity, i.e., the fact that the child is not totally "damaged." But such information may itself (after a frequent response of "seeing the light," as many facts of the child's life fit into place) produce further depression or denial. My own experience is that when these secondary reactions are well established, only a period of intensive psychotherapy can begin to modify them, this quite apart from the patient's specific remedial needs.

The phenomenon of deficit as a nodal point for further symptom formation is seen in the following: "somatic compliance" in psychosomatic illness, whereby biologically weak organs are the ones to show malfunction related to psychological conflict. As bodily deformities or distinctive names "attract" fantasies and become nodal points for the development of symptoms (or, more constructively, interests), so too can specific cognitive disabilities become nodal points for symptom formation. By way of example, let me mention a child with a dyslexic syndrome who experienced inordinate confusion in her struggle with the printed page. Subsequently, when strong aggressive or sexual impulses were aroused, they culminated in similar states of confusion. An anlage for experience had been laid down. The two came together especially in school, where impulse arousal led to "confusion" and thus further learning failure (even in nondeficit areas). This secondary learning failure (in math and history) gave way with interpretation of intrapsychic conflict; but not so the dyslexia. Incidentally, it should be clear that without psychotherapy we are unlikely even to become aware of such subtle interconnections of functioning, let alone to work toward resolving them.

I have just discussed psychological problems secondary to learning problems. Now let me do the reverse.

Learning Problems Secondary to Other Psychological Conditions

In discussing the positions on various developmental lines that a child must have attained in order for learning to take place, I suggested that a child must be able to hold in abeyance those powerful affect states or behavioral impulses that, when present, can disrupt the attentiveness and receptivity requisite for learning. The absence of affect control or impulse control reflects problems which, while not focal to learning, nonetheless may affect it. Some children who show failure to learn need help, not primarily in the area of learning, but in areas that have a secondary impact on the learning process.

Examples, unfortunately, are not hard to find. Janey, an abused and neglected child, was "not doing any work at all" in school, and this, combined with her severe behavior problems and absenteeism, led to her clinic referral. Extremely needy, and preoccupied with wishes for, fears of, and thoughts about her mother, this child on close assessment showed near average intelligence and no specific cognitive disabilities. To put it simply, emotions were her problem; nonlearning was a secondary effect, one of many areas affected by her extraordinarily painful home situation. Preoccupied with her mother and with anxieties linked to that relationship, she was unable to focus on learning. Apart from the sad and frustrating attempts to do something for the home life of such children, I would like to comment on this child's remediation experience. Put in contact with a tutor, the child began to learn. No specialized (deficit-linked) remediation techniques were needed. Rather, the one-to-one relationship itself toned down her neediness and permitted attention to learning; even more, learning became the vehicle for the relationship with the tutor and was fostered by the child herself as a mode of contact.

Other disruptive states operate similarly. An 8-year-old boy would become depressed at recurrent intervals when a favorite pet was given away; learning would cease at these times. (While nonlearning had the secondary gain of an attack on his family, who gave the pets away, the depression was primary and affected many areas beyond learning.) In another case, a school-refusing boy with fragile ego structure was preoccupied with wishes and fears that his mother would be destroyed; he therefore could not learn even when he was in school, and stayed home with the fantasy of protecting her. Similarly, a chronic thought disorder or pervasive behavior problems (e.g., constant fighting and running in the classroom) will obviously have effects on learning.

Each of these children shows a specific learning disturbance that can be understood and worked with therapeutically only by taking into account the broader pathology of which it is a part. This is by no means the case with all psychogenic learning problems, however. Let me turn now to some quite different clinical pictures, ones in which the learning failure is far more central.

Learning Failure as a Specific Symptom

I have described learning failures resultant from deficiencies in the tools of learning (general intelligence or specific deficits) and from the learning process being swamped by other disorders of affect, thought, or behavior. But the process of learning can itself be invested with psychological meaning that leads to interferences. Here we come to more classical neurotic pictures with bound symptoms that eventuate from conflict between impulse and defense. We see interferences with the secondary autonomy of the learning process, an invasion of the process itself or of specific content areas by conflictual fantasies.

Thus, learning can come to be equated with knowing about sexual events or family secrets and, in either case, can succumb to an inhibition (in school) that parallels the repression of ideas connected with sex and secrets. Allen (1967) has described voyeuristic and exhibitionistic conflicts interfering with seeing/knowing or "showing" what one knows, while the group working out of the Judge Baker Child Guidance Center in the 1950s and early 1960s described other essentially neurotic interferences with learning—for example, where success stimulates castration anxiety (Sperry, Ulrich, and Staver, 1958; Grunebaum, Hurwitz, Prentice, and Sperry, 1962). In these instances, learning (as a process) and knowledge (as potentially taboo content) are primary targets of the pathological formation. Just how this comes to be, i.e., the problem of symptom choice, is a question we know little about at the level of general clinical theory but of which we learn a great deal in the in-depth study of each individual when intensive treatment is undertaken.

Sometimes the interference can be much more specific. For example, a child referred because his school grades were falling sharply turned out to have a specific interference with the writing process. He had begun to write so slowly, with such a burden of inhibition, that he never finished his tests and would therefore get low grades. The fantasy that writing was an aggressive act—more specifically, that writing involved "signing a death warrant"—turned out to be central and had taken shape after the death of a relative. In other children, neurotic interference with specific content areas also occurs: difficulty learning about wars in history class in a child struggling with aggressive impulses; failure in English composition in a boy anxious about whether body parts were "long enough," who would feel compelled to make his sentences longer, extending and overextending them until they became "run-on" sentences that were grammatically incorrect and unintelligible. In each of these instances the specific school failure has an intrapsychic "meaning"; something about learning process or content has become involved in intrapsychic fantasy and conflict, has lost its affective neutrality, and has become subject to defensive avoidance or other interference.

Learning Failure as Part of a General Character Trait

I have just described psychological disturbances that have specific impact on particular aspects of learning process or content. I would like now to turn to interference somewhat less precisely directed at learning per se, but yet far more closely tied to learning failure than those conditions (thought disorder, impulse disorder, affect flooding) that interfere with learning in an almost incidental way. I am referring now to maladaptive character traits which subsume aspects of the learning process. That learning is interfered with is no accidental secondary effect; neither is learning itself the focal or original "target" of the psychopathological process. Instead, broad characteristic features of a child such as a generalized inhibition (linked to unconscious active impulses) or avoidance of success or achievement (having roots in oedipal fantasies) will affect modes of play, of movement, of relatedness—and of learning as well. The issues will be structurally similar regarding those other impairments and learning, even though learning itself is not the central focus of the difficulty.

Let me give one example. An 11-year-old girl was referred by her pediatrician, who could find no organic basis for her constant fatigue. Home reports were that she was "lazy," often "lethargic." A picture gradually emerged of a very ambitious and aggressive young girl caught in an oedipal rivalry with a bright and successful stepsister, who defended against her active wishes by a turn to passivity. But the "lethargy" affected her schoolwork as well. Learning became impaired; work output slowed; grades went down. Success, activity, and ambition were in general renounced; learning, one form of activity and success, was drawn into the inhibition.

Learning Failure as a Reflection of Disturbance in Object Relations

While the disturbances of learning that I am now going to describe are of psychogenic origin and can be said to have a "meaning" to the person, I distinguish them from those just described (specific symptoms and character traits) because of what I believe to be in general a greater severity of the diagnostic picture. Based on disturbances in earliest object relations, they show, as do other sequelae of such early disturbances, the profoundly distorting developmental impact of failures and aberrations in the mother-child dyad. I will illustrate two different kinds of interference with learning.

In recent years two female patients, one a middle-aged adult and one a college student, told me about school difficulties in similar terms. Each could not do well because she could not study or do homework. And each could not study because the process, the sustained engagement with inanimate words and books, produced profound and painful feelings of aloneness. The result: flight into sociability, talk, no work, poor grades. Though both patients were well beyond childhood, both dated the problem back to that time. Both were sensitive and articulate patients; I think perhaps it would be quite difficult for a child to verbalize this material. There was, however, an important difference in the early childhood experiences of these two patients, a difference reflected in the further subtleties of the painful feeling of aloneness. One had had early, repeated experiences of object loss; the love object (the mother) was experienced as a differentiated other but was periodically lost. While studying, her experience was one of isolation and the need for contact. The other patient had early experiences that interfered with self-other differentiation; her life showed cycles of panic over merging (loss of differentiation) and moments of a heightened sense of individuality (differentiation) which were accompanied by pained feelings of loss of connectedness to her family. Studying produced that feeling of individuality and was accompanied by feelings not only of isolation but of fear of merging as well. The wish underlying the fear, the wish to terminate the isolation through merging, ultimately became clear. Neither patient had developed that "capacity to be alone" (Winnicott, 1958), here alone with work, that comes from carrying the sense of the mother's presence inside oneself.

A related report, this time of work with young children, shows early disturbances of learning that are linked to pathological mother-child narcissism (Newman, Dember, and Krug, 1973). The children, all bright and precociously verbal, were their mother's pride, shown off by her in such a way that their intellectual functioning (especially the precocious speech) came to be experienced as an extension of the mother's narcissism. When these children reached school, they did poorly. (Admission to this research project was by way of being a "gifted underachiever.") What had happened, broadly, was that intellect had become part of the connectedness to the mother, not a tool for learning about the nonmother world; further, the narcissistic investment in intellectual precocity made failure in the effort to learn too great a risk; the threat to self-esteem was too overwhelming.

Family-Based Disinterest in Learning

Finally, another phenomenon of sociocultural and educational significance should be mentioned, though it rarely comes to us as a clinical problem in its own right. It is seen in children, often of the ghetto poor, for whom there are no family models for the value of learning, little or no family support for learning, and little in the economic-cultural surround holding promise for those who do learn. Many (but by no means all) of these children learn poorly. But to say there is "learning failure" is to presume they share our goals and have failed to meet them. It is not at all clear that this is the case, and we should perhaps speak here instead of motivational, identificatory, and socioeconomic problems.

To sum up regarding disturbances of learning: I have suggested that learning requires the child's adequate movement along developmental lines associated with the growth of the basic cognitive tools of the learning process; the maintenance of the relative autonomy of the learning process such that it does not suffer repression, inhibition, or other malfunction because it has been invested with conflict-ridden symbolic meaning; the harnessing of affective and behavioral flooding that would swamp the attentional and receptive processes requisite for learning; and the development of adequate self-other differentiation, object constancy, and early object relations so that peremptory needs for object contact do not make work in isolation impossible. Along the way I have attempted to be specific regarding both the particular aspect of the learning process or content that is impaired (i.e., the presenting problem and its variations) and the psychological or neuropsychological route to that impairment (i.e., the underlying genetic and structural sources of the problem and their variations). From a clinical-therapeutic point of view I have called attention to issues requiring (1) careful assessment of cognitive skills and capacities;

(2) guidance and education for parent or child; (3) sensitive handling of the affective accompaniments to information regarding deficits; (4) work with children around their secondary reactions to deficits of which they have an inarticulate awareness; (5) recognition of the need at times for remediation, at times for therapy, and at times for both; (6) recognition also that some disturbances of learning are secondary consequences of major affect, thought, behavioral, or even sociocultural disturbances which require primary attention in their own right; and (7) the need for intensive treatment of some learning disturbances that reflect the development of bound and focal symptoms, pathological character traits, or the end result of early disturbances in object relations.

Behavior Disturbances

Behavior is obviously omnipresent in human functioning. Broadly defined, to include "verbal behavior" and "thinking behavior" as well as motor behavior, it becomes practically coterminous with the totality of human psychological functioning. Even with a narrower definition of behavior (as action involving large movements of the voluntary musculature), we are still dealing with phenomena which, like affect, thought, and impulse, are omnipresent; we accept and expect them as part of life.

Though we accept and expect behavior as part of life, we certainly cannot view behavior *disorder* with like equanimity. That is obviously so because pathology involving the behavioral sphere is of great significance for clinical management. At its worst destructive of self or others, even the milder forms of behavioral disturbance have impacts on others. They affect the interpersonal sphere and not only the intrapsychic one. As such, they are highly visible and are often red-flag warnings evoking the concern of parents, teachers, the courts, or others in contact with the child.

In spite of their importance, and perhaps because of their omnipresence, disturbances of behavior do not have any very specific diagnostic significance. They spring from many developmental sources and are found in varying personality contexts. In this section I shall describe and clarify some of the internal features of the broad landscape of behavior disturbances. First, however, I shall narrow the range just a bit and then show the special significance of behavior disturbances for the school-age child.

First, the narrowing: imagine a child who engages in compulsive rituals that involve his walking around his room at bedtime to arrange its contents in particular ways, or a child with tics that involve flailing motions of the arms or posturing of the whole body, or a child who is a sleepwalker, wandering in his home at night. In each of these instances motor behavior (large movements of the voluntary musculature) is enmeshed in some inner psychopathological system, but in none of these instances is the term "behavior disturbance" likely to be applied by working clinicians. Clinical custom reserves the term for disturbed behaviors that have an antisocial or at least interpersonally disruptive component. They are troublesome or dangerous in some way. It is the set of disturbances in the motor sphere that are troublesome to others that I shall focus on here. I shall refer to them simply as actions that are antisocial or interpersonally disruptive. These are often called "behavior disorders," a term that remains imprecise diagnostically (i.e., it fails to indicate what may be going on under the descriptive behavioral surface) but a term I shall try to specify further as we go along.

Behavior disorders are a characteristic form of pathology in the school-age child. Like borderline disturbances and learning disturbances, they present themselves constantly in clinical work with children, though often the term seems rather imprecise. There are at least three reasons why behavior should be a characteristic area of disturbance in the school-age child, all having to do with the child's position on the developmental ladder. First, school makes a great demand for motor restraint. Except in a very few atypical school programs that allow a great deal of free movement, the child is seated at a desk for several hours each day. Not only does this place a great demand on his capacity for motor restraint, but violations of that restraint come to be perceived as socially disturbing acts reflecting individual disturbance. The traditional shouting and running of young children as the end-of-day schoolbell rings well attest the coiled-spring quality of the motor apparatus as that spring tightens through the long school day. Second, if we view development (as I believe we can) as a more or less steady movement toward decreased need for motor activity, or an increased capacity for sedentary activity as cognitive potentials expand, it becomes clear that the school-age child is still at the very early end of that continuum. Starting from the seemingly unending and exuberant capacity for movement in the younger toddler, just learning to crawl and then walk, and culminating in the sedentary lives of the aged a lifetime later, movement plays a declining (though always significant) role in human life. Mittelmann (1954) speaks of an early motor phase in the second year, and Mahler (1972) discusses roughly the same period in terms of a normal motor "practicing" phase of great activity. Motility serves expressive, adaptive, and defensive functions. It gives pleasure, releases tension, serves as communication, and is a basis for peer relationships through play. That the motor apparatus should be involved in disturbed behavior as well comes as no surprise in this context. And the third developmentally linked reason why motor behavior is an expectable area for disturbance in the school-age child—and this is in contrast to the toddler—is that the school-age child is not only very active but has motor capacities for strength and independent action that make his behavior a potential source of concern for others when it goes awry. He can hurt himself or others; he can run away; he can steal; and he can disrupt a classroom. So we have, in the school-age years, the setting for multiple disturbances in the motor domain: a child naturally motoric, with the capacity for motor behavior of wide injurious as well as constructive range, and often (in school) in a setting where motor restraint is emphasized and motor action is disruptive. (I do not, however, mean to imply that these problems would go away if only schools would allow more activity. Would that problems were so easily resolved! Occasionally, yes. But, as I shall discuss, the routes to behavior disturbance are multiple, and here I am describing only the setting for the child's vulnerabilities.)

There is considerable diagnostic confusion in the area of behavior disorders. In 1966 a working committee of the Group for the Advancement of Psychiatry proposed a classification of childhood psychopathology (GAP, 1966) in which they listed (though without endorsing!) no fewer than eleven terms frequently used diagnostically. Their overall definition is compatible with the one I am using here: "Children in this category exhibit chronic behavioral patterns of emotional expression of aggressive and sexual impulses which conflict with society's norms" (p. 254). Among the eleven terms are a number that can be used to highlight some of the sources of confusion in this area. Thus, "antisocial personality," "sociopathic personality," or "dyssocial personality" are all purely descriptive terms; such a "personality" could behave in nonsocialized ways out of allegiance to a deviant subculture, out of neurotic, self-defeating urges, or out of defective development of conscience, among other things. However, other terms in the list (such as "psychopathic personality" or "impulsive character") purport to have specific diagnostic significance (the former in relation to conscience development and the latter in relation to characteristic features of action/delay or drive/defense relationships). Even in the latter instances, however, there is far from complete agreement on the meaning of the terms. In any event, their applicability in any particular case requires a depth-oriented, interior view of the person and not simply a symptom-descriptive approach. Still other terms in the list of eleven, terms such as "affectionless character" and "acting-out personality," have little agreed-upon meaning at all.

The GAP report's very real contribution to clarification is embodied in its delineation of two subtypes. They are (1) impulse-ridden personality (characterized by poor impulse control and little anxiety, guilt, or attachment to others) and (2) neurotic personality disorders whose "behavior often assumes a repetitive character, with unconscious significance to their acts, rather than the predominance of discharge phenomena" (p. 249). A revealing contradiction in this formulation is seen in the report's grouping of these two under the rubric of "tension discharge disorders" even though the second is said not to have a "predominance of discharge phenomena." What the contradiction reveals is the loss of clarity occasioned when disorders are grouped as instances of broader entities in ways that fail to retain sufficient respect for their differences. In any event, let me continue to draw distinctions within the behavior disorders, as the GAP manual does, and as I have done for borderline disturbances and disturbances of learning. Since behavior is in fact omnipresent in human fucntioning, I will begin with a look at the various ways in which it appears inevitably in all development and then at the ways in which it can become implicated in one or another of an unending array of intrapsychic disturbances.

Behavior, then, is inherent in childhood, as indeed it is at every point in the life cycle. Childhood behavior includes exploratory behavior in new situations (Berlyne, 1960; White, 1963); "Functionlust" (Hendrick, 1942), or pleasure in and exercise of capacities for such functioning as grasp or eye-hand coordination early on, and hopping, jumping, and racing in the school years; fight/flight reactions in the face of danger (Bowlby, 1969); and what we on the outside would designate as "appropriate" behavioral expression in the service of need satisfaction or tension reduction (e.g., in eating, going to mother). All of these reflect evolutionary continuity; they are sources of the impetus to action that are characteristic of all of the higher animal species at least. And there is another normal form of behavior that is characteristic of human beings, whether or not it appears in other animal species. Freud (1920) refers to it in his writing as the repetition compulsion; the general tendency to repeat actively what we experience passively; thus, a child is frightened of an operation and then plays doctor, or is frightened of too fast a car ride and then zooms his own cars around his room. Exploration, exercise of capacities, fight/flight, gratification seeking or pain avoiding, and active repetition of things experienced passively—all are expressed in the motor domain (among others), yet no one of them is reflective of behavior disorder. If anything, their absence or inhibition may reflect disorder of another kind. Nonetheless, any one of them may shade over into pathology in ways that may or may not be clear from the outside. Let me give two examples. They are intended as arguments for the need for an inner view of any behavior in order to understand its specifics and to know how to approach it therapeutically. Such an inner view represents the specification I have in mind within the "behavior disorders."

In talking with a mother regarding her 12-year-old son, whom she had brought for help, I learned about his earlier life. She said that "he always ran away." I immediately wondered (silently, to myself) about the solidity of his delay/defense capacities and about the stability of his attachment to his mother. But when I was told, in response to a question about his running away, that it had begun at about 15 to 18 months, when he "would always run down the street and I would have to dash after him to get him," my formulation shifted rapidly. Here seemed to be a mother not only with no understanding of a toddler's normal motor activity, but one, perhaps, who imposed fantasy explanations on it when it occurred. When I next heard that he had also run away (this time more seriously, to various places in the neighborhood, but for short times only) several times at about age 9 or 10, I had to entertain various explanatory notions in the light of his history. Was this a "behavior disorder"? What would that mean? Was he impulsive? Insufficiently aware of the consequences of his acts? Insufficiently attached to his mother? Or was this (as the case turned out) the form of his attachment to her? He acted on her expectations of his "badness" (and in ways specific to her fantasies, such as the running away) and was then punished in the setting of a sadomasochistic mother-child bond. Misbehavior and punishment were essential to their relationship; as he later (at age 13) said to me, "How would I know she loved me if she didn't punish me?" Interestingly, in his mid-teens a new symptomatic act emerged transiently, that of wandering through the streets to fixed locations in a fuguelike obligatory state. Our work revealed this to be a repetition of a forgotten traveling incident with his father, who had disappeared from his life many years before; so "wandering" (a form of running away) had yet another object-related connection in his life—now to his father as well as to his mother. What we see here is neurotic character pathology—structuralized, ego-syntonic, object-related, and characteristic—that expresses itself in seemingly unsocialized behavior as well as in other areas.

Let us look at a second instance, or rather set of instances, where normal behavior (as in the first child's "running away" at 15 months) shades into disturbed behavior. A young child came dangerously close to being hit by a passing truck as he crossed a street with an adult, the adult quickly picking him up out of harm's way as the truck raced past; in his home afterward, he went to play with his trucks, controlling their movements in his play. The passive experience is turned to an active one as a means to mastery. Constructive; hardly pathological. But take another child, for whom the passive experience is one of being beaten and who then goes to school and beats up others. The inner situation is similar to that of the first child—mastery of a passive experience through active repetition—but the second child would present as a "behavior disorder." To proceed hypothetically for a moment, if the first child continued at his truck play for days on end, the play becoming more compulsive, repetitious, less pleasurable, we would begin to consider that a low-grade pathological process was at work, that the movement toward mastery had gone awry. But, though the reflection of the disturbance is in motor play, we certainly would not call it a "behavior disorder," as it does not break social rules. Yet, to switch back now to another actual situation, parallel phenomena (from an intrapsychic viewpoint) would be considered indices of behavior disorder if they did violate social rules. Thus, a particular child who chronically felt weak and unmanly would regularly, in a driven way, climb to high places, race up and down stairs, and in general take risks, as a means of compensatory reversal of those feelings. Such behavior at home or at school leads to the complaint that he is "hyperactive." I adduce these two examples to show how normal behavior shades into disturbed behavior. But I also want to emphasize how much of our labeling of behavior disorders comes about through external, social criteria, even though we know very little about the "disordered behavior" without an understanding of its interior features. With this in mind, I will now describe a number of phenomena that satisfy the external definition (antisocial or interpersonally disruptive action) in order to show differentiations in the interior circumstances underlying them. Which of these are "properly" called "behavior disorders" is an essentially optional matter, though one requiring definition by consensus based on a reasonable rationale. While I shall make a proposal regarding this later on, my principal aim is to describe at least a sample of the array of interior circumstances associated with disruptive action; an understanding of this array is critical to both diagnosis and therapy.

1. We often speak of "tension discharge" through the motor apparatus. Precisely what is meant by either term—tension or discharge—is generally not clear; but "tension discharge" is a phenomenological phrase, on the model of a corked bottle in which pressure builds up and the cork pops. And yet, corks and pressure interact in different ways. A well-corked bottle may indeed build up great pressure and pop the cork; but a cork may incompletely seal the bottle, having a slight air leak, and then pressure will be released through it in a slow leak as the pressure mounts; or, finally, the cork may be on so loose as not to require any real buildup of pressure before it comes off. I would like to describe psychological parallels to each of these three situations.

In its most vivid presentation, "tension discharge" is the "popped cork," an "outburst." A child (or an adult for that matter), ordinarily reasonably self-controlled, "reaches his limit" or "blows his top." In recognition of the atypicality of this response we say that "he wasn't himself." The specific picture may be of a child, reasonably controlled or even inhibited, who is deprived/frustrated, insulted/humiliated, or provoked/injured to the point where he lashes out—hitting, perhaps crying, perhaps cursing, perhaps all of these. There need be no external provocation; the outburst may arise, once or regularly, as the outcome of inner experiences, conflicts, anger, longings. The point that I wish to emphasize, however, is that very real and substantial controls over behavioral expression exist in such instances, even though they may give way episodically, allowing socially disruptive behavior to emerge. In partial contrast, though also with important parallels regarding the presence of inner controls, are those finger-tapping, knee-bouncing children whose motor restlessness if often evident, but whose "contained" restlessness, a kind of overflow phenomenon, is indicative of the presence and maintenance of great control. As with the infant who sucks or rocks, and in contrast to the infant who screams and thrashes around or the toddler who races everywhere, there is a limited motor outlet here that permits a great deal of control to be retained. The parallel is to the cork that maintains pressure, but has an air leak. There is a kind of slow release valve in situations in which major motor restraint is required (e.g., in school). While the motor overflow may have nuisance qualities, it is rarely viewed as a "behavior disorder," having no antisocial, interpersonally disruptive aspect.

2. There is another situation, one that looks superficially like "tension discharge" but where, in actuality, little tension is either built up or "discharged." The cork is not really on tight at all, and it takes no pressure to release it. I refer to children in whom an impulse (to hit, to steal, to grab food, to run out of the classroom) has ready access to action, to motor pathways, with little or no delay, and in whom there is little or no cognitive or defensive working over of the impulse as the mediating process. In Shapiro's work on impulse disorders (1965) he attributes this phenomenon to a defect in planning, a defect in the capacity to envision consequences of action, and reserves the term *impulse disorder* for just this phenomenon. While I believe that the planning/anticipatory defect may be only a part of the picture (albeit a substantial part), I would also propose, following Shapiro, that the term *behavior disorder* is best reserved for this constellation—a constellation of minimal control, of minimal cognitive mediation of impulse, of ready access of impulse to motor pathways. This, in an internal diagnostic sense (rather than simply an external social sense) gives the term some specificity and diagnostic significance; but more on that after I have presented the other constellations. For now let me just note that, although this phenomenon is seen clearly in adolescents and adults, it can already be identified in early and middle childhood, when the normal developmental achievement of delay over automatic motor expression of impulse should have been attained.

3. Turning to quite different internal phenomena that may, however, still be described as behavior disorders from an exterior view, I should like to describe neurotic character disorders or neurotic symptom disorders that culminate in disturbances in the behavioral realm. Freud (1916) first discussed

such a phenomenon—in adults—in his paper on character types met with in psychoanalytic work. There he describes a person whose criminality has the unconscious aim of justifying a preexisting sense of guilt; it creates a cause for an already present affect. By extension, the point I wish to make is that these behavioral disturbances have unconscious meanings in a context of impulse derivatives in fantasy, of guilt, and of compromise formation, just as do other neurotic symptoms. The boy I described earlier (who ran away, who "wandered around") presents such a picture; his running away reflects neither a defect in delay nor a gap in superego, but rather the expression in action of unconscious memories and the form of his attachment both to his mother and to his father. In short, the action expresses a fantasy in compromise (disguised) form.

The phenomenon is not rare. Children whose constant fighting and provocation are attempts to reverse feelings of weakness, damage, and passivity well illustrate it. Similarly, the phenomenon is seen in a child whose stealing reflects not the needy longing for food of a deprived child whose longing is not subject to control and delay, but instead acts out (dramatizes) an oedipal-level fantasy—say, of possessing the mother (taking her "valuables") or of reversing the loss (in fantasy) of a penis by the theft of a water pistol. In each of these instances, the disturbed behavior serves an unconscious aim. As such, the behavior is the end product of a complex cognitive process, reflecting delay, defense formation, and disguise, and is hardly a simple failure of control.

4. In his paper on ego disturbances, Redl (1951) emphasizes how critical it is for us to have a refined conception of the particular area of ego disturbance in individual instances. Relevant to our present concern, he refers to a psychotic child who attacks a child care worker under the delusional idea that the worker is the child's hated father. Redl differentiates this from other forms of attack by a child, though each culminates in disturbed behavior that may look the same from the exterior. Thus, hypothetically in his paper, one child has no delay capacity in the face of some frustration of need and so attacks the frustrating person. Another, with considerable delay capacity, expresses all the pent-up (delayed) rage against the

father, but does so under the sway of the delusional idea and perceptual distortion that a nonfather is the father. If we consider, in addition, that it may be precisely such a distortion that permits the expression of rage, we see here again that considerable cognitive work has gone on between impulse and expression in this psychotic child.

5. Yet another phenomenon often subsumed under the rubric behavior disorder involves expressions of "antisocial" behavior which themselves reflect socialized behavior within a particular deviant subculture. In the case of marijuana use among contemporary adolescents, we can no longer even refer to a "deviant" subculture. Marijuana smoking is part and parcel of identification with a group, acceptance of its values, and connectedness in reliable patterns of relationship to others within it. Within *this* group, some—whose drug use is deemed excessive or otherwise eccentric—may themselves be viewed as outsiders, or at least no longer governed by the values of the group. Some instances of childhood theft, or of childhood gang fighting, similarly reflect socialized behavior within a particular family or group subculture. This does not imply that clinicians need not be concerned with such behavior, or that it might not simultaneously reflect failures in delay, reactions against depression, or the acting out of an unconscious fantasy in a particular individual. To the contrary, it may reflect any of these underlying factors, or still others, which is precisely why the externally identifiable antisocial behavior has so little specific diagnostic value.

In the preceding material I have taken the term behavior disorder loosely to refer to actions that have an asocial or interpersonally disruptive aspect. But I have tried to demonstrate that a number of quite different interior circumstances may underlie such actions. Diagnosis, which I see precisely as the process of understanding external signs through understanding their inner structure and genetic roots, and which then speaks to issues of treatment technique, is obviously enhanced by taking the interior view. Since behavior is omnipresent in human functioning and is certainly a central aspect of the active lives of young children, its disturbances can appear in any pathological context; what I have given here can be regarded as only a sample of the range.

My aim has been to detail some of the wide array of phenomena subsumable under the behavior disorder rubric. But my personal preference, as already noted, is to reserve the term for those children characterized by a failure of delay between impulse and action. I have emphasized failure of delay. The delay of automatic motor or affectomotor expression as need or affect mounts is a major developmental achievement in the period from infancy to early childhood, and its failure has important consequences. In giving my examples above, I have tried to show that some of them reflect such failures of delay, while others reflect a considerable amount of what I have called, for want of a better term, "cognitive working over." In these latter instances, delay, control, and disguise have taken place, and the disordered behavior is embedded in memories, fantasies, cognitive/perceptual distortions, bound symptoms, or character traits.

Just why delay fails to develop is another issue. I believe that delay normally develops from a number of interlocking circumstances. (1) The infant has sufficient experience of gratification and relief following upon need that he begins to trust that relief will come again, and so he can sustain tension states next time around in anticipation of relief; this is already delay. (2) As part of this, the child who is thus developing a "basic trust" in his caretakers can scan his environment expectantly and learn about its features (since he is not in a desperate, panicky, tearful state), thus learning where need satisfaction and tension relief will come from. (3) Though considerably later, a marked additional force is added to the tendency toward control and delay through the internalization of parental standards, the formation of the superego, with its accompanying affect of guilt that tends to accentuate control processes. Following this reasoning, the failure to develop the capacity (or tendency) to delay impulse expression may be seen as the inverse of these normal developments. Paralleling the three points above, respectively, I would suggest that (1) insufficient attachment to, or empathy for, others—reflecting failures in early trusting object relations—can lead a child to express his impulse as he wills it without regard to others; (2) insufficient cognitive elaboration of possibility, of alternatives, and of plans (see Shapiro, 1965) may follow upon the infant's absorption in his unsatisfied inner state, when the surround has insufficiently brought relief and he has not learned to explore it expectantly for relief; and (3) failures in conscience development, involving the absence of guilt, will further permit ready access to impulse expression when those earlier tendencies are present.

Above I suggested reserving the term behavior disorder for instances "characterized by failure of delay." I have discussed the failure of delay, but would now like to say a word also on the phrase "characterized by." I have in mind here the point Fenichel (1945) makes in his distinction between the "neurosis" and the "neurotic conflict." In brief, the latter is a focal conflict between "the drives, that is the id, and the ego" (p. 129); we only speak of a neurosis, however, when that focal conflict has developed further, influencing a larger sphere of behavior, be this symptom or character trait. Similarly, I would suggest that the term behavior disorder might usefully be reserved for those instances of failure of delay between impulse and action, those absences of cognitive working over, which are characteristic of a particular child and are repeated, predictable modes of reaction to an array of impulses and an array of settings.

Concluding Remarks

In this chapter I have tried to do several things. First, I have tried to describe some of the characteristic descriptive features and developmental issues of the period between 7 and 10 years, the later period of latency (Bornstein, 1951), in which the child is normally involved solidly in the world of school and peer relations. Second, I have selected some of the characteristic areas of pathology of that age group (borderline disturbances, learning disturbances, and behavior disturbances) and have tried to show their relation to the developmental issues of the age. Emphasizing that these disturbances are characteristic of but not specific to this period (i.e., they are also seen both earlier and later), I tried to show that they are characteristic precisely because of their tie to the developmental issues of the age. And finally, and in the bulk of the chapter, I have attempted to give a highly differentiated picture of the variations within each of the three domains of pathology, attempting to demonstrate that an interior view adds considerably to our appreciation of the specificity and complexity of particular presenting pictures (see A. Freud, 1970).

At times I have discussed treatment issues in some detail, at times less so, and at times hardly at all. But I have attempted to discuss in considerable detail (1) the developmental failures underlying each pathological presentation (and the normal developmental pathways that these children have been unable to follow) and (2) the many genetic and structural distinctions in varying presenting pictures within each area. A particular view of the therapeutic process underlies these choices—the choice of detailed discussion of development and of diagnostic specificity and a less detailed discussion of treatment technique per se. In this view the two detailed aspects of the discussion are in fact central to the issue of therapeutic technique.

Knowledge of development can be invaluable to the therapeutic enterprise. Elsewhere (Pine, 1976) I have tried to show that therapy (even psychoanalytic therapy as it is traditionally carried out) can be viewed as in part a process of facilitation of normal development; the more customary view sees it only as a process of correction of interruptions and aberrations of development. Certainly in childhood, with developmental change still proceeding rapidly, this view is useful. An understanding of the current developmental tasks of a child can help us understand the continuing pathogenic consequences of particular presenting problems (e.g., learning failure and its implications for self-esteem regulation; or school refusal and its confirmation of attachment to home and mother, making displacement to school, peers, and learning impossible). An understanding of how relevant normal developments that did not take place should have taken place (e.g., delay of impulse expression, neutralization of the learning process, development of signal anxiety and reliable internal structure) can give us clues to the historical loci of the sources of the presenting pathology. And, though developmental failures can by no means always be reversed by a later reexperiencing of the relevant developmental opportunities, an awareness of those normal modes of development can provide cues for technical interventions in individual instances (Pine, 1976).

And finally, knowledge of the specificity of pathological mechanisms is invaluable to the therapeutic enterprise and underlies my having detailed these disorders with such specificity here. When Freud (1912) spoke of the analyst's "evenly suspended attention" to the associative material of the patient, he did not mean that the analyst's mind was blank, unaware of all that he had learned previously. What is intended is that the analyst not be in advance committed to any single idea in the session, thus permitting new and surprising (or perhaps old and familiar) themes to achieve centrality. Our general theory of human functioning, our past knowledge of all our patients, and knowledge of all that has transpired and is presently transpiring with a particular patient are all parts of what the therapist's mind should be "evenly suspended" over; similarly, for diagnostic specificity. Only when we have the full array in mind—in short, only when we have learned from the accumulation of clinical knowledge—can our evenly hovering (uncommitted) clinical minds light upon and recognize the central phenomena in any particular patient or in any particular session. The technical attitude of the therapist has to be one of exploration and discovery; but he has to be a prepared explorer who will recognize relevant variations in the terrain when he sees them. Only then will he understand, and only then will he be able to speak to the patient in descriptive or interpretive words that will help the patient understand the pathological processes at work. Precision in interpretation ultimately follows from precision in understanding. Hence, an informed view of development and of specific pathological mechanisms makes possible a refined therapeutic technique.

References

Alexander, F. (1956), *Psychoanalysis and Psychotherapy*. New York: Norton.

Allen, D.W. (1967), Exhibitionistic and voyeuristic conflicts in learning and functioning. *Psychoanal. Quart.*, 36:546–570.

Anthony, E.J. (1971), Folie à deux. *Separation-Individuation*, ed. J.B. McDevitt & C.F. Settlage. New York: International Universities Press, pp. 253–273.

Benjamin, L. (1971), Learning disorders in children. Report to the Fleischman Commission, New York State.

——— & Finkel, W. (1969), Time disorientation in mildly retarded children with sequencing disorder: Diagnosis and treatment. Paper read at American Orthopsychiatric Association Meetings, April.

——— & Green, B.E. (1968), Differential diagnosis and treatment of childhood aphasic disorder: A case study. In: *Learning Disorders*, ed. J. Hellmuth. Vol. 3. Seattle: Special Child Publications, pp. 225–247.

Berlyne, D.E. (1960), *Conflict, Arousal, and Curiosity*. New York: McGraw-Hill.

Blos, P. (1962), *On Adolescence*. Glencoe, Ill.: Free Press.

Bornstein, B. (1951), On latency. *The Psychoanalytic Study of the Child*, 6:279–285. New York: International Universities Press.

Bowlby, J. (1969), *Attachment and Loss: Vol. I. Attachment*. New York: Basic Books.

Ekstein, R. (1966), *Children of Time and Space, of Action and Impulse*. New York: Appleton-Century-Crofts.

——— & Wallerstein, J. (1954), Observations on the psychology of borderline and psychotic children. *The Psychoanalytic Study of the Child*, 9:344–369. New York: International Universities Press.

Fenichel, O. (1945), *The Psychoanalytic Theory of Neurosis*. New York: Norton.

Freud, A. (1956), The assessment of borderline cases. In: *The Writings of Anna Freud*. Vol. 5. New York: International Universities Press, 1969, pp. 301–314.

——— (1965), *Normality and Pathology in Childhood*. New York: International Universities Press.

——— (1970), The symptomatology of childhood. *The Psychoanalytic Study of the Child*, 25:19–41. New York: International Universities Press.

Freud, S. (1905), Three essays on the theory of sexuality. *Standard Edition*, 7:135–243. London: Hogarth Press, 1953.

——— (1912), Recommendations to physicians practising psycho-analysis. *Standard Edition*, 12:111–120. London: Hogarth Press, 1958.

——— (1916), Some character types met with in psycho-analytic work. *Standard Edition*, 14:311–333. London: Hogarth Press, 1957.

——— (1920), Beyond the pleasure principle. *Standard Edition*, 18:7–64. London: Hogarth Press, 1955.

——— (1933), New introductory lectures on psycho-analysis. *Standard Edition*, 22:7–182. London: Hogarth Press, 1964.

Grunebaum, M.G., Hurwitz, I., Prentice, N.M., & Sperry, B.M. (1962), Fathers of sons with primary neurotic learning inhibitions. *Amer. J. Orthopsychiat.*, 32:462–472.

GAP (1966), *Psychopathological Disorders in Childhood*. New York: Group for the Advancement of Psychiatry.

Hartmann, H. (1939), *Ego Psychology and the Problem of Adaptation*. New York: International Universities Press, 1958.

——— (1952), The mutual influences in the development of ego and id. *The Psychoanalytic Study of the Child*, 7:9–30. New York: International Universities Press.

Hendrick, I. (1942), Instinct and the ego during infancy. *Psychoanal. Quart.*, 11:33–58.

Kanner, L. (1942), Autistic disturbances of affective contact. *Nervous Child*, 2:217–250.

——— (1949), Problems of nosology and psychodynamics of early infantile autism. *Amer. J. Orthopsychiat.*, 19:416–426.

Kernberg, O. (1967), Borderline personality organization. *J. Amer. Psychoanal. Assn.*, 15:641–685.

——— (1968), The treatment of patients with borderline personality organization. *Internat. J. Psychoanal.*, 49:600–619.

Knight, R. (1953a), Borderline states. *Bull. Menn. Clin.*, 17:1–12.

——— (1953b), Management and psychotherapy of the borderline schizophrenic patient. *Bull. Menn. Clin.*, 17:139–150.

Mahler, M.S. (1942), Pseudoimbecility. *Psychoanal. Quart.*, 11:149–164.

——— (1952), On child psychosis and schizophrenia. *The Psychoanalytic Study of the Child*, 7:286–305. New York: International Universities Press.

——— (1968), *On Human Symbiosis and the Vicissitudes of Individuation: Vol. I. Infantile Psychosis.* New York: International Universities Press.

——— (1972), On the first three subphases of the separation-individuation process. *Internat. J. Psycho-Anal.*, 53:333–338.

——— Pine, F., & Bergman, A. (1975), *The Psychological Birth of the Human Infant.* New York: Basic Books.

Masterson, J.F. (1972), *Treatment of the Borderline Adolescent: A Developmental Approach.* New York: Wiley.

Mittelmann, B. (1954), Motility in infants, children and adults Patterning and psychodynamics. *The Psychoanalytic Study of the Child*, 9:142–177. New York: International Universities Press.

Newman, C.J., Dember, C.F., & Krug, O. (1973), "He can but he won't": A psychodynamic study of so-called "gifted underachievers." *The Psychoanalytic Study of the Child*, 28:83–130. New Haven: Yale University Press.

Pine, F. (1974a), On the concept "borderline" in children: A clinical essay. *The Psychoanalytic Study of the Child*, 29:341–368. New Haven: Yale University Press.

——— (1974b), Libidinal object constancy: A theoretical note. *Psychoanal. & Contemp. Sci.*, 3:307–313.

——— (1976), On therapeutic change: Perspectives from a parent-child model. *Psychoanal. & Contemp. Sci.*, 5:537–569.

Rapaport, D. (1967), The theory of ego autonomy. In: *Collected Papers of David Rapaport*, ed. M.M. Gill. New York: Basic Books, pp. 722–744.

Redl, F. (1951), Ego disturbances. In: *Childhood Psychopathology*, ed. S.I. Harrison & J.F. McDermott. New York: International Universities Press, 1972, pp. 532–539.

Rosenfeld, S.K., & Sprince, M.P. (1963), An attempt to formulate the meaning of the concept "borderline." *The Psychoanalytic Study of the Child*, 18:603–635. New York: International Universities Press.

——— (1965), Some thoughts on the technical handling of borderline children. *The Psychoanalytic Study of the Child*, 20:495–517. New York: International Universities Press.

Shapiro, D. (1965), *Neurotic Styles.* New York: Basic Books.

Sperry, B.M., Ulrich, D.N., & Staver, N. (1958), The relation of motility to boys' learning problems. *Amer. J. Orthopsychiat.*, 28:640–646.

Spiegel, L.A. (1951), A review of contributions to a psychoanalytic theory of adolescence: Individual aspects. *The Psychoanalytic Study of the Child*, 6:375–393. New York: International Universities Press.

Stone, J., & Church, J. (1973), *Childhood and Adolescence*. New York: Random House.

Weil, A.P. (1953), Certain severe disturbances of ego development in childhood. *The Psychoanalytic Study of the Child*, 8:271–287. New York: International Universities Press.

——— (1956), Certain evidences of deviational development in infancy and early childhood. *The Psychoanalytic Study of the Child*, 11:292–299. New York: International Universities Press.

White, R.W. (1963), *Ego and Reality in Psychoanalytic Theory*. Psychological Issues Monograph 11. New York: International Universities Press.

Winnicott, D.W. (1958), The capacity to be alone. In: *The Maturational Processes and the Facilitating Environment*. New York: International Universities Press, 1965, pp. 29–36.

Youngerman, J. (1979), The syntax of silence. *Internat. Rev. Psycho-Anal.*, 6:283–295.

19

Blanking Out and Speeding Up Under Stress: An Integrative Disorder in Children and Adolescents

REGINALD S. LOURIE, M.D., MED. SC.D.
CHARLES SCHWARZBECK III, PH.D.

In the following, a new clinical entity is suggested, as well as a hypothetical concept that stems from it. This work grew out of an interrupted research project on criteria for pilot selection in the early days of World War II. A completed phase of that project involved measuring eye function in reading on an ophthalmograph under experimentally induced stress (Strongin, 1941).[1] In "normal" subjects it was found that 6 percent had their reading performance improve under tension, while about 25 percent had their eye function become more or less disorganized. At about the same time, Myrtle McGraw (1943) conducted work at the Normal Child Development Laboratory at Babies Hospital in New York that indicated that in early neuromuscular development some babies appeared to show disorganization of movement under stress.

Having been "sensitized" by such experiences, some children seen in consultation by the authors were found to have their thinking or acting become disorganized or interrupted when anxiety-arousing areas were explored. For example, a 14-year-old describing why he had quit baseball began to tell about

[1] In the experimental situation the subject worked a foot bellows while reading in the ophthalmograph, which takes movies of eye movements. A pipe connected to the bellows ran alongside the subject's head; at the end of the pipe a balloon was being inflated, causing the subject increased tension as it approached the point of bursting.

being at bat against a fast-ball pitcher; suddenly he stopped. Asked why, he answered, "I blanked out just like then. First my legs got rubbery and then it happened. It just happened now." This phenomenon ranged from mild and brief episodes to more severe and prolonged responses. In the more severe instances there is "freezing" and immobilization. For example, an infant videotaped while being tested freezes, staring blankly for 3 full minutes, when a tower he has built falls down. In another instance, a 7-year-old girl suddenly becomes immobilized but anxious while drawing a picture of her mother. Asked about this, she says that it also happens on tests, so she fails even when she knows the subject. Others in the interviews become active instead, speeding up their thinking and activity even to the point of hyperactivity. An 8-year-old boy suddenly stops what he is doing when asked about fears and becomes motorically active and distractible, using rapid-fire speech and flitting from one thing to another. In some, such reactions could be aborted by the examiner's intervention, while in others they persisted until the consultation ended or even continued at home or in school.

In clinical interviews with 645 youngsters from middle and upper middle class families (see Table 1), a surprising 164 (24 percent) reported patterns in which their thinking or acting becomes disorganized or speeded up, making it difficult to function coherently for shorter or longer periods. We therefore felt it important to report this phenomenon, despite its coming from purely clinical observation without the scientifically desirable step of establishing interrater reliability on the operational criteria to be discussed later. Perhaps most important, a corrective approach to these problems has been developed and will be described here.

The clinical diagnostic interviews began with direct observation and notation of the type of situation that triggered the disorganizing response in subjects displaying them in the office. Each individual seen in consultation was also asked a direct question about the process: "Some children tell us that when they are nervous or anxious or upset, as when taking a test, when afraid, or when angry, they suddenly can't think; they say it feels like their minds go blank or speed up. Does that ever happen to you? [or: Did I see it just happen to you?]." The 164 youngsters who answered yes were asked, "When and where does it happen? How does it feel and how long does it last, and what (if anything) helps stop it or get it under control?" This information was supplemented by the usual developmental data; family history (including siblings, parents, etc. who are disorganizers); medical background (including neurological studies when indicated); social information; school performance pattern (requiring school visits and teachers' reports, where indicated); and psychological and neuropsychological testing. When all this information was put together, it did not fit the existing etiological categories. Here was a basic problem in the regulation and organization of thought and behavior.

Illustrative Case Vignettes

Case 1

Clint is a 10-year-old boy referred for study because in spite of normal intelligence he had not responded to three years of intensive special education. He had been diagnosed earlier as having minimal brain dysfunction (MBD) with problems in visual discrimination, perceptual-motor functioning, and auditory recall. In addition, he had poor peer relationships, though he knew how to interest adults in him, including his teachers.

Detailed family and developmental history indicated that Clint had had integrative difficulties from his earliest years, beginning with problems in the regulation of sleep, eating, and self-comforting patterns. He also later showed evidence of MBD manifested in perceptual-motor difficulties. He was preoccupied with dependency, his needs for which had long been fulfilled through his presentation of incapacitating headaches. Despite thorough studies, no organic basis had been found for the headaches, which responded only to rest. He had been in psychotherapy twice a week for a year with little benefit.

In our study Clint appeared relieved to relate that when unable to respond to an anxiety-producing situation his "mind went blank," whether he was at school, on the playground, or at home. He had never been asked about this and had never

TABLE 1
Profile of the Group and Diagnostic Categories
A. Profile of Cases

				Most Common Sources of Anxiety						
1	2	3	4	5	6	7	8	9	10	11. Categories of Major Presenting Symptoms. The first numbers refer to the diagnoses listed below in part B. The numbers in parentheses are the number of patients within each diagnostic category.
Ages	N	Early Homeo. Diff.	Early Hyper-sens.	Sept. Anx.	Perst. Neg.	Body Damage Fears	Aggress. Disorders	Oed. Con.	Soft Neuro. Signs	
3	2	2	1	2	2	2	1	4	1	8c(1) 9(1)
4	4	4		4	4	4	1	5	1	25(2) 7a(2)
5	4	3	1	3	4	3	7	10	3	16a(1) 7a(2) 16c(1)
6	10	3		10	3	10	9	12	7	24a(2) 7a(3) 7b(4) 12b(1)
7	16	7		9	8	16	5	6	7	28a(5) 29(4) 16(2) 7a(2) 25(5)
8	7	5	2	6	5	6	6	6	5	7a(2) 30(1) 13(1) 19(2) 1(1)
9	6	6		6	6	5	8	8	3	25(2) 12b(1) 10(1) 3(2)
10	11	8		11	7	11	10	8	3	2(1) 3(3) 26(2) 10(1) 5(2) 28(2)
11	10	6	1	7	10	10	14	12	5	10(2) 12(2) 1(2) 7(4)
12	15	5		12	10	15	7	11	6	23(1) 24(2) 26(2) 13(1) 4(1) 5(4) 7b(4)
13	11	4	1	7	11	11	6	11	3	10(1) 11(2) 27(2) 31(1) 24(4) 2(1)
14	15	6		13	6	12	6	6	6	2(4) 3(3) 17(1) 12(5) 32(2)

15	9	9		9	3	9	6	6	5	25(1) 32(2) 31(1) 17a(1) 12a(3) 20(1)
16	11	5	2	10	4	11	8	8	6	6(1) 13(1) 28(1) 12a(3) 12b(2) 7(1) 1(2)
17	16	12		8	6	13	12	8	6	27(1) 27a(1) 11(2) 4(1) 24(3) 21(2) 3(2) 28(1) 15(1) 16b(2)
18+	17									
Total	164	105	8	116	89	138	100	115	67	

B. Diagnostic Categories in Column 11
(DSM-II diagnoses have been translated into DSM-III classification)

1. Academic adjustment (7)
2. Adjustment disorder (5)
3. Affective disorder (7)
4. Anorexia nervosa (6)
5. Antisocial behavior (5)
6. Anxiety disorder (1)
7. Attention deficit (MBD)
   a. w/hyperactivity (16)
   b. w/o hyperactivity (8)
8. Atypical personality disorder
   a. dissociative disorder
   b. impulse control disorder
   c. pervasive developmental disorder (1)
9. Autism (1)
10. Avoidant disorder (4)
11. Borderline personality disorder
    a. schizotypal disorder (4)
12. Conduct disorder
    a. unsocialized aggressive (9)
    b. non-aggressive (8)
13. Conversion disorder (3)
14. Dependent personality
15. Depersonalization disorder (1)
16. Disorder of impulse control
    a. intermittent explosive (2)
    b. isolated explosive (2)
    c. pyromania (1)
17. Dissociative disorder
    a. depersonalization (2)
18. Enuresis (2)
19. Encopresis (2)
20. Gender identity disorder (1)
21. Identity disorder (2)
22. Language disorder
23. Mutism-elective (1)
24. Anxiety neurosis (11)
25. Overanxious disorder (8)
26. Oppositional disorder (4)
27. Personality disorder
    a. schizoid (3)
28. Phobic disorder
    a. school phobia (6)
29. Psychosomatic disorder (4)
30. Separation anxiety (171)
31. Schizophrenia (171) (4)
32. Substance abuse (4)

told anyone about it; he felt it meant that something was "wrong" with his head. His headaches were the signal for him that his thinking would be interrupted. When this happened, he felt helpless, "like I'm tied in a plastic bag." He described not being able to think as "feeling dumb and defective, the worst feeling in the world."

Further study indicated that both anxiety and stress triggered the blanking out. The sources of anxiety were found to be unresolved aspects of earlier developmental stages in which anxiety is expectable, particularly separation anxiety and fears of body damage. However, the most frequent "triggers" were his poor self-image and lack of self-confidence, reinforced by a high-achieving older brother who missed no opportunity to point out Clint's deficits. After describing his headaches in detail, he was asked, "If there was somebody magic who could change anything in the world and who gave you three wishes, what would you wish?" He wished first to get rid of blanking out, but none of his wishes were to get rid of his headaches.

Clint was brought into an 8-session remedial program in which, at the first sign that a headache was starting, he would stop himself and concentrate on a clown face painted on his thumbnail. After short periods in which he was in control and able voluntarily to stop his thinking, he was directed to go back to the subject or situation which had been about to bring on the "blanking out." When eventually he could negotiate this return without disorganizing, the headaches disappeared. Work with his school led to his being allowed to have his own brief "time outs," following which he returned more successfully to his remedial tasks. Occupational therapy was brought to bear on the identified sensorimotor problems, and family therapy helped to iron out the boy's dependency and self-image problems. A year later, Clint was successfully mainstreamed in school, was participating in sports, and had developed more appropriate social skills.

Case 2

Diana, age 4, was referred for study because in nursery school she often seemed to forget what she was doing in the middle of a task and then appeared "spacy." At such times she might inappropriately recite rhymes while teachers tried to intervene.

In diagnostic therapeutic play interviews, Diana was found to be a bright, well-related, well-developed, and charming girl whose activity, when she was frustrated, angry, or anxious, would be abruptly halted; she could not be diverted or brought back to the activity and often retreated from interpersonal involvement. It was apparent, however, that she did not retreat into a world of her own, but was simply stunned. When one tried to get her back into the here and now, she turned to something familiar (such as a nursery rhyme) in an attempt to reorganize.

History and developmental information, including home movies made when she was 2, disclosed a pattern of "freezing," of suddenly becoming immobilized for a few minutes when irritable. She had slight language delays, motor awkwardness, and a mild auditory processing disorder. Neurological evaluation showed her to be normal except for slight vestibular imbalance and poor fine motor functioning.

These manifestations of basic integrative difficulties, most of which had been largely overcome at home with practice, led experimentally to a tactic whereby the therapist held her gently, yet firmly, whenever she began to have her thinking and action interrupted, and began her irrelevant speech. This was accompanied by reassurance that this would keep her from "feeling lost" and that help for this was available. Over a period of a month, with twice-weekly sessions, she first stopped her initial fighting off of these interventions. Then she began to enjoy them, offering nonverbal expressions of gratitude. Finally, internalizing the control patterns, she was able to take over the holding function, wrapping her arms around herself briefly whenever she felt the start of "freezing." She was then able to return to the activity that had been interrupted. However, shortly after having mastered this process, she regressed. It became evident that she had been projecting onto others, including the therapist, the responsibility for causing her freezing response. This was resolved by repeating the "holding" pattern, as well as by indicating that others were not making it happen and that she could stop it by wrapping her arms around herself.

Case 3

Willie, age 16, was seen in consultation because he had exhausted the resources for emotionally disturbed youngsters in three school systems. His adjustment difficulties had begun at age 5 with hyperactivity and distractible, aggressive, destructive behavior both at school and at home. Large gaps in knowledge handicapped him in his school work in spite of very superior intelligence and five years in special education classes. Yet he was reported to have periods in which he was calmer and more open to help. More recently, in his stormier periods he had made his parents afraid of him, and he had assaulted one of his school principals, for which he was currently on probation in the juvenile court system. For the past two years his social life was concentrated on a group in the drug scene.

Developmental history included a range of difficult regulatory problems with which he had dealt by dominating the household, leaving them with feelngs of helplessness. Yet at the same time he craved closeness. Talking and toilet training were delayed. Separation fears, fears of body damage, and temper tantrums interfered with his adjustment to nursery school. Hyperactivity of significant degree began in kindergarten and was only partially contained with Ritalin, which was continued for ten years, the last five with little or no benefit. General health and physical development were always good. Neurological study and EEG showed nothing abnormal. Psychological testing highlighted difficulties in sustaining attention. He had been in treatment with three different therapists, averaging two years with each. Family therapy was of little help, with his doggedly faithful parents continuing to be frustrated.

Willie was found to have a borderline character structure, with poor self-confidence under his outward braggadocio. He had an underlying depressive core and many dependency needs which he tried to keep out of sight; he couldn't trust that these needs would be understood and met unless he dictated the terms. When integrative functions were explored, however, he eagerly elaborated on how, particularly when he was angry, his mind went blank. "Then I speed up—I can't tell that it's happening until I've done something stupid and then I get depressed. . . . I don't realize that I speed up but I can't help it. It can last from two minutes to an hour." When he sped up motorically he would strike out at any obstacle in order to free himself from the situation. He had turned to drugs and alcohol because they kept him from feeling anger.

In spite of Willie's interest in his new understanding of his speeding-up process, his ability to work on developing self-organizing techniques was severely limited by defensive patterns set up to keep underlying sources of anxiety out of awareness. His first impulsive reaction was to become angry, project the anger onto another object, and then attack it as a danger to himself, a source of anxiety. His mistrust of dependency unless he was in control of it made a therapeutic relationship difficult. The very fact of having a constitutional handicap increased his depression.

Willie was sent to a wilderness camp where we could work closely with the psychiatric consultant. As the program there created more trust in dependency, the counselors would stop him with the first indications of his "speeding up" and debrief him on the spot in order to build up his self-awareness. As he began to allow himself to experience and tolerate anxiety, the consultant was able to help Willie stop himself by concentrating on a "lucky coin" he carried with him (worry beads didn't work). When he could stop his mind and body from racing, he was able to give up making others feel helpless and afraid instead of himself. It took eight months to bring him to a point where he could be considered ready for participation in a combined treatment and academic program in the community, a task he handled with much improved control.

Diagnostic Patterns, Psychopathology, and Developmental Perspective

In the group of 164, there were nine times as many boys as girls. The largest group was in the 7–13 age range (58 percent). The adolescent group made up 36 percent and those between 3 and 6 accounted for 6 percent. Severity of symptoms, surprisingly, did not always reflect the degree or ease of disruption of thinking under stress.

The presenting symptoms of 147 of the youngsters with evidence of interruption of cognitive functions under anxiety or stress fitted into 29 of the diagnostic categories of DSM-III (see Table 1). Diagnoses of anxiety and attention deficit disorders were most frequent. This placed the children involved into that growing group which falls into the cracks between functional and organic problems, yet shows signs of both.

In considering the evolution of the varied symptom patterns with this constitutional base, it is useful to take a developmental perspective. In individuals with a disorder of integrative function under stress or anxiety, it may be that the organizing capacity has been compromised during early stages of development in which anxiety is expectable or when intrapsychic or environmental stress is encountered. Clinically this is evidenced by such biologically based imbalances as poor tolerance of frustration of instinctual wishes, low threshold of tolerance for anxiety, low sublimation potential, and preponderance of regressive over progressive tendencies (Anokhin, 1964). Poor patterns of response established in the interaction with caretakers in the early stages may complicate appropriate resolutions later on. As for the stages in which anxiety is expectable, if separation anxiety does not satisfactorily organize the beginnings of independence because the presence of an integrative disorder occasions preoccupation with dependency, or lack of trust in it, the situation becomes compounded when heightened anxiety occurs in later stages. The defenses which have evolved can be maladaptive. Thus, for example, poor responses to body damage concerns can lead to a lack of self-confidence and difficulty in dealing with aggression.

The vast majority of our clinical sample showed overt or covert preoccupation with dependency and a poor self-concept. The stage of experimenting with primitive aggressive drives, instead of becoming an organizer of coping strategies for dealing with anger, has left many of these children prone to cognitive handicap as regards the formulation of adaptive responses when anger threatens to surface or cannot be avoided. The type and severity of the resulting psychopathology is in part determined by the intensity and type of inner or outer stimuli which interfere with the individual's regulatory processes. Other individual differences which can occasion disorganization should also be considered; these include unresolved special sensitivities (tactile, auditory, vestibular, and visual) and the integrative problems formerly found under the umbrella of MBD.

The type of symptom pattern which results is determined in the main either by the individual's defensive structure or by learned environmental patterns. Thus, those who respond with anxiety states, phobias, panic reactions, conversion and psychophysiological symptoms, or dissociated states (these are seen rarely) make up one group, while conduct and character disorders make up another. As examples of the latter, 6 children in our study attempted to be in better control by developing strict standards of morality and behavior. The former group includes hyperactive individuals like Willie, whose thinking and acting speed up when cognitive functioning is interrupted. At times this condition overlaps with conduct disorders, including the unsocialized aggressive type.

The defenses in almost all our cases were related to a need to deal with a universal feeling of helplessness in the presence of cognitive disorganization or interruption. This feeling was described as being in a fog, falling into a spider web, being made angry, etc., and sometimes took the form of somatic responses and panic states. Two defensive patterns frequently deployed to deal with this helplessness are (1) making others feel helpless instead and (2) controlling people situations. In some individuals, these defenses could be traced back to a stage of negativism in which oppositional behavior, as an organizer of the will, was perpetuated as a means of control. Avoidance and projection were also frequently seen.

In the differential diagnosis of this clinical entity, particularly when it is not confirmed by the patient's own report or by the examiner's observation, one must consider as alternatives, the voluntary defensive interruption of thinking and acting, as in a conscious form of repression, negativism, avoidance, and regression; the involuntary interruption of consciousness, as in petit mal (where the child is unaware of an interruption);

and the involuntary breakdown of thinking or distortion of reality, as in repression, psychotic dissociative states, alexithymia (Nemiah, 1978), transient thought disorder (Clayer, Campbell, and Ross, 1984), and depersonalization. The speeding up response is considered a reactive form of hyperactivity in contrast to constitutionally based hyperactivity, which is usually from birth. These differential considerations may be supplemented by skilled neuropsychological testing and projective psychological testing using Rapaportean techniques of scoring and interpretation. The diagnostic psychological test profile of children who disorganize typically fits a clearly discernible pattern. However, the most definitive confirmation of the breakdown of cognitive function is the individual's description, upon questioning, of what happens and how it feels.

The Concept of a Central Integrative Disorder (CID)

Although a syndrome has been presented here in order to call attention to a clinical entity, we consider this syndrome to be the result of a disorder in the integrative capacity of the individual. The underlying reasons for this attempt to conceptualize a fundamental, constitutionally based deficit in some individuals' integrative capacity stems from the rather large number of syndromes known to result from integrative malfunction. This malfunction often is evident in the earliest years of life, in babies with regulatory difficulties resulting in problems achieving a state of calm. Such imbalances are well known in pediatric practice: problems include some cases of colic (Cooke and Levin, 1968), apnea of infancy (Deykin, Bauman, Kelly, Hsiah, and Shannon, 1984), mild to severe temperature regulatory disorders (including familial dysautinomia), and some vestibular difficulties, as well as early attachment problems, sleep disorders, eating problems, and chronic irritability (Schwarzbeck, 1984b).

The concept of central integrative disorder (CID) provides a broad clinical perspective in which its derivatives should be seen in combination with any other derivatives. Thus, for example, cognitive disruption under anxiety and stress is viewed as potentially influencing a learning disabled child's ability to respond to a remedial program for dyslexia, as overwhelming the beneficial effects of medication in a hyperactive youngster when stress is encountered, or as forming a basis for intractible compulsions or phobias.

In order to diagnose a central integrative disorder for more systematic research efforts, five pathognomonic operating criteria are suggested.

1. Interruption of cognitive function as evidenced by a clear feeling of going "blank" or "losing onself" (the ability to comprehend one's environment is interrupted), by history, by the patient's own reports, or by clinical observation.

2. A clear physical or mental warning signal experienced before the cognitive interruption begins.

3. An early history, from birth on, of problems in maintaining homeostasis (i.e., evidence of ineffective regulatory capacities).

4. Evidence of other areas of difficulty indicating faulty integration in one or more patterns of functioning (learning disabilities, special sensitivities, difficulties in information processing or motor coordination, etc.) which combined with cognitive disorganization make remedial approaches more difficult.

5. Defenses which appear to have originated for the purpose of covering up, avoiding, or compensating for deficits or related self-esteem problems, before such defenses were elaborated into a psychopathological syndrome.

Of these criteria, the first two are necessary to the diagnosis; the remaining three may or may not be present.

In quantitative terms, the intensity of CID patterns and of the stress that triggers them should be noted, i.e., as mild, moderate, or severe.

Discussion

This clinical report, the first to delineate CID and propose it as a diagnostic entity, is meant to call attention to this phenomenon as a useful and possibly necessary component in the evaluation and treatment of children and adolescents. Against this may be argued that most people subjected to severe stress have a point at which their thinking will become disorganized. But the group described here has a much lower trigger point. A CID may begin in infancy and influence subsequent development; if not corrected, it will affect everyday life, interpersonal relations, and self-image. Though known as an isolated phenomenon for many years, its frequent significance as an underlying contributor to developmental deficits and psychopathology has been insufficiently recognized.

In the 1880s, Cambridge dons wrote of students' "examination paralysis." Head (1923) called attention to problems in maintaining vigilance. Goldstein (1942) wrote of a "catastrophic reaction" when brain damage interferes with cognitive functioning. Kohut (1971) implicated interference with thinking under stress as a major determinant in the borderline personality. Thorne (1976) called attention to a similar phenomenon, but not on a clinical basis. From our studies of these processes, it has become clear that they are based on an integrative disorder. Since such integrative deficits are identifiable in the earliest years, it is hypothesized that we are dealing with the unifying concept of a central integrative disorder, of which cognitive disorganization under stress is one of the earliest manifestations (Kohut, 1971). Later on, problems resulting from faulty integration include, for example, the difficulties grouped under the label of MDB. It is not yet clear which structural patterns in the brain are involved. Current research focuses more on the cellular and molecular levels involved, much of it summarized in the annual *Integrative Control Functions of the Brain* (Tsukahara, Kubota, and Yagi, 1982–1984). Significant earlier contributions are Anohkin's *Systemogenesis* (1964) and Montcastle's article in *The Mindful Brain* (1978).

The prevalence of cognitive disorganization under stress, the ability to identify its pathognomonic features even in infancy (Schwarzbeck, 1984b), and its frequency as a demonstrated interference in therapeutic work with the young have influenced our making this report in this preliminary form. This phenomenon is almost never the presenting complaint—it must be sought if it is to be identified. Much of the resistance to therapy seen in these patients occurs because this correctible, constitutionally based integrative disorder is not taken into consideration; they are understandably reluctant to give up defenses without which they would be left helpless in the face of stress, anxiety, or tension.

The corrective approach suggested is based on a method of interrupting the process of disorganization at the first signal that it is starting. It is easier to find methods of control in the first years of life, methods the young can make their own. When caretakers find the approach a particular infant needs, the picture of dependency and trust produced in that child is a positive one. Many develop their own self-calming methods, such as rhythmic patterns, while others need help in calming down, as by being swaddled or rocked, until they can find their own means.

Not infrequently, children over 6 can report awareness of a physical signal (a headache; bladder pressure; "a feeling" in fingers, eyes, or feet; holding one's breath, etc.) when the process is about to start. Such warning signals, some of which are manifestations of defense mechanisms, can be brought into acute awareness so that better methods of control can be developed. At the appearance of such signals the youngster is helped to find a simple technique to interrupt progression of the interruption of cognitive function and to feel in control of it. One simple method is for the youngster to concentrate on a fixed object such as a special coin, a button, a clown picture, or even just a dot on a thumbnail. This serves the purpose of interrupting the impending cognitive disorganization or speeding up. After a few minutes, when control is reestablished, the youngster can return to the task which triggered it.

Such training in control with a youngster who is ready and available can most often be accomplished in 6 to 8 sessions. The principles involved are similar to those of such approaches as biofeedback, meditation training, or cognitive therapy, or to helping an individual learn to create the first stage of hypnosis on his own. The difference here is in having an instantly available control process on the spot when disorganization threatens and before the child feels defeated. Such approaches can also open these children to more traditional forms of therapy.

There have been good results with this corrective approach

in patients who tend to severe disorganization and who make little or no progress in remedial or psychotherapy programs. Often their resistance to treatment is based on reluctance to give up symptoms and defensive positions if all they are left with is the feeling of helplessness and hopelessness the uncorrected disorganization can bring. Once they can feel themselves in control of the integrative disorder, self-defeating defenses can more effectively be reached. This integrative disorder is an important factor to be considered in the treatment of children with severe physical handicaps. When it is a correctable pattern it can be the basis for an enhanced response to other therapeutic and remedial approaches.

References

Anohkin, A. (1964), Systemogenesis. In: *The Developing Brain,* ed. H.W. Himwich. North-Holland: Elsevier, pp. 315–331.

Chalfont, J.C., & Scheffelin, M.A. (1969), *Central Processing Dysfunctions in Children: A Review of Research.* NINDS Monograph No. 9. HEW.

Clayer, J.R., Campbell, R.L., & Ross, M.W. (1984), Parental rearing and transient thought disorder. *Psychopathology,* 17:9–16.

Cooke, R., & Levin, S. (1968), *Biologic Basis for Pediatric Practice.* New York: McGraw-Hill.

Deykin, E., Bauman, M.L., Kelly, D.H., Hsiah, C., & Shannon, D. (1984), Apnea of infancy and subsequent neurologic, cognitive and behavioral status. *Pediatrics,* 73:638–645.

French, T.M. (1952), *The Integration of Behavior,* Vol. 1. Chicago: University of Chicago Press.

Freud, A. (1983), Editorial. *Amer. J. Psychiat.,* 140:12.

Goldstein, K. (1942), *After-Effects of Brain Injuries in War.* New York: Grune & Stratton.

Gottschalk, L.A., Haer, J.L., & Bates, D.E. (1972), Effects of sensory overload on psychological state. *Arch. Gen. Psychiat.,* 27:451–467.

Greenspan, S.I. (1980), Intelligence and adaptation: An integration of psychoanalytic and Piagetian psychology. *Psychological Issues,* Monograph 47/48. New York: International Universities Press.

——— Lourie, R.S., & Nover, R.A. (1978), A developmental approach to the classification of psychopathology in infancy and early childhood. In: *Handbook of Child Psychiatry,* ed. J. Noshpitz. New York: Basic Books, pp. 157–164.

Head, H. (1923), The conception of nervous and mental energy: II. Vigilance: A physiological state of the nervous system. *Brit. J. Physiol.,* 14:126.

Hertzig, M.E., & Walker, H.A. (1975), Infant psychopathological manifestations of integrative disorders. *J. Autism & Child Schizophrenia,* 5:13–22.

Holtzman, P.S. (1978), Cognitive impairment and cognitive stability: Toward a theory of thought disorder. In: *Cognitive Defects in the Development of Mental Illness,* ed. G. Serban. New York: Brunner/Mazel, pp. 210–241.

Kendall, P.C., & Braswell, L. (1984), *Cognitive Behavioral Therapy.* New York: Guilford Press.

Kohut, H. (1971), *The Analysis of the Self.* New York: International Universities Press.

Lourie, R.S. (1971), The first three years of life: An overview of a new frontier of psychiatry. *Amer. J. Psychiat.,* 127:1457–1463.

——— (1981), A central integrative disorder underlying psychopathology. In: *Annual Proceedings of the Society for Neuroscience.* Bethesda, Md.: Society for Neuroscience, p. 45.

——— & Schwarzbeck, C. (1979), When children feel helpless in the face of stress. *Childhood Education,* 56:134–140.

Luria, A.R. (1966), *Higher Cortical Functions in Man.* New York: Basic Books.

McGraw, M.B. (1943), *The Neuromuscular Maturation of the Human Infant.* New York: Columbia University Press.

Marston, W.M. (1941), *Integrative Psychology.* New York: Harcourt, Brace.

Montcastle, V.B. (1978), An organizing principle for cerebral functions: The unit module and the distributed system. In: *The Mindful Brain,* ed. G.M. Edelman & V.B. Montcastle. Cambridge: MIT Press, pp. 1–3.

Nemiah, J.C. (1978), Alexithymia and psychosomatic illness. *J. Continuing Ed. in Psychiat.,* 39:25–27.

Paulson, G.W. (1981), Transient global amnesia. *Postgrad. Med.,* 69:171–176.

Piaget, J. (1937), Principal factors determining intellectual evolution from childhood to adult life. In: *Organization and Pathology of Thought,* ed. D. Rapaport. New York: Columbia University Press, 1951, pp. 154–175.

Schilder, P. (1958), *Medical Psychology.* New York: International Universities Press.

Schwarzbeck, C. (1984a), A central integrative disorder of synthetic functioning underlying complications in learning and psychopathology. In: *Dyslexia Research and Its Application to the Adolescent,* ed. J. Bath, S. Chinn, & D. Knox. Avon, England: Better Books.

——— (1984b), Reactions to stress in 15 day-old neonates: CID reaction. *Clinical Proceedings, CHNMC,* 40:117–128.

Shagass, C., Boemer, R.A., & Amadeo, M. (1976), Eye tracking performance and engagement of attention. *Arch. Gen. Psychiat.,* 33:121–124.

Sherrington, C.S. (1951), *Man on His Nature.* Cambridge: Cambridge University Press.

Strongin, E.I. (1941), Visual efficiency during experimentally induced emotional stress. *J. Psychol.,* 12:3–6.

Taylor, G.J. (1984), Alexithymia: Concept measurement and implications for treatment. *Amer. J. Psychiat.,* 141:725–732.

Thorne, F.C. (1976), A new approach to psychopathology. *J. Clin. Psychol.,* 32:751–761.

Tsukahara, I.M., Kubota, K., Yagi, K., eds. (1982–1984), *Integrative Control Functions of the Brain.* 3 vols. Tokyo: Kodansha.

Weil, A.P. (1978), Maturational variations and genetic-dynamic issues. *J. Amer. Psychoanal. Assn.,* 26:461–491.

20

Psychological Issues in Accidents and Physical Trauma in Children

IRWIN M. MARCUS, M.D.

Severe physical injury has adverse effects on the mind and the personality; thus it is important to understand its consequences for recovery and healthy adjustment in the future. This chapter distinguishes expected or normal responses from pathological ones.

The Accident Problem

At one time physicians believed there was little they could do to prevent accidents, in contrast to what they could do to prevent disease. Then the concept that accidents are not truly "accidental" attracted considerable attention, particularly when it seemed that they happened more often to certain individuals than to others, and with a greater than average regularity within certain groups. If one were to view accidents as we view disease, it might be possible to identify a susceptible person, a motivating situation, and an environment predisposed to that situation. The notion that accidents may have causes aroused great interest in whether prevention might be feasible. The issue became whether the environment could be made safer and the person less susceptible and, finally, whether the triggering mechanisms could be altered.

Portions of this chapter are reprinted with permission of Aspen Publishers, Inc. from Irwin M. Marcus, "Emotional and Psychological Implications of Trauma in Children." In: *Trauma In Children,* edited by Randall E. Marcus, 1986.

We then began to consider the human factor. Toward this end I initiated a multidisciplinary study (Marcus et al., 1960) that was to cover a period of 4 years. A total of 68 children, 63 mothers, and 47 fathers were studied intensively. Our group wondered if these children, who all suffered repeated accidents, could be distinguished on the basis of personality factors and physical and family issues. Further, we wondered if there might exist a particular emotional disturbance always to be found as the basis of repeated accidents, and leading inevitably to them, or if they might arise from a particular disturbance that under other circumstances can lead to different patterns of behavior. Studies in the past frequently suggested that the so-called human factor is more of a problem than are physical hazards. It has long been known that some individuals have accidents even when environmental hazards are minimal. Also, some individuals have multiple accidents in a relatively short time, whereas others in the same environment have none. Statistical findings and clinical studies have suggested that a large percentage of accidents may occur within a relatively small percentage of the population (Jones, 1954). An illustration would be criminal behavior; most criminals are "repeaters" and account for high statistics on crime in a given community.

Against those who believe that there are accident-prone individuals, we argue, as does Schulzinger (1956), that though a group of persons who have a series of accidents may exist, it is in fact a transient group; accident proneness is not a fixed trait of individuals. Given a significant amount of emotional stress, almost any normal individual might temporarily become susceptible to an accident. We believe that a chronic or even a transient stress situation may increase the tension level for a child or an adolescent, thereby causing a shift of the individual toward the accident-prone group.

The children we studied had all had at least three major accidents requiring medical care. It is known that the probability of an individual's having a serious accident tends to diminish with age, as well as with learning and with physiological and psychological maturation. The children who were studied were between the ages of 6 and 11 and all were white. All had at least normal intelligence. Our study showed that the children had excellent motor development and neuromuscular integration. Motor development in the subjects occurred precociously, as evidenced in their sitting up alone and standing at an early age. The children were compared with two other groups, one of enuretic children and one of children with no apparent physical or mental problems.

In general, the "accident children" seemed to have responded to toilet training even earlier than the control group. The accident-prone group's parents reported in general that their children were very active physically from early on. A protective response to this tended to keep the child in the parental bedroom for a longer period than the children in the two other groups. The accident children seemed to show a persistence of sleep disturbances and a greater tendency toward having nightmares and falling out of bed. These children tended to respond to increased tension with increased motor activity. On the basis of these observations, I suggested use of the term *action-prone*. It seemed to me that the action-prone child is more likely to take chances and to act hastily in order to discharge tension. I believe this is a more accurate description of these behavioral patterns than the term *accident-prone*. Healthy individuals tend to be more reality-oriented, to have a capacity to restrain immediate action responses, and to adapt to the environment in a more cautious manner than do the action-prone children in our study. I believe that this concept can be extrapolated to adults. Certain adults under stress have a tremendous impulse to do something physical, whether it be jumping into an automobile when they are angry and driving carelessly, or kicking or punching a wall, door, or chair.

It is my belief that individuals who are action-prone seem to require taking overt action to reestablish equilibrium when they are under stress. Because of this they seem to be much more willing to accept risky behavior and to express their aggression in the form of hostility toward the environment. This type of individual is more likely to dash across the street suddenly, heedless of automobiles, or to scale high objects with no thought of falling. I have heard parents complain of children who climb high into trees or who walk precariously along the edge of a garage.

The results of our study indicate that the enuretic and the control groups seemed better adjusted than the accident group. They had better perceptions of reality, showed lower levels of tension, and had better social adjustment at home and in school. The child who had a tendency toward accidents was often better coordinated and was frequently skillful in athletics. He was able to perform athletic feats with an abandon not seen in more cautious children. As a result, he often distinguished himself in athletic programs but also had many more serious injuries.

The interaction between mother and child is important to the child's ability to learn caution and to feel a sense of security and diminished anxiety. Thus the mothers and children in the enuretic and control groups showed noticeably more mutual affection and acceptance than was evident in the accident group. This lack was noticeable even when the accident group was observed in the waiting room: the mothers and their children seemed to pay very little attention to each other's presence. (An interesting sidelight regarding these mothers was that they had received very little affection they were aware of during their own childhood, and that their own parents were not demonstrative. However, the sexual adjustment in the marriages of all three groups was similar.) With the other two groups, the closeness was quite noticeable; the parents showed a much more positive attitude toward their children, and they were less likely to express overt criticism. They seemed to take a much more active role in supervising their children's schoolwork, and the fathers were more realistic in their attitudes and expectations. The greater emotional distance between mother and child in the action-prone group was thought to contribute to the child's increased anxiety and difficulty in establishing self-control.

Our findings regarding children who suffered repeated serious injuries did not bear out earlier theories of accident proneness. Freud (1901) thought that many accidents were in effect unconscious self-inflicted injuries. Abraham (1927) held similar beliefs, while Menninger (1936) posited the influence of aggression in those who showed a tendency toward accidents. He thought that these accidents were due to aggression being turned unconsciously and self-destructively against the self.

We found accident-prone behavior to be neither "unconscious suicide" nor hostility turned inward. In fact, our action-prone children seemed more submissive than the two other groups, though they released anxiety through aggressive activity. Both the action-prone group and the enuretic group had much more anxiety than did the healthy control group. In fact, there were some similarities between the action-prone children who had accidents and the enuretic children: both seemed to show more anxiety and had home environments in which there was evidence of less harmony and more unhappiness than the healthy control group. The key issue, then, that seemed to distinguish the action-prone children was that they dealt with anxiety through aggressive activity. They were much more likely to discharge anger and anxiety immediately through action than to show a capacity to moderate these feelings. It is the action-prone child's tendency to regress into immature patterns for release of tension that interfere with the thought process and his vision of potential hazards in the environment. In short, he rids himself of tension by immediate impulsive action.

The action-prone child seems to narrow his range of perception and concentrates on a selected aspect of the environment, excluding many of the important factors that may become potential hazards. Thus, by narrowing the perceptive field, the action-prone child can actually place himself in a situation that is dangerous to his body or life. This behavior represents a type of immaturity in personality function and structure. It appears that action-prone individuals are willing to enter into painful or dangerous situations because of their primary need to release tension. An accident happening to them at such moments is more the product of these factors than of any unconscious wish to punish oneself. In fact, the pleasure principle would seem to operate here, despite the fact that the need to discharge tension through immediate action is not inhibited by the need to avoid physical damage or pain; discharge does, after all, allow the child to avoid the unpleasure or psychic pain generated by the tension.

Education in accident prevention is required for these individuals, who must be taught to recognize their stereotyped patterns of handling tension through impulsive activity and to use anticipatory thought processes to suppress their impulsivity. This work should be done by specialists in mental health.

Finally, a few additional factors must be considered: the adult model in the environment, the child's age, and the child's gender.

The notion that accidents are caused by action-prone persons seeking tension release is applicable to adults as well as children and adolescents. For example, more than one-third of fatal accidents involving automobiles occur when the driver is speeding. Moreover, it is the driver rather than environmental conditions that is the primary cause of automobile accidents. According to the National Safety Council (1982) and insurance company records, approximately 85 percent of fatal and nonfatal automobile accidents occur in clear weather, more than three-fourths of these on dry roads. Adults must try to be aware of any tendency toward action proneness in themselves, and must teach caution and safety to their action-prone children.

The most frequent accidents occurring with children under 16 years of age are falls, blows, and collisions; a smaller number involve cutting and piercing injuries. It is known that during adolescence the influence of conscience and self-control is temporarily diminished in the struggle to assert one's independence. With ego integration thus weakened, action-prone behavior may become much more prominent. As we move up from the preadolescent and early adolescent years into middle and late adolescence, there is a marked increase in accidental deaths; finally, as people mature, the tendency toward accidents declines.

Regarding gender differences, statistics show that throughout their lives men are involved in more accidents than are women. These statistics reflect the fact that in our culture aggressive action tends to be inhibited in women, whereas it is encouraged in men. Boys accounted for three of the four childhood cases of railyard amputations reported by Thompson, Boulourdas, and Marcus (1983). Juvenile amputees tend to come from low socioeconomic urban environments and from problematic family backgrounds, and to have a history of behavioral problems. However, consistent with my earlier studies (Marcus, Wilson, Kraft, Swander, Southerland, and Schulhofer,

1960), Cummings and Molnar (1974) found that juvenile amputees tend to show advanced motor activity.

Trauma Phases

In the *initial impact phase,* every effort is made to work out a live-in arrangement for the mother of a young child faced with hospitalization. Young children respond much more adversely to the psychological stress of separation from the parent than to the physical aspects of their trauma. If a live-in arrangement is impossible, the alternative is long and frequent visits by the parents, who should bring the child's favorite toys, stuffed animals, or dolls. Under these circumstances, parents must be reassured that the child's crying when they leave is normal and to be expected.

During this phase, varying degrees of personality disintegration may occur, even in well-adjusted children and their parents. This phase lasts for the duration of the acute stress.

The child subjected to multiple trauma may not only require prolonged hospitalization but may also be subjected to a series of surgical procedures. Naturally, parents must be informed of complications that may result from prolonged immobilization. Physiological reactions to immediate trauma include an increase in vasomotor response, increased secretion of epinephrine and norepinephrine, dilated pupils, an increase in muscle tension, gluconeogenesis, and the release of antidiuretic and adrenocortical steroid hormone. Central nervous system or peripheral neurological problems may be involved. Emboli, thrombophlebitis, and other significant changes, e.g., in the renal or cardiovascular systems, may lead to death. The cardiovascular system is disrupted not only by trauma and the presence of hemorrhaging, which stimulates tachycardia, but also by the patient's anxiety (Chambers and Reiser, 1953; Dunbar, 1954). Thus it is vitally important that the emotional needs of both the patient and the family be considered. A little girl I saw recently had been struck by an automobile while on her bicycle. Her mother felt guilty that she was not available when authorities tried to reach her after the accident. In addition to concerns for the child's life, the possibility that her face might be permanently scarred created considerable anxiety. Actually, this little 9-year-old girl took the injury far better than her parents did.

A quiet environment with people who are reassuring to the patient is essential if the anxiety reaction is to be allayed. When the patient is able to communicate, the medical team should encourage the expression of fears concerning the injury and the procedures to be used. Patients under acute traumatic stress immediately regress and show a loss of emotional control. Although mild stress causes an increase in alertness, the severe stress of a multiple injury causes decreased alertness, numbness, dulling of sensorium, reduced attention span, loss of memory function, and disorganization of thought processes. Behavior becomes automatic or stereotyped. Accordingly, a patient's disorientation or seemingly psychotic behavior need not occasion undue alarm. These are but transient mental reactions to an overwhelming physical situation (hypoxia, anemia, and electrolyte disturbance) and a high level of anxiety. However, if psychotic reactions continue, the possibility of occult intracranial injury must be considered.

Physiological factors created by the patient's emotional environment may exacerbate the medical condition. Likewise, the physical limitations created by the injury may affect the adjustment. It is well known that electrolyte imbalance is enhanced by the stress reaction (Bernstein, 1971). Fluid retention due to electrolyte imbalance places additional stress on the cardiovascular system. Not only do stress reactions enhance sodium and fluid retention; they also promote the loss of potassium and a nitrogen imbalance. This situation in turn feeds back into the impairment of the cardiovascular, neural, and muscular systems. All children with multiple injuries are necessarily limited in their mobility, and this can have a particularly untoward effect if the child happens to be an action-prone individual who relies on activity to diminish stress.

As damage to the child's body parts and functions creates a tremendous sense of insecurity and helplessness regarding the events going on around him, it is of the utmost importance, as soon as the patient is conscious and capable of communicating, that the significant people around him help to reestablish his reality orientation. Temporal orientation is easily lost under conditions of hospitalization. Depending on the extent of the trauma, the patient more or less quickly begins to adapt to the situation. Children and adolescents who frequently release their anxiety via anger may direct their hostility toward the caretaking personnel. Whereas anxiety makes a person feel helpless, anger gives the patient a sense of power; if anger is present in a patient, its ventilation should be tolerated and understood, rather than criticized or inhibited. During the *recoil phase,* emotional expression, self-awareness, memory, and behavioral controls gradually return. The patient's perspective is still limited, and the need for dependency satisfactions continues. The presence of the foregoing indicates the beginning of a reintegration of adaptive function.

Children and adolescents react in a variety of ways to the loss of body parts. Denial of the injury or of the loss is unhealthy. The medical personnel should help the patient differentiate his handicap from the rest of his personality. They can point out that there is an injury to a specific body part, but that the rest of the person is intact—the injury has not affected his mind. In this manner the patient can be helped to correct distortions in his thinking and to integrate the injury into his total personality. This begins the process of the patient's accepting the reality of what has happened.

The *posttraumatic phase* begins when the child shows that orientation, an appropriate sense of self, motor function, and affective controls are reestablished. The communicative child can share the traumatic experience with others and thereby gradually integrate the emotional stress. What was earlier an intense emotional state is now experienced with diminished intensity. One can expect signs of a return to self-confidence in a mentally healthy child.

The persistence beyond several weeks of anxiety, hostility, aggression, nightmares, and withdrawal or depression reflects a pathological residue perhaps associated with an unfavorably altered self-concept. Under these circumstances, psychiatric consultation is warranted.

Medical personnel should emphasize things the individual

will be able to do rather than the limitations he will have, as each patient discovers his limitations soon enough. If the environment responds with a tragic attitude toward the situation, the child identifies with this attitude and thus increases his anxiety and grief concerning his disability. Depressive reactions in the patient may not only be a response to the loss of certain functions or body parts but may also reflect guilt over having been an active participant in the accident, whether in fantasy or in reality.

In general, children tend to view surgical and medical procedures as invasions and as aggressive attacks on their bodies. Parents as well as medical personnel must understand the patient's perception of medical therapy. Whenever possible, the patient should be prepared for any medical procedures to be performed. Similar preparation is necessary for the parents, as they may otherwise develop pathological responses to the personnel caring for their child.

Repeated nightmares regarding the injury or medical treatment is the natural way in which the mind attempts to integrate mental trauma. Nightmares during the recoil phase should therefore not be viewed with alarm. Rather, the physician should allow the child to talk about his disturbing dreams and should help him see that he is having these scary dreams because of the fright he had due to the injury. He can then be assured that in the next few weeks these dreams will go away.

Because the adjustment of the patient depends on his personality and mental attitude, it is of paramount importance that the mental reaction be taken into account from the beginning of his conscious awareness during the impact phase and all through the recoil and posttraumatic phases of the recovery period.

Families must be treated sensitively from the outset as well. Families react very differently to the dangers that threaten themselves and their children. Some families totally collapse and then gradually recover from the news, whereas others show regressive emotions that are uncontrollable and childish. Some of the most difficult reactions occur when parents respond to their own anxiety or guilt with a hostile attack on the physicians, complaining that they are not doing enough. Calm, understanding, but reality-oriented communication to the family is essential.

Parents must always be advised when the possibility of death exists, and the physician must be alert to their reaction to that information. Sudden death due to accident is much more traumatic to the mind than is death due to chronic illness; in the latter instance people can gradually prepare themselves for the loss. Grief that is protracted over a period of months is more easily integrated than is the suddenness of an accidental death or an injury that leaves a child suddenly and permanently disabled. A severe and life-threatening injury to a child is a tremendous assault on the parents' identities as protectors and providers. Damage and loss have an impact not only on the parents but also on the total family situation. Some parents handle the stress by denying the seriousness of the problem or by becoming hyperactive and agitated, while others withdraw and isolate their emotions. If it seems likely that the child will die, most parents anticipate the loss by beginning the mourning process. This can be an unfortunate experience for the child, because in the mourning process the parents tend to withdraw emotionally from the child, with a pessimistic resignation. By contrast, some parents react with a denial of what they hear and see. They cling to a hope that is totally incompatible with the reality of the situation. If besieged by guilt, the parents may accuse themselves of having been bad parents, believing that now they are being punished. Sometimes when a child dies, parents have divorced or separated because they have become withdrawn, irritable, depressed, and angry with one another. Alternatively, there are families in which the wife, shortly after being confronted with the potential loss of a child, becomes pregnant as a means of dealing with the anticipated loss.

Behavioral and Personality Factors

The patient's reaction to severe trauma naturally influences the way medical personnel handle the situation. The child's developmental stage, his ability to cope with stress, the defenses brought into play, the degree of trauma, the family's reaction, and the child's reaction to the injury are all variables.

Developmental position is a factor of great importance. The infant, of course, is totally dependent on the parents and is frightened of people who are not members of the family. Most children cannot handle separation from their mothers until sometime during the third year of life. Then, between ages 3 and 5, children are not only concerned with separation from their parents but are also capable of having fantasies of body damage. Even bright 2-year-olds are very concerned with any marks on their bodies. The older child has fantasies that his injuries will involve mutilation of his genitals. By contrast, the adolescent can use explanations very concretely, can entertain thoughts of the future, and has available a range of defense mechanisms with which to deal with the catastrophe. Nevertheless, severe trauma causes even adolescents to regress; they too become infantile, demanding, dependent, and depressed. Moreover, older children and adolescents have attained a development of conscience that may generate considerable guilt over the injury itself. They may fantasize about the nature of the injury and their role in having caused it.

A child's ability to cope also must be considered. Children considered well adjusted or normal prior to the injury have the capacity to mobilize inner resources in the face of a catastrophe. Children who are friendly within the family and the peer group may be considered to have coping mechanisms. In general, children who have exhibited problems and difficulties in adjustment prior to the trauma may be presumed to have weaker coping mechanisms; severe trauma usually aggravates their preexisting emotional disturbances. The recoil and posttraumatic stages in such cases may be more problematic than usual, with prolonged dependency, demanding behavior, or other signs of neurotic disturbances in evidence. The new situation of severe injury and hospitalization can then become the trigger for severe and prolonged anxiety reactions and other pathological formations. Unfortunately, children who show marked disturbance during the posttraumatic phase are likely to receive little in the way of understanding and consideration from hospital staff, who tend to regard them as headaches.

Normal developmental processes are dramatically interrupted when the child is confronted with sudden and severe trauma. Depending on the damage done to the child, self-esteem and body-image may be impaired. Chronic physical disability plays havoc with the child's self-esteem and stability.

A number of clinical investigations (Hamburg and Adams, 1967; Hackett and Cassem, 1970; Hocking, 1970; Horowitz, 1976) describe responses to severe stress in terms of phases. But from the patient's point of view, these phases are neither discrete nor subtle; marked variations and changes occur even within each phase, as intense emotional responses to a severe traumatic experience cannot be stably organized. The responses of children and adolescents are particularly complex as compared to those of adults, because of developmental differences as regards coping mechanisms and cognitive and emotional responses. The vulnerability of a relatively immature mental structure renders the youngster subject to easy distortions of reality and to a heavy reliance on repetitious responses and denial. The upset in young people may be walled off and repressed, only to reemerge later in life when emotional responses become organized and return to the surface. The grief felt by a child or adolescent over a permanent disability might be denied for a period of years and then become organized into an angry, hostile response later in life. For all of these reasons there are obvious difficulties in generalizing patterns of response as the inevitable consequences of severe trauma.

Nonetheless, the general response to severe trauma in terms of delineated phases is briefly reviewed here; it must be kept in mind, however, that for the young person certain defense mechanisms and phases may dominate the period from impact to recovery, and other phases may be absent or less salient. Young people, of course, initially react to the acute traumatic or *impact phase* with regression, disorganization, irritability, apprehensiveness, startle reactions, hostility, and anxiety responses such as nightmares. Depending on their state of alertness, they may be docile and extremely submissive because of a natural dependency. Thus, this first phase is influenced by helplessness and panic. Crying and screaming is the most dominant feature of the reflex emotional expression of the suddenly traumatized child.

This phase is followed by a *phase of denial.* Denial mechanisms develop very early in life and are most easily called on in times of stress, not only by young people but throughout life. They offer a means of avoiding recognition of the full extent of the injury and an unconscious means of controlling the intense emotional response.

This phase is often interwoven with or followed by a *phase of intrusiveness* of thoughts that cannot be controlled. This instrusiveness in thinking brings about behavioral reenactments of the traumatic event and its implications. It may be manifest in nightmares or in frightening fantasies or images directly or indirectly related to the traumatic event. Intrusiveness and the repetitious thoughts that intrude are mental efforts to gradually digest and integrate traumatic events.

The phases and features described here are interchangeable within the sequence. Thus in the early stages hypervigilance and startle reactions may be shown toward persons approaching or manipulating the child. These reactions may then alternate with periods or denial or numbness, mental mechanisms that blunt perceptions and diminish the significance of what has been experienced. These may be extended to the point of complete amnesia as regards the trauma. At the opposite extreme, intrusive repetitious thoughts and associated nightmares and sleep disturbances interact with attacks of panic, anxiety, anger, and hostility toward those who manipulate the child for medical purposes. In any case, therapeutic efforts must be directed toward helping the child integrate the traumatic experiences by talking or through play therapy; eventually the defensive mental processes can be worked through and the child's personality function restored.

Certain defenses must be contended with in the face of severe injury. The child under 5 years of age has difficulty differentiating between acute disability and chronic, long-term effects, whereas in later childhood and adolescence he is capable of understanding the nature and severity of the impairment. One of the most difficult pathological reactions to contend with occurs when the older child denies what has been explained to him concerning his disability. This situation is further exacerbated if his parents participate in the denial and fail to cooperate in necessary rehabilitative efforts.

It is important that the physician understand that defense mechanisms such as denial operate unconsciously and automatically. One cannot argue with those who use denial mechanisms. The physician must be aware that these defenses exist and that they are used by the patient or his family to avoid anxiety. Only when the source of this anxiety is understood by the patient and the family can these denial mechanisms be lifted.

With young children, play therapy with toys and other equipment can allow the expression of various fears and reactions to the trauma. This process should lead to adequate catharsis of the pent-up emotion and anxiety that have mobilized the defense mechanism. Play therapy can be conducted by properly trained hospital personnel or by psychiatric social workers, psychologists, or psychiatrists.

Family involvement is another variable; it is wise to gain the full cooperation of the parents. It is important that they emotionally and intellectually accept the nature of the child's injury, the expected course of recovery, and the complications or residual incapacity. When families accept the reality of the situation it is often a comfort, because they can then focus on what the child can accomplish despite the handicap. The "normal" parent is capable of tolerating the regression of his injured child, and so the severe trauma need not seriously upset the family equilibrium. The parents will in a very natural way be able to gratify the child's needs and support his recovery. They will discuss their feelings and reactions with each other and support each other in doing what is necessary. A healthy, well-adjusted father is supportive of his wife, and will not react with competitive jealousy when his wife becomes increasingly involved with their seriously ill child.

Nevertheless, it is normal for parents to experience a certain amount of anxiety during the early impact period. Regression, irritability, demandingness, and frightened or depressed reactions are quite normal for parents during the acute traumatic phase. While overprotectiveness by parents during this phase is a normal reaction to a damaged child, the physician can guide the parents and curb any excessive overprotectiveness that might linger on into the recoil and posttraumatic phases.

If the parents are basically disturbed or unstable, they may react unpredictably. They may become severely depressed or unreasonably enraged at a surgeon or at the hospital staff for not miraculously healing their child. Parents normally identify with their children and have a certain amount of narcissistic investment in them. If the child is severely damaged, so is their narcissism, and they may regress intensely. Such parents require thoughtful therapeutic work to help them clarify the nature of the injury and the prognosis, and to guide them back into a more reasonable approach to their own adjustment. Overreactions by parents, such as severe guilt in the event they had any role in the injury, or felt they might have prevented it, may be devastating to the parents' stability. Sometimes it is not only the child who suffers nightmares; the same thing may happen to the parents. Such reactions are clear signs that psychiatric help is indicated.

The physician's reaction to the child's injury must also be examined. The professional staff may have selective emotional reactions, they may experience empathy, or they may react with countertransference. Some surgeons and their staffs prefer to relate to patients and families who are independent, who demand minimal contact, and who handle things their own way. Others prefer patients and families who are gratifyingly dependent, who show their need for reassurance and explanation. Still a third group, admittedly small, feel more comfortable with patients and families who argue, and who challenge and question them.

Physicians are very human and very sensitive to the needs of their patients, and sometimes emotional involvement with a particular patient or family is unavoidable. If the child's injury is life-threatening, the physician may find himself avoiding contact with the patient or family. This is a defense mechanism we must be alert to, as it is precisely the opposite of what is needed. In such situations physicians should become more responsive than usual to the patient and his family.

If the physician reacts in an irrational way, with hostility and rejection, a countertransference has occurred. It is important for the physician in such a situation to understand the basis for this response. Perhaps it has its origin in reactions the physician may have had to a sibling or to his own children. He may be reacting to the patient's parents just as he did toward his own. Certain situations in the life of a physician might revive earlier life experiences and cause him to lose objectivity when handling the patient or the family.

Another variable influencing the handling of the trauma situation is the degree of the trauma itself. Various studies reveal the striking fact that the social and personality adjustment of a patient do not seem to be greatly dependent on the degree of deformity following severe orthopedic trauma. Other variables bearing on the intensity and nature of the patient's reaction have also been studied.

Kammerer (1940) studied 50 hospitalized children with chronic orthopedic disabilities. His method for collecting data included observing the child in the hospital, interviewing the parents and patients, and performing a battery of psychological tests. The duration of the children's handicaps varied from 9 months to 11 years. He concluded that the duration of a handicap is of some importance but that statistical differences did not indicate that duration could be considered significant as regards behavioral adjustment. On the other hand, his findings indicated a significant relation between severity of the handicap and a tendency toward poor behavioral adjustment. Severe orthopedic injuries, including a chronic disability, apparently do not affect the child's intellectual function. Among children who showed good adjustment, this did not appear to be in any significant way related to chronological age or type of disability. It is evident from his studies that when parents were overprotective and overindulgent toward the disabled child the child showed evidence of greater behavioral disturbance.

Despite severe physical disability, children desire to maintain friendships, to participate in age-appropriate games within their limitations, and in general to grow up and get on with their lives. Available data do not support the Adlerian concept that orthopedic disabilities intensify feelings of inferiority or weakness and occasion compensatory movements toward power-driven behavior. On the contrary, no significant differences from the normal are apparent in terms of the interest shown by these children in such activities as reading, music, drawing, or sports.

One can see that a crippling injury does not necessarily or in itself create a maladjustment in the child. Rather, the disability involves a variety of other problems with which the child must deal, notably the degree to which the child's function is impaired and the outer cosmetic appearance.

This impression is consistent with a study by Gates (1942) of 18 crippled boys and girls. This study examined a variety of orthopedic disabilities, including orthopedic injuries in children with cardiac defects. The study indicated that the child's interpersonal relationships at home, as well as the cultural background, seemed to have more bearing on the type of personality or behavioral change effected than did the crippling injury itself. Along these lines, a study conducted by Nagge and Sayler (1933) of 144 physically disabled students in a special school used a control group of healthy children and found no significant differences. In addition, no correlation was found between duration of the chronic disability and a tendency toward introversion.

In a study of 100 women with a variety of severe disabilities, including orthopedic impairment, Landis and Bolles (1940) found a remarkable similarity in the responses across different disability groups. However, those whose disability occurred before the age of 4 manifested about three times as much dependency on their parents as did those whose disability was of later onset. There was about an equal amount of self-centeredness, but when dependency feelings were compared with degree of disability there was no clear relation. The subjects ranged from teenage to early adulthood.

For individuals faced with a severe handicap, personality adjustment is of course influenced by the fact that certain types of social and physical activity may be limited. In that respect, the handicap becomes a source of frustration. One of the healthier responses by individuals with severe handicaps due to trauma is finding substitutions that allow them to express themselves in ways that bypass the disability. Individuals with higher intelligence who are still young enough to be flexible in their adaptations can adjust very well in this manner. Children and adolescents who come from rather secure homes and who have only mild cosmetic defects may adjust quite well to incapacity, and even to an extreme handicap, by sublimating their activity into educational pursuits. Ambition and a desire for self-improvement often contribute to superior personality adjustment.

Severely injured adolescents who show markedly pathological responses should definitely be referred to a specialist in the personality field. These compensatory reactions may be paranoid responses with projections of feelings of inadequacy onto others, or they may be severe emotional upsets and depressions entailing a pessimistic view of the future. Adolescents who respond with general hostility are much more of a problem than those who compensate with competitive reactions and by substituting for aggressiveness through the educational process.

The influence of a handicap on sexual development was addressed by Landis and Bolles (1940). Their study of physically disabled women found that the women tended to show hyposexuality, almost to the extent of asexuality, and greater dependence on their families. Even though they decreased their heterosexual interest, there was no increase in homosexual attitudes or behavior.

One final variable must be considered in relation to patients' behavior: gender differences. If one may generalize, there seems to be a tendency among boys who receive their injuries during early adolescence to be much more aggressive in their attitudes toward themselves and their handicap and angrier and more negative about their disability. Girls show a similarly angry response if their disability has its onset later on in adolescence but seem in general more readily able to accept their disability.

Social Attitudes Toward Physical Disability

The attitudes of others, particularly parents, toward a child or adolescent who has experienced severe orthopedic trauma is a significant influence on his behavior. The harmful responses of parents were identified in a study by Allen and

Pearson (1928): (1) parents with very inconsistent attitudes who provide necessary care for the child but are resentful because of the burden placed on them; (2) parents who openly reject the child; and (3) parents who are overprotective.

The most desirable behavior toward the injured child, of course, is to show a realistic acceptance of the limitations brought about by the injury, to give necessary loving care and security, and not to encourage a high degree of emotional dependency on the parent. This behavior includes helping the child develop realistic goals, understand his physical and mental condition, and design a proper education program. This recommendation is consistent with previous studies: Kammerer (1940) found children to be less well adjusted if they were indulged and overprotected; Landis and Bolles (1940) found that of women with severe handicaps about 23 percent tended to be overly dependent on their families; and Meng concluded that the family environment of a severely disabled child was of marked importance (Barker, Wright, and Gonick, 1946).

One can see then that it is not the physical impairment as such that brings about distortions in personality, but rather the manner in which the environment responds to the patient. Both indulgence and its opposite—neglect—can be markedly pathogenic. It is important that parents be given a thorough understanding of the physical and emotional requirements of a child or adolescent who has been severely traumatized and who may have some degree of orthopedic disability later on. It is very important that adults realize that if a child has a physical disability due to severe trauma this in no way indicates that his personality has been equally altered. They should know, too, that strong parental favoritism toward a disabled child can have an adverse effect on other children in the family, thus altering intrafamily relationships.

The attitudes of parents who have in some way been complicit in their child's injury present a special situation. These parents often have severe feelings of guilt and responsibility, which tend to contribute to parental overindulgence and overprotection of the child.

Cultural differences in attitudes toward severely handicapped people range from those who are respectful, affectionate, and admiring of a good adjustment to physical impairment to those whose superstitious attitudes have been handed down through the ages; the latter may believe that physical deformity is a punishment for evil, an attitude depicted in *The Hunchback of Notre Dame*.

Conclusion

Certain approaches should come into play during the initial stages following a traumatic injury. Supportive care is modified according to the child's developmental phase and degree of injury. It is necessary to understand the patient's mental state, to recognize the need to provide therapeutic answers to allay the prevalent anxiety, and to plan for future adaptation. The medical team should be oriented toward *listening* to the patient's concerns about what has happened and what will happen in the near future. Information gleaned from them helps the therapeutic team see things more clearly and renders them truly capable of empathic and helpful responses.

Patients of all ages and all degrees of injury need to feel trust and an effective rapport with their caretakers in order to cooperate in achieving their goal of recovery, both mental and physical. Moreover, they must be helped to realize that attention to their mental attitude is part of their total medical care.

Two special situations must be considered. One is that of the patient whose personality problems exceed expectations for the degree of injury incurred: unmanageable behavioral problems or severe withdrawal and depression. Here the physician should consult mental health professionals who are qualified in child care (a psychiatric social worker, a child psychologist, or a child psychiatrist). A variety of psychological tests and interviewing techniques may be employed to evaluate the problem and institute therapeutic counseling and treatment.

The second special situation is that of the patient who will be left with a permanent handicap. It is especially important that efforts be made to prepare this individual to live in a manner that provides substitutions and sublimations for the physical limitation. When a prosthesis is necessary, the focus should be on its usefulness so as to forestall the patient's balking at its aesthetic deficiencies. Participation in group therapy can prepare a patient with a physical deformity to handle social reactions to his condition.

Finally, it should be stressed once again that it is essential in this work that the patient's attitudes and adjustments be given as high a priority as is his physical recovery.

References

Abraham, K. (1927), *Selected Papers on Psycho-Analysis.* London: Hogarth Press.

Allen, F.H., & Pearson, G.H.J. (1928), The emotional problems of the physically handicapped child. *Med. Psychol.,* 8:212–235.

Barker, R.G., Wright, B.A., & Gonick, M.R. (1946), *Adjustment to Physical Handicap and Illness: A Survey of the Social Psychology of Physique and Disability.* New York: Social Science Research Council.

Bernstein, I.A., ed. (1971), *Biochemical Responses to Environmental Stress.* New York: Plenum.

Chambers, W.N., & Reiser, M.F. (1953), Emotional stress in the precipitation of congestive heart failure. *Psychosom. Med.,* 15:38–60.

Cummings, V., & Molnar, G. (1974), Traumatic amputations in children resulting from "train–electric-burn" injuries: A social-environmental syndrome? *Arch. Phys. Med. Rehabil.,* 55:71–73.

Dunbar, F. (1954), *Emotions and Bodily Changes.* New York: Columbia University Press.

Freud, S. (1901), The psychopathology of everyday life. *Standard Edition,* 6:1–279. London: Hogarth Press, 1960.

Gates, M.F. (1942), A comparative study of some prroblems of social and emotional adjustment of crippled and non-crippled girls and boys. Masters thesis, University of Wisconsin.

Gratz, R.R. (1979), Accidental injury in childhood: A literature review on pediatric trauma. *J. Trauma,* 19:551–555.

Hackett, T., & Cassem, N. (1970), Psychological reactions to life threatening illness: Acute mental illness. In: *Psychological Aspects of Stress,* ed. H. Abram. Springfield, Ill.: Charles C Thomas.

Halsey, M.N., & Joliet, P.V., ed. (1961), Home safety. In: *Accident Prevention: The Role of Physicians and Public Health Workers.* New York: McGraw-Hill, pp. 93–116.

Hamburg, D., & Adams, J.E. (1967), A perspective on coping behavior, seeking, and utilizing information in major transitions. *Arch. Gen. Psychiat.,* 17:277–284.

Hocking, F. (1970), Extreme environmental stress and its significance for psychopathology. *Amer. J. Psychother.,* 24:4–26.

Horowitz, M.J. (1976), *Stress Response Syndromes.* New York: Aronson.

Jones, E.R. (1954), A Study of accident proneness with special reference to aircraft Accidents. Masters thesis, Washington University, St. Louis.

Kammerer, R.C. (1940), An exploratory study of crippled children. *Psychol. Rev.*, 4:47–100.

Kiefer, N.C. (1973), Accidents: The foremost problem in preventive medicine. *Prev. Med.*, 2:106–122.

Landis, C., & Bolles, M.M. (1940), *Sex in Development.* New York, Hoeber.

Marcus, I.M., Wilson, W., Kraft, I., Swander, D., Southerland, F., & Schulhofer, E. (1960), An interdisciplinary approach to accident patterns in children. *Monograph of the Society for Research in Child Development*, 76. Yellow Springs, Oh.: Antioch Press.

Menninger, K.A. (1936), Purposive accidents as an expression of self-destructive tendencies. *Internat. J. Psycho-Anal.*, 17:6–16.

Nagge, J.W., & Sayler, R.H. (1933), Physical deficiency and extroversion-introversion. *J. Social Psychol.*, 4:239–244.

National Safety Council, (1982), *Accident Facts.* Chicago: National Safety Council.

Schulzinger, M.S. (1956), *The Accident Syndrome.* Springfield, Ill.: Charles C Thomas.

Suchman, E.A., & Scherzer, A.L. (1960), *Current Research in Childhood Accidents.* New York: Association for the Aid of Crippled Children.

Thompson, G.H., Bolourdas, G.M., & Marcus, R.E. (1983), Railyard amputations in children. *Pediat. Orthoped.*, 3:443–448.

21

Hypersensitivity and Insensitivity: Allergic Disposition and Developmental Disturbance

HAROLD P. BLUM, M.D.

Infantile allergy, given the frequency of its occurrence and its developmental implications, is a subject deserving of further psychoanalytic study. Allergy can be constitutional and inherited, with familial determinants and multiple symptoms, periods of remission and exacerbation, local or systemic involvement of mild to severe intensity, and acute as well as chronic complications. Allergy may be a determinant of psychological disturbance, which may in turn precipitate, perpetuate, or aggravate allergic attack. The allergic disposition is protean; in its various manifestations it may influence all phases of development. An infantile allergic syndrome raises complex analytic questions concerning pathogenesis, repetition, developmental transformation, and reconstruction. Sequelae may involve any area of the personality. The emphasis here is on developmental interference, and on narcissistic and affective disorders.

Many patients have a history of eczema of variable duration, severity, and association with other allergic phenomena. I shall discuss the instructive analysis of one such patient with an allergic disposition particularly manifest in attacks of eczema and mild rhinitis. The eczema probably began in the first month of life, with a presumed allergic reaction to her formula. The allergies persisted and recurred throughout development and were major factors straining and disturbing development and contributing to the form and content of the infantile neurosis. The repetitive allergic reactions were associated with recurrent infantile conflicts, with major affective disorder and multiple impairments and inhibitions, including severe narcissistic hypersensitivity and emotional insensitivity. The patient was not the type of patient who usually seeks analysis; not psychologically minded, she was inhibited in curiosity and indisposed to think in terms of a long-range, intensive analytic treatment with distant goals. There was, however, a definite sense of relatedness and affective resonance.

She began analysis in her mid-thirties, presenting with clinical depression manifested in insomnia, appetite disturbance with some weight loss, an inability to concentrate or meet responsibilities, and a feeling that she could not respond to requests, answer telephone calls, or organize her household. She tended to scratch her face, at times during sleep, and was worried about her self-image and the damage to her appearance. The skin problem was related, she felt, to her childhood eczema, which had been severe for her first three years, less frequent and intense during the next two, and occasionally recurrent thereafter. There was a family history of allergies, and, though she stressed the constitutional factor, the patient was aware that emotional stress may trigger allergic reactions. Subject to atopic dermatitis, she was wary of contact allergens and of spicy foods; she also reported a "sensitive stomach." Anything she touched, breathed, or ate could be a threat, unconsciously animated in fantasies of a threatening object world. Although vigilant, she tended to be depressed and detached rather than paranoid in response to stress and feelings of injury. Her facial expression was characterized by a rather drawn look that faded into subdued sadness. Her emotions were generally subdued, and constricted, but she could recognize and express differentiated affects. Rather stereotyped remarks were offered about her relationships with her family. Surprisingly, for a southern woman of her particular academic subculture, she seemed little concerned with intellectual or cultural pursuits. She was unaware of jealousy of her brothers and of their academic and professional careers. She was frightened of her depression, her facial scratching, and her depressive, depressing inability to function.

The onset of her current depression was precipitated by

parenthood. Her only child, a daughter then 1 year old, had been wanted and long awaited, but received with no great enthusiasm on arrival. The patient had tendencies toward the "postpartum blues" and felt that her functioning had declined throughout the first year of her baby's life. There was affection, but also worry about her relationship with the baby; her excitement in playing with the baby or in observing developmental advances was diminished. She emphasized family values, how much she invested in cleaning and arranging the house, and how much she now needed the support of her family. In effect, she wished the family was available to help mother her and the baby. In the initial interviews prior to beginning analysis, her isolation of feelings and thoughts was readily evident. When not pressed, she was inclined to superficial and impersonal discourse, preferring to discuss petty household details rather than interactions with people. At times her empathic communication seemed blocked. But there was never any indication of loss of cohesion, logic, or reality, or of inappropriate affect. She searched for outside direction, regularly sought the analyst's approval or disapproval, and searched for cues evincing the analyst's preferences or judgments; she avoided spontaneity and free association. It became clear that for her emotional contact was a dangerous prospect involving a fear of losing control. She readily regressed to passive dependence, or withdrawal at once clinging and resentful. In the early phase of analysis, she often transiently retreated into silence while lying rigid and relatively immobile on the couch. She struggled against free association and interpretation. She was angry at times but could express little hostility, and the notion of death wishes against the analyst and members of her family was beyond her conscious imagination.

Extensive discussion of her isolation of affect and thought, her inhibition to touch on sensitive issues and emotionally significant areas, and her feeling itchy and sensitive to being touched shed light on her skin disorder. The eczema tended to appear primarily on her face, and secondarily on neck, elbows, knees, and hands. The skin would not feel quite right, and was easily irritated and discolored. Itching and scratching were recurrent in adolesence and adult life, usually when she was drowsy or asleep, and not necessarily in association with overt eczema. The itch could be premonitory to, concomitant with, or a consequence of the atopic dermatitis. Her scratching was consciously experienced as relatively painless. If she did feel pain on scratching it was experienced as less unpleasant than the intense itch it replaced. This itch-scratch-pain sequence was linked to paradoxical relief and gratification, as well as to injury and punishment. The itching was not remembered as intractable, and had greatly diminished by the time she began school.

The allergic phenomena, and the associated itching and scratching, were interwoven into a constellation of somatic and psychosomatic disorders, conversion symptoms, and self-injurious actions related to unconscious conflicts and overdetermined compromise formations (Rangell, 1959). The allergic disorder preceded conflict, and the preverbal disturbance probably contributed to dysphoric tendencies having a neurobiological substructure (Weil, 1985). Such disturbances, occurring during earliest infancy and proceeding through the formation and consolidation of psychic structure, are likely to affect many aspects of later personality organization and function. The allergic attacks and chronic eczema doubtless constituted repeated and cumulative trauma, occasioning pathogenic strain, exacerbated conflict, and both regressive and aggressive reactions. The physical illness, maternal care, and medical treatment so often mediated through the mother had complex psychological consequences for both child and parents (A. Freud, 1952). The somatization acquired secondary symbolic meanings superimposed on the relatively undifferentiated and prerepresentational psyche-soma, ego-id matrix (Schur, 1955). It may be noted that we have much to learn concerning the later fate of infantile sensorimotor and affective patterns, their symbolic representation and transformation, and their translation into the sphere of verbalization.

The patient's relative bodily rigidity and inhibited hand movements led to questions of internal and external restraint. Her mother confirmed that on doctor's orders her daughter's hands had been tied to prevent scratching; this probably occurred in her second year. The dermatitis waxed and waned, with a week's hospitalization during the third year of life for observation and tests. By then she had been subjected to physical restraint, dietary restriction and manipulation, and external and internal medication.

The allergic syndrome was constitutionally based, but was also influenced by the surround, including objects, climate, and season. Interestingly, the analysis resumed each year in September, following vacation and a new outbreak of allergic symptoms, as this is the season for hay fever and rhinitis. The patient's symptoms also intensified premenstrually and during her period. She tended to blush and had wondered, as a teenager, if a mild acne did not announce her period to her family and peers. Attacks of rhinitis with congestion, sneezing, red and tearing eyes, and itching of eyelids was common, often disrupting sleep. During an episode of severe regression, this patient imagined herself covered with a skin of potato chips. She had not been feeding or otherwise attending to her family, had little appetite for anything, and picked at her food. When I remarked on the potato-chip skin image, she recalled certain scaly feelings and peculiarities of temperature, pressure, and touch and was able to recognize that she was picking at both her food and her skin. She wanted to be in the chips—to have all the oral-phallic chips for herself. Her husband's career conflicts and fantasies of returning to a life of southern comfort converged with her own inner conflicts. The onset of her depression meant that she was being flayed, her skin and insulation taken from her. She could not save her own skin, her security blanket.

Following colds, asthmatic tendencies may have contributed toward bronchitis. It should be emphasized that the experience of allergic reactions during childhood may have been much more distressing for the patient than she consciously recalls. The effect of the allergic syndrome could readily be seen in the transference. Following an allergic reaction the patient was clinging and whining, passively dependent, and lethargic. She would become needy and greedy, intolerant of frustration. The analyst's silence was a void, and she craved intervention, explanation, and direction; alternatively, she would withdraw into a protective and resentful reticence. Separations were more threatening than usual, and the patient was chronically anxious and angry. She was deeply ambivalent toward her family, particularly her increasingly assertive infant daughter. Her parents, living afar, were ambivalently and inconsistently supportive and complained of travel hardships to visit their expanded family. But even as she complained of this, the patient, herself conflicted over nurturance and her own oral demands, could not tolerate close emotional or physical contact. During periods of severe depression it was necessary for mother surrogates to undertake some of the baby's feedings, as the patient required more time and attention for herself. The early dreams and daydreams she reported featured themes of generosity and withholding, affluence and indigence, clinging and separation. A recurrent dream of a dress with a long, transparent scarf and of being denuded held a range of meanings, and her associations were replete with metaphorical references to the skin and similar surfaces. Yet it was initially difficult for this patient to understand metaphor and to follow abstract analytic interpretation. For example, she did not easily grasp the connections between being touchy, speaking of ticklish matters, and "scratching the surface," or between not being allowed to touch her skin, her sexual organs, and certain forbidden subjects. Her thinking was not really concrete, but her capacity for abstraction and for the expression of complex affects was either inhibited or impaired.

She had hidden from herself and from me both the fact of her family wealth and her distrust of her "mercenary analyst with sticky fingers." Her parents were modest, reticent, secretive. Southern aristocrats, they had concealed their affluence and their political influence. Her father, described as a benign student of ancient philosophy, and the patient confused magic with medicine. The theme of repair and restitution through magic and mysticism influenced the transference. Her mother could be critical of her father, as also of anything less than the patient's very proper, very regulated behavior. She had insisted on high standards of cleanliness, had forbidden the touching of valuable and fragile objects in the house, and was protective of furniture that might be scratched. The patient herself imposed many stringent prohibitions in her home, including very strict standards of cleanliness for the children, covers for furniture and rugs, and almost restrictive provisions for the use of her beautiful living room chairs. As her defenses loosened, she gradually became more permissive, toward both herself and the family, and her husband noticed that analysis was having a favorable effect in terms of lifting her depression and allowing her to be lighter and brighter in spirit, more tolerant of play and regressive behavior. More of her personality strengths and former interests reappeared. Her self-denigration was gradually muted, though she continued with some self-effacement and self-reproach. In the somatic realm, her self-inflicted excoriations still occasionally occurred, especially in relation to her periods, unwelcome interpretations, and times of billing or separation. She kept her fingernails cut very short, but tended to bite them, as well as her cuticles, although she had stopped picking her nose, which now was less itchy and congested.

Comparing me with an analyst who had business interests with his patients, she tested the waters for possible financial or romantic manipulation in the transference. When she realized that I would not relinquish the analytic positions, I became an "untouchable," like the patient. The patient had concretely "untouchable" skin, and I was metaphorically untouchable, immune to bribery. After a defensive idealization of the incorruptible and unperturbable object, her underlying resentment returned. She then picked on me, on herself, and on her husband, gradually realizing that she was tearing us down, and was "scratching" us. The "untouchable" label referred both to the maintenance of impulse control and moral values, as exemplified in not rubbing and scratching (masturbation) or stealing, and to the anal devaluation of doctors who were filthy rich. Transference attacks on my competence and consistency began more and more to center on issues of mutilation and castration. After a series of insults she would picture me as mutilated and bloody. She associated to her nosebleeds, to bleeding, weepy skin, and finally to menstruation. There were nightmarish dreams of picking at the skin on her abdomen, leaving gaping, bleeding holes. She had the fantasy that she had castrated herself during masturbation and also that she had been castrated as a punishment for it; this was reinforced by the tying of her hands and the disapproving, restraining attitudes of her mother. At the same time she had a fantasied hidden female phallus, a symbol of power and influence. The long sash which hung from her dress was both a security blanket and an aggressive phallic whip. She unconsciously held the whip hand over her husband, identifying with the phallic mother she felt dominated her household.

What kind of child had she been? Analytic reconstruction revealed a very sensitive and anxious child, difficult to comfort because of the eczema and other allergies. The itchy child was both self-absorbed and excessively demanding, and in response her mother had become apprehensive, overprotective, and overcontrolling. Her baby's allergy had hypersensitized the mother in some areas and deformed the mother-child relationship in others. Parental and sibling tensions were increased. Rebuffed in her efforts to comfort and soothe, she seemed to have compensated through auditory-verbal contact with her infant. Separations were experienced as dangerous both by the beleaguered little girl and by her anxious mother, who worried that her daughter would not be handled or comforted properly by a maid or babysitter. The patient was a "difficult," wriggly child, clinging and then pushing away, demanding to be picked up and then either disappointed or irritated by the very contact. Oversensitive not only to touch but to other forms of stimulation, she cried and fussed, both wanting and opposing the maternal ministrations. The same pattern was seen in her scratching, which both relieved the itching and intensified the skin disorder, thereby increasing the itching. The allergy had overtaxed the mother and child relationship, at times probably leaving both depleted and exhausted.

A rather willful child in her second year, by her third and fourth she was timid, rather compliant and conforming, perhaps passively manipulative, and lacking effervescence or great interest in play or exploration. In latency she was a quiet and conforming little girl, too well-behaved and serious, but in adolescence she could "let her hair down" with the permission of friends and other peers. She thought she had had a basically warm and friendly relationship with her siblings, but transference jealousy of other patients, as well as a recurrent dream image, indicated long-standing problems related to the arrival of her younger sibling. In one mirror dream she looks and sees not her own face but that of her sibling. Upstaged by her younger sibling's arrival, she had wanted to obliterate the newcomer's identity while simultaneously identifying with this child she regarded as favored, as having replaced her in their mother's affection. The attacks she inflicted on her own face were punishment for having wanted to attack this "betraying" mother, and for having wanted to efface and destroy her younger sibling rival. Her own identity was both defined and eradicated as she negotiated separation-individuation complicated by her sibling's birth, by regression, and by heightened pregenital aggression. The 1-week hospitalization for study of the allergic syndrome had apparently occurred within months of her sibling's birth, and the eczema was intermittently severe and generalized. At the same time—and continuing into the oedipal phase—the patient identified with both parents, both in their parenting roles and in the primal scene. The allergic disorder, particularly the eczema (and the itching, scratching, and bleeding associated with it) had left her feeling damaged, deprived, and defaced. She saw women as damaged and castrated and entertained compensatory fantasies of phallic grandeur.

The insults of life, expressions of ordinary disapproval, and the hypercritical attitudes of her mother, who sometimes chastized the patient for her disorderly house, were too much for her. She felt she needed to be better insulated. She had no protective hide. In common parlance, she was too thin-skinned and hypersensitive, though at the same time she was too thick-skinned and unempathic. Her insensitivity, which defended against her hypersensitivity in certain areas, was also rooted in an infantile adaptation to the allergic syndrome and chronic eczema. As allergic symptoms were recurrent and came often without warning, barriers to overstimulation and affect storms had vigilantly to be maintained. Early traumatic experience could be reactivated and validated by allergic attacks in later life. Surmounting a more generalized ego constriction, her insensitivity did not extend to all areas of her personality, and was reciprocal to her object-related hypersensitivity. She could be relatively sensitive to the feelings of others, though hypersensitive to their feelings toward her.

As analysis progressed her associations became freer, and she could be more attuned to the analytic work, better able to utilize interpretations and understand metaphor. She did not spontaneously generalize but could benefit from my synthesis of her isolated thoughts and affects. She could now refer to herself as soft-shelled and crabby. Early dreams of novocaine injections and emotional numbing could now be integrated with the patient's expanding self-knowledge. Whereas previously she had lamented her lot and tended to blame her husband and her parents for their failures, now she saw herself as rather selfish, self-centered, and withholding of affection. Her sexual fantasies came into the analysis, and she began to relate her marital problems to her inner conflicts. She had always been sexually inhibited and relatively frigid. She preferred her husband's penis rubbing against her clitoris to being penetrated, and had wished that she could be more interested in her husband's pleasure or emotional fulfillment. She suffered from vaginismus, which made penetration difficult and sometimes impossible. She fought her husband "every inch of the way" and struggled with conflicts about his being "under her skin." Her problems with close contact, holding, and sensitivity interfered with the intimacy and relaxation she consciously desired. She realized that these conflicts also affected her mothering, and her receptivity to the analytic work and her willingness to listen and learn. Contrasting husband and analyst, Christian and Jew, she knew her husband was uncircumcised. She fantasied that a Jew's missing foreskin must represent a conflicted identity: both a skin lesion and a mastery of loss. These reactions disguised and represented unconscious incest and castration conflict—the patient's husband (and analyst) representing her father, and her own damaged self. Identifying with the comforter, with maternal and medical care, she could soothe the injured partner and heal the damage. Her identification with the comforter was indicative of her having experienced "good enough mothering" and soothing support. But in the area of her psychopathology she identified primarily with the victim. She needed to suffer oedipal defeat and humiliation; she could not permit herself to compete with her mother or attempt to engage her remote father. She had been too dependent on her mother to risk any expression of rivalry, jealousy, and rage. These oedipal conflicts, however, condensed the preoedipal sadomasochistic conflicts expressed in the fantasy of a denuded organ—excoriated skin and foreskin—and in oral aggressive assault.

Before analysis sexual relations had been very infrequent, and fantasies were generally forbidden. She now acknowledged affection and attachment felt toward the analyst, occasional romantic-erotic thoughts about him, and greater tolerance for her own sexual interests and those of her husband. She was embarrassed by the songs that at times ran through her head during intercourse, and then became curious about their meaning. These songs included commercial jingles such as "Fly the Friendly Skies of United" and the Schaefer beer ditty, "When You're Having More Than One." But she was particularly embarrassed and excited by the chorus "Glory, glory, hallelujah," which was also a response to ideas of termination. She felt deeply moved and touched by this stirring song. First struggling to recall that this was the chorus from "The Battle Hymn of the Republic," she was then flustered by its references to her childhood Christian themes as well as to war. She reacted with both dismay and humor when she realized that the first line of the song was "Mine eyes have seen the glory of the coming of the Lord." Sexual intimacy and contact was also a call to battle, and threatened castration, mutilation, and subjugation or, alternatively, vanquishing and victimizing the partner. With preoedipal, narcissistic regression, orgasm represented fusion with the omnipotent idealized object, as well as dangerous engulfment.

It was now possible to comprehend further her splitting of self- and object representations into idealized and denigrated, phallic and castrated, intact and damaged. In terms of the earlier transformation of narcissistic and preoedipal developmental issues, interpenetrating and codetermining oedipal conflict and the infantile neurosis (Mahler, Pine, and Bergman, 1975). The patient's physical and psychological hypersensitivity, her repeated traumata followed by heightened aggression and dependence, and the danger of touch on all developmental levels contributed to intensified isolation, numbing and splitting. She was severely damaged and magically intact; pursued by threatening and punitive objects as well as magically repaired and restored by contact with the idealized object to whom omnipotence was delegated. Her preoedipal problems were determinants also of her conflicted fears of desertion or engulfment, masochistic surrender or sadistic control.

In terms of oedipal and adolescent conflict, the TV jingles referred to selling herself (unacceptable incestuous prostitution fantasies) as well as to the acquisition of wealth, power, and a penis. Instead of the sash she waved the banner of analysis, and glorified the analyst—"His truth is marching on." She utilized the subliminal sexual meaning of the commercials as transference messages, e.g., "fly me." Narcissistic exhibitionism compensated for the damage inflicted when "the sexual itch was scratched." She had unconsciously struggled against surrender to itching, rubbing, and sexual stimulation; these were forbidden. Shame and humiliation for narcissistic injury were condensed with oedipal guilt in her inhibition and self-denigration, though she retained healthy strivings for self-realization. She was torn between religious piety and sacrilegious incest, between victim and aggressor, female and male. To be male meant to be castrating, scratching, and destructive but also to be intact, whole, and unmutilated. She had been warned of destructiveness by her mother, had reproached herself, and was probably told that she was bringing allergies on herself by eating inappropriate foods or through contact with irritants, and that her scratching was reprehensible; finally, the allergies themselves were perceived as punishments, as attacks by punitive objects.

What about the songs and their earlier antecedents? As an adult this patient was not musically inclined to any great degree. She enjoyed melody and rhythm and had sung popular tunes in adolescence. It did appear, however, that lullabies had been used in attempts to sooth the distressed, allergic-itchy, and occasionally asthmatic child who suffered sleep disturbance early in life. Cooing and music may well have tapped both preverbal and nonverbal affective and sensorimotor experience, with which music resonated and articulated. The comforting musical qualities of the songs could again imply successful early comforting, and alternate pathways of maternal contact and communication. The words were also very significant, and verbalization was synthesized with the sensoriaffective musical medium. There were genetic links between rhythmic play, early songs, and the songs in her adult sexual fantasies. The child's experience of lullabies, nursery rhymes, musical games, and dance were all determinants.

Soothing sounds, familiar friendly words, and pious hymns may have had facilitating meanings that were adaptive, comforting, and—most important—approving. Children and adults will hum and sing to themselves as depression lifts, playfulness resumes, and positive self-regard is restored along with the love object and the object's love. The songs were associated with rhythm and harmony, as well as with anxiety, anger, and the discordant voice of conscience (Goldings, 1974). Both soothing and stimulating, the songs also represented freedom from allergy, breathing free, and the temptation, danger, and punishment associated with having "a free hand." "The Battle Hymn of the Republic" is a Civil War song, a song of freedom from enslavement, a song designed to mobilize the forces of liberation. In the patient's case, the song functioned more as seduction than distraction, blending with her excitement even while linked to ego control of regression and painful affect. The rhythm of the song helped her organize earlier overstimulation and diffuse excessive tension related to allergic attack, the itch-scratch cycle, and masturbation. For similar reasons, music and dance therapy probably help patients with dysphoric affects and diffuse tensions. The songs were inferred to be repetitive phenomena, serving binding and mastery with inner speech leading to internal and external communication and analytic verbalization. The songs probably derived from the preoedipal period, and were altered with the accretions and modifications of later development. However, the patient's fantasy life had determinants from her entire life experience, including her current analytic experience. Analysis precluded physical touch but provided initial empathic soothing and then essential understanding and the integration of idea and affect, past and present, cause and effect. The patient did overcome crippling inhibitions, characterological rigidity, and self-punitive depression. She stopped scratching and became more cheerful, showing greater capacity for spontaneous give-and-take, controlled regression, and independent aims.

She had entered treatment for symptom relief rather than for personality change. At termination it was clear that she again expected a magical transformation, the sort depicted in her dream image of "a new bearskin or deerskin hung over a balcony as a trophy." The anticipated transformation represented a narcissistic victory—she could cover herself with the skin of the glorified analyst, with whom she identified. The magic of transference coexisted with the repetitive analysis of her entrenched infantile omnipotence. Her depression and self-excoriation were alleviated, but she was left with a tendency to idealize the treatment and the analytic relationship. I wondered how much analytic understanding and structural change would be retained. The patient made definite gains in her capacity to link psychological cause and effect, to recognize and express affect, and to explore the inner and the outer world with modest curiosity. Her range of affective and abstract expression expanded, and she showed greater spontaneity and sparkle, without the need for scratching. She could understand the sexual and aggressive meanings of her itching and scratching; her inhibition of touch gave way to being able to "feel," to have feelings, and to tolerate physical and emotional contact. On the negative side, however, she lacked initiative and used active modes of mastery and integration.

The case is striking in that the allergy contributed to trauma and developmental strain throughout infancy and childhood. It is probably significant that her dominant but distorted oedipal organization, which reorganized the preoedipal phases (Rangell, 1959; Abrams, 1984), was characterized by less intense and intrusive allergic tendencies than was the earlier organization. The oedipal reorganization, then, exerted a beneficial and corrective developmental influence. Developmental strain and fixation to trauma probably led to some phase disruption, with such persistent infantile features as narcissistic fragility and heightened separation anxiety, as well as tendencies toward fixation and regression. The preoedipal disorder colored oedipal development and paved the way for intense castration anxiety, massive repression and isolation, and characterological rigidity. The eczema and allergic disorders were not only manifest on the skin, but infiltrated her body image, her self- and object representations, and her ego and superego identifications. She appeared to have been excessively depleted and deflated as a toddler, and the flattened affect and loss of initiative persisted into adult life (Blum, 1978). The bodily concerns usurped her investment in the object world. The body was a damaged phallus and self, but also an object that could be comforting, punishing, stimulating, etc.

Body and organ language, difficulties in communication and empathy, and tendencies to enact rather than verbalize were all related to her early traumata and developmental disturbance (Greenacre, 1967). Conflicts were prominent, though subtle deficits in affective, cognitive, and synthetic functions cannot be ruled out. Regressive tendencies and fixation could be severe, but appeared to be closely related or secondary to conflict.

Her improved functioning consequent on analytic treatment points to the importance of modifying existing psychic structure rather than removing deficits. The case is reminiscent of several already in the literature. Arlow (1977) reported a patient who had eczema and like mine had her hands tied in infancy to prevent scratching; regressive and affective disturbance in later life resulted. Biven (1977) presented a case involving similar skin preoccupations, self-injury, and related conflicts. Pollock (1964) described a patient with a history of infantile eczema and asthmatic bronchitis who as an adult suffered from pruritus ani, pruritus vulvae, and neurodermatitis. The analytic elucidation of her skin symptoms revealed a regressive defense against separation stemming from oedipal conflict, as well as a dependent symbiotic tie to her mother. My patient's itching, rubbing, and excoriation represented conflicts on all developmental levels, social alienation, and fears of castration and loss of the object and of the object's love. They were also a sadomasochistic tie to the object in a sickly, resentful dependence. Being hospitalized and immobilized a few months after a sibling's birth led to disruption of the anal phase and to a rapprochement subphase marked by intensified ambivalence, narcissistic and object-directed rage, splitting of representations, and traumatic separation-annihilation anxiety. Her sibling's fantasied annihilation also defended against hostility toward her mother, and was later linked to guilt over death wishes toward her oedipal rival. Her phallic and oedipal phase development appear to have been more benign and benevolent, though still infiltrated by unresolved preoedipal problems.

To the extent that the skin is the container, the boundary between self and object, the envelope and boundary of the body ego (Freud, 1923), the eczema impeded the development of mature narcissism and object relations (Spitz, 1965). The eczema did improve gradually, consistent with greater differentiation of psyche and soma as maturation and development proceeded, and with increasing ego regulation of stimulation and tension. There was heightened skin sensitivity and vulnerability, but not the maternal avoidance of touch or cutaneous gratification that Spitz reported in institutional cases.

As an organ of touch, temperature, and pain perception, the skin is linked to the body image and self-definition. The skin comes to represent the self as well as objects and their attributes. Development may be impeded or deviant when tactile stimulation is absent or inappropriate. The experience of attachment and stimulation (both affectionate and aggressive) of the skin surface is a basic area of infant-mother exchange (Anzieu, 1980). Skin and touch convey the caregiver's love and warmth, holding, soothing, and security. Primitive identifications involving adhesive skin surfaces may derive from the symbiotic tie to the primary object (Bick, 1968). Contact, caresses, massages (as in affectionate cuddling and foreplay), or aggressive scratching and digging become significant aspects of object relations and communication. As an envelope, the skin is both protective and vulnerable, a barrier, buffer, receptor, and filter. Skin attributes are associated with age, health, affect and feelings, intactness and loss. The association of the skin with pleasure or pain, erotization or attack, security or injury, is dependent on both constitutional factors and the child's experience with skin disorders such as eczema or scabies.

The patient had repeatedly confronted her vision of omnipotent damage—the feeling she had botched everything. She could control neither her allergy nor her mother's attempts to control the infant and the illness. Her passive omnipotence, defensive idealization, and narcissistic hypersensitivity and insensitivity were reactivated during the termination phase of her analysis. At termination, a royal blue curtain descended. The analytic drama would finish with restored skin and sovereignty. The depressive blues were both dramatized and denied. She fantasied rebirth as an ideal and intact, phallic woman; she identified with the analyst, acquiring his skin and his strength. Redecorating her home, she recommended that I replace my frayed turquoise draperies with new blue fabric. Her molting and metamorphosis was to be a shared analytic experience.

This patient's allergic disposition, interacting in a complemental series with the environment (Freud, 1916–1917), contributed to pathogenesis and strain throughout development. A biologically based hypersensitivity led to narcissistic fragility, defensive insensitivity and early disturbance of affect and object relations. Her narcissistic-affective insensitivity had been mended and in many respects mastered, but the physical and psychological hypersensitivity to stress and injury remained, with a potential for regressive reactivation of pathogenic conflict and trauma. It would be valuable to collect and compare cases of similar allergic syndromes with eczema, though usually these are highly variable, in order to determine what clinical and theoretical inferences might appropriately be generalized, and if psychological intervention in infancy would have marked beneficial effects on subsequent development.

References

Abrams, S. (1984), Fantasy and reality in the oedipal phase: A conceptual overview. *The Psychoanalytic Study of the Child,* 39:83–100. New Haven: Yale University Press.

Anzieu, D. (1980), Skin ego. In: *Psychoanalysis in France,* ed. S. Lebovici and D. Widlocher. New York: International Universities Press, pp. 17–32.

Arlow, J. (1977), Affects and the psychoanalytic situation. *Internat. J. Psycho-Anal.,* 58:157–170.

Bick, E. (1968), The experience of the skin in early object relations. *Internat. J. Psycho-Anal.,* 49:484–486.

Biven, B. (1977), A violent solution: The role of skin in a severe adolescent regression. *The Psychoanalytic Study of the Child,* 32:327–352. New Haven: Yale University Press.

Blum, H. (1978), Reconstruction in a case of postpartum depression. *The Psychoanalytic Study of the Child,* 33:335–362. New Haven: Yale University Press.

Freud, A. (1952), The role of bodily illness in the mental life of children. In: *The Writings of Anna Freud,* Vol. 4. New York: International Universities Press, 1968, pp. 260–279.

Freud, S. (1916–1917), Introductory lectures on psycho-analysis. *Standard Edition,* 15/16. London: Hogarth Press, 1963.

——— (1923), The ego and the id. *Standard Edition,* 19:12–66. London: Hogarth Press, 1961.

Goldings, H. (1974), Jump-rope rhymes and the rhythm of latency development in girls. *The Psychoanalytic Study of the Child,* 29:431–450. New Haven: Yale University Press.

Greenacre, P. (1967), The influence of infantile trauma on genetic patterns. In: *Psychic Trauma,* ed. S. Furst. New York: Basic Books, pp. 108–153.

Mahler, M., Pine, F., & Bergman, A. (1975), *The Psychological Birth of the Human Infant.* New York: Basic Books.

Pollock, G. (1964), On symbiosis and symbiotic neurosis. *Internat. J. Psycho-Anal.,* 45:1–30.

Rangell, L. (1959), The nature of conversion. *J. Amer. Psychoanal. Assn.,* 7:632–662.

Schur, M. (1955), Comments on the metapsychology of somatization. *The Psychoanalytic Study of the Child,* 10:119–164. New York: International Universities Press.

Spitz, R. (1965), *The First Year of Life.* New York: International Universities Press.

Weil, A. (1985), Thoughts about early pathology. *J. Amer. Psychoanal. Assn.,* 33:335–352.

22

The Psychology and Psychotherapeutic Treatment of Borderline and Psychotic Conditions of Childhood

RUDOLF EKSTEIN, PH.D.

While descriptions of borderline and psychotic conditions can be found even in ancient literature, only with the onset of modern psychiatry in the middle of the last century were systematic attempts made to understand and treat these conditions. Within two years, three great men were born who changed the picture of psychiatry: Freud and Kraepelin, born in 1856, and Bleuler, born in 1857. Kraepelin's primary contribution (1900) was in the area of diagnosis and classification of symptomatology, although he also studied the progress and the process of diseases and did not hold a static point of view. He was pessimistic, feeling that the prognosis of severe mental illness was hopeless. Bleuler's concern (1911) was with thought and affect disorders in schizophrenia, and basically he held a similarly pessimistic view concerning outcome. Freud's major contribution in this area can be traced to his 1924 article, "The Loss of Reality in Neurosis and Psychosis," in which he emphasized the structural aspects of psychosis, specifically the loss of reality testing and of the capacity for normal object relations. While these different views seem concerned primarily with etiological issues concerning the cause of the illness, they also contain latent positions concerning the cause *of the cure*. One might say that each stated a disguised commitment to a specific treatment philosophy and technique.

Kraepelin, who assumed that mental patients were hopelessly ill and required permanent hospitalization, provided them with a hospital order based on different diagnostic pictures. Bleuler was so pessimistic regarding treatment that in his classic, *Dementia Praecox* he devoted only one chapter to treatment and stated that it would be "unjust if we try to prevent hopeless schizophrenics from suicide." Freud's emphasis on reality testing and object relations is, I would argue, an expression of his commitment to a psychoanalytic technique based on a therapeutic relationship making use of transference, resistance, etc.

Freud (1916–1917) once spoke about three narcissistic blows that science delivered to mankind. The first was the change from the Ptolemaic view of the universe, a geocentric one comparable to the infant's omnipotent fantasies, to the Copernican theory of a heliocentric universe. The second blow Freud ascribed to Darwin, whose theory of evolution challenged religious beliefs about the creation of man as the unique, rational homo sapiens, different from the unreasoning animals. Freud saw himself as the deliverer of the third narcissistic blow—his discovery of the unconscious, which overturned the idea of man's rational uniqueness, and his assertion that man, like the other animals, is driven by nonrational forces.

Could one speak of a fourth narcissistic blow to mankind, implicit in Freud's third blow, and suggest that there is no basic difference between the psychotic and the neurotic, between ordinary conditions and those described as borderline and psychotic? With such a view, psychosis and borderline conditions can be considered treatable, thereby allowing greater optimism in the prognosis of such patients.

The survey of the literature on serious childhood disorders reveals that during the last forty years we have moved from mere etiological considerations, and from diagnostic pessimism, to a new optimism concerning psychotherapy. Often exaggerated, this optimism is based on creative and enthusiastic pioneering efforts which increase the probability of recovery, provided society as a whole supports therapeutic efforts and research in this area.

The complex area of serious childhood disorders has a roster of distinguished pioneers. Bender (1953) emphasized constitutional factors, the neurological lag and deficit, and medical treatment, surgical techniques, and retraining programs. Kanner (1944) was concerned with childhood autism, and he too emphasized reeducation techniques in treatment. Among psychoanalytic workers in this field was Szurek, a student of Sullivan, who with his collaborators saw psychiatry as the science of interpersonal relations (Szurek and Berlin, 1973). Rank (1949), most of whose work was done with very young children, contributed the concept of ego fragmentation. While her work was guided by psychoanalytic thinking, her techniques were more akin to educational work in nursery schools. Perhaps the most powerful contribution was made by Mahler, who together with her coworkers (Mahler, Pine, and Bergman, 1975), contributed to an understanding of symbiotic and autistic phases, the problem of individuation, and the birth of the psychological self. My own work (Ekstein, 1966), and that of my colleagues, is concerned with fluctuating ego states, visible in schizophrenia as well as in borderline conditions of childhood. My contributions are concerned mainly with psychotherapeutic techniques and the causes of recovery. Bettelheim's work (1974) is concerned with the total psychotherapeutic treatment program, including the use of the environment, that he and his colleagues practice at the Orthogenic School.

The Diagnostic Process

We deliberately do not speak of diagnosis but rather of *process,* the interaction between doctor and patient. We speak about this process as a movement that leads from the family's first awareness that something is wrong to the final decision of commitment to a treatment program. We have in mind a "social diagnosis," a phrase borrowed from social casework, which examines not only the psychological world of the sick child but also the social forces contributing to illness and to recovery. The diagnostic categorization is not an accusation or a threat by virtue of naming the illness but rather serves as a decision, a program toward a curative process. The diagnostician does not merely look through a microscope, as one might in a laboratory examination. Rather, he is involved with the patient and the family in solving a task that moves from the emergency of an emerging process toward the resolution of the conflict or the restoration or rebuilding of lost capacities.

One might well say that the diagnostic process is a kind of trial treatment, a way of seeing whether one can get child and family to participate in the process. An illustration of diagnostic interaction leading to the beginning of psychotherapy with a severely disturbed 10-year-old boy may clarify what is meant by the diagnostic process. The first contact occurred when the father telephoned the therapist concerning his boy, whom he considered psychotic. He spoke of the child as being split into two persons, and later—during the first session, before the child was seen—gave more details. The father is a professional man in the engineering field. There are three other children in the family, the patient the second oldest boy. Mother and father gave somewhat different versions of the child's difficulties. The mother obviously identified with the role of defender of the child and had more patience with him. The father constantly stressed the seriousness of the illness and betrayed more anxiety. One could feel the underlying competition for the therapist's ear and the wish on the part of each to have the therapist's support.

They had just interrupted their son's treatment by a child psychiatrist. They thought the treatment was useless; the child was not improving, and in fact seemed to be getting sicker. The psychiatrist had demanded that they, too, be treated by him. Their overt opposition was concerned with the question of fees, but what seemed uppermost in their minds was that the psychiatrist had suggested that they were really the cause of the difficulty. Allegedly, he had said to the child during one of the treatment sessions that the parents had a bad marriage. The child quoted him and set off a flood of ambivalence and the search for a new therapist. When the therapist suggested that he ought to talk with their son's psychiatrist, the parents objected: They had lost all confidence in him. They had gotten the therapist's name through an analyst far up north and obviously were frantically searching for someone they could trust at a period in their lives when they did not trust themselves, the child, or the various sources they had consulted previously.

The parents described nights of terror. The boy could not go to sleep, would keep them awake, was riddled by panic and deepening anxiety attacks, saw himself persecuted by all kinds of monsters, and would "freak out." This description was used by the parents as well as the boy, who identified with the parents' way of describing him. The first impression was that these "freaking out" experiences might be descriptions of fluctuating states of consciousness. The parents had followed the suggestion of the psychiatrist (and their pediatrician) and were giving the boy heavy doses of chlorpromazine hydrochloride (Thorazine) and other drugs. He often seemed in a stuporous state and could not be maintained in any school program. This state of affairs had been going on for a number of months. The parents were quite ready to have the therapist see the child, perhaps use psychological testing, and have him confer with the pediatrician, but did not want him to make contact with the psychiatrist.

The therapist tried to suggest, first, that they not interrupt the treatment; that he would want merely to act as a consultant; that they must understand that treatment techniques today require immense patience and take a very long time, so that the psychiatrist could not be expected to be helpful in as short a time as they had anticipated. While he tried to maintain the role of the consultant, the parents insistently cast him as the psychotherapist. The interplay between his wish for cautious evaluation and their wish for commitment went on throughout the two sessions in which he saw the parents alone. They did not give up, and, in the long run they prevailed.

The child came, accompanied by the father, who could not really allow the psychotherapist to be alone, either with him or with the child; nor could he keep from explaining the child's difficulties in front of the child. He brought along a number of the child's drawings and told the child to take these up with the psychotherapist. The father also gave the psychotherapist a tape he had made the night before while talking to the boy; it would illustrate to the therapist the child's psychotic maladjustment.

The tape was most interesting, inasmuch as it documented the fact that the father was an intrusive parent who did not permit the boy to have his own inner life and tried to force explanations out of him. The father acted more or less like the caricature of a psychitrist who wants to get to the bottom of things. The boy indeed gave the impression of a youngster flooded by psychotic delusional material, perhaps from drug-induced states, and suffering endless pain.

The father had also directed the boy to make a drawing that would tell the therapist about the problem. This drawing was made on the reverse side of computer paper. With that paper, the therapist felt as if he had both sides of the family coin. The engineering mind of the father, wanting everything orderly and exact, was presented on one side of the paper that he provided the boy, who then made a psychoticlike drawing on the other side. Obsessional exactness struggled with primary process on a single sheet of paper.

The drawing depicted a little boy lying in his bed full of fear, saying to his father who is standing nearby at the bedroom door: "Don't always scream at me. I am just asking for you to come because I am scared." In response, the father yells at the boy: "What you think about does not exist. There are no such things." During the next few sessions the boy brought the therapist other drawings, all of them representing terrible monsters. They seemed to be archaic animals from the past, vicious creatures from science fiction, evil monsters engaged in brutal internecine war. They represented a psychotic version of oedipal material, a struggle between father and son, interlocked in an endless war desperately waged for the prize of pursuing what each wanted. One could not help but feel the invisible presence of the mother, who tried to build a bridge between the boy's panic and the father's rage.

The child requested the use of the tape recorder so that he and the therapist could enact a radio broadcast. The child would be introduced by the psychotherapist to the imaginary radio audience as one who had exciting stories to tell about the struggle of the monsters, their fears, their hopes, and their solutions to problems. The boy freely interacted with the psychotherapist, and the material that came out now was immensely different from the tape the father had provided. From the father's tape one got the impression of a delusional boy overcome by private monsters and unable to return to reality. Now he appeared to be deliberately inventing and telling stories: a master teller of science fiction rather than a devoured victim of his own fantasy creations.

Shall we believe the material that the boy provided for the psychotherapist or the material on the earlier tape? In the first instance, we would be dealing with a boy in neurotic conflict, whose use of science fiction and fantasy indicated that reality testing was not lost and whose anxiety nowhere approached psychotic panic. But if we were to believe the father's account and the earlier taped material, we would have much evidence for thinking him psychotic. Moreover, we have a third alternative: we might think of him as borderline, as someone who fluctuates between psychotic and neurotic states with no control over the fluctuation, as if from time to time he were compelled to experience the world like a dream and, unable to step out of the dream to cope with reality, could only distort it into a psychotic nightmare. The issue thus becomes one of differential diagnosis.

Enough has been said about the parents, particularly the father, to make us wonder whether his anxiety and the child's panic states do not create a kind of symbiotic folie à deux. Could the father avoid his intrusive behavior? Could he stop trying to get into the child's inner world, taking it so seriously that he himself was overwhelmed by his overidentification? Could he not simply be reassuring and direct the situation in such a way that the child would bring the illness to the therapist rather than have to face a father who tries to scream his mental anguish out of him? The father promised that he would not try to intrude any longer. Every hour he asked for advice on what he ought to do. Although he experienced the therapist as reassuring and tried to follow suggestions, at one critical moment his wife, having become more aware of her husband's difficulty, telephoned. During this introductory period in the diagnostic process, the therapist tried to be reassuring and did not require that the parents get help for themselves, though he realized the problems this course of action entailed.

In the meantime, the work with the child went on. He brought a few more drawings and dwelt on his monsters, but after a while, he lost interest in them. More and more his behavior became that of his age group. The fantasies very rarely took on psychotic dimensions, and he looked forward to his hours. All this took place at the beginning of the school year, and now a new problem had to be considered. The parents wondered what school to use. Did it have to be a private school, or could he go to public school? Would he have to go to a special class? What did the therapist recommend? They were utterly convinced that the boy could not be placed in the public school system. They wanted to protect him from that. At the same time, however, they wanted to protect him from being in a school system that maintained only very regressed children. The public school was called in, and the boy was given some special testing. A special program was worked out with the school psychologist, according to which he would first be given some tutoring and would then start on a limited program with youngsters of his own age in a "regular" class. The psychotherapist endorsed that procedure. The limited testing done by the school psychologist did not really provide the picture that a complete battery of projective tests would have afforded. As a matter of fact, the testing revealed more about the parents' anxiety than the boy's pathology. The psychotherapist did not want to administer additional tests, however, feeling that the boy was already under too much pressure.

The child himself was asked by the therapist if he meant to cooperate with that program. He was now being dosed with Thorazine and experiencing less "freaking out." But there were enough upsetting nights and enough disturbance that the parents did not want him to go beyond the tutoring. The child would sometimes do excellently with the tutor, but sometimes he would utterly fail. The parents' response was to delay any attempt at adjustment in the school setting.

This short summary illustrates the strengths and weaknesses of these diagnostic processes. We are not ready to give the boy a diagnostic label, but we know enough to proceed with the treatment. He should continue to be seen by the psychotherapist twice a week, and the parents should be permitted to move slowly around the issue of school attendance (though the therapist, if he were responsible for the decision, would allow him to start some schooling right away). There is a great deal of strength in this boy. His drawings and stories show talent; he is an endurance swimmer who sometimes swims miles to strengthen himself. Sometimes, however, he is overwhelmed by anxiety and cannot quite describe what he means by "freaking out," though he is aware of increased anxiety and of a desperate wish that his parents not scream at him. Sometimes he begs his mother not to scream at him, even though she never does and has no intention of doing so. It is as if he constantly thinks his parents might develop into monsters who would hurt him. Feeling completely dependent on them, he sees them sometimes as his only reliable protectors and at other times as dangerous enemies. The ambivalence occasionally takes on psychotic proportions.

One must have sympathy for the parents, who—regardless of how often they do not respond well to the child and bring on their own discomfort—are under endless pressure from him. At times his behavior almost suggests that he has a diabolical knowledge of how to keep them in check and how to tyrannize them, so that he seems to become the monster trying to prevail against them.

At moments of deepest distress he seems to be as ill as the artist whom Freud (1922) described in his work on a seventeenth-century devil neurosis. This artist painted himself into a psychotic depression, a position of isolation and of confrontation with the devils within him—archaic monster figures which at times represented the psychotic process within him, his own monster identity, and at times the images of the father and the mother. But these productions went hand in hand with normal behavior and with sufficient if somewhat intermittent ego strength that could be tapped.

It is interesting that the pediatrician who prescribed the Thorazine based his decision on the parents' description of the boy's behavior. He himself never saw the boy in the kind of psychotic state the parents described. Neither did the therapist, though he witnessed moments that indirectly verified the parents' observations.

Once the boy stood before the huge glass window of the therapist's consulting room, which is on the seventh floor of a high-rise building. From there he could see the whole city, with huge buildings in the background. He wondered how it would be if the glass broke and he could freely step out into the air and fly, reach these other buildings, and control the city like a powerful, monstrous bird.

The therapist thought of Plato's definition of play. He saw the inception of play, children's or animal's, as a big leap into the air. This desire to leap, to fly, to be independent, to have total autonomy, to be free of gravity, Plato suggests, is typical for the young. But the higher they jump and the abler they are, the more they are concerned about coming safely back to the ground. He only jumps rightly who can safely fall back on his feet on the safe ground. The myth of Daedalus and his son Icarus tells of how they built wings so they could fly. As Icarus came nearer to the sun, however, the wax used in constructing the wings melted, and his short-lived autonomy in the air ended not in safety on the ground but in destruction. Mother Sun destroys and Mother Earth gives strength.

The patient here, full of the wish to leap, to play with fantasies in which he has superhuman strength or creates enemies of superhuman strength, describes a leap that constitutes dangerous play. The therapist thought for a moment that such a boy might jump through an open window in order to reach the sun or the high rises and could fall to his doom. There are people who give the impression that they may leap without having a place to safely land.

Like many such people, this boy could be suffering from a borderline condition; at times his leaps are based on a realistic assessment of how high he can jump without hurting himself, while at other times his leaps exceed his capacity to test reality, and to recognize his fantasies as such.

We may assume that his parents are torn by their own anxiety that the boy may really leap into space with no means of landing safely. The therapist's task is to help this child restore the connection between leaping into autonomy, into freedom, with the capacity to fall back on safe ground. The diagnosis is not a final one. Ongoing diagnostic work shows the existence of deep pathology that may be increasing, thereby bringing into prominance underlying psychotic structures which permit leaping without considerations of safety. The diagnosis also suggests that such behavior can be kept in check and that psychotherapy can restore or build these security systems of the self, thereby adding to the fantasies the strength of reasoning and reality testing.

In one of his more recent works, *Toys and Reasons* (1977), Erikson quotes William Blake's lines, "The Child's Toys and the Old Man's Reasons/are the Fruits of the Two Seasons." Our patient's fantasies, his toys, are sometimes stronger than his reasoning power. The parents' reasons are sometimes stronger than their capacity to deal with the child's fantasies. In the interactions so far, we have a process that allows for a beginning but not yet for a clear prognosis, a simple classification, or a completed plan of treatment.

Anna Freud once suggested to me that a true diagnosis can be made only after treatment, when one knows, so to speak, all the facts. But when does one ever know all the facts? We should not, therefore, expect the diagnostic process to afford us more than a fairly clear beginning. In this child's life we can see autistic isolation, symbiotic yearnings, touches of a thought disorder, oedipal anxieties, preoedipal panics, strong islands of ego strengths, a will to struggle with his outer and inner monsters, and a capacity to take hold of the therapeutic situation, to transfer to the therapist expectations of trust and worries lest he fail him. Can the therapist's knowledge and enthusiasm, and the parents' willingness to participate in the treatment, overcome the child's emotional and mental difficulties? There is hope but no certainty.

Psychotherapeutic Techniques

An old English proverb suggests that "speech is the picture of the mind." Today, the word "language" would have to be substituted for "speech"; and language has to be understood not only as verbal discourse but as including all the forms of communication of which the human being is capable. If the therapist is capable of developing a system of communication between himself and the patient, he will open the door to the mind of the patient, to his interpersonal and intrapsychic life. He will gain a picture of the mind, analogous perhaps to the picture that an X ray specialist can gain of the body. One fault in the analogy is the fact that the X ray is a "still picture," not a movie; but the things our patients tell us, as we develop them in psychotherapeutic dialogue, are more like a movie, a process. Perhaps one needs to say that language can be used to learn about the processes of the mind, not simply to obtain a static picture of it.

Nevertheless, we often try to suggest a still picture of the mind. In that case, we refer to the structure of the mind, to personality order or disorder. (Personality disorder has its own order, the order of the pathological process.)

Unlike Pallas Athene, who is said to have sprung from the head of Zeus fully armed and educated, the human being develops slowly, as do his language capacities and, often, language pathologies. The speech used by the patient, the language system developed, and the capacity for communication tell us something about the phases of normal and abnormal development. When there is no normal speech, as for example in the autistic child, we search for other forms of communication. These forms can include withdrawal, escape, autistic speech, echolalia, echopraxia, and other forms of speech pathology, such as stuttering, stammering, psychotic speech, delusional speech, etc. A study of the development of speech helps one to know more about its meaning and function, in terms of interpersonal situations and intrapsychic conditions.

The first language of the child is *appeal language,* the screaming and yelling of the small baby. This is the signal the infant gives to the mother who "understands" it as a request for food or comfort, and she usually responds by an act such as feeding. Much of the language of very disturbed children is appeal language, signal language. Even advanced speech, advanced communications—as the psychotherapist listens to the psychotherapeutic communication—are frequently dominated by mere appeal. Patients often start out with complaints, expressions of suffering; they wish to prove the validity of their need for help. We are to stop the pain, to reassure, to promise, or to gratify in one way or another.

Psychotic children often do not respond to *interpretive language.* Such language can only be acquired and understood by the child if he has moved forward to symbolic communication, the hallmark of mature human speech. Psychotic children, in beginning therapy, therefore, do not respond to the ordinary interpretive language of the psychotherapist. The system of communication between a therapist and such a child has to take other forms.

The first appeal of the hungry baby leads not to communication, but to communion. The baby is once more, in some form, united with the mother. The mouth finds the nipple of the breast, and that is the goal of the first communication. Can the psychotherapist allow himself to respond to appeal language, to understand the patient on his own level? How often will he have to make the kind of overture which aims at the restoration of communion rather than at the establishment of communication?

We have no difficulty in responding to an infant's baby talk and are willing periodically to regress with him without fearing the consequences. We know that he will grow up and identify with our higher modes of speech; we know that our identifying with him, using baby talk, will help him to respond and learn our language.

While we have no difficulty in accepting the needs of the infant, we find it difficult to respond similarly to psychotic and borderline children who take from us our achievement of symbolic, interpretive, explanatory systems of communication. Here we have a situation where we must be "bilingual." Only he who understands baby talk can help the baby to wish to learn our language. The developmental schemata tell us that there is a long way from appeal language to representational and symbolic language. A message might be an appeal, an expression without appeal character, symbolic communication, or all at the same time. No symbolic communication is entirely free of the other forms of communication, and therefore we frequently find behind the manifest content of a communication its deeper meaning.

Freud (1900) characterized the dream as the royal road to the unconscious of the patient; Erikson (1950) saw the play of the child as the royal road to the unconscious of the child. Both stressed what they considered the best therapeutic communications available. In the treatment of psychotic and borderline conditions of childhood, the psychotherapeutic dialogue is best characterized by the use of metaphor, analogy, simile, or allusion. A kind of twilight language is used, which is neither the language of reality in pure daylight, nor the language of the dream during the night, but a language based on fusion and confusion of the poetic and the commonplace.

When the young patient described earlier speaks about monsters, he speaks about his internal world of panic, an almost dreamlike, often hypnogogic preoccupation with himself and the adult figures in his life. This language becomes threatening to the father, who, needing to express his rage, his own unconscious fantasies, withdraws into the world of computer exactness, itself a kind of metaphoric communication concerning the way his mind feels safest. While at times the child tends to return to an autistic position, not quite successfully, and never gives up the search for the maternal matrix, the father, who wants him to be realistic, reasonable, logical, tries to impose on him a different language. Different styles of existence are in combat with each other.

The language of metaphor creates a bridge between these two worlds. It becomes a language which means something to both, even though each attaches slightly different meanings to what is said. The demand for absolute clarity gives way to a language which is vague and allows for different interpretations. It is the bridge between two different minds, using different systems of communication, searching to communicate with the other while trying desperately to keep their inner worlds hidden from each other.

What are scientific models or models of the mind but metaphors? Robert Frost (1949) suggested that "All thinking is metaphorical," and C.S. Lewis (1939) wrote that "all our truths, or all but a few fragments, are won by metaphor." Certainly, all psychological truth, insight into self or into interpersonal relationships, is won by metaphoric means of communication.

The earliest systems of communication, such as the contact between mother and baby, can also be considered as metaphors—action metaphors. The screaming of the baby is to tell the mother that he needs her, that he loves her in his particular way; her act of feeding him is a way of telling him that she protects and loves him. But the telling is not yet the customary language of speech. It is a telling through the act.

The neglected baby, like the children Spitz (1946) described as suffering from anaclitic depression, moves from human contact, turns to the wall, and gives up the search for the mother—gives up the appeal function—and regresses in despair. He assumes an autistic position that is also language, an attempt to be independent in his way, to have autistic autonomy, and indirectly, to accuse the mother. Thus, autistic withdrawal is also a communication system, a warning that ordinary communication is being given up and that a protective wall is being built. Therefore, we see autistic children who have acquired some language using it not as a basis for direct communication but as a way of withdrawing, as a way of having merely intrapsychic communication. Such autistic children talk, but to themselves. The psychotherapist, the wise educator, teacher, or nurse, or the reeducated parent—anyone trying to make contact with such a child—tries to break through the autistic barrier. The withdrawal from interpersonal contact, the apparent giving up of the love object, is the child's desperate struggle to maintain himself against objects that are experienced as dangerous, as devouring—often the projection of his own wishes to devour the object—and against being overrun by the other. The struggle of the boy described earlier is one against the intruding parent, against the "yelling" mother, and at the same time, an appeal for a safe object. Projection and identification are interchanged, often fused, at war with each other, before there is clear differentiation between them.

The way the child "speaks" helps the psychotherapist decide on a possible bridge of communication. A good many of these bridges have to be thought of as auxiliary bridges, at least until the more permanent ones can be restored or—if they have never existed—built for the first time.

It should be clear by now that certain revisions of psychoanalytic methods in the treatment of psychotic and borderline children are aided by a study of language. We are not speaking about sheer linguistics but rather about the considerations which permit us to deduce, from the special use that a sick child makes of communication, how to establish a bridge to him. It is a special bridge, sometimes unsafe, sometimes one that immediately breaks again, sometimes one that lasts; the attempt to bridge differences, lack of understanding, and lack of communication must be made over and over using ever-changing methods. This contact may sometimes be effected by communion, a kind of feeding of the patient, sometimes by action and action metaphor, sometimes by primitive language, and sometimes by metaphoric communication which appeals to affect, builds a bridge to the preconscious or unconscious mind, and opens a way for mutual identification, as in incorporation. The way of speaking, of communicating, may be preverbal or verbal. It may serve not only to establish a diagnosis, but also indirectly to indicate the kind of object relationships of which the child is capable, the kind of avoidance of object relationships that is used, and any precursors of object relationships that might be present. It provides a measure of the individual's ability to distinguish between self and nonself.

During the different phases of the establishment of speech we find that sick children have particular difficulties in going beyond imitation, as in echolalia and echopraxia, to identification. We also find children whose overidentification is so firmly established that they remain on a symbiotic level where self and nonself are not differentiated.

Individuation, the development of the self, is a slow process. Our work in psychotherapeutic tasks has given us much insight into the relation between the development of language and the development of the self as differentiated from the nonself. One is impressed by the degree to which studies of early development, especially those involving severely sick children, have helped us in our psychotherapeutic work with adults. A rich literature, initiated by Kohut (1971), concerning the development of the self and the overcoming of primitive narcissism, has been influenced, we believe, by these studies.

Differentiation, however, may go so far that it drives the patient into autistic positions, into distance from the object. This does not always express itself in a lack of speech. For such a patient has problems concerning not only symbolic communication but also the experience of normal emotional response. Many an autistic child may "communicate" with us but may be far away, without the capacity for emotional response. There is the logic of speech, the secondary process of thinking, and there is also the question of appropriate affect. Many a mother cannot establish emotional contact with such a child. The child uses the mother as an anaclitic object, literally uses her for gratification without moving on to more advanced forms of emotional contact; there is no capacity for the experience of love and hate, of turning toward and away from the object. We are referring to primitive fixations and regressions that are frequently characteristic of our child patients. In the earlier days of psychoanalytic theory, these phenomena were understood merely in terms of psychosexual and psychoaggressive development. Our concern with systems of communication has moved us beyond the consideration of basic conflicts, of positions of sexuality and aggression, and toward the consideration of ego psychology, the different steps of self-development, and the different forms of object relationships.

We have touched on methods of approach, of keeping appropriate distance, of optimal systems of communication, and have advanced notions concerning the use of language. Presymbolic language, symbolic language, communication based on action metaphor or metaphor, each can provide a system of language which allows the patient either to move toward contact and object relationships in a way that is appropriate for him, or to keep him equidistant from external objects and the not fully integrated or accepted inner world.

At times the therapist cannot use symbolic language with the psychotic child. He is tempted himself to use only signal language, almost an imitative echolalic language, which at least satisfies the child's yearnings for contact and allays some of the fantastic anxiety attendant on the failure to achieve such contact. However, if the child gets back only an echo, he can never learn that there is both a self and an object, a Me and a You. Therefore the therapist gradually pushes the process in such a way that he does not merely act as an echo. He needs to open an avenue for two-way communication, at first a kind of mirroring, an indication for imitation. His contact development must eventually lead to symbolic communication based on mutual identification. Thus, echoing and mirroring are followed by the slow development of symbolic communication, accompanied by the capacity to observe and to communicate about the inner world and the interpersonal world.

For years, one such patient had allowed contact only on a metaphoric basis, a basis which does not touch the issue of clear differentiation between self and nonself. Then she began to challenge the therapist and wondered why they always talked indirectly about a topic rather than speaking more directly. By so doing, she demonstrated that she had achieved the capacity for symbolic language and no longer needed the distancing device of metaphoric communication. Her capacity for a relationship had developed in the transference struggle with the therapist.

When we speak of the "transference" of psychotic children, we must keep in mind that here the concept must be understood within a special theoretical context. Ordinarily, transference involves relating to the psychotherapist in a way that recalls earlier experiences with significant adults. Repressed early attitudes, feelings, recollections, etc., vis-à-vis parent figures are reexperienced with the therapist in the transference. But for many psychotic children these early relationships were not usual object relationships. They dealt with part objects, often with fusion states, often with no clear differentiation between parent and self. These early fusion states are now transferred to the psychotherapist, who becomes the heir of very primitive early complexes.

An example will illustrate. The child wondered how he could be sure the therapist really existed. Perhaps the psychotherapist was no more than a picture, a dream picture or a television-screen picture, and his words were not really communication with the patient but prewritten stage scripts for a television show. As he developed these fantasies, his anxiety mounted and he became panicky. How could he restore reality testing? How could he be sure that the psychotherapist truly existed and that he, the patient, was not alone in his nightmare world of panic? The therapist suggested that perhaps their present give-and-take could establish that both of them were "real." But the panic mounted, and as the child lost contact with the object and decathected it, he slowly described and experienced depersonalization. This open psychotic experience of depersonalization lasted for a little while, until the patient came toward the therapist and touched him. As soon as he touched him, the anxiety evaporated, and contact was restored.

During this interlude, symbolic speech, the discussion together, had no value whatsoever as convincing evidence of reality. But the touch did, as if this patient had suddenly returned to an early system of communication consisting of direct physical contact. We are reminded of a panic-stricken child who comes running to the mother crying. She lifts him up and holds him close to her. His tears disappear as the union with the mother is restored. Under such circumstances this is the only convincing "language"; it is action language, evidence based on touch, on being held, on feeling the body. Its power is evident in the case of our youngster, who from time to time was overwhelmed by psychotic episodes involving loss of contact with the internal object, the internal parent who makes it truly possible for him to transfer trust to another person. As soon as he lost the intrapsychic object, he could not experience the therapist as being alive, despite reassuring verbal communication. He then regressed to a level of primitive object relationships, a level of primitive communication, where touch and communion are dominant and later functions of communication, never firmly established, have lost their strength, as if drained away.

How quickly can a psychotherapist become an integral part of the ever-changing communication systems of his severely disturbed patients? How capable is he of learning linguistic systems of communication which, once part of his own life, he has forgotten, given up, and repressed, and which he now finds anxiety-provoking as he attempts to cope with countertransference experiences? Yet the therapist can work with such patients only if he feels himself in their world and privy to their system of communication. Hence he sometimes may feel overwhelmed by the burdens of his task.

Another patient, experiencing herself as first identifying with Christ, and as then being driven to experience merger with Him, accused the therapist of having blasphemous thoughts. The therapist, feeling anxiety, understood it as the consequence of being accused by the patient of thinking of himself as omnipotent, as being a deity himself. Further, he felt a kind of guilt, as if he were thinking of himself as more powerful than the deity and struggling with the patient over whether she was going to work with him or whether she was going to rely entirely on religious experience. As soon as he understood himself, the therapist was able to communicate again. He was able to help the patient see that he was not attacking her religious beliefs, but rather wanted her to know that he understood her difficulty in identifying with an ideal. She felt in danger when her experience of self was invaded by symbiotic experience, a merging of self and nonself. She could not allow herself this experience since she could not move beyond it toward self-realization.

Such psychotherapeutic techniques require immense support by parents, other relatives, school and church, and cooperating agencies; they are very rarely useful without therapeutic alliances beyond that of patient and doctor. Bettelheim (1974) talks about the therapeutic environment. Others talk about forms of behavior modification, reeducation, and the necessity of bringing the parents into the treatment process. Certain parents, however, as Bettelheim suggests, should be kept out of the treatment process, and this usually requires hospitalizing the child or providing some alternative therapeutic environment. Other authors, such as Bowen (1975), suggest that the parents be included in the hospital setting, and that the whole family including siblings, be treated. And finally, those of us who work in clinics and in private practice develop ways of working with parents, either seeing the parents in psychotherapeutic treatment or involving them in casework treatment. The most difficult aspect of work with severely disturbed children, based on our experience over the last few decades, is the length of treatment. Occasionally the very ill respond favorably in a very short time. But most cases demand endless patience, time, experimentation, and cooperation with the parents. Treatment processes may last from a few years to much more than a decade. In some cases treatment seems interminable.

Freud's early work with psychoanalytic patients (1900) was

often clarified by his use of Greek mythology, psychological insights based on metaphor. One of the most powerful themes he used was that of Oedipus, the rejected child who left his surrogate parents, killed his father, and married his mother. This is a beautiful representation of the unconscious conflict over patricide and incest which the child must overcome in order to gain the capacity for mature object relationships.

To describe the difficulties of those who work with borderline or psychotic children, we call attention to another Greek myth. One of the heroes of the Trojan War, Achilles, was considered by all to be invulnerable. Thetis, a sea goddess, and the mother of Achilles, wished him to become a great hero, but she was also anxious to protect him from all physical harm. So that he might become a hero without risk to his life, she took him as an infant to the river Styx, knowing that immersion in its waters would render him forever invulnerable. To prevent the baby from drowning, however, she held him by his heel, and in so doing established the legendary Achilles' heel, the unprotected area. Achilles did indeed become a hero, but died in battle from a wound to the single vulnerable spot. It is interesting at this point to remember that Oedipus had a deformed foot, a fact implicit in his name, that his mother sent her infant away, and that his father feared his son's potential rivalry. The fatal flaw, the basic weakness that everyone possesses, is different for the two heroes. That of Oedipus centers about the triad, the triangle which is father, mother, and son. That of Achilles is in the preoedipal, dyadic relationship of mother and son. The ambition of Thetis was a premature attempt to determine the goal, the future identity of her baby.

The story of Thetis and Achilles, the story of a mother who held on in the wrong way, may be taken as a metaphor for the problem of psychotic children. They are caught in the phase of separation-individuation and cannot get out of it. Their struggle is between the wish for eternal attachment and counterphobic separation. In modern terms, attachment and separation (Bowlby, 1969) are a struggle between the autistic and the symbiotic position (Mahler and Furer, 1968); involved here may be maternal deprivation (Spitz, 1965), a failure of early environment (Szurek and Berlin, 1973), or a biological deficit, a maturational lag (Bender, 1953).

Etiological controversy seems to be but a disguised description of the technical interventions by means of which these pathological states can be cured, improved, or at least temporarily altered.

At times one has the impression that the synthetic and integrating function of self, of ego, cannot be fully restored. There are children who are in permanent need of help. Such children forever need a protective environment, a kind of halfway house between the first home, which they must leave, and the adult community they can never fully reach.

Work with Parents

Parental collaboration is always necessary in child psychotherapy, but it is particularly difficult to achieve in dealing with severely ill children. The parents frequently experience themselves as the cause of the illness. They feel guilty, alarmed, and desperate, and are self-accusatory. They waver between deep guilt and hate toward the child and a wish to find help and the proper resources, even if doing so means sacrificing everything. Most of us who treat such children find that the parents have made many previous efforts before coming to us; they frequently regard us as a last resort; often they lose confidence in us, or have magical expectations of us, hoping that we can do the impossible. They love and hate us at the same time; are completely dependent on us and challenge us constantly with their doubts and their displaced or open hostility.

For years they may have denied any awareness of their child's pathology, only slowly admitting that something is wrong. We spoke about our own difficulties in dealing with such parents. Overidentification with the child leads us to believe, if not consciously, in the parents' incompetence, and we often believe it would be desirable to move the parents away from the situation, allowing ourselves complete control over the child. Feeling the need for complete control over the child leads us to a variety of assumptions which can hardly be proved. Each sick child faces a different social situation with a different set of parents, and our plans can never be based on omnipotent prescription giving, demanding this or that kind of sacrifice, but must be based on a diagnostic awareness that takes into account the total situation.

It may be true that the parents have contributed to the pathology. Or, as Goldfarb (1961) has suggested, they may have been so overwhelmed by the illness that they could not cope with it, even though otherwise they proved to be fairly competent adults, having done quite well with other children in the family. A static view as to what one should do with parents, or what they ought to do in order to help us, is contraindicated, especially since the very same parents who contributed to the illness are also the ones who will contribute to recovery. But they must be helped to help us achieve that.

The nature of that help depends on the kind of help they need. Frequently we think of them as auxiliary personnel who ought to do whatever we demand in terms of the child's needs, thus overlooking their own needs. They could be parents who are not able to maintain the child because of their own physical or emotional illness or because of a precarious balance in the marriage or the presence of other children who should not be growing up with a very sick sibling. Or they may be parents who are capable of sacrifice and insight into the child's difficulty and able to provide—if guided correctly—immense help in the child's upbringing.

The child not only needs treatment; he needs living space, a home, and an education. While often we cannot precisely differentiate between the tasks of education and the tasks of psychotherapy, between rearing a child and resolving inner conflicts, we must believe that in most cases the parents have a place in the treatment program. Even when the child must be hospitalized or placed in a residential setting, or when the parents, overanxious and distraught, must be freed of a burden they cannot carry, we deal with a process to be developed rather than a prescription to be given or demands to be made.

It may be a long time before the parents become capable of facing the fact that they have to give up the illusion of a healthy child. At first they may deny the pathology; then they may deny their wish to get rid of the child. They have to work through their own conflict and have to learn to accept the pathology and the need for separation.

Whenever we think of a child going to the hospital, we think of the child's trauma, but separation is as traumatic for the parents as it is for the child. It is difficult for us to think through this trauma experienced by parents who must let go. The letting go is not only the child's problem; it is also the parents'. Yet how can a mother let go if she is attached to the child in a symbiotic way? Parents who let go of their child and apply to a treatment center have to go through a process of helplessness, of mourning, and of deep disappointment, as they experience the narcissistic blow of having parented a severely sick child.

We therefore assume as a matter of course that a parallel process of helping is necessary. Just as the child needs help, so do the parents. It is hard to make clear how children of the type we describe produce and revive immense anxiety and rage in a parent. Only those who have treated such children and have experienced the hate in the countertransference so well described by Winnicott (1947), as well as the helplessness in the countertransference, can sympathize and identify with these parents.

The task of the psychotherapist is to remain equidistant from the needs of the parents and the needs of the child, so that he may keep the child in treatment and help the parents to permit him to continue. Often the therapist is not able to meet the task alone. He needs collaborators to work with the parents.

These collaborations are endlessly difficult, as each worker, concentrated as he is on either the parent or the child, tends to overidentify with his own task so as not to see that of the other. He may thus create in the total situation a kind of fragmentation which will be neither more nor less than the replica of the internal, fragmented world of the sick child. Such treatment programs, carried out in institutions, in social agencies, and in hospitals, are in constant danger. Sometimes the whole staff is caught up in the countertransference and organized hate, forcing the end of treatment for such a child. In an attempt to meet the endless provocations from such children, therapeutic programs frequently include group psychotherapy for parents and staff, group meetings with parents, and endless staff meetings and consultations.

In the end, the parents may see improvement in the child but may have to accept that they have lost years of valuable contact with him; that with him it will never be the same, even when he returns to the family; and that they may have to give him up prematurely. Sometimes a child, kept for years in a therapeutic environment, grows up, goes through school, and enters college, never returning to his childhood home except as an adult. He has become a stranger to the family, having more life contacts with the institution, the foster home, the therapist, and the social worker, who have become the real world of his childhood.

The letting-go process is always a painful one. The most complex act of true parental love is the one that permits the child to move away toward his own life. This act of letting go is an act of love. Frequently we think of love in terms of "forever, until death do us part." Parental love, however, suggests that if we are to love forever, love must include letting go, separation, and giving up. That act is even more painful when the child is seriously ill.

Parents need children just as children need parents. In the case of these children, however, the needs of the parents are frequently of a pathological order, and therefore we must work with them as well as with the children in order to help them to turn pathological needs or anxiety reactions into appropriate responses contributing to the autonomy of the child. Unlike adult psychotherapy, work with this category of child is a kind of tie-in sale. We must take the parents with the child, even though we often feel that we want to work only with the child. Today the work with parents is perhaps the weakest link in our technical armamentarium; yet we must remember that we need them as much as they need us. They are a significant part of a new triad: the therapeutic forces, the parental forces, and the growing adaptive forces of the child patient. These act in constant collaboration or, sometimes, in deadly conflict, in an endless process of working toward the uncertain goal of recovery.

Most people who have worked for a long time with such children have reported occasional successes in the literature. Some of our psychotic or borderline child patients have made immense achievements in the world. But there are also total failures. The same holds true of our work with parents. Are they the failures? Is our lack of technical skill or theoretical understanding the cause for the interruption of work? We should be careful, not dogmatic, with our answers, as our experiences so far are but beginning efforts in the work of solving extremely complex problems.

Training and Research

Jones (1913) suggested that every psychotherapist unconsciously feels that he is God. He dreams and fantasizes about omnipotence. His curative abilities allow him to do what no one else can. Those of us who dedicate much of our time to psychotic or borderline children know that our sense of omnipotence is frequently accompanied by an experience of helplessness. We vacillate, not unlike our patients, between a sense of omnipotence and a sense of omni-*im*potence.

We are usually alone and fight the battle of pioneers in treating this group of patients, and so live in a world in which there is still considerable lack of knowledge, an enormous lack of resources, limited facilities, and little support by community or government agencies.

Because of our special interests, we do not always get along well with our colleagues. Much of what we do arouses in us or in others enormous conflict. We are hardly easier to live with than the children with whom we work. We have to learn to work in institutions with other colleagues, and we deal with a body of knowledge that sometimes gives us the feeling that we are the possessors of absolute truth—which makes us dogmatic—and sometimes the feeling that we are in a jungle of dangerous uncertainty.

We must also cope with students who are interested in this field and who bring us similar fantasies of rescue and omnipotence as well as helplessness. They are willing to believe in miracle cures, to turn to schools of thought which are the newest, the most revolutionary, and which promise immediate answers. They are often reluctant to learn and unwilling to participate in slow training programs which frequently seem dull or prosaic. They prefer fast prescriptions to slow insight. Surrounded by emergencies, they are not yet quite ready to allow ideas for treatment techniques to emerge slowly.

One would wish that those who choose to engage in psychoanalytic work with children would undergo a thorough personal analysis, but even that is not enough. Besides the need to know oneself, there is also the need to understand the patient; this requires long hours of supervision, a tedious process of developing insights into the psychotherapeutic process.

As noted earlier, the treatment of the psychotic child or the borderline condition in childhood is a kind of intertwining of patient and therapist. The lines of the interpretive process and the associative process of the patient—psychotic acting out, psychotic plays, dreams, and fantasies—all frequently merge. Often the words of the patient and the therapist merge: the psychotherapeutic notes of therapists who do such work are frequently unclear as to what was said by the patient and what they themselves said. Their memory becomes unreliable. These constant fusion experiences are in part necessary in order to understand the patient, but they also make the recording of data unreliable and create an intense, yet vague situation with the supervisor. The demands made on the supervisor are a kind of parallel process, showing in reverse what takes place between patient and psychotherapist. Transferences and countertransferences blur and merge. Frequently we have the impression that the process of communication regresses to symbiotic communion. It is difficult for the supervisor to distinguish between interpretive interventions and the patient's material. The records of such treatment often seem to picture and recreate the mother-child symbiosis, or autistic conditions, rather than to communicate about these processes.

The supervisor frequently experiences himself as so immersed in the process that he wants to relinquish his supervisory task and take over the treatment himself. Wanting to take the patient away from the treating therapist is a kind of counter-identification with the parents, who occasionally lose trust in the work of the therapist. In short, the blurring between the supervisor's task and that of the therapist resembles the blurring of the object relationship.

The drain on the psychotherapist is enormous and endless. The frustrations and the lack of tangible success create a special problem. It seems that the only vital counteractivity which helps to sustain the psychotherapist, as he faces difficulties that invite pessimism, is involvement in research. The best supervisor, the best seminar leader in the training of child psychotherapists in this area, is not one who insists on certain answers, but one who experiences his work with supervisees as a process of joint discovery. It is necessary for both to avoid any sharp differentiation between teacher and student, and to accept each other as scientific collaborators. Both are searching. Neither knows everything. Master teachers in this field are usually surrounded by devoted students who soon become their collaborators. The few programs doing consistent work with psychotic and borderline children are small and dedicated. They tend to form into cultlike groups where the leaders are surrounded by devotees—not merely students seeking credit—who identify with the task of the primary investigators.

This form of training has many advantages and brings forth productive and creative students. At the same time, these small circles suffer certain limitations. The hold on each other is powerful. Group cohesion around such a leader is deep and strong. Frequently such groups develop their own language, their own conceptualizations, their own system of communication, and thus they become a kind of advanced replica of their patients. They create autistic islands that are an exaggerated version of the situation normally obtaining between different psychotherapeutic schools. Only slowly is it possible to build bridges between these schools.

We have found that in working with psychotic and borderline children the issue of "worthwhileness" arises. One need only reflect on how difficult it is to refer such a patient to realize the significance of this issue. Usually we try to "sell" such a patient to someone else, speaking about the worthwhileness of the case, as if expecting such great hostility to arise in the treatment that the therapist must be fortified in advance. To treat such children it is essential that the therapist himself feel worthwhile and able to commit himself, without time limitations or other conditions, to situations where there is no end in sight and where it is difficult to be optimistic. Those who need the patient to be worthwhile are most likely searching for worthwhileness in themselves. Only if they experience themselves as worthwhile can they make such a commitment.

Erikson (1950) suggested that frequently such children, as well as their parents, lack "sending" power. They do not "turn each other on," nor do they turn us on. We who work with children and try to treat them also lack this power and therefore need to create in ourselves a sustaining power. Only those of us who have such a sense of personal worthwhileness can live without the guarantees of positive outcome, success, precise and simple techniques.

Only clinical research makes it possible to sustain such treatment situations. Formal research is oriented toward the establishment of truth. Here, however, we advocate the kind of research that helps to free these patients and helps them overcome their illness and move toward some form of autonomy. We therefore need to build into our treatment models, unclear and unfinished as they often are, clinical research directed toward the development of techniques for the facilitation of treatment—research which is not objective but tied to an attitude about the work itself, which must, in part, be based upon faith, an identification with humanism. This faith needs to be based on one's own worthwhileness as a therapist so that one can develop the capacity to make no demands on the patient to be worthwhile. He cannot be the evidence for our own worthwhileness. We must not be like Thetis, who plunged her infant son into the river to protect him from all harm, while at the same time she planned for him to be a great warrior. We must not set goals for the child, but must do what is needed to help him set his own goals.

How can one teach such an attitude? How can such attitudes become part of our training program? Some of our students, seeking identity models, as all students do, may be able to identify with us. They use us for professional self-realization.

Those who cannot, leave such training. We do with them what we do with our patients: initiate a process—the treatment process there, the educational process here. Our strength as teachers, and as therapists, depends on developing the capacity to participate in these therapeutic and educational processes without the illusion of omnipotence and to accept the limits and uncertainties as well as the challenges of a new dimension in treatment.

References

Bender, L. (1953), Childhood schizophrenia. *Psychiat. Quart.*, 27:663.

Bettelheim, B. (1974), *A Home for the Heart.* New York: Knopf.

Bleuler, E. (1911), *Dementia Praecox, or the Group of Schizophrenias,* trans. J. Zinken. New York: International Universities Press, 1950.

Bowlby, J. (1969), *Attachment and Loss: Vol. 1. Attachment.* New York: Basic Books.

——— (1973), *Attachment and Loss: Vol. 2. Separation, Anxiety and Anger.* New York: Basic Books.

Bowen, M. (1975), Family therapy after 20 years. In: *American Handbook of Psychiatry,* ed. S. Arieti, Vol. 5. New York: Basic Boboks, pp. 367–392.

Ekstein, R. (1966), *Children of Time and Space, of Action and Impulse.* New York: Appleton-Century-Crofts.

Erikson, E.H. (1950), *Childhood and Society.* Rev. ed. New York: Norton, 1963.

——— (1977), *Toys and Reasons: Stages in the Ritualization of Experience.* New York: Norton.

Freud, S. (1900), The interpretation of dreams. *Standard Edition,* 4/5. London: Hogarth Press, 1953.

——— (1916–1917), Introductory lectures on psycho-analysis. *Standard Edition,* 15/16. London: Hogarth Press, 1961.

——— (1922), A seventeenth-century demonological neurosis. *Standard Edition,* 19:72–105. London: Hogarth Press, 1961.

——— (1924), The loss of reality in neurosis and psychosis. *Standard Edition,* 19:183–187. London: Hogarth Press, 1961.

Frost, R. (1949), Education by metaphor. In: *Selected Prose of Robert Frost,* ed. E. Latham & H. Lot. New York: Holt, Rinehart, & Winston.

Goldfarb, W. (1961), The mutual impact of mother and child in childhood schizophrenia. *Amer. J. Orthopsychiat.,* 31:738.

Jones, E., ed. (1913), The god complex. In: *Essays in Applied Psycho-Analysis,* Vol. 2. London: Forsythe Press, and The Institute of Psychoanalysis, 1951.

Kanner, L. (1944), Early infantile autism. *J. Pediat.,* 25:211.

Kohut, H. (1971), *The Analysis of the Self.* New York: International Universities Press.

Kraepelin, E. (1900), *Einführung in die Psychiatrische Klinik* (*Introduction to the Psychiatric Clinic*), Vol. 3. Leipzig: Verlag von Johann Ambrosius Barth, 1916.

Lewis, C.S. (1939), Bluspels and flalansferes. In: *Rehabilitations and Other Essays.* New York: Oxford University Press, pp. 135–158.

Mahler, M., & Furer, M. (1968), *On Human Symbiosis and the Vicissitudes of Individuation.* New York: International Universities Press.

——— Pine, F., & Bergman, A. (1975), *The Psychological Birth of the Human Infant.* New York: Basic Books.

Rank, B. (1949), Adaption of the psychoanalytic technique for the treatment of young children with atypical development. *Amer. J. Orthopsychiat.,* 19:130–139.

Spitz, R. (1946), Anaclitic depression. *The Psychoanalytic Study of the Child,* 2:313–342. New York: International Universities Press.

——— (1965), *The First Year of Life.* New York: International Universities Press.

Szurek, S., & Berlin, I. (1973), *Clinical Studies in Childhood Psychoses.* New York: Brunner/Mazel.

Winnicott, D. (1947), Hate in the countertransference. In: *Collected Papers: Through Paediatrics to Psycho-Analysis.* New York: Basic Books, 1958, pp. 194–203.

Name Index

Subject Index